Transformative Impact of Artificial Intelligence on Management Information Systems

Muhammad Ramzan
Emerson University, Multan, Pakistan

Muhammad Farooq
Emerson University, Multan, Pakistan

Hina Adeeb
University of Central Punjab, Pakistan

IGI Global
Scientific Publishing
Publishing Tomorrow's Research Today

Vice President of Editorial	Melissa Wagner
Director of Acquisitions	Mikaela Felty
Director of Book Development	Jocelynn Hessler
Production Manager	Mike Brehm
Cover Design	Jose Rosado

Published in the United States of America by
IGI Global Scientific Publishing
701 East Chocolate Avenue
Hershey, PA, 17033, USA
Tel: 717-533-8845
Fax: 717-533-7115
Website: https://www.igi-global.com E-mail: cust@igi-global.com

Library of Congress Cataloging-in-Publication Data

LCCN: 2025020210 (CIP Data Pending)
ISBN13: 9798337305134
Isbn13Softcover: 9798337305141
EISBN13: 9798337305158

British Cataloguing in Publication Data
A Cataloguing in Publication record for this book is available from the British Library.

This manuscript is dedicated to the students, faculty and researchers of management and administrative sciences.

Table of Contents

Foreword

In today's dynamic business environment, maintaining a competitive edge demands more than just adaptability. It necessitates a profound comprehension of how technology can drive success. "Transformative Impacts of Artificial Intelligence in Management Information Systems" offers a comprehensive exploration of essential topics crucial for navigating the complexities of contemporary business landscapes. A continuing improvement of information technology innovations is transforming the traditional business world. Authored by Prof. Dr. Rukhsar Ahmed and Prof. Dr. Muhammad Ramzan, the book takes readers on a journey into the core of modern business information strategy. Drawing upon their extensive expertise and experience, the authors provide a detailed roadmap for navigating the complexities of management information systems, ranging from foundational principles to advanced applications.

In the 21st century, with the adoption of modern technologies into operation, firms will be achieving operational excellence, developing new products and services, improving decision-making, and achieving competitive advantage. In this backdrop, the book will help students and industry practitioners find the most up-to-date knowledge related to the modern technologies used by business firms.

In addition, integrating advanced technologies like automation, collection of operational data, artificial intelligence tools, mobile digital business platforms based on smartphones, tablets, ultrabooks, the Internet of Things (IOTs) and the emergence of cloud computing enables organizations to achieve unprecedented levels of efficiency, productivity, and innovation. These innovations allow entrepreneurs and innovative traditional firms to create new products and services and develop new business models. In addition to examining opportunities, this book addresses the critical concerns of knowledge management, E-business, E-commerce, mobile technologies, supply chain management, cybersecurity-related issues, and risk management.

The authors beautifully elaborate that the telecom reform in Pakistan has seen substantial changes, moving away from a monopolistic setup led by PTCL towards a competitive environment. Mobile telephony is the cornerstone of the industry, driven by the widespread adoption of smartphones and the evolution of network technologies such as 3G, 4G, and the upcoming 5G. Management Information Systems (MIS) are vital in the telecom sector, as they strengthen operational efficiency and strategic decision-making and facilitate the deployment of effective customer relationship management systems. One of the significant advancements is the increasing utilization of business intelligence and data analytics within organizations. I congratulate the authors on writing a phenomenal book and lightening the readers with emerging trends in management information systems. Moreover, I strongly recommend reading this book which contains valuable insights and important technological information.

Qaiser Abbas
University of Sargodha, Pakistan

Foreword

Transformative Impacts of Artificial Intelligence in Management Information Systems" by Prof. Dr. Rukhsar Ahmed and Prof. Dr. Muhammad Ramzan, is an important contribution towards contextualizing the significance of the evolving landscape of Management Information Systems (MIS). This book, published by Great Britain Press in 2024, serves as a comprehensive guide through the complexities of MIS, elucidating its foundational principles, its transformative role in modern organizations, and the future directions in which the field is heading. The authors, R. Ahmed and M. Ramzan, have brought forward a wealth of experience and expertise, drawing upon their extensive academic and professional backgrounds to offer readers a deep dive into the subject matter.

The text begins with an exploration of the foundational elements of MIS, emphasizing the structures and frameworks that enable these systems to function effectively within organizations and connecting stakeholders. The authors then guide the reader through the evolution of information systems, highlighting key theoretical frameworks that have shaped the field over time. Through practical examples, Ahmed and Ramzan explain the critical role of MIS in enhancing decision-making, optimizing operations, and fostering innovation within modern businesses.

One of the core themes of the book is the strategic integration of MIS with organizational objectives, underscoring the importance of alignment for achieving competitive advantage. The discussion extends to emerging technologies such as blockchain, artificial intelligence, and the Internet of Things, showcasing how these innovations are redefining the possibilities within the MIS domain.

The comprehensive coverage of MIS challenges and opportunities, from cybersecurity risks to the adoption of enterprise resource planning systems, reflects the authors' commitment to providing a holistic view of the field. The book concludes by looking forward to the role of MIS in digital transformation and the future of work, offering strategic insights and best practices for navigating the digital age.

This foreword aims to underscore the significance of "Transformative Impacts of Artificial Intelligence in Management Information Systems" as an indispensable resource for students, professionals, and academics alike. With its extensive coverage of topics, practical insights, and forward-looking perspective, the book stands as a testament to the dynamic and ever-evolving nature of MIS. As we stand on the cusp of a new era in digital transformation, the insights presented by Ahmed and Ramzan will undoubtedly serve as a beacon for navigating the challenges and seizing the opportunities that lie ahead in the realm of Management Information Systems.

Zahid Hussain Khand

Aror University, Sukkur, Pakistan

Foreword

In today's fast-paced and hyper-connected world, businesses are constantly confronted with a deluge of data and technological advancements that shape the landscape of decision-making. From the emergence of Artificial Intelligence (AI) to the integration of Enterprise Resource Planning (ERP) systems, the realm of Management Information Systems (MIS) has evolved into a complex ecosystem of interconnected tools and methodologies.

In this book, the author(s) embark on a journey through the intricate terrain of MIS, Data Analytics, and Emerging Technologies, exploring how these elements converge to empower organizations in making informed and strategic decisions. Through a comprehensive examination of topics ranging from AI-driven predictive analytics to the intricacies of ERP implementation, we delve into the core principles and practical applications that drive success in today's digital age.

The chapters within this book serve as navigational beacons, guiding readers through the multifaceted realm of MIS and emerging technologies. We explore how organizations can leverage the vast reservoirs of data at their disposal, utilizing advanced analytics techniques to extract actionable insights that drive innovation and growth. From understanding the fundamentals of Knowledge Management to harnessing the power of Decision Support Systems (DSS), each section provides valuable insights and real-world examples that illuminate the path toward organizational excellence.

Furthermore, author(s) examined the ethical considerations and societal implications inherent in the adoption of emerging technologies, emphasizing the importance of responsible and sustainable practices in the digital era. By fostering a deeper understanding of the intersection between technology and humanity, organizations can navigate the digital frontier with integrity and purpose.

Whether you are a seasoned executive seeking to enhance your organization's competitive edge or a student eager to explore the cutting-edge developments in MIS and technology, this book offers a comprehensive road-map for success in the digital age. By embracing innovation, harnessing the power of data, and leveraging emerging technologies, organizations can chart a course toward a future defined by informed decision-making and sustainable growth.

I highly recommend this book to students to unlock the potential of MIS, Data Analytics, and Emerging Technologies, transforming challenges into opportunities and shaping a brighter tomorrow for businesses worldwide.

Rauf I Azam

Punjab University of Technology, Rasul, Pakistan

Foreword

"In the dynamic landscape of modern business, staying ahead requires not just adaptability but also a deep understanding of how technology can be leveraged to drive success. "Insight into Management Information System: Navigating Data for Business Success " provides a comprehensive overview of crucial topics that are essential for navigating the complexities of contemporary business environments. Authored by Prof. Dr. Muhammad Ramzan, Dr. Muhammad Farooq and Hina Adeeb who are experts in the field, this book serves as a valuable resource for graduate students seeking to grasp the intricacies of management information systems (MIS) and related disciplines.

One of the book's strengths lies in its structured approach, beginning with foundational concepts in management information systems. From there, it delves into the realms of data analytics and business intelligence, emphasizing the critical role of data-driven decision-making in today's competitive landscape. Each chapter is meticulously crafted to provide not just theoretical insights but also practical applications, making it an invaluable companion for students looking to bridge the gap between academia and industry. Moreover, the book explores how information systems can be strategically deployed to gain a competitive advantage. It elucidates the significance of emerging technologies such as artificial intelligence, blockchain, and the Internet of Things (IoT) in reshaping business processes and fostering innovation. By examining real-world case studies and industry trends, it equips readers with the knowledge needed to harness these technologies effectively. In addition to exploring opportunities, this book addresses the pressing issue of cybersecurity and risk management. In an era where data breaches and cyber threats pose significant challenges to organizations, understanding how to safeguard sensitive information is paramount. The book provides actionable insights into developing robust cybersecurity frameworks and mitigating potential risks.

This book is an indispensable resource for graduate students embarking on careers in business and technology. Its comprehensive coverage of foundational concepts, emerging technologies, and strategic applications makes it essential reading for anyone seeking to thrive in today's digital era. Whether you're pursuing a degree in business administration, information systems, or related fields, this book provides a roadmap for success in an ever-evolving business environment.

Here's why students should study this book:

1. **Comprehensive Coverage:** The book covers a wide range of topics relevant to modern business environments, from foundational management information systems to emerging technologies and future trends. This breadth ensures that students gain a holistic understanding of the field, equipping them with the knowledge needed to excel in their careers.
2. **Practical Application:** Each chapter includes practical applications and real-world case studies, bridging the gap between theory and practice. This hands-on approach enables students to apply theoretical concepts to solve real-world business challenges, enhancing their problem-solving skills and readiness for the workforce.
3. **Strategic Insight:** Understanding how information systems can be strategically deployed to gain a competitive advantage is crucial for success in today's business landscape. This book delves into strategies for leveraging technology to drive organizational growth, providing students with strategic insight that is invaluable in their future roles as business leaders and decision-makers.
4. **Relevance to Industry Trends:** The book explores emerging technologies and their impact on business, including data analytics, cybersecurity, e-commerce, and mobile technologies. By staying abreast of industry trends, students are better prepared to adapt to changing market dynamics and contribute meaningfully to their organizations from day one.
5. **Preparation for Evolving Role:** As technology continues to reshape the business landscape, professionals with expertise in management information systems are in high demand. Studying this book prepares students for a variety of roles, including data analysts, IT consultants, business strategists, and more, opening up diverse career opportunities upon graduation.
6. **Interdisciplinary Perspective:** Management information systems intersect with various disciplines, including business, technology, and data science. By studying this book, students gain an interdisciplinary perspective that enriches their understanding of how different components of an organization work together to achieve strategic objectives.
7. **Future-Focused:** The book concludes by examining future trends in information management, offering students insights into emerging technologies and their potential impact on business practices. By understanding these future trends, students can position themselves as forward-thinking professionals capable of driving innovation within their organizations.

Ghulam Ali Bhatti
University of Sargodha, Pakistan

Preface

In an era of transformative technological advances, management information systems (MIS) are no longer mere facilitators; they are essential engines of business growth and competitive advantage. This book, Transformative Impact of Artificial intelligence on Management Information Systems, explores the unprecedented opportunities and challenges that artificial intelligence (AI) brings to the field of MIS. Written for students, scholars, and industry professionals, this work seeks to illuminate how the evolving landscape of AI-enhanced information systems can empower organizations, redefine strategies, and reshape the business world.

Our journey begins with a comprehensive exploration of MIS foundations, spanning critical areas such as data analytics, strategic advantage, cybersecurity, customer relationship management (CRM), and more. Each chapter is thoughtfully designed to provide readers with a nuanced understanding of the synergies between AI and MIS. By diving into specific applications, emerging technologies, and ethical considerations, this book aims to equip readers with both theoretical insights and practical tools for success.

CHAPTER OVERVIEW

Chapter 1: Foundations of Management Information Systems in the Era of AI and Beyond

Setting the stage, we begin by laying out the foundations of MIS, detailing the discipline's evolution from early data processing systems to today's sophisticated AI-driven platforms. MIS supports decision-making, optimizes operations, and drives strategic initiatives, playing a pivotal role in modern organizations. This chapter discusses the importance of aligning MIS with corporate strategy to harness information systems for competitive advantage. We also examine the challenges and opportunities involved, emphasizing the critical nature of adaptability as technology continues to evolve.

Chapter 2: Transformative Impact of Artificial Intelligence in Data Analytics and Business Intelligence

Chapter 2 delves into the revolutionary influence of AI on data analytics and business intelligence. By examining the fundamentals of data analytics, we highlight how AI has become indispensable for interpreting vast datasets. This chapter introduces readers to advanced tools and techniques, showcasing AI's impact on data visualization, predictive analytics, and big data management. With a focus on case studies, we illustrate how AI-driven analytics enable organizations to generate valuable insights, make informed decisions, and achieve strategic goals.

Chapter 3: Transformative Impacts of AI in Information Systems for Strategic Advantage

AI-enhanced MIS is a powerful tool for gaining strategic advantage, as discussed in Chapter 3. By aligning IT infrastructure with business strategy, companies can harness information systems to achieve measurable competitive gains. This chapter provides a roadmap for integrating AI within MIS frameworks to enhance strategy, drawing on real-world case studies that underscore the transformative potential of AI-driven MIS. Organizations looking to optimize their strategic approach can leverage this chapter to understand the role of information systems in achieving sustained growth.

Chapter 4: Transformative Impacts of AI on Emerging Technologies in Business

Emerging technologies like blockchain, machine learning, and the Internet of Things (IoT) are reshaping the business landscape. Chapter 4 explores these technologies and their applications, illustrating how decentralized systems can improve transparency and security. We examine the role of AI in automating business processes, from IoT-enabled smart devices to virtual and augmented reality in customer engagement. Ethical considerations are also discussed, urging readers to approach these innovations responsibly.

Chapter 5: Transformative Impacts of AI on Cybersecurity and Risk Management

As technological capabilities grow, so do security challenges. In Chapter 5, we cover cybersecurity fundamentals, focusing on AI's role in enhancing security measures. Organizations must prioritize cybersecurity and develop comprehensive risk management frameworks, as discussed in this chapter. Emerging threats, countermeasures, and policies on cybersecurity compliance are explored in depth, providing insights into creating a culture of security awareness that safeguards organizations against data breaches and cyberattacks.

Chapter 6: Transformative Impacts of AI on Enterprise Resource Planning (ERP) Systems

Enterprise Resource Planning (ERP) systems play a crucial role in organizational efficiency. Chapter 6 offers a comprehensive overview of ERP systems, detailing their components, architecture, and the advantages of integrating AI. By exploring ERP deployment challenges and solutions, this chapter provides lessons from successful and failed ERP implementations. Case studies demonstrate how AI can streamline ERP systems, enabling companies to adapt more quickly to changing market demands.

Chapter 7: Transformative Impacts of AI in Future Trends in Management Information Systems

In our concluding chapter, we look toward the future, analyzing the trends that will shape MIS beyond AI. We explore digital transformation, the future of work, quantum computing, and advanced robotics. This chapter emphasizes the need for continuous learning, agility, and readiness for disruptive innovations. Preparing for the future means anticipating changes and developing strategies that align with emerging technological advancements.

Chapter 8: Transformative Impacts of AI on Customer Relationship Management (CRM) Systems

Chapter 8 underscores the importance of CRM in cultivating strong customer relationships. With AI, CRM systems can deliver personalized customer experiences, analyze data for insights, and enhance customer loyalty. This chapter covers CRM technologies, applications, and integration with other business systems, providing strategies to strengthen customer relationships. Organizations can leverage AI-driven

CRM insights to meet customers' evolving needs, fostering long-term loyalty and retention.

Chapter 9: Transformative Impacts of AI on Supply Chain Management (SCM) Systems

Global supply chain efficiency is crucial, and Chapter 9 discusses how AI enhances SCM by improving visibility, agility, and sustainability. Readers will learn about the fundamentals of SCM, AI-driven sourcing, procurement, and risk management. This chapter highlights sustainable supply chain practices, emphasizing how AI can forecast disruptions and optimize resource allocation. By improving operational efficiency, AI-driven SCM strengthens businesses' resilience and responsiveness.

Chapter 10: Transformative Impacts of AI on Knowledge Management and Decision Support Systems

Knowledge is one of the most valuable assets of any organization. Chapter 10 focuses on knowledge management, examining decision support systems (DSS) that integrate AI for enhanced decision-making. AI-driven DSS processes large volumes of data, enabling managers to make informed, data-backed decisions. This chapter also shares best practices in knowledge management, helping organizations retain, share, and utilize knowledge effectively to maintain a competitive edge.

Chapter 11: Transformative Impacts of AI om Cloud Computing and Information Systems Infrastructure

Cloud computing has redefined IT infrastructure, offering scalability and cost efficiency. Chapter 11 introduces the fundamentals of cloud services, such as IaaS, PaaS, and SaaS, emphasizing the role of AI in securing cloud environments and enhancing functionality. We explore the future directions of cloud computing, like edge computing, highlighting AI's role in optimizing cloud services. This chapter underscores how AI-driven cloud solutions offer a flexible foundation for digital transformation.

Chapter 12: Transformative Impacts of AI on E-Business and E-Commerce Systems

In the digital age, e-business and e-commerce systems are fundamental to reaching customers worldwide. Chapter 12 examines how AI is transforming the e-commerce landscape through personalization, recommendation systems, and improved customer experience. This chapter explores e-commerce business models, legal and security considerations, and emerging trends, emphasizing how companies can leverage AI to drive success in the digital marketplace.

Chapter 13: Transformative Impacts of AI on Mobile Technologies and Applications in Business

Mobile technologies have become integral to cutomer engagement and operational efficiency. Chapter 13 examines the evolution of mobile applications, focusing on how AI enhances their functionality. Readers will explore mobile marketing strategies, security challenges, and future trends like 5G. This chapter illustrates how mobile technologies, when paired with AI, enable businesses to connect with customers and optimize workflows.

Chapter 14: Transformative Impacts of AI on Social Media and Corporate Communication Strategies

Social media's reach and influence in shaping corporate communications are unparalleled. Chapter 14 explores the role of social media in business, particularly AI's contribution to content strategy, audience targeting, and engagement analytics. We also discuss reputation management and legal considerations, urging companies to harness AI for responsible social media strategies that strengthen brand presence and corporate communication.

Chapter 15: Transformative Impacts of AI on Ethics, Privacy, and Regulatory Compliance in MIS

With AI's rise comes the need for strong ethical standards and regulatory compliance. Chapter 15 delves into the ethical implications of AI in information systems, covering privacy laws, data protection, and ethical decision-making frameworks. Through case studies, we highlight compliance challenges, emphasizing the importance of ethical responsibility in AI implementation. Organizations that prioritize these issues gain trust and reduce risks associated with data mismanagement.

FINAL THOUGHTS

Management Information Systems in the Era of AI and Beyond offers a comprehensive look at the synergies between AI and MIS, merging foundational knowledge with forward-thinking perspectives. By balancing theoretical foundations with practical applications, we provide readers with a valuable resource to thrive in an increasingly complex digital landscape. Our aim has been to help readers understand the transformative potential of AI in MIS and to equip them with tools and knowledge for leading in a time of rapid technological change.

Whether you are a student, professional, or academic, this book is an essential guide to understanding AI's impact on MIS and the broader business environment. We hope the material will inspire you to innovate, adapt, and harness the power of technology to drive positive change. As we navigate this new era, let us embrace the opportunities AI brings to information systems and strive to use these tools to create meaningful progress. Thank you for embarking on this journey with us—together, we can shape a future where technology and humanity advance hand in hand.

Chapter 1
Foundations of Management Information Systems in the Era of AI and Beyond

ABSTRACT

The hardware infrastructure, the structural backbone that underpins an organization's digital nerve center, is the cornerstone of these foundations. The structural foundation of MIS is made up of computers, servers, storage devices, and networking equipment (Dahiya et al., 2022). This allows MIS to expand its capabilities. The system's ability to manage large datasets and process information reliably and efficiently depends on how strong this foundation is. Hardware development has had a significant impact on MIS's responsiveness and agility, helping businesses to adapt to the constantly shifting demands of their operations (L. M. Jiang et al., 2023).

1.1 CHAPTER INTRODUCTION

The software architecture, a complex ecosystem of applications and programs that give the hardware framework life, complements the physical infrastructure. Together, database management systems, operating systems, and application software convert unprocessed data into insightful knowledge. The MIS's software component changes to meet the changing demands of businesses as technology advances with it (J. Gao et al., 2024). A robust MIS foundation is built on the symbiotic interaction between

DOI: 10.4018/979-8-3373-0513-4.ch001

hardware and software, which allows for smooth integration and communication across a range of organizational tasks (Prandel & Barreto, 2024).

The heartbeat of every information system is data, which travels via MIS. Data collection, archiving, retrieval, and analysis are all included in the foundation's data management procedures. Ensuring the data's integrity and security is crucial in protecting the company from possible attacks and weaknesses. The fundamentals of MIS combine modern data management methods, such data warehousing, and data mining, to extract useful insights and improve decision making skills as businesses struggle with an ever-expanding amount of data(K. J. Wang & Simarmata, 2024).

The network infrastructure, or circulatory system of the management information system, connects the hardware, software, and data components. Networks provide smooth interaction and cooperation between many parts, guaranteeing immediate data transmission and availability. Strong networking protocols and security measures are essential to prevent unwanted access and data breaches, as stated in the foundations of MIS. In order to create a unified information environment, dismantle departmental silos, and promote departmental cooperation, network infrastructure is essential(Fang et al., 2024).

1.2 Management Information Systems (MIS) Infrastructure and Its Structural Foundations

Management Information Systems (MIS) play an integral role in modern organizations by providing tools that facilitate decision-making, data processing, and strategic planning (Karim et al., 2024; León-Romero et al., 2024) . At its core, MIS infrastructure comprises several foundational components, including hardware, software, data, and network infrastructure (Chatzimichailidou et al., 2024; Chenyang et al., 2024; Okada et al., 2024). Together, these elements form a synergistic ecosystem that enables an organization to process, manage, and analyze data effectively, ultimately contributing to achieving organizational goals (J. Xie et al., 2024; Zhai & Chen, 2024). Each component's role is vital, as it impacts the system's ability to scale, adapt, and integrate emerging technologies.

1.2.1 Hardware Infrastructure: The Structural Backbone

Hardware infrastructure is the physical foundation of MIS, encompassing computers, servers, storage devices, and networking equipment (Farooq et al., 2024c). These elements form the structural backbone of an organization's digital nerve center, providing the computational power and storage capabilities necessary to support and expand MIS functionalities(Farooq et al., 2024a, 2024g). Hardware influences the capacity and speed of data processing, which in turn affects how well an organization can adapt to changes, handle large datasets, and ensure the efficient flow of information across departments.

Hardware advancements play a critical role in enhancing the performance and reliability of MIS. Powerful processors, high-capacity storage, and efficient memory modules all contribute to faster and more efficient data processing. For example, the adoption of solid-state drives (SSDs) over traditional hard disk drives (HDDs) has significantly reduced data access times, thereby increasing overall system responsiveness(Farooq et al., 2024i, 2024j). High-speed servers and data centers equipped with efficient cooling and power systems further support the operational requirements of MIS by enhancing processing speeds and ensuring continuous availability (Jiang et al., 2023).

Scalability is another crucial feature of hardware infrastructure. Organizations constantly adapt to shifting demands, such as increased data loads or the need for faster processing times. Hardware that can scale to meet these demands allows MIS to evolve without compromising performance(Farooq et al., 2024h). The importance of robust and scalable hardware is even more pronounced in today's business environment, where the volume of data continues to grow exponentially (Farooq et al., 2024e). The impact of hardware on MIS agility cannot be overstated, as it enables businesses to swiftly pivot to meet changing needs, ensuring continuity and responsiveness in an ever-evolving landscape.

1.2.2. Software Architecture: The Heart of MIS

While hardware provides the structural foundation, software architecture breathes life into the MIS. This ecosystem of applications, programs, and databases complements the hardware by enabling data processing, management, and analytics functions(Farooq et al., 2024d, 2024f). Software architecture includes operating systems, database management systems, and specialized application software that transforms raw data into actionable insights (Gao et al., 2024). The ability of the MIS to adapt to organizational requirements hinges on the flexibility and efficiency of its software components.

At the core of software architecture lies the operating system, which manages hardware resources and provides an interface for other software applications. This layer ensures that all processes within the MIS function harmoniously, optimizing the use of hardware resources. Database Management Systems (DBMS) are equally important, as they provide the tools necessary for storing, retrieving, and managing vast quantities of data(Farooq et al., 2024b; Gupta & Panigrahi, 2023). Effective DBMS solutions are designed to handle structured and unstructured data, a capability that is essential in today's data-driven environments.

Application software represents another key layer within the software architecture. These applications are tailored to perform specific functions, such as financial reporting, inventory management, and customer relationship management (CRM) (Godoy et al., 2023). As organizations evolve, so do their software needs. Regular updates and the adoption of new software solutions enable MIS to stay current with technological advancements and industry standards. For instance, the integration of artificial intelligence (AI) and machine learning algorithms into MIS software has improved decision-making capabilities by providing predictive insights and automation options (Prandel & Barreto, 2024).

The interaction between hardware and software in MIS creates a symbiotic relationship that enhances system performance and supports organizational tasks(Y. Wang et al., 2023). This seamless integration fosters communication and data flow across various departments, contributing to more cohesive and streamlined business operations. As a result, the organization can efficiently manage resources, optimize processes, and achieve greater operational flexibility.

1.2.3. Data Management: The Lifeblood of MIS

Data serves as the lifeblood of MIS, flowing through each component to drive decision-making and support strategic initiatives. The data management aspect of MIS encompasses processes related to data collection, storage, retrieval, and analysis(Dalloul et al., 2023; Zhidong, 2023). Ensuring data integrity, accuracy, and security is paramount, as any compromise can expose the organization to risks, including data breaches and cyber threats (W. Liu & Wei, 2022).

Data management practices in MIS have evolved to address the complexities of modern data environments. The adoption of data warehousing, for instance, has enabled organizations to consolidate data from various sources into a centralized repository(Song, 2022). This approach not only improves data accessibility but also allows for more comprehensive analysis, as users can view and interpret data holistically. Data mining techniques further support data management by enabling the extraction of valuable insights from large datasets (K. J. Wang & Simarmata, 2024).

In today's digital landscape, where data generation rates are accelerating, effective data management is essential for organizations seeking to maintain a competitive edge(R. Liu & Wang, 2022). The ability to process and analyze data in real-time allows businesses to respond to market changes and make informed decisions(Lian, 2022). However, the integrity of data is equally important. Ensuring data accuracy and consistency across different systems prevents errors and ensures that MIS outputs are reliable(C. Liang & Wang, 2022).

Data security measures are a critical aspect of data management. Organizations must implement robust cybersecurity protocols to protect sensitive information from unauthorized access and potential data breaches(Fu & Xu, 2022). This is particularly important as organizations handle increasingly sensitive information, such as customer data and financial records. The integration of encryption, access controls, and regular security audits within the MIS framework helps safeguard data, providing a secure environment for data-driven decision-making(G. Wang et al., 2022).

1.2. 4. Network Infrastructure: The Circulatory System

The network infrastructure of MIS acts as the circulatory system, linking hardware, software, and data components to ensure smooth communication and data flow within the organization(B. Guo & Shuai, 2022). Network infrastructure comprises the physical and logical structures that facilitate connectivity, enabling data transmission between devices, databases, and users. A robust network is essential for providing reliable access to information and supporting collaboration across various organizational levels (Fang et al., 2024).

Networks support real-time data sharing, a crucial feature for organizations operating in fast-paced environments. With a reliable network infrastructure, employees across different departments can access and share information instantaneously, enabling more efficient workflows and collaboration (Tian et al., 2022). This capability reduces information silos within the organization, allowing departments to work cohesively toward shared objectives.

The network infrastructure also plays a pivotal role in supporting remote access, a feature that has become increasingly important in the context of remote work. Virtual Private Networks (VPNs) and cloud-based solutions have expanded the reach of MIS beyond the physical boundaries of an organization, allowing employees to access resources from anywhere (Xiaobao et al., 2022). This flexibility not only enhances productivity but also supports business continuity, as employees can maintain access to MIS resources even in unforeseen circumstances(Y. Zhang, 2022).

Security within the network infrastructure is equally vital, as data breaches and unauthorized access can compromise the entire MIS(Jian, 2022). Firewalls, intrusion detection systems, and data encryption are standard security measures that protect the network from external threats(Haiying, 2022; J. Xie & Luo, 2022). Network segmentation is another strategy that enhances security by isolating sensitive data, reducing the risk of widespread damage in the event of a security breach.

1.2.5. The Interconnectedness of MIS Components: A Holistic Approach

The components of MIS—hardware, software, data, and network infrastructure—do not operate in isolation(Khan et al., 2022). Instead, they form an interconnected system where each element supports and enhances the others. The effectiveness of MIS depends on this interdependence, as each component's functionality is amplified by the synergy created through their integration(Shin & Choi, 2022).

Hardware infrastructure provides the necessary computational power, while software enables the processing and analysis of data(C. Zhang et al., 2022). Data management ensures that this information is accurate and readily available, while network infrastructure facilitates the flow of information across the organization(Zekun et al., 2022). Together, these components create a cohesive MIS framework that supports data-driven decision-making and enables the organization to respond dynamically to market demands(Na & Shon, 2022).

A holistic approach to MIS also considers scalability and adaptability. As organizations grow and technology evolves, the MIS framework must be flexible enough to accommodate new tools, software updates, and increased data loads(Iliescu, 2022). This adaptability is critical for maintaining the relevance of MIS in a rapidly changing digital landscape(Y. Wang, 2022). By designing an MIS framework that is both scalable and adaptable, organizations can ensure that their information systems continue to support their strategic objectives.

1.2.6 Emerging Trends and the Future of MIS Infrastructure

The field of MIS is continuously evolving, driven by advancements in technology and changing business needs(L. Huang, 2022). Emerging trends such as cloud computing, artificial intelligence, and big data analytics are reshaping the landscape of MIS infrastructure (Kamenska et al., 2022). Cloud computing, for example, offers a scalable and cost-effective solution for data storage and processing, reducing the need for extensive on-site hardware. This shift toward cloud-based solutions allows organizations to allocate resources more efficiently and access MIS functionalities from any location(Pereira et al., 2022).

Artificial intelligence and machine learning are also transforming MIS by providing tools for predictive analysis and automation. These technologies enable organizations to make proactive decisions by identifying patterns and trends in data(X. Li et al., 2022). For example, AI-powered MIS can forecast market demand, optimize inventory levels, and personalize customer experiences, all of which contribute to improved operational efficiency (Koo et al., 2021; Siyao & Bin, 2021).

In addition, the rise of the Internet of Things (IoT) is expanding the scope of data available to MIS. IoT devices generate vast amounts of data, which can be integrated into the MIS framework to provide real-time insights into various aspects of business operations. For example, IoT sensors can monitor equipment performance in real-time, enabling predictive maintenance and reducing downtime(Y. Chen, 2021; Xuelei et al., 2021).

The MIS infrastructure, comprising hardware, software, data, and network components, forms the foundation of an organization's information system(Jin et al., 2021; Xuelei et al., 2021). Each component plays a distinct yet interconnected role in ensuring that MIS supports the organization's strategic goals. Hardware infrastructure provides the physical foundation, while software enables data processing and analysis. Data management ensures accuracy and security, and network infrastructure facilitates communication and collaboration.

As MIS continues to evolve, organizations must stay informed about emerging trends and adopt technologies that enhance the system's capabilities. A well-designed MIS infrastructure not only supports current operational

Figure 1. Management Information System MIS core components

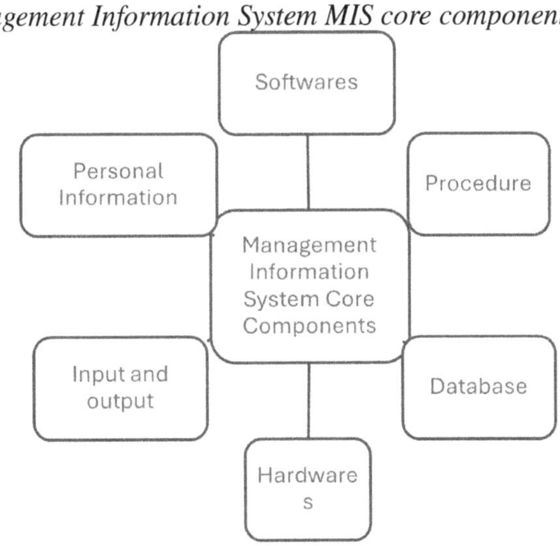

Figure 2. Mind map of foundations of management systems (Author self-made based on literature)

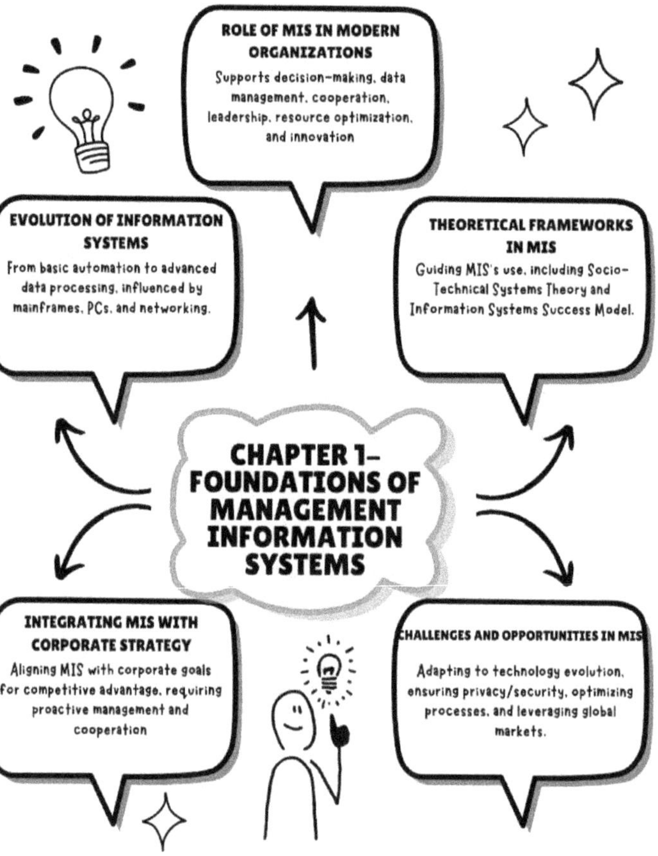

1.2 Evolution of Information Systems

The development of Information Systems (IS) represents a noteworthy advancement in the fields of business and technology. It is clear from studying the historical evolution of information systems that the environment has changed dramatically, influencing how businesses operate and handle data (Schoormann et al., 2023).

Information systems were primitive in the early days of computers and were concerned with automating manual tasks. Basic data storage and retrieval capabilities, mostly for administrative purposes inside companies, were the hallmark of early information systems. These systems were compartmentalized and operated separately, with little to no integration, to handle certain tasks(Xuan et al., 2023).

The development of mainframe computers at the start of the 20th century resulted in a paradigm change. Large-scale data processing and storing became possible during this period because to the concentration of processing power. Organizations started to see how information technology might improve decision-making and streamline operations. The emphasis switched from simple automation to effective data processing and analysis, setting the stage for more complex information system(Prabhavathy & Umamaheswari, 2022).

When personal computers were introduced in the 1980s, the progress proceeded. The accessibility of computer resources was transformed by this decentralized model, which empowered individual users inside businesses. Information systems therefore developed to include user-friendly applications and interfaces, creating an environment that is more focused on the needs of the user(S. Lee, 2022).

The development of networking technology in the 1990s allowed for smooth communication across previously unconnected systems. The growth of enterprise-wide information systems, which encouraged departmental cooperation and data exchange, was made possible by this networked architecture. Information systems evolved into dynamic, linked ecosystems as a result of the integration of databases and the expansion of the internet(Z. Huang, 2022).

Management Information Systems (MIS) have their conceptual foundations shaped in large part by theoretical frameworks. There is now a framework for analyzing the elements impacting the adoption and success of information systems inside businesses thanks to theories like the Technology Acceptance Model and the Information Systems Success Model. These frameworks highlight the significance of perceived utility, system quality, and user happiness in assessing the efficacy of information systems(X. Zhang, 2022).

The function of management information system (MIS) in modern firms is complex in today's corporate environment. Since information systems provide real-time data analysis and insights, they have become essential to decision-making processes. Effective communication, teamwork, and knowledge management are made easier by MIS, which promotes organizational flexibility and agility in a setting that is changing quickly(Kamenska et al., 2022).

MIS integration with corporate strategy has become essential for businesses looking to gain a competitive advantage. Information systems are guaranteed to be in line with the organization's overarching aims and objectives via strategic alignment(X. Li et al., 2022; Pereira et al., 2022). In a world driven by data and digitization, MIS helps firms remain ahead of the curve by supporting both strategic planning and daily operations (L. J. Zhao et al., 2022).

There are difficulties in integrating MIS with company strategy. Organizations deal with problems relating to privacy, data security, and the quick speed at which technology is developing(Z. Huang, 2022; S. Lee, 2022). For contemporary businesses, maintaining a safe and dependable information infrastructure while yet requiring innovation is a constant problem.

Figure 3. Evolution of information systems

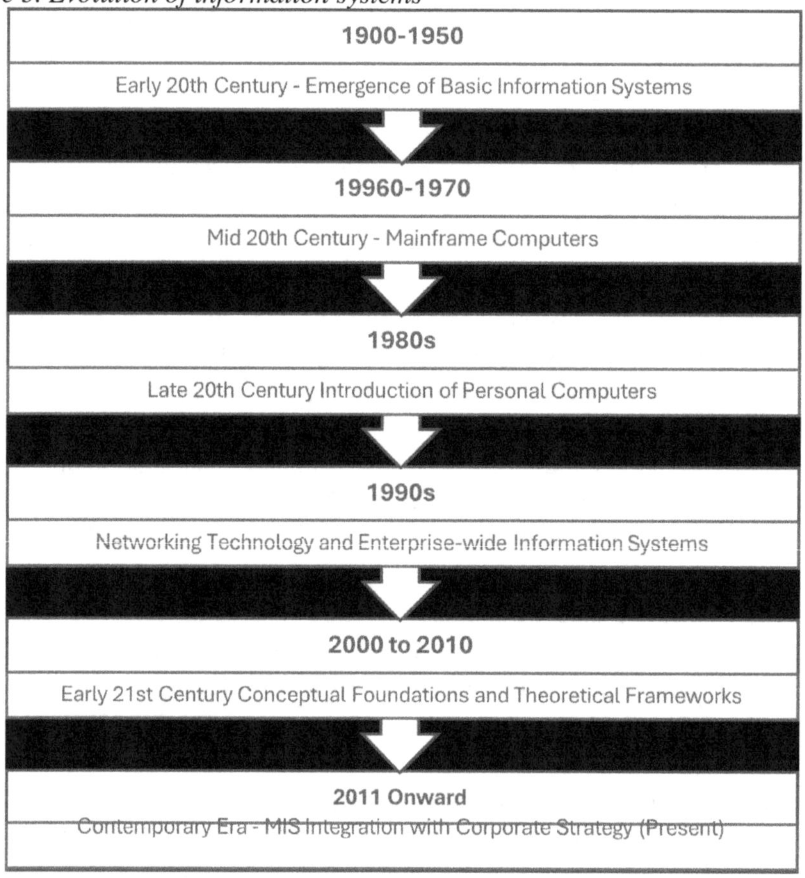

The evolution of Information Systems (IS) marks a transformative journey in both the realms of business and technology. Since their inception, information systems have dramatically evolved, reflecting and driving shifts in how organizations handle data, communicate, and make strategic decisions (Schoormann et al., 2023). This evolution can be traced through different phases, each characterized by advances in technology, changes in organizational needs, and the continuous development of new theoretical frameworks(Runge et al., 2022; X. Zhang, 2022). Together, these advancements have transformed information systems from basic automation tools into complex, integrated platforms crucial for strategic planning and decision-making.

1.2.1 Early Days: Basic Automation and Data Storage

Information systems in their infancy were rudimentary, primarily focused on automating manual processes to increase efficiency and reduce errors. Early IS applications were compartmentalized, functioning in isolation from one another and primarily limited to basic data storage and retrieval tasks (Xuan et al., 2023). For instance, payroll processing, inventory tracking, and simple record-keeping were typical examples of early applications. During this period, data was often manually inputted and organized in a straightforward way, and the primary goal was to streamline repetitive tasks(Y. Liu, 2022; Shi et al., 2022).

Initially, these systems lacked the integration that characterizes modern information systems. As such, they were limited to performing specific tasks and did not facilitate cross-functional data sharing or collaboration(Hu & Shi, 2021; B. Zhao & Tu, 2021). Despite these limitations, the ability to store and retrieve information in an automated way was an invaluable development, marking the first step toward more sophisticated data management systems.

1.2.2 Mainframe Era: Centralized Data Processing

The advent of mainframe computers in the mid-20th century signaled a paradigm shift in the development of information systems. Mainframes introduced centralized data processing, which allowed organizations to store, process, and retrieve larger volumes of data with greater efficiency. This era witnessed a focus on enhancing the capability of information systems to process high volumes of data, making them ideal for supporting administrative functions and large-scale data management tasks.

The mainframe era established a foundation for more complex IS applications, where organizations could use data not only for administrative purposes but also to support decision-making processes. Centralized processing enabled more comprehensive and efficient data handling, empowering organizations to analyze data at scale and generate meaningful insights (Prabhavathy & Umamaheswari, 2022). This shift highlighted the importance of IS as a tool for improving productivity and marked the beginning of a new understanding of how technology could support organizational goals.

Despite the efficiency gains brought by mainframes, the technology was largely inaccessible to smaller organizations due to its high cost and the specialized skills required for operation. Consequently, IS development during this period remained limited to large organizations with the necessary resources to invest in and maintain mainframe systems.

1.2.3 The PC Revolution: Decentralization and User Empowerment

The introduction of personal computers (PCs) in the 1980s democratized access to computing resources, ushering in a new era for information systems. PCs empowered individual users within organizations, giving them direct access to computing power that was previously centralized and restricted to specialized departments. This decentralization had a profound impact on the evolution of IS, enabling a shift from large, centralized mainframes to more accessible, user-friendly platforms.

With the advent of PCs, information systems evolved to include applications with intuitive interfaces and functionalities that catered to end-users' needs. For example, spreadsheet software, word processors, and databases were introduced, providing users with powerful tools for data analysis and document management. These developments transformed information systems into more versatile and accessible resources within organizations, fostering an environment where employees at various levels could utilize data and technology in their daily tasks.

The PC revolution also catalyzed the development of user-centric applications that could run independently on individual computers. This shift toward usability and accessibility was a key factor in advancing IS, enabling organizations to expand their reliance on technology for more strategic purposes. By making technology more accessible, the PC revolution laid the groundwork for more collaborative and integrated information systems in the future.

1.2.4 The Networking Age: Connectivity and Integration

The 1990s brought about another pivotal transformation in IS with the development of networking technology. Networks enabled the interconnection of previously isolated systems, facilitating communication and data sharing across departments and organizational boundaries. This advancement marked the beginning of enterprise-wide information systems, allowing organizations to unify their data management and communication functions in a more cohesive manner.

Networking technology paved the way for the development of more dynamic, integrated information systems. For instance, enterprise resource planning (ERP) systems emerged during this period, enabling organizations to integrate various functions—such as finance, human resources, and inventory management—into a single, unified platform. This connectivity allowed information to flow freely across different departments, promoting collaboration and data-driven decision-making on an enterprise scale.

The rise of the internet further enhanced the connectivity of information systems. With web-based applications and online databases, organizations could access real-time data and communicate with clients, suppliers, and partners across the globe.

This expansion facilitated the globalization of business processes and allowed organizations to manage their operations with greater agility and responsiveness.

1.2.5 Conceptual Foundations: Theoretical Frameworks Shaping MIS

The evolution of information systems has been influenced by several theoretical frameworks, which provide a foundation for understanding the adoption, use, and impact of IS in organizations. Two prominent frameworks that have shaped the conceptual foundation of Management Information Systems (MIS) are the Technology Acceptance Model (TAM) and the Information Systems Success Model (ISSM).

The Technology Acceptance Model, developed by Davis in 1989, posits that user acceptance of technology is determined by two primary factors: perceived usefulness and perceived ease of use. This model underscores the importance of user-centric design in the development of information systems, as user satisfaction and perceived utility are critical determinants of successful IS adoption. As technology continues to advance, the TAM framework remains relevant, guiding the development of IS that meets the evolving needs of users (Schoormann et al., 2023).

The Information Systems Success Model, proposed by DeLone and McLean in 1992, provides a multidimensional framework for evaluating IS effectiveness. According to the ISSM, information systems' success can be measured based on factors such as system quality, information quality, user satisfaction, and the impact on organizational performance. This model has been instrumental in shaping the assessment of MIS, emphasizing the importance of alignment between technology, user experience, and organizational goals.

Together, these frameworks have provided a structured approach to analyzing MIS adoption and success, offering insights into how organizations can leverage information systems to achieve their objectives. By applying these theoretical models, businesses can better understand the factors that influence IS effectiveness and make informed decisions regarding technology investments.

1.2.6 Modern MIS: Integration and Strategic Alignment

In today's business environment, the role of MIS is multifaceted, as information systems have become integral to decision-making, collaboration, and strategic planning. Modern MIS are characterized by real-time data analysis, seamless integration with other systems, and enhanced capabilities for knowledge management and communication. These features enable organizations to adapt swiftly to market changes, respond to customer needs, and improve operational efficiency.

Strategic alignment has become a crucial aspect of MIS, as organizations seek to leverage technology to gain a competitive advantage. This alignment ensures that information systems are directly linked to the organization's overarching goals, supporting both strategic planning and day-to-day operations. MIS plays a critical role in facilitating this alignment by providing the tools necessary for data analysis, reporting, and decision-making.

However, the integration of MIS with corporate strategy also presents challenges. Organizations must address issues related to data security, privacy, and the rapid pace of technological change. Ensuring that MIS infrastructure remains secure while supporting innovation requires a balanced approach that considers both operational needs and potential risks. This challenge is particularly significant in a data-driven world where organizations are increasingly reliant on information systems to maintain their competitive position (Zhao et al., 2022).

1.2.7 The Future of MIS: Emerging Trends and Challenges

The evolution of information systems continues as organizations adopt new technologies and respond to changing business needs. Emerging trends, such as artificial intelligence (AI), big data analytics, and the Internet of Things (IoT), are shaping the future of MIS and presenting new opportunities for innovation. These advancements are transforming how organizations manage information, enabling more sophisticated data analysis, automation, and predictive capabilities.

Artificial intelligence, for example, offers tools for machine learning, natural language processing, and predictive analytics, which allow organizations to gain deeper insights into customer behavior, operational efficiency, and market trends. AI-driven MIS can support strategic decision-making by identifying patterns in large datasets, enabling organizations to anticipate changes and respond proactively.

Big data analytics is another area of growth, as organizations harness the power of vast amounts of data to improve decision-making and operational efficiency. Data from various sources—such as customer interactions, supply chains, and social media—can be integrated and analyzed to provide a holistic view of business performance. This data-driven approach allows organizations to make informed decisions based on real-time insights, supporting more effective strategic planning.

The Internet of Things (IoT) is expanding the scope of data available to MIS by connecting physical devices, sensors, and systems to the internet. This connectivity enables the collection of data from a wide range of sources, such as equipment, vehicles, and production lines, providing organizations with real-time information on operational conditions. IoT-powered MIS can support predictive maintenance, improve resource allocation, and optimize production processes.

As information systems continue to evolve, organizations face new challenges related to data privacy, security, and ethical considerations. With the increasing volume of data being collected and processed, ensuring compliance with regulations and protecting sensitive information has become a top priority. Organizations must implement robust security measures, including encryption, access controls, and regular audits, to safeguard their MIS infrastructure.

The evolution of information systems reflects the dynamic interplay between technological advancement, organizational needs, and theoretical insights. From basic automation and data storage to the development of sophisticated, integrated platforms, MIS has undergone a transformative journey. The progression from mainframe computers to networked systems and the emergence of user-centric applications have enabled organizations to harness the power of information systems for strategic and operational success

The future of MIS is marked by rapid technological advancement and the increasing importance of data-driven decision-making. As organizations adopt new technologies, they must navigate challenges related to data security, privacy, and strategic alignment. By leveraging emerging trends and aligning MIS with their organizational goals, businesses can position themselves for success in a competitive, data-driven world.

The conceptual foundations that direct the planning, creation, and use of information systems within enterprises are found in Management Information Systems (MIS) theoretical frameworks (Carayannis & Morawska-Jancelewicz, 2022). By using these conceptual frameworks, academics and practitioners may better comprehend, evaluate, and enhance the way MIS operates in many organizational settings.

The Socio-Technical Systems Theory is a well-known theoretical framework in MIS. The interdependence of social and technological components inside an organization is highlighted by this viewpoint. This idea holds that well integrated social and technological elements lead to efficient information systems. It acknowledges that information systems are intricately woven with an organization's social structure and are more than just technical objects (Farooq & Raju, 2019). As a result, for MIS implementation to be effective, social, and technical factors such as organizational culture, structure, and human behavior as well as hardware and software must be considered.

The Resource-Based View (RBV), which emphasizes the strategic use of resources to obtain a competitive advantage, is another important theoretical paradigm. Organizations use technology and information as useful resources to improve their competitive position in the setting of MIS. The RBV viewpoint, which acknowledges the importance of MIS in establishing and maintaining a competitive advantage, pushes businesses to invest in distinctive and priceless information resources(D. H. Chen et al., 2022).

Another well-known theoretical framework that evaluates the efficacy of information systems based on user happiness, system quality, and the influence on organizational performance is the Information Systems Success Model.

According to this paradigm, satisfying user requirements and expectations, guaranteeing the system's technical perfection, and having a beneficial impact on organizational results are all necessary for a MIS installation to be successful. In order to increase overall performance, this paradigm helps firms assess and improve their information systems. The acceptance and deployment of new technologies inside businesses is also clarified by the Diffusion of Innovations hypothesis(Cobbs et al., 2017).

According to this idea, the steps of knowledge, persuasion, decision-making, implementation, and confirmation are all included in the diffusion process. By using this approach, MIS practitioners may better understand how information system innovations are embraced and dispersed throughout an organization, reducing opposition and promoting a more seamless integration process (Priyashantha & Priyangaa, 2022).

The Transaction Cost Economics viewpoint, which emphasizes the examination of costs related to transactions in information sharing, is equally pertinent to MIS. According to this idea, companies should choose governance structures that reduce transaction costs. MIS is essential for enabling effective information sharing and lowering transaction costs inside companies.

1.3 Theoretical Frameworks in MIS and Artificial Intelligence

The study of Management Information Systems (MIS) benefits from a range of theoretical frameworks that guide the design, development, and implementation of information systems within organizations. These frameworks provide insights into how information systems function within various organizational contexts, highlighting the complex interplay between technology, people, and processes (Carayannis & Morawska-Jancelewicz, 2022). Through these frameworks, researchers and practitioners can examine how different factors influence the effectiveness and success of MIS, ultimately allowing organizations to harness technology for competitive advantage.

1.3.1 Socio-Technical Systems Theory

The Socio-Technical Systems (STS) Theory is one of the foundational theoretical frameworks in MIS, emphasizing the interdependence of social and technical components within an organization. STS posits that an effective information system is not only technologically sound but also harmoniously integrated with the organization's social structure (Farooq & Raju, 2019c). This theory suggests that an MIS implementation will be more successful when both the technical (hardware, software, network infrastructure) and social (organizational culture, human behavior, leadership) factors are adequately aligned.

STS Theory challenges the view that technology alone can drive organizational efficiency, emphasizing the human aspects of information systems. It recognizes that employees, their motivations, behaviors, and interactions with technology play a pivotal role in MIS outcomes. For instance, a highly advanced technological system may not yield the desired results if the employees lack the skills to use it effectively or if the organizational culture resists change. Therefore, a socio-technical approach to MIS implementation requires organizations to consider factors like training, change management, and leadership, alongside the technical aspects of the system.

An example of STS in action can be seen in the implementation of collaborative software platforms in companies. These platforms are designed to enhance teamwork, but without fostering a collaborative culture and ensuring employees understand the platform's features, the software alone cannot achieve meaningful collaboration. By emphasizing both social and technical elements, STS Theory helps MIS professionals design systems that are better integrated into the organizational structure, ultimately increasing their efficacy and adoption rates.

1.3.2 Resource-Based View (RBV)

The Resource-Based View (RBV) offers another important lens through which MIS can be examined, focusing on the strategic use of organizational resources to gain a competitive advantage. RBV posits that certain resources, particularly those that are valuable, rare, inimitable, and non-substitutable (often referred to as VRIN resources), can enable an organization to outperform its competitors (D. H. Chen et al., 2022). When applied to MIS, RBV suggests that information technology and data are critical resources that, when managed effectively, can provide a sustainable competitive advantage.

MIS serves as a strategic resource within the RBV framework by enabling organizations to optimize their operations, improve decision-making, and support innovation. For example, an organization with an advanced MIS that provides real-time data analysis can respond to market changes faster than competitors, creating a unique advantage. Similarly, a well-maintained database of customer information can enable personalized marketing strategies that enhance customer loyalty and satisfaction, which competitors may struggle to replicate.

RBV encourages organizations to invest in building and maintaining distinctive information resources, such as proprietary databases, analytics capabilities, and skilled personnel, which can become unique assets over time. By viewing MIS as a critical organizational resource, businesses can better justify investments in advanced technologies and IT infrastructure, as these resources are integral to achieving a competitive edge. Consequently, RBV provides a strategic perspective on MIS, urging organizations to consider information systems not merely as tools but as valuable assets that contribute to long-term success.

1.3.3 Information Systems Success Model (ISSM)

The Information Systems Success Model (ISSM), introduced by DeLone and McLean in 1992, is another widely used framework in the study of MIS. ISSM measures the success of information systems based on several key dimensions, including system quality, information quality, user satisfaction, and the impact on organizational performance. The model posits that an information system can only be deemed successful if it meets user needs, functions with technical excellence, and contributes positively to organizational outcomes.

ISSM is a comprehensive approach that helps organizations evaluate and improve their MIS. For example, an MIS that provides accurate, timely, and relevant information is likely to improve user satisfaction and support better decision-making. System quality is also critical, as a reliable, secure, and user-friendly system can enhance productivity and reduce the likelihood of errors. Additionally, ISSM highlights the importance of user satisfaction, recognizing that even the most advanced systems can fail if users are unhappy with their experience.

The ISSM is particularly useful for organizations seeking to assess the effectiveness of their MIS and identify areas for improvement. By examining user satisfaction, information quality, and system impact, organizations can make targeted adjustments to enhance performance. For instance, if users report dissatisfaction due to poor system usability, the organization might invest in a more intuitive interface or additional training to address this issue. Overall, ISSM provides a structured framework for assessing MIS success, ensuring that the system aligns with organizational goals and delivers tangible benefits.

1.3.4 Diffusion of Innovations Theory

The Diffusion of Innovations (DOI) Theory, developed by Everett Rogers, provides valuable insights into how new technologies are adopted within organizations. DOI suggests that the adoption of innovations follows a process consisting of several stages: knowledge, persuasion, decision, implementation, and confirmation. This theory is particularly relevant for understanding how MIS innovations are integrated within an organization, as it sheds light on the factors that influence the adoption and spread of new technologies (Priyashantha & Priyangaa, 2022).

In the context of MIS, DOI Theory suggests that successful adoption requires careful attention to how information about the system is communicated to potential users. During the knowledge stage, users become aware of the new system, while the persuasion stage involves convincing them of its benefits. Decision, implementation, and confirmation follow as users decide to adopt, implement, and eventually validate the effectiveness of the system.

The DOI framework highlights the importance of managing the human aspect of technology adoption. For instance, an organization implementing a new MIS may face resistance from employees who are accustomed to existing systems. By focusing on education, training, and clear communication, the organization can ease the transition and reduce resistance. Furthermore, DOI suggests that opinion leaders—individuals within the organization who are respected and trusted—can play a critical role in influencing adoption. By engaging these opinion leaders early in the process, MIS practitioners can facilitate smoother adoption and ensure the technology is more widely embraced.

1.3.5 Transaction Cost Economics (TCE) Perspective

Transaction Cost Economics (TCE) is another perspective that contributes to our understanding of MIS. Developed by economist Ronald Coase, TCE focuses on the costs associated with economic transactions, such as search, negotiation, and enforcement costs. In an organizational context, TCE posits that companies should structure their operations in a way that minimizes transaction costs, thereby improving efficiency and profitability. MIS plays a vital role in this process by streamlining information sharing, reducing coordination costs, and improving decision-making.

MIS helps organizations reduce transaction costs in various ways, such as through automated workflows, data-sharing platforms, and communication tools that facilitate collaboration. For instance, an MIS can automate routine transactions, such as purchase orders or inventory tracking, reducing the time and effort required to complete these tasks manually. This reduction in transaction costs enables organizations to focus their resources on more strategic activities, such as innovation or customer service.

The TCE perspective is particularly relevant in large organizations, where coordination costs can be high due to complex operations and diverse stakeholders. By leveraging MIS, organizations can simplify processes, reduce redundancies, and improve overall efficiency. TCE encourages businesses to consider the economic implications of their information systems, evaluating how technology can minimize transaction costs and support cost-effective operations.

1.3.6 Technology Acceptance Model (TAM)

The Technology Acceptance Model (TAM) is another influential theoretical framework in MIS, particularly for understanding user adoption of technology. Developed by Fred Davis in 1989, TAM suggests that two primary factors—perceived usefulness and perceived ease of use—determine whether users will accept or reject a new system. According to TAM, if users believe a technology will improve their job performance (usefulness) and is easy to use, they are more likely to adopt it.

TAM is especially useful in the context of MIS, as it highlights the importance of user-centric design. For example, an MIS that is perceived as complex or difficult to use may face low adoption rates, even if it offers significant functionality. Conversely, a system that is user-friendly and demonstrably beneficial to job performance is more likely to be embraced by employees.

Organizations can apply TAM principles when designing or selecting MIS solutions by focusing on usability and aligning the system's capabilities with users' needs. Training and support are also critical, as they can enhance perceived ease of use and increase user confidence. By addressing both usefulness and usability, organizations can improve the likelihood of successful MIS adoption, ensuring that the system provides value and aligns with user expectations.

1.3.7 Unified Theory of Acceptance and Use of Technology (UTAUT)

The Unified Theory of Acceptance and Use of Technology (UTAUT) builds on TAM, incorporating additional factors that influence technology adoption. UTAUT identifies four key determinants of user acceptance: performance expectancy, effort expectancy, social influence, and facilitating conditions. Performance expectancy refers to the extent to which a user believes the system will help achieve better outcomes, while effort expectancy relates to the ease of using the system. Social influence encompasses the impact of others' opinions on the user's decision, and facilitating conditions involve the resources and support available for using the technology.

UTAUT provides a comprehensive framework for examining the factors that influence MIS adoption, particularly in complex organizations where multiple stakeholders are involved. For instance, social influence may play a significant role in adoption if employees perceive that using the MIS aligns with organizational norms or expectations. Facilitating conditions, such as training and technical support, are also critical, as they provide users with the resources needed to overcome any barriers.

By applying UTAUT, organizations can identify potential obstacles to MIS adoption and develop

strategies to address them. For example, if employees are resistant due to low performance expectancy, the organization might demonstrate the MIS's value through case studies or pilot programs. By understanding the determinants of acceptance, organizations can create an environment that supports successful MIS implementation, ensuring that the system is embraced and utilized to its full potential.

The theoretical frameworks in MIS provide valuable insights into how information systems are designed, implemented, and adopted within organizations. From the socio-technical perspective, which emphasizes the importance of aligning technology with social structures, to the Resource-Based View, which positions MIS as a strategic asset, these frameworks offer diverse perspectives on the role of information systems in modern businesses. By understanding and applying these frameworks, MIS professionals can create systems that not only meet technical requirements but also align with organizational goals, support user needs, and deliver sustainable value. In an increasingly complex and technology-driven business environment, these frameworks serve as essential tools for navigating the challenges and opportunities associated with MIS.

1.4 Role of MIS in Modern Organizations

To support informed decision-making processes, MIS plays a diverse role in modern organizations by integrating technology, data, and human knowledge. The foundation of organizational operations is MIS, which offers an organized method for managing information resources and boosts the general efficacy of corporate procedures (Yoo, 2010).

The contribution of MIS to data management is a key component of that function. Organizations get enormous volumes of data from many sources in today's data-driven world. MIS makes ensuring that this data is efficiently gathered, stored, and retrieved in order to convert it into information that is useful for operational and strategic planning decisions. MIS helps businesses to use data to obtain insights, spot patterns, and predict future trends by using strong databases and information systems (Karinshak & Jin, 2023).

Within organizations, MIS promotes cooperation and communication. MIS guarantees smooth information flow between departments, facilitating effective staff coordination and cooperation via the integration of communication technology and collaborative platforms. Because of this interconnection, organizations are more agile and can react to opportunities and changes in the market more quickly (Chekotilo et al., 2020).

Organizational leaders are empowered by MIS with timely and relevant information. MIS supports strategic decision-making by giving executives access to real-time data and analytical tools, which helps them negotiate uncertainty and make decisions that support company goals. In a corporate environment that is changing quickly, this strategic alignment is essential for companies looking to gain a competitive advantage.

Resource optimization is a part of MIS's responsibilities. MIS optimizes operational processes by automating repetitive procedures, which minimizes mistakes and human labor. In addition to increasing productivity, this efficiency enables firms to deploy resources more wisely, concentrating on tasks that have a higher potential impact on the overall company plan (Effah et al., 2023).

Innovation inside organizations is stimulated by MIS. MIS specialists aid in the discovery and application of novel solutions by using cutting-edge technology and remaining current with market developments. By taking a proactive stance, companies may take advantage of emerging possibilities and maintain a competitive edge in a constantly evolving business landscape.

Although MIS offers many chances to improve a company, it is not without difficulties. For MIS personnel, security concerns, data privacy problems, and the quick speed of technology improvements provide constant hurdles. In the field of management information systems, finding a balance between using technology to gain a competitive edge and reducing related risks is a continuous task.

Management Information Systems (MIS) play a foundational role in modern organizations, enhancing operational efficiency, supporting strategic decision-making, and driving innovation. MIS combines technology, data, and human knowledge to create structured pathways for managing information resources, allowing organizations to achieve a competitive edge (Yoo, 2010). In today's data-driven environment, MIS is more relevant than ever, as it not only streamlines processes but also facilitates the integration of advanced technologies such as Artificial Intelligence (AI), which further amplifies its transformative impact. This section explores the multifaceted role of MIS in data management, communication, decision-making, resource optimization, innovation, and the transformative influence of AI in these domains.

1.4.1 Data Management in a Data-Driven Era

One of the primary roles of MIS in modern organizations is efficient data management. Organizations today deal with enormous volumes of data from various sources, including customer interactions, market analysis, and internal processes. MIS plays a crucial role in collecting, storing, processing, and transforming this raw data into valuable information that supports operational and strategic planning (Karinshak & Jin, 2023).

Through robust databases and efficient information systems, MIS enables organizations to derive actionable insights, recognize patterns, and make data-driven predictions about future trends. This capacity to convert data into useful information is essential in an era where businesses rely on analytics to guide their growth strategies. For instance, with the help of MIS, retail businesses can analyze purchasing behaviors to forecast demand and manage inventory, leading to cost savings and improved customer satisfaction. Furthermore, MIS enables real-time data management, allowing companies to monitor performance indicators and react promptly to market changes.

Artificial Intelligence (AI) significantly enhances the data management capabilities of MIS by enabling advanced analytics, machine learning, and predictive modeling. AI-powered MIS can process large volumes of unstructured data, such as social media feeds or customer reviews, transforming it into structured insights that support decision-making. This automation of data analysis not only speeds up the process but also uncovers hidden insights, giving companies a clearer understanding of customer preferences, market trends, and operational efficiencies. For instance, an AI-enhanced MIS in the healthcare sector can analyze patient data to predict disease patterns and optimize treatment plans, ultimately improving patient outcomes.

1.4.2 Facilitating Communication and Collaboration

MIS also plays a pivotal role in fostering communication and collaboration within organizations. By integrating communication technologies and collaborative platforms, MIS ensures that information flows seamlessly across departments, which promotes effective coordination among staff. This interconnected environment increases organizational agility, enabling teams to respond swiftly to market opportunities and operational challenges (Chekotilo et al., 2020).

In the past, departments often operated in silos, creating barriers to information sharing and collaboration. Modern MIS, however, integrates tools such as intranets, instant messaging platforms, and project management systems, which bridge these gaps. Employees can access and share data instantly, eliminating the delays associated with manual information transfer. For example, a finance team can seamlessly collaborate with the marketing department to analyze campaign budgets and assess return on investment in real-time, facilitating more aligned and timely decision-making.

AI further enhances communication within MIS by implementing intelligent systems that can streamline interactions. AI chatbots and virtual assistants can manage routine inquiries, freeing up time for human resources to focus on complex tasks. Additionally, AI-driven tools like natural language processing (NLP) can analyze communication patterns and provide insights into team dynamics, helping management improve organizational communication strategies. This ability to analyze and optimize communication fosters a more collaborative environment, which is crucial in today's highly interconnected workspaces.

1.4.3 Empowering Strategic Decision-Making

One of the most valuable functions of MIS is empowering leaders with relevant and timely information to support strategic decision-making. By providing access to real-time data and advanced analytical tools, MIS helps executives navigate uncertainties and make informed decisions that align with the organization's goals. In a rapidly changing business environment, this strategic alignment is essential for organizations aiming to maintain a competitive advantage.

MIS achieves this by providing executives with dashboards and reporting tools that consolidate key performance indicators (KPIs) and other metrics into visual formats, allowing for quick assessment of the company's performance. With tools like predictive analytics, MIS can help leaders anticipate future trends and identify potential risks, which supports more proactive and forward-thinking decision-making. For example, a manufacturing company can leverage MIS to monitor supply chain data, identifying potential bottlenecks before they disrupt production.

AI integration within MIS takes strategic decision-making to new heights by offering deeper insights through advanced analytics. AI algorithms can analyze past performance, current trends, and external factors to generate predictions with a high degree of accuracy. This predictive power enables executives to anticipate market shifts, optimize resource allocation, and make data-driven decisions. For instance, in the finance industry, AI-enabled MIS can analyze stock market data in real-time, helping investment firms make quick, informed decisions that align with client goals and market trends.

1.4.4 Resource Optimization and Operational Efficiency

MIS plays a crucial role in optimizing resources by automating repetitive tasks, reducing errors, and minimizing human effort. Automation not only boosts productivity but also enables organizations to allocate resources more effectively, allowing them to focus on tasks that align with their strategic objectives (Effah et al., 2023). Through resource optimization, MIS helps companies achieve greater operational efficiency and cost-effectiveness.

For instance, MIS can automate payroll processes, inventory tracking, and other routine administrative tasks, which not only reduces errors but also frees up human resources for higher-value work. Automated workflows in MIS improve turnaround times and ensure consistency in operations, which is essential for maintaining high-quality standards. An optimized MIS can also provide insights into resource allocation, such as identifying underutilized assets or suggesting ways to optimize production schedules in manufacturing, thereby reducing waste and costs.

The impact of AI on resource optimization is transformative. AI-powered MIS can use machine learning algorithms to predict demand, optimize inventory levels, and automate complex scheduling tasks. For example, in logistics, AI can analyze traffic patterns, weather forecasts, and shipping routes to determine the most efficient delivery schedules, minimizing fuel consumption and improving delivery times. Such AI-driven optimization not only reduces operational costs but also enhances customer satisfaction by ensuring timely service delivery.

1.4.5 Driving Innovation and Competitiveness

MIS fosters innovation by providing organizations with the tools and insights needed to develop new products, processes, and business models. MIS professionals help organizations stay up-to-date with technological advancements, applying innovative solutions that give companies a competitive edge. In a constantly evolving market, innovation fueled by MIS enables organizations to seize emerging opportunities and maintain their market position.

For instance, MIS can support research and development (R&D) by offering data-driven insights that inform product design and market positioning. By analyzing customer feedback, competitive data, and market trends, MIS provides organizations with a clear understanding of customer needs, which can guide product development and marketing strategies. An innovative MIS can even help companies identify potential areas for expansion, such as new markets or untapped customer segments.

AI accelerates the innovation potential of MIS by enabling data-driven experimentation and faster iteration cycles. AI algorithms can analyze data from R&D efforts, helping companies refine their products and processes based on real-time feedback.

For example, in the pharmaceutical industry, AI-driven MIS can analyze clinical trial data to accelerate drug development, improving the chances of regulatory approval and bringing new treatments to market faster. Additionally, AI can support creative processes, such as generating product design ideas or recommending modifications based on consumer preferences, thereby fostering continuous innovation.

1.4.6 Enhancing Security and Addressing Challenges

While MIS offers numerous opportunities for enhancing organizational performance, it also presents challenges, particularly in terms of security and data privacy. MIS professionals face the constant task of securing data against cyber threats and ensuring compliance with data protection regulations. In an era where data breaches can have severe financial and reputational consequences, maintaining a secure information infrastructure is essential.

To address these challenges, MIS incorporates advanced security protocols, such as encryption, access controls, and intrusion detection systems, to protect sensitive information. Additionally, MIS professionals must stay updated on regulatory requirements, such as the General Data Protection Regulation (GDPR) and industry-specific standards, to ensure compliance. Regular security audits and employee training also play a vital role in mitigating risks and maintaining data integrity.

AI has transformed the way organizations approach security within MIS. AI-powered security systems can detect anomalies in real-time, allowing organizations to respond to potential threats proactively. Machine learning algorithms can identify patterns associated with malicious activity, such as unusual login locations or abnormal transaction volumes, and alert security teams. This real-time threat detection and response capability is invaluable for safeguarding sensitive information and maintaining customer trust.

The role of MIS in modern organizations is multifaceted, encompassing data management, communication, decision-making, resource optimization, and innovation. By providing structured and efficient methods for managing information, MIS enables organizations to operate more effectively and respond to challenges with agility. The integration of AI into MIS amplifies these capabilities, transforming traditional MIS functions and offering unprecedented opportunities for insight, efficiency, and security.

In a rapidly evolving digital landscape, the combination of MIS and AI positions organizations to leverage data as a strategic asset, facilitating data-driven decisions and innovative practices. AI-enhanced MIS systems allow companies to anticipate market shifts, optimize operations, and maintain robust security protocols, all of which are essential for achieving long-term success. As organizations continue to adopt AI within their MIS frameworks, the transformative potential of this technology will only grow, offering new ways to enhance competitiveness, improve performance, and drive innovation. Together, MIS and AI form a powerful foundation for organizations striving to navigate the complexities of the modern business environment and capitalize on the opportunities of the future.

1.5 Integrating MIS with Corporate Strategy

The process of integrating MIS with corporate strategy entails matching the information systems' technical prowess with the organization's broader objectives and vision. This alignment affects decision-making structures, business processes, and company culture as a whole; it goes beyond simple technological considerations. A MIS that is properly integrated acts as a catalyst, encouraging productivity, creativity, and flexibility within the company.

The identification of information systems as strategic assets as opposed to just support functions is a basic component of this integration. Information systems were formerly thought of as back-office instruments whose main purpose was to automate repetitive work. But as the digital environment changed, businesses saw how revolutionary MIS might be for developing and carrying out corporate plans.

Strategic MIS deployment requires a deep comprehension of the particular requirements of the firm as well as the dynamics of the industry. Identifying the crucial business procedures that information technology may improve or optimize is part of this. Organizations may achieve a competitive advantage, optimize processes, and improve their ability to adapt to changing market circumstances by using MIS strategically to support essential activities.

Proactive information management is required when integrating MIS with company strategy. When handled correctly, data sometimes referred to as the lifeblood of modern organizations becomes a strategic asset. MIS makes it easier to gather, process, and analyze data, allowing decision-makers at all organizational levels to make wellinformed choices. Employing data strategically enables firms to see patterns, predict changes in the market, and take advantage of new possibilities.

Cross-functional cooperation is required for the integration of MIS with business strategy. Information systems now penetrate every aspect of the company and are not limited to the IT department. In light of this, it is crucial to promote a collaborative culture and make sure that technology is in sync with several departments and business divisions. A key component of a successful MIS integration is the synergy between technology and human capital, wherein staff members participate actively in the strategic use of information rather than only being consumers.

This integration path is not without its hurdles. Concerns including data security, system interoperability, and the need for ongoing technological adaptation are challenges that organizations must face. In order to make sure that MIS supports corporate strategy without jeopardizing the security and resilience of the company, it is essential to strike the correct balance between innovation and stability.

Integrating Management Information Systems (MIS) with corporate strategy is a transformative process that requires aligning an organization's technological capabilities with its broader business objectives. This integration influences decision-making structures, business processes, and corporate culture, extending beyond purely technical considerations to shape how the organization achieves its vision. When properly integrated, MIS serves as a powerful catalyst, fostering productivity, innovation, and adaptability within the organization. With advancements in Artificial Intelligence (AI), the integration of MIS and corporate strategy is further empowered, enabling a dynamic, data-driven approach that enhances both operational and strategic outcomes.

1.5.1 Viewing Information Systems as Strategic Assets

A key aspect of integrating MIS with corporate strategy is recognizing information systems as strategic assets rather than mere support functions. Traditionally, MIS was seen as a back-office tool, primarily used to automate repetitive tasks and streamline administrative functions(Zeng & Yanchao, 2021). However, as the digital landscape evolved, companies began to recognize MIS's transformative potential in shaping and executing corporate strategies. Modern organizations view MIS as a central component in creating a competitive advantage, capable of driving key functions like product development, customer relations, and resource allocation (Dongfang et al., 2021).

For instance, MIS enables data-driven decision-making across departments, helping companies predict market trends and refine product offerings based on customer data. In the retail sector, a well-integrated MIS can identify shifts in customer preferences and enable agile adjustments in product positioning, pricing, or inventory management(Lili et al., 2021; Zheng et al., 2021). By treating MIS as a strategic asset, organizations move beyond merely automating tasks, leveraging MIS to generate actionable insights and align business activities with strategic goals.

1.5.2 AI's Transformative Role in Strategic MIS Integration

Artificial Intelligence further transforms MIS by providing sophisticated tools for data analysis, pattern recognition, and predictive modeling. AI-powered MIS systems can process vast amounts of data in real-time, generating insights that inform strategic decisions and enable proactive responses to market changes. For example, in financial services, AI-enabled MIS can analyze market data to identify investment opportunities, predict economic trends, and optimize portfolio management. This level of strategic insight would be nearly impossible to achieve through traditional MIS alone(Kazemi et al., 2021; Yuan & Yicun, 2021).

Moreover, AI enhances MIS's capability to adapt to new data streams and changing conditions. Machine learning algorithms can refine predictive models based on real-time data, allowing businesses to adjust their strategies dynamically(L. Huang, 2021; Rusakov V et al., 2021). AI-powered chatbots and virtual assistants also streamline customer service processes, enhancing customer satisfaction and loyalty, which are key strategic objectives for many companies. By integrating AI into MIS, organizations create a feedback loop where data informs strategy and strategy, in turn, guides data utilization, driving continuous improvement and competitive advantage.

1.5.3 Aligning MIS with Key Business Processes

Strategic integration of MIS requires a deep understanding of the organization's unique needs and industry dynamics. This includes identifying key business processes that can be optimized through MIS. In today's fast-paced business environment, the ability to streamline workflows, reduce operational costs, and enhance customer experiences is crucial(Gang et al., 2021; Z. Guo et al., 2021). MIS facilitates these objectives by providing tools for process automation, data analysis, and cross-functional collaboration.

For example, in the manufacturing sector, MIS can monitor supply chain processes, track production efficiency, and manage inventory levels. AI can further enhance this integration by enabling predictive maintenance, where algorithms analyze equipment data to predict failures and schedule maintenance before disruptions occur(S. Liu, 2021; YOUNG, 2021). This level of process optimization reduces downtime, improves production schedules, and contributes to the overall strategic goal of maximizing operational efficiency.

In the healthcare industry, an integrated MIS can manage patient data, streamline appointment scheduling, and ensure regulatory compliance. AI can enhance MIS capabilities by analyzing patient records to identify patterns, predict health outcomes, and suggest treatment plans(X. Li, 2021; Zhigang, 2021). Such strategic MIS integration allows healthcare providers to deliver higher-quality patient care while optimizing resources and reducing costs.

1.5.4 Proactive Information Management and Data as a Strategic Asset

Integrating MIS with corporate strategy necessitates a proactive approach to information management. Data, often considered the lifeblood of modern organizations, becomes a critical strategic asset when managed effectively(Kuzovkova et al.,

2021). Through MIS, organizations can collect, process, and analyze data, enabling decision-makers at all levels to make well-informed choices. Strategic use of data allows organizations to recognize patterns, predict market shifts, and capitalize on emerging opportunities(W. Jiang & Xie, 2021; Thorpe et al., 2021).

AI amplifies the value of data by enabling advanced analytics, predictive modeling, and real-time decision support. For instance, AI algorithms can analyze customer behavior patterns, providing insights into preferences, purchasing behaviors, and market trends(H. Cai et al., 2021; Han et al., 2021). Retail companies can leverage this data to personalize marketing strategies, predict inventory needs, and optimize pricing. This data-driven approach allows organizations to act proactively rather than reactively, creating a significant strategic advantage in highly competitive markets(Doutcheva, 2021).

Furthermore, proactive information management enables organizations to pivot their strategies as market conditions change. AI-powered MIS can detect shifts in consumer sentiment or emerging risks, allowing companies to adjust their strategies promptly(Junru et al., 2021; Park et al., 2020). In finance, for example, AI algorithms can assess market volatility and suggest investment adjustments in response to real-time economic changes. This agility is essential for organizations aiming to maintain resilience and adaptability in an unpredictable business environment(-Bukunov, 2020; Y. Zhu & IEEE, 2020).

1.5.5 Fostering Cross-Functional Collaboration

MIS integration with corporate strategy requires cross-functional collaboration, as information systems now permeate every part of the organization rather than being confined to the IT department. This calls for a collaborative culture in which technology aligns with the goals of various departments and business units(Long et al., 2020; Yaroslavtsev & Matukhina, 2020). In a successful MIS integration, the synergy between technology and human capital is paramount. Employees are not merely users of information but are active participants in the strategic deployment of MIS, leveraging it to achieve their departmental objectives and the organization's broader goals(C. Xie, Luo, & IEEE, 2020; Zhongkai et al., 2020).

AI further facilitates cross-functional collaboration by breaking down communication barriers and promoting data sharing. AI-powered analytics tools enable departments to access and interpret data relevant to their functions, allowing them to work together more effectively(C. Yang & Sun, 2020; X. Zhang, 2020a). For instance, a marketing team can use AI-driven insights from customer service data to refine campaigns, while product development teams can adjust their designs based on real-time customer feedback(Q. Chen, 2020; Genchev, 2020). By enabling seamless collaboration and data sharing, AI-enhanced MIS supports a cohesive strategy that aligns all departments toward shared organizational goals.

Additionally, AI tools such as natural language processing (NLP) and machine learning can analyze communication patterns and suggest improvements for collaboration(Leventhal & Schreyer, 2020; Sukhorukov et al., 2020). In large organizations with complex hierarchies, AI can identify communication bottlenecks and recommend process improvements, ensuring that information flows efficiently between teams(C. Xie, Luo, Yu, et al., 2020)s. This enhances organizational agility, as departments can respond quickly to internal and external changes, fostering a more resilient and adaptable corporate strategy.

1.5.6 Addressing Security and Compliance Challenges

While the integration of MIS with corporate strategy offers significant benefits, it also poses challenges related to security, data privacy, and compliance. As organizations rely more heavily on data to inform strategic decisions, they become more vulnerable to cyber threats. A single security breach can have severe financial and reputational consequences, making it essential for organizations to prioritize data protection and regulatory compliance.

MIS plays a critical role in addressing these challenges by implementing robust security protocols, such as encryption, multi-factor authentication, and access controls. Regular security audits and employee training on data privacy practices further strengthen the organization's defenses. Compliance with regulations like the General Data Protection Regulation (GDPR) and industry-specific standards is also vital, as non-compliance can result in substantial fines and legal repercussions(Nedzelskay et al., 2020; X. Zhang, 2020b).

AI offers transformative potential in managing security and compliance within an integrated MIS. AI-powered security systems can detect anomalies in real time, allowing organizations to respond to potential threats proactively(Changcheng & Chaohu, 2020; Yousefnezhad et al., 2020). For instance, machine learning algorithms can analyze network traffic patterns to identify suspicious activity, such as unauthorized access attempts or unusual data transfers. By automating threat detection and response, AI enhances the organization's ability to safeguard sensitive data and maintain compliance with regulatory standards(Chan et al., 2020).

Furthermore, AI-driven compliance tools can automate regulatory reporting, reducing the administrative burden on employees and minimizing the risk of human error (Le Queau et al., 2020; J. Liang, 2020). For example, in the healthcare sector, AI can monitor patient data access to ensure compliance with privacy regulations, such as the Health Insurance Portability and Accountability Act (HIPAA). This level of automated compliance management enables organizations to focus on strategic objectives without compromising data security.

1.5.7 Balancing Innovation and Stability

A critical aspect of integrating MIS with corporate strategy is finding the right balance between innovation and stability. On one hand, organizations need to adopt new technologies and innovative practices to remain competitive (LE et al., 2020; Luo et al., 2020). On the other hand, constant technological changes can disrupt operations and create risks. Achieving this balance requires a strategic approach to MIS that promotes innovation while ensuring operational stability (Matsumoto & Shigeyasu, 2020; Mohd et al., 2019).

MIS enables this balance by providing a structured framework for adopting and implementing new technologies. For example, when introducing AI-driven MIS tools, companies can use pilot programs to test their effectiveness and identify potential challenges before full-scale deployment(Shtangret et al., 2019; Zhaorong et al., 2019). This phased approach allows organizations to embrace innovation at a manageable pace, reducing disruption and minimizing risks(C. Zhang & IOP, 2019).

AI plays a crucial role in maintaining this balance by offering predictive insights that guide innovation efforts (Wan et al., 2019). AI algorithms can simulate the potential impact of new technologies on organizational processes, helping companies assess whether the benefits of innovation outweigh the associated risks (Lin, 2019; Mu et al., 2019). For example, in the logistics industry, AI can simulate the impact of autonomous vehicles on delivery times and costs, allowing companies to make informed decisions about adopting this technology.

1.5.8 A Strategic Imperative in the Digital Age

The integration of MIS with corporate strategy is not merely a technological undertaking but a strategic imperative in today's digital age(X. Gao et al., 2019; Miyazaki et al., 2019). By aligning MIS capabilities with organizational goals, companies can create a cohesive approach that drives operational efficiency, enhances decision-making, and fosters a culture of innovation(Teplicka, 2019; Yi-Jia et al., 2019). The integration process requires proactive information management, cross-functional collaboration, and a balanced approach to technology adoption, all of which contribute to a robust and adaptable corporate strategy(Y. M. Chen & Liu, 2019; G. Li et al., 2019).

The transformative power of AI within MIS amplifies these benefits, providing organizations with advanced tools for data analysis, process optimization, and risk management (Kokoeva et al., 2019; Tarigan et al., 2019). AI-enabled MIS systems enable organizations to make data-driven decisions, optimize resource allocation, and maintain resilience in an unpredictable business environment(Guan et al., 2019; Hongrui et al., 2019). As organizations continue to embrace AI and other emerging technologies, the strategic integration of MIS will become even more essential for achieving long-term success and maintaining a competitive advantage.

In the coming years, the integration of MIS with corporate strategy will play a defining role in how organizations adapt to evolving market conditions, leverage data as a strategic asset, and remain at the forefront of innovation(Nasrulloh et al., 2019). By recognizing the strategic value of MIS and embracing AI's transformative potential, companies can create a sustainable path toward growth, resilience, and competitive success in an increasingly complex and dynamic business landscape.

1.6 Challenges and Opportunities in MIS

The fact that technology is always evolving is one of the main issues facing MIS. Organizations must constantly adapt to new tools and platforms as information systems develop quickly in order to stay competitive. For MIS specialists, this is a never-ending task since they have to keep up with the latest technical advancements, evaluate their organizational value, and execute them with ease. In addition, integrating these technologies with current systems presents new difficulties that must be carefully planned and carried out to guarantee a seamless transition.

Privacy and data security are related issues to the technology problem. The growing dependence of enterprises on digital platforms for information processing and storage raises the continual risk of data breaches and cyberattacks. Complying with strict data security rules and strengthening systems against possible attacks present challenges. MIS specialists have to maneuver through this intricate environment, putting strong security measures in place and making sure that private data is used in an ethical and legal manner. One important area of focus is the strategic alignment of MIS with company objectives. MIS may be used by organizations to improve decision-making processes by offering data driven, real-time insights (Kuts & Makarchuk, 2023). Organizations are able to make well-informed strategic choices by using MIS to identify operational inefficiencies, consumer preferences, and market trends via efficient data analysis. Technology will assist organizational goals by acting as an enabler when MIS and business strategy are seamlessly integrated. Business process optimization is yet another noteworthy possibility. Routine chores may be automated with the help of MIS, which streamlines operations and boosts productivity. Organizations may spend resources more wisely and create a more responsive and agile corporate environment by automating repetitive and monotonous operations. Consequently, this leads to decreased expenses and enhanced overall efficiency. Business internationalization offers MIS possibilities as well as difficulties. Global market interconnection creates opportunities for cooperation and innovation even as it calls for complex information systems to handle a variety of functions. By facilitating cross-border coordination, cooperation, and communication, MIS enables businesses to take advantage of the skills of varied teams and successfully adapt to the global market.

The evolving technological landscape has created an ongoing challenge for Management Information Systems (MIS), demanding organizations to constantly adopt new tools and platforms to remain competitive. For MIS specialists, this requires staying current with technological advancements, assessing their value to the organization, and integrating them effectively to drive strategic goals. Artificial Intelligence (AI) has introduced transformative possibilities within MIS, reshaping how organizations process, analyze, and act upon information. However, this evolution also brings challenges in privacy, data security, and the strategic alignment of MIS with business objectives. With AI as a pivotal enabler, MIS is equipped to address these challenges, enhance decision-making, and create a responsive, agile environment for global business operations.

1.6.1 The Role of AI in Enhancing MIS Adaptability and Innovation

MIS is continually evolving to keep pace with rapid technological changes, creating a need for agility in how information systems are managed and deployed(Masuin et al., 2019; Setiawan et al., 2019). AI has redefined adaptability within MIS, providing intelligent tools that enable organizations to automate routine tasks, streamline workflows, and gain insights from vast amounts of data. With AI, MIS can move beyond traditional functions, integrating machine learning, natural language processing, and predictive analytics to create systems that adapt and learn over time.

For example, in customer service, AI-powered chatbots can handle a significant portion of customer interactions, enabling MIS to support an around-the-clock service model without additional human resources(N. Jiang et al., 2019; Luma & Abazi, 2019). AI-driven sentiment analysis tools can further enhance customer interactions by analyzing feedback and identifying areas for improvement in real time, leading to a more responsive and customer-centric organization(H. Cai et al., 2019; Z. Liu et al., 2019). In logistics, AI optimizes supply chain operations by predicting demand, managing inventory, and automating delivery schedules, all of which contribute to an efficient and adaptable MIS structure that supports strategic objectives

1.6.2 Addressing Privacy and Data Security Challenges with AI-Enhanced MIS

One of the most pressing issues facing MIS today is data security, especially as digital platforms play an increasingly central role in information processing and storage (Brunner et al., 2019; Qian et al., 2019). The risks of data breaches and cyberattacks are constant, requiring MIS professionals to implement robust security measures(J. Chen et al., 2019). AI offers advanced tools for safeguarding sensitive data, enhancing security measures, and ensuring compliance with data privacy regulations(P. Cai & Jiang, 2019; Hoeffner et al., 2019). Through AI, MIS can employ techniques like anomaly detection, where machine learning algorithms identify unusual patterns in data access or network traffic that could indicate a security breach(Fadillah et al., 2019; Mukhtar et al., 2019).

AI-powered cybersecurity systems can learn from each interaction, refining their ability to detect and respond to threats (kang-hyun-wook et al., 2019; B. Li et al., 2019). For example, AI can automatically recognize potential phishing emails, alert employees, and block the compromised communications. In terms of regulatory compliance, AI tools help organizations adhere to laws such as GDPR by automating data audits and access management (Iskanderov & Pautov, 2019; Yong et al., 2019). By streamlining these processes, AI enables MIS to focus on other strategic initiatives while ensuring data security and regulatory compliance remain top priorities (Chin et al., 2019; Manzhurov et al., 2019). Moreover, AI supports MIS in developing ethical frameworks for data usage, as algorithms can be programmed to prioritize transparency and accountability (X. Liu, 2019; D. Yang et al., 2019). As privacy concerns grow, AI-enabled MIS can enforce policies around data minimization and user consent, ensuring that organizations adhere to both legal requirements and ethical standards(C. L. Huang, 2019; Shmeleva et al., 2019). This helps to build trust with customers, an increasingly important factor in sustaining competitive advantage in data-driven industries.

1.6.3 Strategic Alignment of MIS with Organizational Objectives Using AI

To achieve sustainable growth, organizations must strategically align their MIS with business objectives, ensuring that technology acts as an enabler rather than a standalone asset (Fuaddi & Sabarguna, 2019; Vidal Carvalho et al., 2019). AI has transformed how organizations can use MIS for strategic alignment by offering data-driven, real-time insights into consumer behavior, market trends, and operational inefficiencies (Y. Huang et al., 2019; Ramachandran & Karthick, 2019). With AI,

MIS systems can provide dynamic, actionable insights that empower leaders to make informed strategic decisions (Rozhkova et al., 2018; Zagornaya et al., 2018).

AI-driven analytics allow MIS to process vast datasets quickly, identifying patterns and trends that inform decisions on product development, marketing strategies, and customer engagement (Chelyshkov & Aralkin, 2018; Ionescu et al., 2018). For instance, AI-enabled MIS can analyze sales data to reveal customer preferences and purchasing trends, guiding product positioning and pricing strategies. In finance, predictive analytics can assess investment risks and optimize portfolio strategies, allowing organizations to manage risk more effectively while aligning financial decisions with broader corporate(X. Chen et al., 2018; Fatimah et al., 2018) goals (Azarov et al., 2018; D. G. Lee et al., 2018). MIS further supports strategic alignment through AI-powered decision-support systems that simulate potential outcomes of various strategies. For example, retail companies can use AI to predict the impact of seasonal trends on inventory management, helping to prevent stockouts or overstock situations (Lamboglia et al., 2018; Xiaosong et al., 2018). This proactive approach enables organizations to remain agile in dynamic markets, ensuring MIS capabilities are in sync with strategic objectives and organizational growth (Hwang et al., 2018; Olson, 2018).

1.6.4 AI-Driven Business Process Optimization in MIS

A key advantage of integrating AI into MIS is the optimization of business processes. AI-powered MIS can automate routine tasks, enhance workflow efficiency, and enable organizations to allocate resources more effectively (Velmakina et al., 2018; Yi-Lin et al., 2018). By automating repetitive activities, AI helps MIS eliminate inefficiencies, allowing employees to focus on higher-impact tasks that require human creativity and decision-making (Ding, 2018; Xiaofang & Machinery, 2018).

For instance, in HR departments, AI-driven MIS can automate the recruitment process, screening resumes, and matching candidates based on predetermined criteria, allowing HR professionals to focus on interviews and culture fit (H. Wang, 2018; W. Zhu et al., 2018). In financial departments, AI can streamline accounting processes by categorizing transactions and identifying anomalies, leading to more accurate financial reporting and fraud detection (K. Chen et al., 2018; G. Yang et al., 2018). The resulting efficiency reduces operational costs, improves accuracy, and enhances productivity, positioning the organization for sustainable growth (Code, 2018; Ogiela & Ogiela, 2018).

Additionally, AI enables predictive maintenance in sectors like manufacturing and energy, where equipment performance is critical to productivity (Lijun, 2018; Morozov et al., 2018). MIS systems can leverage AI to monitor machine health, predict equipment failures, and schedule maintenance before issues arise(Kratov,

2018; Wu et al., 2018). This proactive approach reduces downtime, minimizes repair costs, and extends the lifecycle of assets, contributing to a more resilient and efficient business model.

1.6.5 The Role of AI-Enabled MIS in Supporting Globalization Efforts

The interconnected global market presents both opportunities and challenges for organizations, requiring sophisticated information systems to manage diverse functions across regions(Burkov et al., 2018; S. Chen, 2018). AI-enhanced MIS systems facilitate globalization by enabling cross-border coordination, collaboration, and communication. By leveraging AI, MIS can provide a standardized platform for global operations, allowing companies to operate seamlessly across multiple markets and adapt to regional nuances effectively (Mateer & Jones, 2018).

For example, AI-enabled translation tools support communication between multinational teams, removing language barriers and enhancing collaboration (Ma et al., 2018; Min & IEEE, 2018). In addition, AI-powered data analytics provide insights into regional market conditions, customer preferences, and regulatory requirements, allowing companies to tailor their strategies to specific markets(Oh Seh-La et al., 2018; J. Zhang, 2018). In supply chain management, AI helps optimize logistics, reduce delivery times, and manage cross-border regulatory compliance, all of which are essential for efficient global operations.

AI-driven MIS further supports globalization by enabling organizations to create a more inclusive and diverse work environment. Through AI-powered talent acquisition platforms, companies can attract skilled professionals from around the world, building a workforce that brings varied perspectives and expertise. By facilitating global talent integration, AI-enhanced MIS enables organizations to tap into diverse skills and knowledge, strengthening their competitive edge in an interconnected market.

1.6.6 AI's Role in Balancing Technological Innovation and Stability in MIS

As organizations embrace new technologies to maintain competitiveness, they must balance innovation with stability to avoid disruptions in critical operations. MIS provides the structure necessary to adopt new technologies while maintaining operational continuity, and AI plays a pivotal role in achieving this balance. By using AI-driven simulations, MIS can assess the impact of new technology implementations on existing processes, helping organizations make informed decisions about adoption.

For example, a retail company considering augmented reality for enhancing customer experiences can use AI to simulate the technology's impact on current sales processes, customer engagement, and inventory management. Through this approach, MIS ensures that technology integration supports strategic objectives without compromising stability. In financial services, AI-driven risk assessment tools evaluate the potential impact of new digital banking platforms, helping to mitigate risks associated with technology adoption.

AI also supports MIS in managing change by providing predictive insights that allow organizations to proactively address challenges. In healthcare, for instance, AI-driven MIS can simulate the impact of telemedicine platforms on patient outcomes, resource allocation, and regulatory compliance. This ability to test and evaluate technology enables healthcare organizations to innovate responsibly, ensuring that new solutions align with both clinical and operational goals.

1.6.7 Navigating AI-Driven MIS Challenges: Ethical Considerations and Workforce Adaptation

While AI offers numerous advantages to MIS, it also presents challenges that require careful management. Ethical considerations surrounding AI, such as bias in algorithms and the need for transparency, are particularly relevant. For MIS specialists, addressing these ethical concerns requires a commitment to developing AI systems that are fair, accountable, and transparent. Ensuring that AI-driven MIS adheres to ethical guidelines builds trust among employees, customers, and stakeholders, which is crucial for long-term organizational success.

Moreover, as AI automates tasks traditionally performed by employees, organizations must consider the impact on the workforce. AI-enabled MIS systems reduce the need for manual data entry, transaction processing, and other administrative tasks, but they also create a demand for skills in AI management, data analytics, and cybersecurity. MIS departments play a key role in supporting workforce adaptation, providing training programs and resources that help employees develop the skills needed to thrive in an AI-driven environment.

Organizations that address these challenges responsibly can foster a culture of innovation while minimizing potential disruptions. MIS specialists can implement guidelines for ethical AI use, ensuring that AI aligns with the organization's values and strategic goals. By prioritizing workforce adaptation, MIS departments enable organizations to build a skilled, resilient workforce that is well-equipped to leverage AI for strategic advantage.

1.6.8 Conclusion: AI's Transformative Potential in Shaping the Future of MIS

The transformative impacts of AI on MIS extend beyond operational efficiencies to strategic alignment, innovation, and competitive advantage. AI enhances the adaptability of MIS, enabling organizations to respond to changing market dynamics, optimize processes, and manage global operations effectively. By addressing privacy and security challenges, AI strengthens MIS's role in protecting sensitive information and maintaining regulatory compliance, which is crucial in today's data-driven business landscape.

AI's ability to provide real-time insights and predictive analytics supports decision-making at all levels of the organization, aligning MIS with corporate strategy and empowering leaders to make informed, data-driven choices. As organizations navigate the balance between innovation and stability, AI-driven simulations and predictive tools offer a path to responsible technology adoption that supports long-term growth.

In an increasingly globalized economy, AI enables MIS to manage cross-border operations.

1.7 CHAPTER CONCLUSION

The chapter thoroughly examines the fundamental components of Management Information Systems (MIS) and investigates their progression throughout history, theoretical frameworks that shape their advancement, functions within contemporary businesses, alignment with corporate strategy, and the obstacles and possibilities they offer.

The hardware infrastructure is the fundamental support system for MIS, providing the essential framework for its operations. The software architecture enhances the hardware by allowing the processing and analysis of data, while the network infrastructure facilitates smooth communication and collaboration across different system components. Collectively, these factors constitute the fundamental constituents of administration Information Systems (MIS), which are important for the effective administration of information and the facilitation of decision-making processes in organisations.

The progression of information systems has been characterized by notable breakthroughs, starting with the rudimentary mechanization of human processes and culminating with the incorporation of intricate networks and databases. The creation and implementation of Management Information Systems (MIS) are guided by theoretical frameworks, such as Socio-technological Systems Theory and

Resource-Based View. These frameworks highlight the significance of incorporating both social and technological variables to ensure efficient implementation.

MIS is essential in contemporary organisations for managing data, facilitating communication, making informed decisions, optimizing resources, and fostering innovation. Nevertheless, the process of incorporating Management Information Systems (MIS) into business strategy presents obstacles such as privacy apprehensions, data protection dilemmas, and the requirement for continuous technical adjustment. Although there are difficulties, when there is strategic alignment between Management Information Systems (MIS) and company objectives, it may result in enhanced decision-making processes, operational efficiency, and a competitive edge.

In the future, Management Information Systems (MIS) provide organisations the chance to utilise technology to make well-informed decisions, optimize company processes, and adapt to the global market. Nevertheless, MIS professionals continue to face continual hurdles in dealing with the ever-changing technical environment and assuring the ethical and legal use of data. By efficiently navigating these hurdles and seamlessly integrating Management Information Systems (MIS) with larger organisational plans, firms may fully leverage the potential of information systems to propel growth and achieve success in the digital era.

REFERENCES

Al Karim, R., Rabiul, M. K., Ahamed, T., Karim, D. N., & Mehzabeen, M. (2024). Integrating Green Entrepreneurial Orientation, Green Information Systems, and Management Support with Green Supply Chain Management to Foster Firms' Environmental Performance. *Sustainability (Basel)*, *16*(12), 4921. DOI: 10.3390/su16124921

Azarov, V. N., Mayboroda, V. P., & Leokhin, Y. L. (2018). The Approaches to the Design of Integrated Quality Management Systems for the Digital Enterprise. In S. Shaposhnikov (Ed.), *2018 IEEE INTERNATIONAL CONFERENCE QUALITY MANAGEMENT, TRANSPORT AND INFORMATION SECURITY, INFORMATION TECHNOLOGIES (IT&QM&IS)* (Issue IEEE International Conference on Quality Management, Transport and Information Security, Information Technologies (IT and QM and IS) CL-St Petersburg Electrotechn Univ LETI, St Petersburg, RUSSIA PU-IEEE PI-NEW YORK PA-345 E 47TH ST, NEW YORK, NY 10017 USA, pp. 3–8). DOI: 10.1109/ITMQIS.2018.8525047

Brunner, M., Mussmann, A., Breu, R., & Machinery, A. C. (2019). Enabling Change-Driven Workflows in Continuous Information Security Management. In *SAC '19: PROCEEDINGS OF THE 34TH ACM/SIGAPP SYMPOSIUM ON APPLIED COMPUTING* (Issues 34th ACM/SIGAPP Annual International Symposium on Applied Computing (SAC) CL-Univ Cyprus, Limassol, CYPRUS PU-ASSOC COMPUTING MACHINERY PI-NEW YORK PA-1601 Broadway, 10th Floor, NEW YORK, NY, UNITED STATES, pp. 1924–1933). DOI: 10.1145/3297280.3297468

Bukunov, A. (2020). Functional Modeling of an Integration Information System for Building Design. In D. G. Arseniev, L. Overmeyer, H. Kalviainen, & B. Katalinic (Eds.), *CYBER-PHYSICAL SYSTEMS AND CONTROL* (Vol. 95, Issue International Conference on Cyber-Physical Systems and Control (CPS and C) CL-Peter Great St Petersburg Polytechn Univ, St Petersburg, RUSSIA PU-SPRINGER INTERNATIONAL PUBLISHING AG PI-CHAM PA-GEWERBESTRASSE 11, CHAM, CH-6330, SWITZERLAND, pp. 525–535). DOI: 10.1007/978-3-030-34983-7_51

Burkov, V. N., Burkova, I. V., Rossikhina, L. V., & Meshcheryakova, T. V. (2018). Information Technologies for Development Management Systems. *Automation and Remote Control*, *79*(10), 1813–1822. DOI: 10.1134/S0005117918100065

Cai, H., Li, G., Zhao, H., & Liu, Y. (2019). Research on application of information system to nursing management. In *Proceedings - 2019 11th International Conference on Measuring Technology and Mechatronics Automation, ICMTMA 2019* (Issues 11th International Conference on Measuring Technology and Mechatronics Automation (ICMTMA) CL-Qiqihar, PEOPLES R CHINA PU-IEEE PI-NEW YORK PA-345 E 47TH ST, NEW YORK, NY 10017 USA, pp. 561–563). DOI: 10.1109/ICMTMA.2019.00129

Cai, H., Ouyang, M., Wang, H., & Ma, Z. (2021). Civil Engineering Process File Information Management System. In Z. Li & F. Cen (Eds.), *INTERNATIONAL CONFERENCE ON SMART TRANSPORTATION AND CITY ENGINEERING 2021* (Vol. 12050, Issue International Conference on Smart Transportation and City Engineering CL-Chongqing, PEOPLES R CHINA PU-SPIE-INT SOC OPTICAL ENGINEERING PI-BELLINGHAM PA-1000 20TH ST, PO BOX 10, BELLINGHAM, WA 98227-0010 USA). DOI: 10.1117/12.2613749

Cai, P., & Jiang, Q. (2019). GIS spatial information sharing of smart city based on cloud computing. *Cluster Computing*, *22*(S6), 14435–14443. DOI: 10.1007/s10586-018-2311-z

Carayannis, E. G., & Morawska-Jancelewicz, J. (2022). The Futures of Europe: Society 5.0 and Industry 5.0 as Driving Forces of Future Universities. *Journal of the Knowledge Economy*, *13*(4), 3445–3471. Advance online publication. DOI: 10.1007/s13132-021-00854-2

Chan, Z., Yuxia, X., Chang, L., Guoping, Y., & Zhijun, H. (2020). Design and practice of clinical trial management information system. *Chinese Journal of Clinical Pharmacology and Therapeutics*, *25*(5), 555–558.

Changcheng, X., & Chaohu, H. (2020). Research on university scientific research patent management information system based on BS mode. *Journal of Intelligent & Fuzzy Systems*, *38*(2), 1371–1379. DOI: 10.3233/JIFS-179500

Chatzimichailidou, M., Whitcher, T., & Suzic, N. (2024). Complementarity and Compatibility of Systems Integration and Building Information Management. *IEEE Systems Journal*, *18*(2), 1198–1207. DOI: 10.1109/JSYST.2024.3387064

Chekotilo, E. Y., Abramkina, D. A., & Kichigina, O. Y. (2020). Financial Resources Management Information System of Flagship University Projects. In A. D. Nazarov (Ed.), *PROCEEDINGS OF THE 2ND INTERNATIONAL SCIENTIFIC AND PRACTICAL CONFERENCE - MODERN MANAGEMENT TRENDS AND THE DIGITAL ECONOMY: FROM REGIONAL DEVELOPMENT TO GLOBAL ECONOMIC GROWTH (MTDE 2020)* (Vol. 138, Issue 2nd International Scientific and Practical Conference on Modern Management Trends and the Digital Economy-from Regional Development to Global Economic Growth (MTDE), pp. 1212-1218 WE-Conference Proceedings Citation In). DOI: 10.2991/aebmr.k.200502.201

Chelyshkov, P., & Aralkin, K. (2018). The practice of building an information system for managing the operation of an industrial facility. In A. Volkov, A. Pustovgar, & A. Adamtsevich (Eds.), *MATEC Web of Conferences* (Vol. 251, Issues 6th International Scientific Conference on Integration, Partnership and Innovation in Construction Science and Education (IPICSE) CL-Moscow, RUSSIA PU-E D P SCIENCES PI-CEDEX A PA-17 AVE DU HOGGAR PARC D ACTIVITES COUTABOEUF BP 112, F-91944 CEDEX A, FRANCE). DOI: 10.1051/matecconf/201825103059

Chen, D. H., Esperanca, J. P., & Wang, S. F. (2022). The Impact of Artificial Intelligence on Firm Performance: An Application of the Resource-Based View to e-Commerce Firms. [WE - Social Science Citation Index] [SSCI]. *Frontiers in Psychology*, *13*, 884830. Advance online publication. DOI: 10.3389/fpsyg.2022.884830 PMID: 35465474

Chen, J., Lv, Z., & Song, H. (2019). Design of personnel big data management system based on blockchain. *Future Generation Computer Systems*, *101*, 1122–1129. DOI: 10.1016/j.future.2019.07.037

Chen, K., Chen, W., Li, C. T., Chan, K. Y., & Cheng, J. C. P. (2018). Developing a Location Aware Building Information Modeling System for Facility Maintenance Management. In C. Wang, C. Harper, Y. Lee, R. Harris, & C. Berryman (Eds.), *CONSTRUCTION RESEARCH CONGRESS 2018: INFRASTRUCTURE AND FACILITY MANAGEMENT* (Issue Construction Research Congress CL-Louisiana State Univ, Bert S Turner Dept Construct Management, New Orleans, LA PU-AMER SOC CIVIL ENGINEERS PI-NEW YORK PA-UNITED ENGINEERING CENTER, 345 E 47TH ST, NEW YORK, NY 10017-2398 USA, pp. 111–120). DOI: 10.1061/9780784481295.012

Chen, Q. (2020). Research on the Implementation Method of Database Security in Management Information System Based on Big Data Analysis. In L. Yang & Z. Xu (Eds.), *2020 INTERNATIONAL CONFERENCE ON ENERGY, ENVIRONMENT AND BIOENGINEERING (ICEEB 2020)* (Vol. 185, Issue International Conference on Energy, Environment and Bioengineering (ICEEB) CL-ELECTR NETWORK PU-E D P SCIENCES PI-CEDEX A PA-17 AVE DU HOGGAR PARC D ACTIVITES COUTABOEUF BP 112, F-91944 CEDEX A, FRANCE). DOI: 10.1051/e3sconf/202018502033

Chen, S. (2018). Understanding of the Management Information System Based on MVC Pattern. In L. Liu, C. Yang, & J. Ke (Eds.), *ADVANCES IN MATERIALS, MACHINERY, ELECTRONICS II* (Vol. 1955, Issues 2nd International Conference on Advances in Materials, Machinery, Electronics (AMME) CL-Xian, PEOPLES R CHINA PU-AMER INST PHYSICS PI-MELVILLE PA-2 HUNTINGTON QUADRANGLE, STE 1NO1, MELVILLE, NY 11747-4501 USA). DOI: 10.1063/1.5033678

Chen, X., Huang, R., Shen, L., Chen, H., Xiong, D., Xiao, X., Liu, M., Xu, R., & IOP. (2018). Intellectual Production Supervision Perform based on RFID Smart Electricity Meter. In *3RD INTERNATIONAL CONFERENCE ON ENERGY EQUIPMENT SCIENCE AND ENGINEERING (ICEESE 2017)* (Vol. 128, Issues 3rd International Conference on Energy Equipment Science and Engineering (ICEESE) CL-Beijing, PEOPLES R CHINA PU-IOP PUBLISHING LTD PI-BRISTOL PA-DIRAC HOUSE, TEMPLE BACK, BRISTOL BS1 6BE, ENGLAND). DOI: 10.1088/1755-1315/128/1/012050

Chen, Y. (2021). Optimization of Clinical Nursing Management System Based on Data Mining (Retracted Article). *Complexity, 2021*. Advance online publication. DOI: 10.1155/2021/2110154

Chen, Y. M., & Liu, M. (2019). Construction of Service-Oriented Postgraduate Management Information System. In H. Wang (Ed.), *2019 4Th International Workshop on Materials Engineering and Computer Sciences (Iwmecs 2019)* (Issue 4th International Workshop on Materials Engineering and Computer Sciences (IWMECS), pp. 564–567). https://doi.org/DOI: 10.25236/iwmecs.2019.108

Chenyang, X., Piao, W., Zilun, L., Qing, L., & Yadong, K. (2024). Research on Science and Technology Management Information Security Guarantee System. *Journal of Information Security Research, 10*(7), 675–681.

Chin, S.-H., Chen, C., Ko, P.-C., & Lin, S.-Y. (2019). Design of museum advertisement picture management system based on web. *Journal of Visual Communication and Image Representation, 63*, 102595. Advance online publication. DOI: 10.1016/j.jvcir.2019.102595

Cobbs, J., Tyler, B. D., Jensen, J. A., & Chan, K. (2017). Prioritizing Sponsorship Resources in Formula One Racing: A Longitudinal Analysis. *Journal of Sport Management, 31*(1), 96–110. http://10.0.4.99/jsm.2016-0115. DOI: 10.1123/jsm.2016-0115

Code, L. (2018). Design and Implementation of. *2018 13th World Congress on Intelligent Control and Automation (WCICA), 7*(7), 507–511.

Dahiya, S., Goyal, Y., & Sharma, C. (2022). Designing Delivery of Healthcare Services with Health Management Information System, Artificial Intelligence, Big Data, and Innovative Digital Technologies. [WE - Emerging Sources Citation Index] [ESCI]. *Journal of Young Pharmacists : JYP, 14*(4), 366–371. DOI: 10.5530/jyp.2022.14.74

Dalloul, M. H. M., binti Ibrahim, Z., & Urus, S. T. (2023). Financial Crises Management in Light of Accounting Information Systems Success: Investigating Direct and Indirect Influences. *Sustainability (Basel), 15*(10), 8131. Advance online publication. DOI: 10.3390/su15108131

Ding, H. (2018). Design and Implementation of Vehicle Management System. *IOP Conference Series. Materials Science and Engineering, 398*(1), 012014. Advance online publication. DOI: 10.1088/1757-899X/398/1/012014

Dongfang, S., Jiping, C., Yu, Z., Wanqi, Q., & Weiying, L. (2021). Building and application of urban water supply network information management system. *Jishui Paishui, 47*(1), 96–102.

Doutcheva, N. Z.-. (2021). *Information Management of Family Caregivers of Children with Medical Complexity.*

Effah, D., Bai, C. G., Asante, W. A., & Quayson, M. (2023). The Role of Artificial Intelligence in Coping With Extreme Weather-Induced Cocoa Supply Chain Risks. *IEEE Transactions on Engineering Management*. Advance online publication. DOI: 10.1109/TEM.2023.3289258

Fadillah, A. P., Fitriana, D., & IOP. (2019). Design of Project Data Management Information System. In *2ND INTERNATIONAL CONFERENCE ON INFORMATICS, ENGINEERING, SCIENCE, AND TECHNOLOGY (INCITEST 2019)* (Vol. 662, Issues 2nd International Conference on Informatics, Engineering, Science, and Technology (INCITEST)-Building Competitive Advantage to Face Industry 4.0 CL-Bandung, INDONESIA PU-IOP PUBLISHING LTD PI-BRISTOL PA-DIRAC HOUSE, TEMPLE BACK, BRISTOL BS1 6BE, ENGLAND). DOI: 10.1088/1757-899X/662/2/022014

Fang, J., Lee, V. C. S., & Wang, H. Y. (2024). Optimal service resource management strategy for IoT-based health information system considering value co-creation of users. *Industrial Management & Data Systems, 124*(3), 1132–1154. DOI: 10.1108/IMDS-03-2023-0173

Farooq, M., & Raju, V. (2019). Impact of Over-the-Top (OTT) Services on the Telecom Companies in the Era of Transformative Marketing. *Global Journal of Flexible Systems Management*. DOI: 10.1007/s40171-019-00209-6

Farooq, M., Ramzan, M., & Yen, Y. Y. (2024a). AI in Consumer Behavior Management. In *Transformative Impacts of AI in Management* (pp. 281–294). IGI Global., DOI: 10.4018/979-8-3693-4322-7.ch011

Farooq, M., Ramzan, M., & Yen, Y. Y. (2024b). AI in Customer Service, HR, and Administration. In *Transformative Impacts of AI in Management* (pp. 45–70). IGI Global. DOI: 10.4018/979-8-3693-4322-7.ch002

Farooq, M., Ramzan, M., & Yen, Y. Y. (2024c). AI in Quality Management. In *Transformative Impacts of AI in Management* (pp. 295–312). IGI Global., DOI: 10.4018/979-8-3693-4322-7.ch012

Farooq, M., Ramzan, M., & Yen, Y. Y. (2024d). Artificial Intelligence and Customer Experiences. In *Transformative Impacts of AI in Management* (pp. 95–114). IGI Global., DOI: 10.4018/979-8-3693-4322-7.ch004

Farooq, M., Ramzan, M., & Yen, Y. Y. (2024e). Artificial Intelligence in Administration Sciences. In *Transformative Impacts of AI in Management* (pp. 115–156). IGI Global., DOI: 10.4018/979-8-3693-4322-7.ch005

Farooq, M., Ramzan, M., & Yen, Y. Y. (2024f). Artificial Intelligence in Business and Law. In *Transformative Impacts of AI in Management* (pp. 71–94). IGI Global., DOI: 10.4018/979-8-3693-4322-7.ch003

Farooq, M., Ramzan, M., & Yen, Y. Y. (2024g). Artificial Intelligence in Ethical Business Decision Making. In *Transformative Impacts of AI in Management* (pp. 265–280). IGI Global., DOI: 10.4018/979-8-3693-4322-7.ch010

Farooq, M., Ramzan, M., & Yen, Y. Y. (2024h). Exploring the Impact of Artificial Intelligence on Brand Management. In *Transformative Impacts of AI in Management* (pp. 157–188). IGI Global., DOI: 10.4018/979-8-3693-4322-7.ch006

Farooq, M., Ramzan, M., & Yen, Y. Y. (2024i). Exploring the Impact of Ethical Leadership and Employee Engagement on Knowledge Sharing Attitudes in the Asian Digital Economy. In *Transformative Impacts of AI in Management* (pp. 241–264). IGI Global., DOI: 10.4018/979-8-3693-4322-7.ch009

Farooq, M., Ramzan, M., & Yen, Y. Y. (2024j). Transformative Impact of AI in Education Management. In *Transformative Impacts of AI in Management* (pp. 189–216). IGI Global., DOI: 10.4018/979-8-3693-4322-7.ch007

Fatimah, D. D. S., Supriatna, A. D., & Kurniawati, R. (2018). Design of personnel information systems using rapid application development method. In A. G. Abdullah & A. B. D. Nandiyanto (Eds.), *MATEC Web of Conferences* (Vol. 197, Issues 3rd Annual Applied Science and Engineering Conference (AASEC) CL-Univ Pendidikan Indonesia, Bandung, INDONESIA PU-E D P SCIENCES PI-CEDEX A PA-17 AVE DU HOGGAR PARC D ACTIVITES COUTABOEUF BP 112, F-91944 CEDEX A, FRANCE). DOI: 10.1051/matecconf/201819703016

Fu, S., & Xu, B. (2022). Facial Expression Recognition and Beauty Health Management Based on Image Feature Analysis. *Mobile Information Systems*, *2022*, 1–11. Advance online publication. DOI: 10.1155/2022/4336840

Fuaddi, M., & Sabarguna, B. S. (2019). Web-based Maintenance Information System in Medical Equipment Management. In M. Gozan, S. Astutiningsih, P. Wulan, G. Ramahdita, R. Dhelika, & P. Kreshanti (Eds.), *3RD BIOMEDICAL ENGINEERING'S RECENT PROGRESS IN BIOMATERIALS, DRUGS DEVELOPMENT, AND MEDICAL DEVICES* (Vol. 2092, Issues 3rd International Symposium of Biomedical Engineering (ISBE) on Recent Progress in Biomaterials, Drugs Development, and Medical Devices CL-Jakarta, INDONESIA PU-AMER INST PHYSICS PI-MELVILLE PA-2 HUNTINGTON QUADRANGLE, STE 1NO1, MELVILLE, NY 11747-4501 USA). DOI: 10.1063/1.5096736

Gang, S., Xiaoming, W., Junfeng, W., Shufang, L., Zhuowen, L., & Wang, X. (2021). Analysis of the information management system in the manufacturing process of cigarette enterprises using fuzzy AHP. *Journal of Intelligent & Fuzzy Systems*, *40*(4), 8257–8267. DOI: 10.3233/JIFS-189648

Gao, J., Li, J., & Duan, P. L. (2024). The application of machine learning and artificial intelligence technology in the production quality management of traditional Chinese medicine decoction pieces. *INTERNATIONAL JOURNAL OF INTERACTIVE DESIGN AND MANUFACTURING - IJIDEM*, *18*(1), 239–251. DOI: 10.1007/s12008-023-01448-9

Gao, X., Wu, Y., Li, Y., & IOP. (2019). Research on Information Integration of Construction Project Management Based on BIM. In *2019 3RD INTERNATIONAL WORKSHOP ON RENEWABLE ENERGY AND DEVELOPMENT (IWRED 2019)* (Vol. 267, Issues 3rd International Workshop on Renewable Energy and Development (IWRED) CL-Guangzhou, PEOPLES R CHINA PU-IOP PUBLISHING LTD PI-BRISTOL PA-DIRAC HOUSE, TEMPLE BACK, BRISTOL BS1 6BE, ENGLAND). DOI: 10.1088/1755-1315/267/3/032069

Genchev, P. (2020). An approach to support information security risk assessment. In V. Markova & T. Ganchev (Eds.), *PROCEEDINGS OF THE 2020 INTERNATIONAL CONFERENCE ON BIOMEDICAL INNOVATIONS AND APPLICATIONS (BIA 2020)* (Issue International Conference on Biomedical Innovations and Applications (BIA) CL-Varna, BULGARIA PU-IEEE PI-NEW YORK PA-345 E 47TH ST, NEW YORK, NY 10017 USA, pp. 125–128). DOI: 10.1109/BIA50171.2020.9244516

Godoy, M. P., Rusu, C., Hatibovic, F., Granollers, T., & Ugalde, J. (2023). Addressing Information Consumer Experience through a User-Centered Information Management System in a Chilean University. *Sustainability (Basel)*, *15*(22), 15998. Advance online publication. DOI: 10.3390/su152215998

Guan, Q., Zhang, F., & Zhang, E. (2019). Application Prospect of Knowledge Graph Technology in Knowledge Management of Oil and Gas Exploration and Development. In *2019 2nd International Conference on Artificial Intelligence and Big Data, ICAIBD 2019* (Issues 2nd International Conference on Artificial Intelligence and Big Data (ICAIBD) CL-Chengdu, PEOPLES R CHINA PU-IEEE PI-NEW YORK PA-345 E 47TH ST, NEW YORK, NY 10017 USA, pp. 161–166). DOI: 10.1109/ICAIBD.2019.8837003

Guo, B., & Shuai, L. (2022). Research on Object-oriented Data Model Technology in Tourism Information Management. In S. F. ElZoghdy & M. K. Mohiddin (Eds.), *THIRD INTERNATIONAL CONFERENCE ON ELECTRONICS AND COMMUNICATION; NETWORK AND COMPUTER TECHNOLOGY (ECNCT 2021)* (Vol. 12167, Issues 3rd International Conference on Electronics and Communication; Network and Computer Technology (ECNCT) CL-Xiamen, PEOPLES R CHINA PU-SPIE-INT SOC OPTICAL ENGINEERING PI-BELLINGHAM PA-1000 20TH ST, PO BOX 10, BELLINGHAM, WA 98227-0010 USA). DOI: 10.1117/12.2629214

Guo, Z., Zhang, X., Gao, Y., Hao, W., Zhang, S., & Du, X. (2021). Design of Information Management System for Large Modular Manned Spacecraft. In *Proceedings of the 16th IEEE Conference on Industrial Electronics and Applications, ICIEA 2021* (Issues 16th IEEE Conference on Industrial Electronics and Applications (ICIEA) CL-Chengdu, PEOPLES R CHINA PU-IEEE PI-NEW YORK PA-345 E 47TH ST, NEW YORK, NY 10017 USA, pp. 655–659). DOI: 10.1109/ICIEA51954.2021.9516303

Gupta, B. B., & Panigrahi, P. K. (2023). Analysis of the Role of Global Information Management in Advanced Decision Support Systems (DSS) for Sustainable Development. *Journal of Global Information Management*, *31*(1), 1–13. Advance online publication. DOI: 10.4018/JGIM.320185

Haiying, J. (2022). Conceptual model construction of building information management system based on BIM architecture. *Soft Computing*, *26*(16), 7925–7931. DOI: 10.1007/s00500-022-06851-0

Han, Y., Lei, Y., Bao, Z., & Zhou, Q. (2021). Research and Implementation of Mobile Internet Management Optimization and Intelligent Information System Based on Smart Decision. *Computational Intelligence and Neuroscience*, *2021*(1), 5144568. Advance online publication. DOI: 10.1155/2021/5144568 PMID: 34925490

Hoeffner, K., Jahn, F., Loerke, A., Pause, T., Schneider, B., Ammenwerth, E., & Winter, A. (2019). Open and Linkable Knowledge About Management of Health Information Systems. In L. OhnoMachado & B. Seroussi (Eds.), *MEDINFO 2019: HEALTH AND WELLBEING E-NETWORKS FOR ALL* (Vol. 264, Issues 17th World Congress of Medical and Health Informatics (MEDINFO) CL-Int Med Informat Assoc, Lyon, FRANCE PU-IOS PRESS PI-AMSTERDAM PA-NIEUWE HEMWEG 6B, 1013 BG AMSTERDAM, NETHERLANDS, pp. 1678–1679). https://doi.org/DOI: 10.3233/SHTI190593

Hongrui, B., Haiguang, H., Qinsi, Y., Feng, J., & IEEE. (2019). Design of security evaluation system for mobile Internet Information management platform based on BOPPPS model. In *2019 INTERNATIONAL CONFERENCE ON ROBOTS & INTELLIGENT SYSTEM (ICRIS 2019)* (Issue International Conference on Robots and Intelligent System (ICRIS) CL-Haikou, PEOPLES R CHINA PU-IEEE PI-NEW YORK PA-345 E 47TH ST, NEW YORK, NY 10017 USA, pp. 216–220). DOI: 10.1109/ICRIS.2019.00063

Hu, B., & Shi, W. (2021). Design of a Flexible Exhibition Management Information System for Exhibition Services. *Scientific Programming*, *2021*, 1–10. Advance online publication. DOI: 10.1155/2021/4789408

Huang, C. L. (2019). Bayesian recommender system for social information sharing: Incorporating tag-based personalized interest and social relationships. *Intelligent Data Analysis*, *23*(3), 623–639. DOI: 10.3233/IDA-183910

Huang, L. (2021). Applications of Small and Medium Enterprise Management System Using Edge Algorithm. *Mobile Information Systems*, *2021*, 1–11. Advance online publication. DOI: 10.1155/2021/8730413

Huang, L. (2022). Research and Application of Business Law Information Management System Based on Big Data. *Journal of Sensors*, *2022*, 1–12. Advance online publication. DOI: 10.1155/2022/5885451

Huang, Y., Debnath, J., Iorga, M., Kumar, A., & Xie, B. (2019). CSAT: A User-interactive Cyber Security Architecture Tool based on NIST-compliance Security Controls for Risk Management. In S. Chakrabarti & H. N. Saha (Eds.), *2019 IEEE 10th Annual Ubiquitous Computing, Electronics and Mobile Communication Conference, UEMCON 2019* (Issue IEEE 10th Annual Ubiquitous Computing, Electronics and Mobile Communication Conference (UEMCON) CL-Columbia Univ, New York, NY PU-IEEE PI-NEW YORK PA-345 E 47TH ST, NEW YORK, NY 10017 USA, pp. 0697–0707). DOI: 10.1109/UEMCON47517.2019.8993090

Huang, Z. (2022). Integrated Management System of Instrument and Equipment in University Financial Media Laboratory Based on Hybrid Cloud Architecture. In S. Liu & X. Ma (Eds.), *ADVANCED HYBRID INFORMATION PROCESSING, PT I* (Vol. 416, Issues 5th EAI International Conference on Advanced Hybrid Information Processing (ADHIP) CL-ELECTR NETWORK PU-SPRINGER INTERNATIONAL PUBLISHING AG PI-CHAM PA-GEWERBESTRASSE 11, CHAM, CH-6330, SWITZERLAND, pp. 587–600). DOI: 10.1007/978-3-030-94551-0_46

Hwang, Y., Lin, H., & Shin, D. (2018). Knowledge system commitment and knowledge sharing intention: The role of personal information management motivation. *International Journal of Information Management*, *39*, 220–227. DOI: 10.1016/j.ijinfomgt.2017.12.009

Iliescu, D. (2022). Some Considerations on Conceptual Modeling for a Laboratory Information Management System. In D. Popescu, L. Barbulescu, E. Popescu, M. Roman, & D. Sendrescu (Eds.), *2022 23RD INTERNATIONAL CARPATHIAN CONTROL CONFERENCE (ICCC)* (Issues 23rd International Carpathian Control Conference (ICCC) CL-Sinaia, ROMANIA PU-IEEE PI-NEW YORK PA-345 E 47TH ST, NEW YORK, NY 10017 USA, pp. 19–24). DOI: 10.1109/ICCC54292.2022.9805898

Ionescu, R. C., Ceausu, I., & Ilie, C. (2018). Considerations on the implementation steps for an information security management system. In *PROCEEDINGS OF THE INTERNATIONAL CONFERENCE ON BUSINESS EXCELLENCE* (Vol. 12, Issues 12th International Conference on Business Excellence (ICBE) CL-Bucharest, ROMANIA PU-SCIENDO PI-WARSAW PA-BOGUMILA ZUGA 32A, WARSAW, MAZOVIA, POLAND, pp. 476–485). DOI: 10.2478/picbe-2018-0043

Iskanderov, Y., & Pautov, M. (2019). Security of Information Processes in Supply Chains. In A. Abraham, S. Kovalev, V. Tarassov, V. Snasel, & A. Sukhanov (Eds.), *PROCEEDINGS OF THE THIRD INTERNATIONAL SCIENTIFIC CONFERENCE INTELLIGENT INFORMATION TECHNOLOGIES FOR INDUSTRY (IITI'18), VOL 2* (Vol. 875, Issues 3rd International Scientific Conference on Intelligent Information Technologies for Industry (IITI) CL-Sochi, RUSSIA PU-SPRINGER INTERNATIONAL PUBLISHING AG PI-CHAM PA-GEWERBESTRASSE 11, CHAM, CH-6330, SWITZERLAND, pp. 13–22). DOI: 10.1007/978-3-030-01821-4_2

Jian, L. (2022). Design of enterprise human resources decision support system based on data mining. *Soft Computing*, *26*(20), 10571–10580. DOI: 10.1007/s00500-021-06659-4

Jiang, L. M., & Liu, X. L. (2023). Application Research of Computer Artificial Intelligence Face Recognition Technology in Student File Management Information System. In *2023 3RD ASIA-PACIFIC CONFERENCE ON COMMUNICATIONS TECHNOLOGY AND COMPUTER SCIENCE, ACCTCS* (Issues 3rd Asia-Pacific Conference on Communications Technology and Computer Science (ACCTCS), pp. 571–574). WE - Conference Proceedings Citation Index - Science (CPCI-S) DOI: 10.1109/ACCTCS58815.2023.00112

Jiang, N., Zhao, X., & Zhang, J. (2019). An empirical study on the impact of information system absorption on the performance of troops' logistics organization. *Cluster Computing*, *22*(2), 4109–4118. DOI: 10.1007/s10586-017-1516-x

Jiang, W., & Xie, Z. (2021). The Information Management System of China Forest Products International Trade Based on Internet Platform. In *Proceedings - 2021 6th International Conference on Smart Grid and Electrical Automation, ICSGEA 2021* (Issues 6th International Conference on Smart Grid and Electrical Automation (ICSGEA) CL-Kunming, PEOPLES R CHINA PU-IEEE PI-NEW YORK PA-345 E 47TH ST, NEW YORK, NY 10017 USA, pp. 343–346). DOI: 10.1109/ICSGEA53208.2021.00084

Jin, Y., Zhao, J., Yu, W., Li, H., Liu, B., Sun, Y., Zheng, Y., He, C., Duan, S., & IOP. (2021). Research on Image Data Management System of Power Transmission Project Based on Geographic Information. In *2020 ASIA CONFERENCE ON GEOLOGICAL RESEARCH AND ENVIRONMENTAL TECHNOLOGY* (Vol. 632, Issue Asia Conference on Geological Research and Environmental Technology (GRET) CL-ELECTR NETWORK PU-IOP PUBLISHING LTD PI-BRISTOL PA-DIRAC HOUSE, TEMPLE BACK, BRISTOL BS1 6BE, ENGLAND). DOI: 10.1088/1755-1315/632/4/042038

Junru, Z., Bo, Y., Yanfeng, G., Jian, X., & Dingding, L. (2021). Research Status and Prospects of Intelligent Monitoring Technology and Information Management System for Tunnel Engineering. *Chinese Journal of Underground Space and Engineering*, *17*(2), 567–579.

Kamenska, L., Moiseenko, V., Shendryk, V., Kamenskyi, S., & Shendryk, S. (2022). Implementation of Distributed Information Systems in Solving Problems of Energy Consumption Monitoring. In I. Karabegovic, A. Kovacevic, & S. Mandzuka (Eds.), *NEW TECHNOLOGIES, DEVELOPMENT AND APPLICATION V* (Vol. 472, Issue International Conference on New Technologies, Development and Application CL-Acad Sci & Arts Bosnia & Herzegovina, Sarajevo, BOSNIA & HERCEG PU-SPRINGER INTERNATIONAL PUBLISHING AG PI-CHAM PA-GEWERBESTRASSE 11, CHAM, CH-6330, SWITZERLAND, pp. 758–767). DOI: 10.1007/978-3-031-05230-9_90

Karinshak, E., & Jin, Y. (2023). AI-driven disinformation: A framework for organizational preparation and response. *Journal of Communication Management (London)*, *27*(4), 539–562. Advance online publication. DOI: 10.1108/JCOM-09-2022-0113

Kazemi, P., Lau, F., Matava, C., & Simpao, A. F. (2021). An Environmental Scan of Anesthesia Information Management Systems in the American and Canadian Marketplace. *Journal of Medical Systems*, *45*(12), 101. Advance online publication. DOI: 10.1007/s10916-021-01781-0 PMID: 34661760

Khan, M. S., Khan, M., Bughio, M., Talpur, B. D., Kim, I. S., & Seo, J. (2022). An Integrated HBIM Framework for the Management of Heritage Buildings. *Buildings (Basel, Switzerland)*, *12*(7), 964. Advance online publication. DOI: 10.3390/buildings12070964

Kokoeva, L. T., Kolieva, A. E., Gaytova, L. K., & Khadikov, M. K. (2019). The Necessity for Legal Regulation of Usage of New Information Technologies in Management. In E. G. Popkova & V. N. Ostrovskaya (Eds.), *PERSPECTIVES ON THE USE OF NEW INFORMATION AND COMMUNICATION TECHNOLOGY (ICT) IN THE MODERN ECONOMY* (Vol. 726, Issues 5th National Scientific and Practical Conference on Perspectives on the Use of New Information and Communication Technology (ICT) in the Modern Economy CL-Pyatigorsk, RUSSIA PU-SPRINGER INTERNATIONAL PUBLISHING AG PI-CHAM PA-GEWERBESTRASSE 11, CHAM, CH-6330, SWITZERLAND, pp. 403–408). DOI: 10.1007/978-3-319-90835-9_48

Koo, J., Kim, S.-H., & Kim, Y.-S. (2021). Effects of the Government Performance Evaluation System on the Organization Effectiveness of Public Organizations: A Focus on the Interaction Effect of Performance Information. *Socail Science Review*, *52*(1), 33–57. DOI: 10.31502/SSRI.52.1.3

Kratov, S. (2018). On providing the fault-tolerant operation of information systems based on open content management systems. In *Journal of Physics: Conference Series* (Vol. 944, Issue 1). DOI: 10.1088/1742-6596/944/1/012067

Lamboglia, R., Cardoni, A., Dameri, R. P., & Mancini, D. (2018). Business information systems in a networked, smart and open environment. In R. Lamboglia, A. Cardoni, R. P. Dameri, & D. Mancini (Eds.), *Lecture Notes in Information Systems and Organisation* (Vol. 24, Issues 13th Annual Conference of the Italian-Chapter of Association-for-Information-Systems (ItAIS)-ICT and Innovation-A Step Forward to a global Society CL-Verona, ITALY PU-SPRINGER INTERNATIONAL PUBLISHING AG PI-CHAM PA-GEWERBESTRASSE 11, CHAM, CH-6330, SWITZERLAND, pp. 1–20). DOI: 10.1007/978-3-319-62636-9_1

Le, Q. B., Nguyen, M. D., Bui, V. C., & Dang, T. M. H.LE. (2020). The Determinants of Management Information Systems Effectiveness in Small- and Medium-Sized Enterprises. *The Journal of Asian Finance, Economics and Business*, *7*(8), 567–576. DOI: 10.13106/jafeb.2020.vol7.no8.567

Le Queau, C., Ann Phillips, W., & Srinivasan, A. (2020). Practical use of biobank information management system (BIMS) for clinical-biological annotations in biobanks. *Medecine Sciences*, *36*(3), 285–288. DOI: 10.1051/medsci/2020044 PMID: 32228852

Lee, D. G., Park, J. Y., & Song, S. H. (2018). BIM-Based Construction Information Management Framework for Site Information Management. *Advances in Civil Engineering*, *2018*(1), 5249548. Advance online publication. DOI: 10.1155/2018/5249548

Lee, S. (2022). A Study on the Improvement Model of Administrative Information Dataset Records Management Environment: Focused on the Dataset of Picture Archiving and Communication System. *Journal of Korean Society of Archives and Records Management*, *22*(2), 51–73. DOI: 10.14404/JKSARM.2022.22.2.051

León-Romero, L. P., Aguilar-Fernández, M., Luque-Sendra, A., Zamora-Polo, F., & Francisco-Márquez, M. (2024). Characterization of the information system integrated to the construction project management systems. *Heliyon*, *10*(11), e31886. Advance online publication. DOI: 10.1016/j.heliyon.2024.e31886 PMID: 38841493

Leventhal, E. L., & Schreyer, K. E. (2020). Information Management in the Emergency Department. *Emergency Medicine Clinics of North America*, *38*(3), 681–691. DOI: 10.1016/j.emc.2020.03.004 PMID: 32616287

Li, B., Feng, C., & Gu, J. (2019). Thoughts about the smart architecture of the new generation of traffic management system for public security. In L. Zhang, J. Ma, P. Liu, & G. Zhang (Eds.), *CICTP 2019: Transportation in China - Connecting the World - Proceedings of the 19th COTA International Conference of Transportation Professionals* (Issues 19th COTA International Conference of Transportation Professionals (CICTP)-Transportation in China 2025 CL-Nanjing, pp. 5831–5842). DOI: 10.1061/9780784482292.501

Li, G., Liu, Y., Zhao, H., Cai, H., & IEEE. (2019). Researchon Application of Network System to Nursing Management. In *2019 11TH INTERNATIONAL CONFERENCE ON MEASURING TECHNOLOGY AND MECHATRONICS AUTOMATION (ICMTMA 2019)* (Issues 11th International Conference on Measuring Technology and Mechatronics Automation (ICMTMA) CL-Qiqihar, pp. 705–707). DOI: 10.1109/ICMTMA.2019.00161

Li, X. (2021). Design and Implementation of Project Cost Management Information System Based on Web. In *Proceedings - 2021 6th International Conference on Smart Grid and Electrical Automation, ICSGEA 2021* (Issues 6th International Conference on Smart Grid and Electrical Automation (ICSGEA) CL-Kunming, pp. 288–292). DOI: 10.1109/ICSGEA53208.2021.00070

Li, X., Wang, L., & Fang, L. (2022). Optimal Design of an Information Management System for Government: A Bridge between Government and Citizens. *Mathematical Problems in Engineering*, *2022*, 1–10. Advance online publication. DOI: 10.1155/2022/3127858

Lian, J. (2022). Optimization of Music Teaching Management System for College Students Based on Similarity Distribution Method (Retracted Article). *Mathematical Problems in Engineering*, *2022*, 1–11. Advance online publication. DOI: 10.1155/2022/6444554

Liang, C., & Wang, C. (2022). Coding structure of highway engineering information model. In *Shenzhen Daxue Xuebao (Ligong Ban)/Journal of Shenzhen University Science and Engineering* (Vol. 39, Issue 4, pp. 424–431). DOI: 10.3724/SP.J.1249.2022.04424

Liang, J. (2020). Research on the Quality Evaluation of Higher Education Information Management Based on Weighted Topsis. In *Proceedings - 2020 5th International Conference on Smart Grid and Electrical Automation, ICSGEA 2020* (Issues 5th International Conference on Smart Grid and Electrical Automation (ICSGEA) CL-Zhangjiajie, pp. 380–387). DOI: 10.1109/ICSGEA51094.2020.00088

Lijun, Z. (2018). Construction of Education Management Information System Based on Cloud Computing. In A. Wu (Ed.), *2018 5TH INTERNATIONAL CONFERENCE ON ELECTRICAL & ELECTRONICS ENGINEERING AND COMPUTER SCIENCE (ICEEECS 2018)* (Issues 5th International Conference on Electrical & Electronics Engineering and Computer Science (ICEEECS) CL-Beijing, pp. 311–315).

Lili, S., Xiaoping, L., Zhen, Y., Yanru, C., & Xianhong, H. (2021). Improvement and effects evaluation of the information system of nursing hierarchy management. *Chinese Journal of Nursing Education*, *18*(11), 1018–1022.

Lin, P. (2019). Design and Implementation of Financial Accounting Information Management System of Shipping Companies Based on ERP. *Journal of Coastal Research*, *94*(sp1), 470–474. DOI: 10.2112/SI94-093.1

Liu, R., & Wang, L. (2022). Information Resource Sharing Based on University Dance Big Data Management and Utilization System Design. *Mathematical Problems in Engineering*, *2022*, 1–9. Advance online publication. DOI: 10.1155/2022/4325984

Liu, S. (2021). Design and Implementation of High-Skilled Talent Information Management System Based on Multisensor Information Fusion. *Journal of Sensors*, *2021*(1), 3812145. Advance online publication. DOI: 10.1155/2021/3812145

Liu, W., & Wei, S. (2022). Design and Management of Comprehensive Art Student Information Database from the Perspective of Internet plus Education (Retracted Article). *Security and Communication Networks*, *2022*, 1–9. Advance online publication. DOI: 10.1155/2022/6494404

Liu, X. (2019). Research on Intelligent Retrieval Technology of User Information in Medical Information System Under the Background of Big Data. In G. Gui & L. Yun (Eds.), *ADVANCED HYBRID INFORMATION PROCESSING, ADHIP 2019, PT I* (Vol. 301, Issues 3rd European-Alliance-for-Innovation (EAI) International Conference on Advanced Hybrid Information Processing (ADHIP) CL-Nanjing, pp. 310–316). DOI: 10.1007/978-3-030-36402-1_33

Liu, Y. (2022). Design of Financial Information Management System and IoT Application Based on Fuzzy Comprehensive Evaluation (Retracted Article). *Wireless Communications and Mobile Computing*, *2022*, 1–11. Advance online publication. DOI: 10.1155/2022/2483306

Liu, Z., Liu, L., Fan, W., & IEEE. (2019). Design and Application of Rural Road Lifecycle Management Information System. In *2019 4TH INTERNATIONAL CONFERENCE ON INTELLIGENT TRANSPORTATION ENGINEERING (ICITE 2019)* (Issues 4th International Conference on Intelligent Transportation Engineering (ICITE) CL-Singapore, pp. 136–140). DOI: 10.1109/ICITE.2019.8880171

Long, F., Chuan, W., Yufen, D., Chuanyong, L., Junjie, Y., & Qiang, L. (2020). Information System of Marine Survey Part 2: The Application Software. In *Hydrographic Surveying and Charting* (Vol. 40, Issue 4, pp. 72–76).

Luma, A., & Abazi, B. (2019). The importance of integration of information security management systems (ISMS) to the organization's Enterprise Information Systems (EIS). In M. Koricic, Z. Butkovic, K. Skala, Z. Car, M. CicinSain, S. Babic, V. Sruk, D. Skvorc, S. Ribaric, S. Gros, B. Vrdoljak, M. Mauher, E. Tijan, P. Pale, D. Huljenic, T. G. Grbac, & M. Janjic (Eds.), *2019 42nd International Convention on Information and Communication Technology, Electronics and Microelectronics, MIPRO 2019 - Proceedings* (Issues 42nd International Convention on Information and Communication Technology, Electronics and Microelectronics (MIPRO) CL-Opatija, pp. 1205–1208). DOI: 10.23919/MIPRO.2019.8756645

Luo, M., Fan, Z., & Yu, T. (2020). Marine Information Management Service Platform: A GIS Based Study. *Journal of Coastal Research*, *557–561*(sp1), 557. Advance online publication. DOI: 10.2112/SI106-126.1

Ma, L., Zhao, H., You, S., & Ge, W. (2018). Analysis and Design of Hospital Management Information System Based on UML. In D. Fang, S. Zhu, & T. Kuang (Eds.), *6TH INTERNATIONAL CONFERENCE ON COMPUTER-AIDED DESIGN, MANUFACTURING, MODELING AND SIMULATION (CDMMS 2018)* (Vol. 1967, Issues 6th International Conference on Computer-Aided Design, Manufacturing, Modeling and Simulation (CDMMS) CL-Busan. DOI: 10.1063/1.5039086

Manzhurov, I. L., Antonov, K. L., Kit, M., Berg, D. B., & Denisov, D. (2019). Information system for decision support in waste management in the Arctic region of Russia. In T. Simos & C. Tsitouras (Eds.), *AIP Conference Proceedings* (Vol. 2116, Issue International Conference on Numerical Analysis and Applied Mathematics (ICNAAM) CL-Rhodes. DOI: 10.1063/1.5114447

Masuin, R., Latief, Y., & Zagloel, T. Y. (2019). Development of information systems in integrated management systems in order to increase organisational performance in a construction company. In L. Nulhakim, N. D. G. Drantantiyas, R. Ikhwanuddin, Sunarsih, & H. T. Yudistira (Eds.), *INTERNATIONAL CONFERENCE ON SCIENCE, INFRASTRUCTURE TECHNOLOGY AND REGIONAL DEVELOPMENT* (Vol. 258, Issue International Conference on Science, Infrastructure Technology and Regional Development CL-Inst Teknologi Sumatera Campus, Lampung. DOI: 10.1088/1755-1315/258/1/012012

Mateer, J. E., & Jones, R. W. (2018). Information systems, indirect risks and safety: An 8-step safety management process. In *Proceedings of the 13th IEEE Conference on Industrial Electronics and Applications, ICIEA 2018* (Issues 13th IEEE Conference on Industrial Electronics and Applications (ICIEA) CL-Wuhan, PEOPLES R CHINA PU-IEEE PI-NEW YORK PA-345 E 47TH ST, NEW YORK, NY 10017 USA, pp. 352–357). DOI: 10.1109/ICIEA.2018.8397741

Matsumoto, N., & Shigeyasu, T. (2020). A New Mobile Agent System for Sharing Disaster Information Under Unstable Network Conditions. In L. Barolli, P. Hellinckx, & T. Enokido (Eds.), *Lecture Notes in Networks and Systems* (Vol. 97, Issues 14th IEEE International Conference on Broadband Wireless Computing, Communication and Applications (BWCCA) CL-Univ Antwerp, Antwerp, pp. 222–230). DOI: 10.1007/978-3-030-33506-9_20

Min, G., & IEEE. (2018). Information Management System for Comprehensive Quality Evaluation of Students Based on the Fusion of Information Exchange Model. In *2018 10TH INTERNATIONAL CONFERENCE ON MEASURING TECHNOLOGY AND MECHATRONICS AUTOMATION (ICMTMA)* (Issues 10th International Conference on Measuring Technology and Mechatronics Automation (ICMTMA) CL-Changsha, pp. 424–428). DOI: 10.1109/ICMTMA.2018.00110

Miyazaki, T., Anazawa, K., Maruyama, Y., Kobayashi, S., Segawa, T., & Li, P. (2019). Resilient Information Management for Information Sharing in Disaster-Affected Areas Lacking Internet Access. In M. R. Palattella, S. Scanzio, & S. C. Ergen (Eds.), *Lecture Notes in Computer Science (including subseries Lecture Notes in Artificial Intelligence and Lecture Notes in Bioinformatics): Vol. 11803 LNCS* (Issues 18th International Conference on Ad-Hoc Networks and Wireless (AdHoc-Now) CL-Luxembourg, pp. 3–17). DOI: 10.1007/978-3-030-31831-4_1

Mohd, S., Syazli Fathi, M., & Nahar Harun, A. (2019). Information management for humanitarian aid distribution system in Malaysia. In *IOP Conference Series: Materials Science and Engineering* (Vol. 513, Issue 1). DOI: 10.1088/1757-899X/513/1/012012

Morozov, V., Kalnichenko, O., Khrutba, A., Steshenko, G., Liubyma, I., & IEEE. (2018). Managing of Change Streams in Projects of Development Distributed Information Systems. In *2018 IEEE SECOND INTERNATIONAL CONFERENCE ON DATA STREAM MINING & PROCESSING (DSMP)* (Issues 2nd IEEE International Conference on Data Stream Mining and Processing (DSMP) CL-Lviv, pp. 346–351).

Mu, Z., Li, X., & IEEE. (2019). Analysis and Design of Property Management System Based on B/S. In *2019 INTERNATIONAL CONFERENCE ON INTELLIGENT TRANSPORTATION, BIG DATA & SMART CITY (ICITBS)* (Issue International Conference on Intelligent Transportation, Big Data & Smart City (ICITBS) CL-Changsha, pp. 381–384). DOI: 10.1109/ICITBS.2019.00100

Mukhtar, M., Fransiska, A. B., & Wahyudi, M. (2019). Management Information Systems Doctorate Program of Educational Management (DOCPEM). In *2018 6th International Conference on Cyber and IT Service Management, CITSM 2018* (Issues 6th International Conference on Cyber and IT Service Management (CITSM) CL-Parapat, pp. 282–286). DOI: 10.1109/CITSM.2018.8674314

Na, S.-H., & Shon, T.-S. (2022). A Study on the Development of Information Security Management System Using RMF. *Journal of Digital Contents Society*, *23*(5), 977–983. DOI: 10.9728/dcs.2022.23.5.977

Nasrulloh, M. Y., Putra, Y. H., & IOP. (2019). Student Data Management Information System Using the Zachman Framework. In *2ND INTERNATIONAL CONFERENCE ON INFORMATICS, ENGINEERING, SCIENCE, AND TECHNOLOGY (INCITEST 2019)* (Vol. 662, Issues 2nd International Conference on Informatics, Engineering, Science, and Technology (INCITEST)-Building Competitive Advantage to Face Industry 4.0 CL-Bandung. DOI: 10.1088/1757-899X/662/2/022101

Nedzelskay, O. N., Moiseyev, V. V., Bikineeva, A. N., & Bulakina, E. N. (2020). Infrastructure management of software systems of modern "iT" in the automation of production processes. In *IOP Conference Series: Materials Science and Engineering* (Vol. 865, Issue 1). DOI: 10.1088/1757-899X/865/1/012017

Ogiela, L., & Ogiela, M. R. (2018). Towards cognitive service management and semantic information sharing in the Cloud. *Multimedia Tools and Applications, 77*(14), 18625–18635. DOI: 10.1007/s11042-017-5302-9

Okada, K., Sugimoto, K., Wada, S., Konishi, S., Manabe, S., Matsumura, Y., & Takeda, T. (2024). Development of the Clinical Specimen Information Management System for Multicenter Clinical Studies. In J. Bichel-Findlay, P. Otero, P. Scott, & E. Huesing (Eds.), *MEDINFO 2023 - THE FUTURE IS ACCESSIBLE* (Vol. 310, Issues 19th World Congress on Medical and Health Informatics (MEDINFO) CL-Sydney, pp. 119–123). DOI: 10.3233/SHTI230939

Olson, D. L. (2018). View of IJPR contributions to knowledge management in supply chains. *International Journal of Production Research, 56*(1–2), 733–742. DOI: 10.1080/00207543.2017.1398427

Pereira, J., Varajao, J., & Takagi, N. (2022). Evaluation of Information Systems Project Success - Insights from Practitioners. *Information Systems Management, 39*(2), 138–155. DOI: 10.1080/10580530.2021.1887982

Prabhavathy, M., & Umamaheswari, S. (2022). Prevention of runtime malware injection attack in cloud using unsupervised learning. *Intelligent Automation & Soft Computing, 32*(1), 101–114. Advance online publication. DOI: 10.32604/iasc.2022.018257

Prandel, P. C., & Barreto, P. S. (2024). Age of information optimization in cyber-physical systems with stateful packet management techniques. *Ad Hoc Networks, 154*, 103358. Advance online publication. DOI: 10.1016/j.adhoc.2023.103358

Priyashantha, K. G., & Priyangaa, Y. (2022). Impact of Green Human Resource Management on Employee Green Behavior: The Mediating Role of Green Attitude. [WE - Emerging Sources Citation Index] [ESCI]. *INDONESIAN JOURNAL OF SUSTAINABILITY ACCOUNTING AND MANAGEMENT, 6*(2), 378–389. DOI: 10.28992/ijsam.v6i2.674

Qian, X., Tu, J., & Lou, P. (2019). A general architecture of a 3D visualization system for shop floor management. *Journal of Intelligent Manufacturing, 30*(4), 1531–1545. DOI: 10.1007/s10845-017-1335-1

Ramachandran, K. K., & Karthick, K. K. (2019). Digital technology and quality management. In S. Shaposhnikov (Ed.), *International Journal of Recent Technology and Engineering* (Vol. 8, Issue 2 Special Issue 3, pp. 1651–1654). DOI: 10.35940/ijrte.B1299.0782S319

Rozhkova, N., Blinova, U., & Rozhkova, D. (2018). The Concept of Management Accounting Based on the Information Technologies Application. In T. Antipova & A. Rocha (Eds.), *INFORMATION TECHNOLOGY SCIENCE* (Vol. 724, Issue International Conference on Information Technology Science (MosITS) CL-Moscow, pp. 89–95). DOI: 10.1007/978-3-319-74980-8_8

Runge, M., Reiche, L. T., Niemann, K. H., & Fay, A. (2022). Universal energy information model for industrial communication. In *IEEE International Conference on Emerging Technologies and Factory Automation, ETFA* (Vols. 2022-September, Issue IEEE 27th International Conference on Emerging Technologies and Factory Automation (ETFA) CL-Stuttgart. DOI: 10.1109/ETFA52439.2022.9921557

Rusakov, V. D., Loseva, D. M., & IEEE. (2021). Development of an Information System for Managing User Requests Using Bitrix. In *PROCEEDINGS OF THE 2021 IEEE CONFERENCE OF RUSSIAN YOUNG RESEARCHERS IN ELECTRICAL AND ELECTRONIC ENGINEERING (ELCONRUS)* (Issue IEEE Conference of Russian Young Researchers in Electrical and Electronic Engineering (ElConRus) CL-Saint Petersburg Electrotechn Univ, pp. 1055–1058). DOI: 10.1109/ElConRus51938.2021.9396631

Schoormann, T., Strobel, G., Möller, F., Petrik, D., & Zschech, P. (2023). Artificial Intelligence for Sustainability-A Systematic Review of Information Systems Literature. *Communications of the Association for Information Systems*, *52*, 52. DOI: 10.17705/1CAIS.05209

Seh-La, Oh., Park, S., & Yim, J. H. (2018). A Case Study of Dataset Records in Information Management System. *Journal of Korean Society of Archives and Records Management*, *18*(2), 109–133. DOI: 10.14404/JKSARM.2018.18.2.109

Setiawan, R., Kurniadi, D., Aulawi, H., & Kurniawati, R. (2019). Asset management information system for higher education. In A. G. Abdullah, A. B. D. Nandiyanto, I. Widiaty, A. A. Danuwijaya, & C. U. Abdullah (Eds.), *Journal of Physics: Conference Series* (Vol. 1402, Issue 2). DOI: 10.1088/1742-6596/1402/2/022083

Shi, Y., Ying, J., Shi, D., & Yan, J. (2022). Service-Oriented Modeling for Blockchain-Enabled Supply Chain Quality Information Systems. *Security and Communication Networks*, *2022*, 1–16. Advance online publication. DOI: 10.1155/2022/1987933

Shin, J., & Choi, B. (2022). Design and Implementation of Quality Information Management System for Modular Construction Factory. *Buildings (Basel, Switzerland), 12*(5), 654. Advance online publication. DOI: 10.3390/buildings12050654

Shmeleva, A. G., Ladynin, A. I., Smirnova, E. E., & Ryabchik, T. A. (2019). Transport logistics management information system. In *Proceedings of the 2019 IEEE Conference of Russian Young Researchers in Electrical and Electronic Engineering, ElConRus 2019* (Issue IEEE Conference of Russian Young Researchers in Electrical and Electronic Engineering (EIConRus) CL-St Petersburg Electrotechn Univ, pp. 1471–1473). DOI: 10.1109/EIConRus.2019.8657007

Shtangret, A., Melnyk, N., Shevchuk, I., Sydoruk, I., & Shyra, T. (2019). Information Support for the Management of the Economic Security of High-Tech Enterprises. In *Proceedings - International Conference on Advanced Computer Information Technologies, ACIT* (Issues 9th International Conference on Advanced Computer Information Technologies (ACIT) CL-Ceske Budejovice, pp. 350–353). DOI: 10.1109/ACITT.2019.8779922

Siyao, G. U. O., & Bin, X. I. E. (2021). An Education Management Assessment Model Based on Information Control Theory. In *Proceedings - 2021 13th International Conference on Measuring Technology and Mechatronics Automation, ICMTMA 2021* (Issues 13th International Conference on Mcasuring Technology and Mechatronics Automation (ICMTMA) CL-Beihai, pp. 531–534). DOI: 10.1109/ICMTMA52658.2021.00122

Song, Q. (2022). Design and Application of Land Resource Management System Based on Internet of Things. *Wireless Communications and Mobile Computing, 2022*, 1–14. Advance online publication. DOI: 10.1155/2022/2726673

Sukhorukov, A., Koryagin, N., Sulyagina, J., Ulitskaya, N., & Eroshkin, S. (2020). Digital Transformation of Airline Management as the Basis of Innovative Development. In Z. Popovic, A. Manakov, & V. Breskich (Eds.), *VIII INTERNATIONAL SCIENTIFIC SIBERIAN TRANSPORT FORUM, VOL 1* (Vol. 1115, Issues 8th International Scientific Siberian Transport Forum (TransSiberia) CL-Novosibirsk, pp. 845–854). DOI: 10.1007/978-3-030-37916-2_83

Tarigan, Z. J. H., Siagian, H., Bua, R. R., & IOP. (2019). The Impact of Information System Implementation to the Integrated System for Increasing the Supply Chain Performance of Manufacturing Companies. In *2018 5TH INTERNATIONAL CONFERENCE ON ADVANCED MATERIALS, MECHANICS AND STRUCTURAL ENGINEERING (AMMSE)* (Vol. 473, Issues 5th International Conference on Advanced Materials, Mechanics and Structural Engineering (AMMSE) CL-Seoul. DOI: 10.1088/1757-899X/473/1/012050

Teplicka, K. (2019). Significance of implementation of Management Information Systems in the IPO chain for SMEs. In *INFORMATICS 2019 - IEEE 15th International Scientific Conference on Informatics, Proceedings* (Issue IEEE 15th International Scientific Conference on Informatics (INFORMATICS) CL-Poprad, pp. 183–188). DOI: 10.1109/Informatics47936.2019.9119251

Thorpe, D., Aghili, N., van Neuren, C., & IEEE. (2021). Managing Sustainable Asset Networks using Advanced Information Systems. In *2021 INTERNATIONAL CONFERENCE ON MAINTENANCE AND INTELLIGENT ASSET MANAGEMENT (ICMIAM)* (Issue International Conference on Maintenance and Intelligent Asset Management (ICMIAM) CL-Ballarat. DOI: 10.1109/ICMIAM54662.2021.9715219

Tian, J., Liu, Y., Yang, M., Sun, R., & Zheng, X. (2022). Blockchain Information Sharing Mechanism Based on Embedded System in Project Management System (Retracted Article). *Computational Intelligence and Neuroscience*, *2022*, 1–13. Advance online publication. DOI: 10.1155/2022/1835626 PMID: 35965759

Velmakina, Y. V., Aleksandrova, S. V., & Vasiliev, V. A. (2018). Basics of Forming an Integrated Management System. In S. Shaposhnikov (Ed.), *2018 IEEE INTERNATIONAL CONFERENCE QUALITY MANAGEMENT, TRANSPORT AND INFORMATION SECURITY, INFORMATION TECHNOLOGIES (IT&QM&IS)* (Issue IEEE International Conference on Quality Management, Transport and Information Security, Information Technologies (IT and QM and IS) CL-St Petersburg Electrotechn Univ LETI, St Petersburg, pp. 77–78). DOI: 10.1109/ITMQIS.2018.8524955

Vidal Carvalho, J., Rocha, Á., & Abreu, A. (2019). Maturity of hospital information systems: Most important influencing factors. *Health Informatics Journal*, *25*(3), 617–631. DOI: 10.1177/1460458217720054 PMID: 28720012

Wan, C., Zhou, Z., Li, S., Ding, Y., Xu, Z., Yang, Z., Xia, Y., & Yin, F. (2019). Development of a bridge management system based on the building information modeling technology. *Sustainability (Basel)*, *11*(17), 4583. Advance online publication. DOI: 10.3390/su11174583

Wang, G., Li, D., Ge, J., & Wang, T. (2022). Medical informatization of management system for admission office under convolutional neural network. *Expert Systems: International Journal of Knowledge Engineering and Neural Networks*, *39*(3), e12780. Advance online publication. DOI: 10.1111/exsy.12780

Wang, H. (2018). Information Platform Framework for the Integrated Management of Intercity Arterial Roads. In L. Jia, Y. Qin, J. Suo, J. Feng, L. Diao, & M. An (Eds.), *PROCEEDINGS OF THE 3RD INTERNATIONAL CONFERENCE ON ELECTRICAL AND INFORMATION TECHNOLOGIES FOR RAIL TRANSPORTATION (EITRT) 2017: TRANSPORTATION* (Vol. 483, Issues 3rd International Conference on Electrical Engineering and Information Technologies for Rail Transportation (EITRT) CL-Changsha, pp. 995–1003). DOI: 10.1007/978-981-10-7989-4_101

Wang, K. J., & Simarmata, M. T. A. (2024). Fuzzy activity-based costing: An investment evaluation approach for management information system of a smart factory. [WE - Science Citation Index Expanded] [SCI-EXPANDED] [WE - Social Science Citation Index] [SSCI]. *The Engineering Economist*, *69*(1), 66–86. DOI: 10.1080/0013791X.2024.2314673

Wang, Y. (2022). Optimization of the Music Teaching Management System Based on Emotion Recognition. *Computational Intelligence and Neuroscience*, *2022*, 1–9. Advance online publication. DOI: 10.1155/2022/4568041 PMID: 35586091

Wang, Y., Xue, W., & Zhang, A. (2023). Application of Big Data Technology in Enterprise Information Security Management and Risk Assessment. *Journal of Global Information Management*, *31*(3), 1–16. Advance online publication. DOI: 10.4018/JGIM.324465

Wu, Q., Liu, Y., Wen, B., Zhou, A., Chen, Z., & IEEE. (2018). Research of Cross-regional Vulnerability Governance for Power Grid Enterprise Information System. In *2018 11TH INTERNATIONAL SYMPOSIUM ON COMPUTATIONAL INTELLIGENCE AND DESIGN (ISCID), VOL 2* (Issues 11th International Symposium on Computational Intelligence and Design (ISCID) CL-Hangzhou, pp. 181–184). DOI: 10.1109/ISCID.2018.10143

Xiaobao, L., Shumin, L., & Kunyan, L. (2022). Establishment and application of hospital clinical trial management information system for improving clinical trial quality. *Chinese Journal of New Drugs and Clinical Remedies*, *41*(3), 146–150.

Xiaofang, Z., & Machinery, A. C. (2018). Design and Implementation of Student Information Management System Based On Java. In *PROCEEDINGS OF THE 2018 INTERNATIONAL CONFERENCE ON INFORMATION SCIENCE AND SYSTEM (ICISS 2018)* (Issue International Conference on Information Science and System (ICISS), pp. 90–92). DOI: 10.1145/3209914.3226153

Xiaosong, L., Bin, L., Zhenhua, X., & IEEE. (2018). Design Military and Civil Information Exchange Organization Management System Based on Structural Entropy. In *PROCEEDINGS OF THE 30TH CHINESE CONTROL AND DECISION CONFERENCE (2018 CCDC)* (Issues 30th Chinese Control and Decision Conference (CCDC) CL-Shenyang, pp. 2080–2085).

Xie, C., Luo, Y., & IEEE. (2020). Research and Design of College Educational Resource Sharing Information System in Military Civilian Integration Based on .NET Platform. In *2020 5TH INTERNATIONAL CONFERENCE ON ELECTROMECHANICAL CONTROL TECHNOLOGY AND TRANSPORTATION (ICECTT 2020)* (Issues 5th International Conference on Electromechanical Control Technology and Transportation (ICECTT), pp. 231–235). DOI: 10.1109/ICECTT50890.2020.00059

Xie, C., Luo, Y., Yu, X., & IEEE. (2020). Research on the Construction of the Dynamical Mechanism Model for the Military Civilian Integration Sharing of College Educational Resources of Hubei Province. In *2020 16TH INTERNATIONAL WIRELESS COMMUNICATIONS & MOBILE COMPUTING CONFERENCE, IWCMC* (Issues 16th IEEE International Wireless Communications and Mobile Computing Conference (IEEE IWCMC), pp. 1208–1212). DOI: 10.1109/IWCMC48107.2020.9148562

Xie, J., Jablonski, M., Smith, J., & Navedo, A. (2024). A Graphical Interface to Support Low-Flow Volatile Anesthesia: Implications for Patient Safety, Teaching, and Design of Anesthesia Information Management Systems. *Journal of Medical Systems*, *48*(1), 36. Advance online publication. DOI: 10.1007/s10916-024-02055-1 PMID: 38532235

Xie, J., & Luo, W. (2022). General Surgery Clinical Information Management System Based on Intelligent Data Management (Retracted Article). *Computational Intelligence and Neuroscience*, *2022*, 1–11. Advance online publication. DOI: 10.1155/2022/8601164 PMID: 35958777

Xuan, Y. L., Yu, X. N., Wang, Y., Liu, D. H., Ma, Q., & Xue, X. (2023). A self-evolving network-based artificial society model for the experiment analysis of complex social system. *Information Sciences*, *640*, 119057. Advance online publication. DOI: 10.1016/j.ins.2023.119057

Xuelei, L., Enjing, L., Yuetian, L., Kai, H., Yongyi, Z., & Kexin, L. (2021). Research on Function Optimization of University Laboratory Security Access System Information System Based on Environmental Monitoring Laboratory. In *Environmental Monitoring in China* (Vol. 37, Issue 1, pp. 23–28).

Yang, C., & Sun, Z. (2020). Data Management System based on Blockchain Technology for Agricultural Supply Chain. In G. DiFatta, V. Sheng, A. Cuzzocrea, C. Zaniolo, & X. Wu (Eds.), *IEEE International Conference on Data Mining Workshops, ICDMW* (Vols. 2020-November, Issues 20th IEEE International Conference on Data Mining (ICDM), pp. 907–911). DOI: 10.1109/ICDMW51313.2020.00130

Yang, D., Duan, R., Guan, S., Sun, J., & Xue, H. (2019). Trilateral game aided information management for open complex giant systems. In Q. Liang, J. Mu, M. Jia, W. Wang, X. Feng, & B. Zhang (Eds.), *Lecture Notes in Electrical Engineering* (Vol. 463, Issues 6th International Conference on Communications, Signal Processing, and Systems (ICCSPS) CL-Tianjin Normal Univ, Harbin, pp. 1758–1766). DOI: 10.1007/978-981-10-6571-2_213

Yang, G., Liu, K., Di, Y., & Ma, J. (2018). Design of Drilling Sensor Information Management System Based on UHF RFID. In J. B. Li (Ed.), *2018 EIGHTH INTERNATIONAL CONFERENCE ON INSTRUMENTATION AND MEASUREMENT, COMPUTER, COMMUNICATION AND CONTROL (IMCCC 2018)* (Issues 8th International Conference on Instrumentation and Measurement, Computer, Communication and Control (IMCCC) CL-Harbin Inst Technol, Harbin, pp. 128–131). DOI: 10.1109/IMCCC.2018.00034

Yaroslavtsev, A. V., & Matukhina, O. V. (2020). Crcating the Web Service of the Laboratory Information and Management System for Analytical Quality Control. In A. V Bogoviz & Y. V Ragulina (Eds.), *Lecture Notes in Networks and Systems* (Vol. 115, Issue Scientific and Practical Forum on Industry, Science, Competences, Integration CL-RUDN Univ, Moscow, pp. 643–649). DOI: 10.1007/978-3-030-40749-0_77

Yi-Jia, H., Xing-hua, L., Yong-Cong, C., & IOP. (2019). Research on Optimization Retrieval Technology of Multimedia Information Management System Based on Fuzzy Control. In *2018 INTERNATIONAL CONFERENCE ON COMPUTER INFORMATION SCIENCE AND APPLICATION TECHNOLOGY* (Vol. 1168, Issue International Conference on Computer Information Science and Application Technology (CISAT) CL-NE Petr Univ, Daqing. DOI: 10.1088/1742-6596/1168/3/032074

Yi-Lin, W., Jun, W., & IEEE. (2018). onstruction of Interlibrary Loan Information System Based on SaaS Mode. In *2018 NINTH INTERNATIONAL CONFERENCE ON INFORMATION TECHNOLOGY IN MEDICINE AND EDUCATION (ITME 2018)* (Issues 9th International Conference on Information Technology in Medicine and Education (ITME) CL-Hangzhou, pp. 432–436). DOI: 10.1109/ITME.2018.00103

Yong, S., Donglei, W., Yuquan, Z., Yuan, Z., & IOP. (2019). Design and Research on the Information Management System of Qinhuai River Intelligent Pump Station. In *2019 3RD INTERNATIONAL WORKSHOP ON RENEWABLE ENERGY AND DEVELOPMENT (IWRED 2019)* (Vol. 267, Issues 3rd International Workshop on Renewable Energy and Development (IWRED) CL-Guangzhou. DOI: 10.1088/1755-1315/267/3/032020

Yoo, Y. (2010). Computing in everyday life: A call for research on experiential computing. *MIS Quarterly: Management Information Systems, 34*(SPEC. ISSUE 2), 213–231. DOI: 10.2307/20721425

YOUNG, C. J. (2021). Study on the Health Information Management Practice Program Model for EMR Certification System Education -Focus on Patient Information Management-. *Journal of The Health Care and Life Science, 9*(1), 1–9. DOI: 10.22961/JHCLS.2021.9.1.01

Yousefnezhad, N., Malhi, A., Kinnunen, T., Huotari, M., & Framling, K. (2020). Product Lifecycle Information Management with Digital Twin: A Case Study. In *IEEE International Conference on Industrial Informatics (INDIN)* (Vols. 2020-July, Issues 18th IEEE International Conference on Industrial Informatics (INDIN), pp. 321–326). DOI: 10.1109/INDIN45582.2020.9442208

Yuan, C., & Yicun, H. (2021). Management Information System for Compensation under Multihoming Network Architecture. *Wireless Communications and Mobile Computing, 2021*(1), 6168947. Advance online publication. DOI: 10.1155/2021/6168947

Zagornaya, T. O., Panova, V. L., Berg, D. B., Medvedev, M., & Medvedev, N. (2018). Mathematical tools of the architectural decisions efficiency assessment in the system of the enterprise development information support. In *AIP Conference Proceedings* (Vol. 1978, Issue International Conference of Numerical Analysis and Applied Mathematics (ICNAAM) CL-Thessaloniki. DOI: 10.1063/1.5044052

Zekun, W., Yakun, Z., Xuteng, Z., Wenzhe, T., & Maoshan, Q. (2022). Information management of water conservancy project partnering. *Qinghua Daxue Xuebao. Ziran Kexue Ban, 62*(8), 1351–1356.

Zeng, L., & Yanchao, W. (2021). The internet of things integrated management system of civil engineering laboratory. In Z. Li & F. Cen (Eds.), *INTERNATIONAL CONFERENCE ON SMART TRANSPORTATION AND CITY ENGINEERING 2021* (Vol. 12050, Issue International Conference on Smart Transportation and City Engineering CL-Chongqing, p. 59). DOI: 10.1117/12.2613743

Zhai, Q., & Chen, X. (2024). Design and application of optical communication technology based on machine learning algorithms in physical education teaching information management system. *Optical and Quantum Electronics*, *56*(1), 111. Advance online publication. DOI: 10.1007/s11082-023-05717-5

Zhang, C., & IOP. (2019). Research on life cycle of bulk port production environmental management information system. In *2018 INTERNATIONAL CONFERENCE ON CONSTRUCTION, AVIATION AND ENVIRONMENTAL ENGINEERING* (Vol. 233, Issue International Conference on Construction, Aerotropolis, Aviation and Environmental Engineering (ICCAE) CL-Taoyuan. DOI: 10.1088/1755-1315/233/5/052037

Zhang, C., Xu, X., Duan, L., & Liu, S. (2022). Research on Information Assets Security Management of Electric Power Enterprise Based on Cloud Edge Collaboration Technology. In *2022 4th International Conference on Smart Power and Internet Energy Systems, SPIES 2022* (Issues 4th International Conference on Smart Power and Internet Energy Systems (SPIES) CL-Beijing, pp. 2266–2270). DOI: 10.1109/SPIES55999.2022.10082089

Zhang, J. (2018). Optimization design of university information management platform based on B/S framework and APP. In *Proceedings - 2018 3rd International Conference on Mechanical, Control and Computer Engineering, ICMCCE 2018* (Issues 3rd International Conference on Mechanical, Control and Computer Engineering (ICMCCE) CL-Huhhot, pp. 584–588). DOI: 10.1109/ICMCCE.2018.00128

Zhang, X. (2020a). The design and implementation of geologic hazard information management system. *Arabian Journal of Geosciences*, *13*(17), 854. Advance online publication. DOI: 10.1007/s12517-020-05874-x

Zhang, X. (2020b). The design and implementation of geologic hazard information management system. *Arabian Journal of Geosciences*, *13*(17), 854. Advance online publication. DOI: 10.1007/s12517-020-05874-x

Zhang, X. (2022). Design and Implementation of Management Information System Based on Network Environment. In D. Zhou & Z. Y. Du (Eds.), *Lecture Notes in Electrical Engineering: Vol. 827 LNEE* (Issue International Conference on Information Technology and Industrial Engineering CL-Wuhan, pp. 1076–1080). DOI: 10.1007/978-981-16-8052-6_147

Zhang, Y. (2022). Development Strategy of College Sports Information Management System Using Data Mining in Mobile Internet Environment (Retracted Article). *Journal of Environmental and Public Health*, *2022*. Advance online publication. DOI: 10.1155/2022/3895555 PMID: 36159766

Zhao, B., & Tu, C. (2021). Research and Development of Inventory Management and Human Resource Management in ERP. *Wireless Communications and Mobile Computing, 2021*(1), 3132062. Advance online publication. DOI: 10.1155/2021/3132062

Zhao, L. J., Nazir, M. S., Nazir, H. M. J., & Abdalla, A. N. (2022). A review on proliferation of artificial intelligence in wind energy forecasting and instrumentation management. *Environmental Science and Pollution Research International, 29*(29), 43690–43709. DOI: 10.1007/s11356-022-19902-8 PMID: 35435552

Zhaorong, Y., Yiwen, C., & IEEE. (2019). Design And Application Of Adolescent Mental Health Data Mining And Management System. In *2019 INTERNATIONAL CONFERENCE ON SMART GRID AND ELECTRICAL AUTOMATION (ICSGEA)* (Issue International Conference on Smart Grid and Electrical Automation (ICSGEA) CL-Xiangtan, pp. 490–492). DOI: 10.1109/ICSGEA.2019.00117

Zheng, H., Zhang, T., Fang, C., Zeng, J., & Yang, X. (2021). Design and implementation of poultry farming information management system based on cloud database. *Animals (Basel), 11*(3), 1–15. DOI: 10.3390/ani11030900 PMID: 33809835

Zhidong, L. (2023). Construction of management mechanism model of soil and water conservation information system. In *Science of Soil and Water Conservation* (Vol. 21, Issue 5, pp. 106–110).

Zhigang, W. (2021). Research on the Framework of Library Management System Based on Internet of Things. In *Proceedings - 2021 13th International Conference on Measuring Technology and Mechatronics Automation, ICMTMA 2021* (Issues 13th International Conference on Measuring Technology and Mechatronics Automation (ICMTMA) CL-Beihai, pp. 384–388). DOI: 10.1109/ICMTMA52658.2021.00089

Zhongkai, L., Gui, L., & Yaodong, L. (2020). Management method and management system of non-model informationin in product design process. *Chinese Journal of Engineering Design, 27*(1), 13–18.

Zhu, W., Jia, Y., & IOP. (2018). The Research on Safety Management Information System of Railway Passenger Based on Risk Management Theory. In *2017 3RD INTERNATIONAL CONFERENCE ON ENVIRONMENTAL SCIENCE AND MATERIAL APPLICATION (ESMA2017), VOLS 1-4* (Vol. 108, Issues 3rd International Conference on Environmental Science and Material Application (ESMA) CL-Chongqing. DOI: 10.1088/1755-1315/108/4/042067

Chapter 2 Transformative Impact of Artificial Intelligence in Data Analytics and Business Intelligence

ABSTRACT

Analyzing raw data systematically in order to find patterns, draw conclusions, and generate forecasts that make sense is known as data analytics. This process entails sorting through the enormous datasets that corporations amass using sophisticated algorithms, statistical models, and machine learning approaches (Li & Wu, 2021). Businesses may uncover the hidden story by combining apparently unrelated data pieces into coherent tales via the lens of data analytics. Producing reports is not the only objective; another is to draw out useful information that spurs strategic decision-making, (Farooq, Yuen, et al., 2024; León-Romero et al., 2024).

2.1CHAPTER INTRODUCTION

Business intelligence refers to the more comprehensive framework that includes the instruments, systems, and procedures used in gathering, examining, and displaying business data. It acts as the general framework that makes it easier to incorporate data analytics into organizational processes(Farooq et al., 2025c, 2025a, 2025g). Business intelligence provides stakeholders with user-friendly dashboards and reports that condense complicated information into easily understood forms, acting as a translator between raw data and actionable solutions. This makes it possible

DOI: 10.4018/979-8-3373-0513-4.ch002

for leaders at all levels to take well informed choices that promote creativity and performance (Niesler, 2020).

A symbiotic relationship between business intelligence and data analytics is being played out in a variety of industries, including manufacturing, retail, healthcare, and finance. Predictive analytics, for example, may be used in the financial sector to minimize risks, improve investment portfolios, and anticipate market trends. Data analytics is used in healthcare to enable customized medication, clinical decision support, and epidemiological pattern recognition. Business intelligence technologies improve supply chain visibility, simplify inventory management, and optimize production operations in the manufacturing sector(Farooq et al., 2025i, 2025j).

Figure 1. Mind map of data analytics and business intelligence

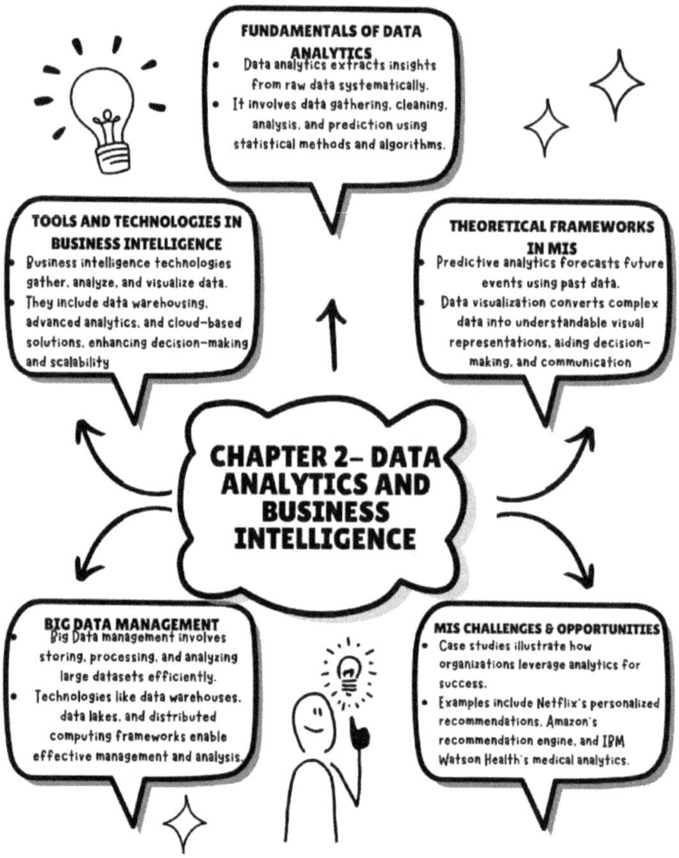

The integration of artificial intelligence (AI) in data analytics and business intelligence (BI) has reshaped how businesses approach data and make strategic decisions. This transformation hinges on the power of AI to handle vast data volumes, unveil hidden patterns, generate insights, and drive forecasts that are crucial in a data-driven world. The purpose of AI-enhanced data analytics extends beyond report generation; it enables organizations to distill meaningful insights from raw data, facilitating strategic planning and operational efficiencies across diverse industries, including healthcare, finance, retail, and manufacturing.

2.1.1 Data Analytics: A Systematic Approach to Understanding Data

Data analytics involves a structured approach to examining raw data to uncover patterns, draw insightful conclusions, and predict future trends. At its core, data analytics leverages advanced algorithms, statistical models, and machine learning to sift through complex datasets. The ultimate goal of this process is not just to identify trends but to synthesize data into meaningful narratives, enabling organizations to see the hidden "story" within numbers and statistics (Q. P. Li & Wu, 2021).

Using techniques such as clustering, regression, and classification, data analytics combines otherwise disparate pieces of data to create a cohesive picture. Machine learning, a key component of AI, plays a central role in predictive analytics, empowering businesses to make data-driven predictions about customer behavior, product demand, and potential risks. With machine learning, systems can identify complex patterns that are difficult, if not impossible, for humans to detect. For instance, clustering algorithms can group similar customers, revealing buying patterns that drive targeted marketing strategies. Regression analysis can uncover correlations that suggest future sales trends, while classification algorithms can categorize customer feedback to reveal emerging market trends.

By leveraging data analytics, organizations gain access to actionable insights that extend beyond traditional reporting functions. A retail company, for example, may analyze customer data to understand seasonal trends, optimize product placement, and adjust pricing strategies. In finance, predictive analytics can help banks assess credit risk, reducing the likelihood of loan defaults. In healthcare, data analytics enables physicians to make informed decisions, drawing on patient data to customize treatment plans and improve patient outcomes.

2.1.2 Business Intelligence: The Framework for Informed Decision-Making

Business intelligence is a comprehensive framework that involves the collection, analysis, and presentation of business data. It combines technology, processes, and systems that support the data-driven decision-making process. BI tools such as dashboards, reporting systems, and data visualization platforms serve as conduits for converting raw data into a form that is understandable, actionable, and valuable for organizational decision-making (Niesler, 2020).

BI provides stakeholders with a user-friendly interface, often presenting complex information in graphical formats like charts, graphs, and dashboards. These visualizations make it easier for leaders and decision-makers to interpret data at a glance. For example, in a manufacturing setting, a BI dashboard might display key metrics related to production rates, inventory levels, and supply chain performance. Decision-makers can use this consolidated view to identify bottlenecks, adjust workflows, and ultimately improve efficiency and output.

In essence, BI bridges the gap between data analytics and actionable solutions. It enables organizations to go beyond mere data collection and instead fosters an environment where data-driven decision-making becomes an integral part of the business process. BI tools facilitate cross-departmental communication, ensuring that insights generated from data analytics reach relevant stakeholders across the organization. Whether it's a finance department analyzing budget allocations or a marketing team assessing campaign effectiveness, BI systems provide a common platform for shared insights.

2.1.3 The Symbiotic Relationship Between Data Analytics and Business Intelligence

The relationship between data analytics and business intelligence is a symbiotic one, where each complements and enhances the other. Data analytics serves as the engine that drives BI, feeding BI systems with refined, meaningful data that BI tools then convert into actionable insights. This relationship enables businesses to incorporate real-time data analysis into their decision-making processes.

For instance, in the retail industry, BI tools can integrate with data analytics models to track customer purchasing patterns in real-time. Retailers can use this data to adjust pricing, offer promotions, and manage inventory in response to changing consumer demand. In the healthcare sector, data analytics enables personalized medicine by analyzing patient data, while BI dashboards provide physicians with a visual representation of a patient's medical history, making diagnosis and treatment planning more efficient.

Furthermore, predictive analytics—a branch of data analytics focused on forecasting future outcomes—can be seamlessly integrated into BI platforms. Predictive models can be used to anticipate market trends, identify high-risk customers, and even detect fraud in financial transactions. By embedding predictive analytics within BI tools, organizations can take proactive measures based on anticipated scenarios, thereby reducing risks and improving outcomes.

2.1.4 AI's Role in Enhancing Data Analytics and Business Intelligence

AI has significantly amplified the capabilities of both data analytics and BI, allowing organizations to automate data processing, generate insights faster, and make more accurate predictions. AI-driven analytics frameworks allow for real-time analysis of massive datasets, something that would be impossible to achieve manually. Machine learning, a subset of AI, enables data systems to learn and improve over time, ensuring that models and algorithms evolve in response to new data.

One of the key areas where AI has transformed data analytics is through predictive and prescriptive analytics. Predictive analytics focuses on forecasting future outcomes based on historical data, while prescriptive analytics goes a step further, recommending actions that should be taken to achieve desired outcomes. For example, an AI-powered predictive model in retail might predict an increase in demand for winter clothing, while a prescriptive model could recommend specific stock adjustments or marketing strategies to capitalize on this trend.

Moreover, natural language processing (NLP), another AI technology, has made it possible to analyze unstructured data, such as social media posts, customer reviews, and feedback forms. NLP can extract valuable insights from this data, helping companies understand consumer sentiment, detect emerging trends, and tailor products or services to meet customer needs. By converting unstructured data into actionable insights, NLP expands the scope of data analytics, allowing businesses to consider a broader array of data sources in their decision-making processes.

2.1.5 Cross-Industry Applications of AI-enhanced Data Analytics and Business Intelligence

The application of AI-enhanced data analytics and BI varies across industries, with each sector leveraging these technologies to meet unique challenges and goals. Here are a few examples of how different industries benefit from these advancements:

Finance

In finance, AI-powered data analytics helps manage risk, optimize investments, and predict market fluctuations. Predictive models analyze factors such as economic indicators, interest rates, and historical price movements, allowing financial institutions to forecast market trends and make informed investment decisions. BI dashboards aggregate these insights, presenting them to portfolio managers who can quickly adjust strategies based on real-time data.

Healthcare:

In healthcare, AI-driven analytics support clinical decision-making, enable personalized treatment plans, and assist in epidemiological studies. Data from electronic health records (EHRs), wearables, and other medical devices can be analyzed to predict patient outcomes, detect early warning signs of diseases, and personalize treatments. BI systems then present this information in a way that healthcare professionals can readily interpret, improving both patient outcomes and operational efficiency.

Retail

Retailers use AI-powered data analytics to understand customer behavior, optimize inventory management, and personalize marketing. By analyzing purchase histories, browsing behavior, and demographic information, data analytics tools can generate personalized product recommendations and promotions. BI tools provide a consolidated view of these insights, helping retail managers make decisions on stock levels, pricing, and store layouts based on consumer demand.

Manufacturing

In the manufacturing sector, AI-powered analytics optimize production processes, enhance quality control, and improve supply chain management. Predictive maintenance algorithms analyze data from machinery sensors to identify patterns that signal potential failures, reducing downtime and extending equipment life. BI tools visualize this data, enabling managers to monitor production performance, assess bottlenecks, and make data-driven improvements to the manufacturing process.

2.1.6 Challenges and Ethical Considerations

While the integration of AI in data analytics and BI has transformative potential, it also presents unique challenges and ethical considerations(Karim et al., 2024; Wang et al., 2023). One key issue is data privacy. AI systems often require access to vast amounts of personal data, which raises concerns about how this data is collected, stored, and used. Organizations must ensure compliance with data privacy laws, such as the General Data Protection Regulation (GDPR), to protect individuals' privacy rights and maintain trust.

Bias in AI algorithms is another ethical concern. If an AI model is trained on biased data, it can perpetuate or even amplify that bias, leading to unfair outcomes. For example, a predictive model used in hiring could favor certain demographics if the training data reflects historical biases. Ensuring that AI models are fair and transparent is critical to avoiding discrimination and building ethical AI systems.

Additionally, there are challenges related to transparency and explainability. Complex AI models, especially deep learning networks, are often difficult to interpret, making it challenging for organizations to understand how specific decisions were made. This "black-box" nature of AI can be problematic, particularly in regulated industries where decision-making transparency is essential.

2.1.7 The Future of AI in Data Analytics and Business Intelligence

Looking ahead, the role of AI in data analytics and BI is expected to grow as new advancements emerge. Future developments may include fully autonomous BI systems capable of generating insights and recommendations with minimal human intervention. Augmented analytics, which combines AI, machine learning, and natural language processing, is likely to democratize BI by making data insights accessible to non-technical users.

Moreover, as AI models become more sophisticated, they will provide even more accurate and actionable predictions, enabling businesses to make proactive decisions. For instance, AI-driven demand forecasting could help businesses preemptively adjust inventory or staffing based on anticipated demand changes. In healthcare, AI could predict patient health outcomes with even greater precision, enabling more targeted interventions.

The transformative impact of artificial intelligence on data analytics and business intelligence cannot be overstated. By enhancing data processing capabilities, AI enables businesses to uncover insights, make more accurate predictions, and facilitate data-driven decision-making across industries. AI-powered data analytics offers a systematic way to understand and leverage data, while BI tools translate these insights into actionable information for stakeholders. Despite challenges related to privacy, bias, and transparency, the future of AI in data analytics and BI is promising, with continued advancements set to further reshape how organizations operate and thrive in a data-driven world.

2.2 TRANSFORMATIVE IMPACT OF AI ON FUNDAMENTALS OF DATA ANALYTICS

Modern business strategies are fundamentally based on data analytics, which gives firms the ability to glean insightful information from massive amounts of data. For businesses looking to gain a competitive advantage in the rapidly changing digital era, knowing the foundations of data analytics is essential (Ram & Zhang, 2022).

Analyzing raw data systematically to find patterns, trends, and important information is known as data analytics. This procedure is essential to making well-informed decisions because it enables companies to base their strategic decisions on data rather than gut feeling. Essentially, it converts data into meaningful insights that firms can use to improve productivity, spur innovation, and optimize procedures(Munodawafa & Johl, 2022).

The gathering and preparation of data is the initial component of the foundations of data analytics. Prior to analysis, raw data which often comes from several sources must be selected and cleansed. In order to guarantee the precision and dependability of the insights obtained, this stage is essential. It includes data transformation, loading, and cleaning (ETL) procedures, which provide the groundwork for reliable analytical results.

After the data is produced, patterns and linkages within the dataset are found using statistical methods and algorithms. A crucial element is descriptive analytics, which is analyzing and interpreting historical data to comprehend historical patterns more deeply. Prescriptive and predictive analytics are made possible by the use of this retrospective study as the foundation for more sophisticated analytics methods(Huang et al., 2020).

One popular subcategory, predictive analytics, makes use of machine learning models and statistical algorithms to predict future trends and results. Organizations may support proactive decision-making by generating well-informed forecasts via the analysis and identification of trends in past data. This kind of insight is very beneficial in a variety of sectors, from manufacturing to retail, where it may be used to forecast consumer behavior or anticipate equipment faults.

In the field of business intelligence, technology and tools are essential for facilitating efficient data analytics. Organizations have a wide range of options, from cutting-edge cloud-based solutions to conventional relational databases. By the use of graphical representations, these solutions help stakeholders understand complicated information via data visualization. An organization's data-driven culture may be fostered by giving people the natural ability to study data via interactive dashboards and reports (Zhang et al., 2022).

In modern data analytics, large data management integration is essential. Businesses need to implement scalable solutions to manage enormous datasets as the volume, velocity, and diversity of data keep growing rapidly. Large amounts of heterogeneous data can be processed thanks to big data technologies like Hadoop and Spark, which open up new avenues for analysis and insight creation.

Figure 2. Fundamentals of data analytics

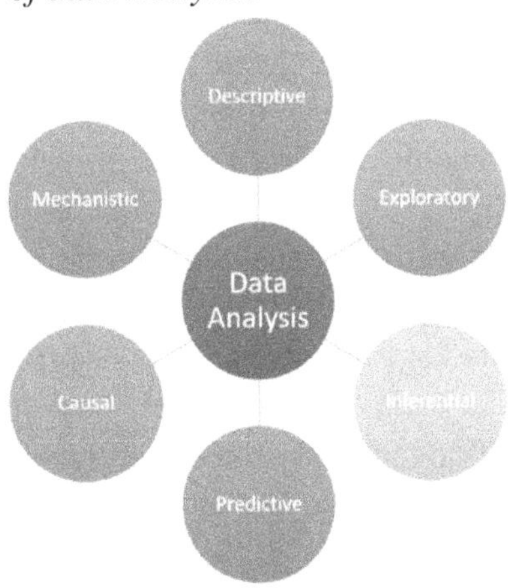

Modern business strategies are deeply embedded in data analytics, empowering organizations to derive critical insights from enormous datasets. As businesses seek a competitive edge in today's data-driven environment, understanding the foundations of data analytics has become indispensable (Ram & Zhang, 2022). Data analytics entails the systematic examination of raw data to uncover patterns, trends, and significant information, allowing organizations to make data-driven decisions that are rooted in evidence rather than intuition. This transformation of raw data into actionable insights aids in improving productivity, fostering innovation, and optimizing operational processes (Munodawafa & Johl, 2022).

Artificial Intelligence (AI) has had a profound impact on data analytics, fundamentally transforming each stage of the process—data gathering, data cleaning, analysis, visualization, and decision-making. AI-powered techniques and tools have redefined the possibilities within data analytics, enabling businesses to harness the full potential of their data and make forward-looking decisions.

2.2.1 Data Collection and Preparation: The First Stage of Data Analytics

Data collection and preparation constitute the foundation of data analytics. Before data analysis can occur, raw data—often collected from a multitude of sources—needs to be aggregated, cleansed, and structured. This is essential for ensuring the accuracy and reliability of subsequent insights. The process, which includes data extraction, transformation, and loading (ETL), is critical for creating dependable analytical outcomes.

AI technologies have significantly enhanced the ETL processes. By automating tasks such as data cleaning and integration, AI reduces the time and effort required for data preparation. Machine learning algorithms identify and correct anomalies, handle missing values, and remove duplicate entries more effectively than manual processes. For instance, AI-driven ETL tools can recognize patterns in historical data to detect outliers or anomalous data points, ensuring that only high-quality data is used in the analysis.

Additionally, AI algorithms play a role in data transformation, standardizing data formats, and facilitating integration from disparate sources. This is particularly important in today's data landscape, where businesses gather information from multiple channels—such as social media, transactional systems, IoT devices, and external databases. By unifying these diverse data sources, AI-driven ETL systems create a comprehensive dataset that enables holistic analysis and richer insights.

2.2.2 Statistical Methods and Algorithmic Analysis

Once data is collected and prepared, the next step in data analytics is to identify patterns and relationships within the dataset. This phase relies on statistical methods and algorithms, which provide a foundation for descriptive, predictive, and prescriptive analytics. Descriptive analytics focuses on interpreting historical data to gain insights into past behaviors and trends. This retrospective analysis forms the basis for more advanced analytics approaches, enabling organizations to make sense of historical patterns and their implications.

AI has transformed statistical analysis by automating complex calculations, allowing analysts to conduct descriptive analytics on a much larger scale. AI-powered tools perform computations and recognize trends within large datasets in seconds, offering businesses a quicker pathway to insights. In addition to traditional statistical methods, machine learning algorithms bring a predictive dimension to data analytics.

For example, clustering algorithms group similar data points, revealing patterns that are essential for customer segmentation, while association algorithms uncover relationships between variables. In retail, these algorithms can analyze purchase histories to identify items frequently bought together, leading to optimized inventory strategies and cross-selling opportunities.

2.2.3 Predictive Analytics: Leveraging AI for Forward-looking Insights

Predictive analytics, a subset of data analytics, employs machine learning models and statistical algorithms to predict future outcomes based on historical data. It enables organizations to make informed forecasts, facilitating proactive decision-making. Predictive analytics is widely applicable across industries, from manufacturing to retail, as it can help predict customer behavior, optimize inventory, and even anticipate equipment failures.

AI enhances predictive analytics by leveraging deep learning, neural networks, and other machine learning algorithms that improve over time. Deep learning, in particular, is capable of recognizing complex, non-linear relationships within data, enabling more accurate predictions. For example, in the financial industry, AI models analyze historical market data to predict stock prices or identify potential investment risks. In retail, predictive analytics helps in demand forecasting, which allows businesses to adjust their inventory based on anticipated trends and customer preferences.

AI models continually improve as they are exposed to new data, making them more accurate and reliable over time. These self-learning systems, fueled by advancements in AI, bring significant value to businesses by reducing uncertainty and allowing them to make data-informed, strategic choices. With AI-driven predictive analytics, companies can respond quickly to changing market conditions, adapting their strategies in real-time to maintain a competitive advantage.

2.2.4 Prescriptive Analytics: Recommending Optimal Actions

Building on predictive analytics, prescriptive analytics goes a step further by recommending specific actions that can lead to desired outcomes. It not only predicts what might happen in the future but also suggests the best course of action to achieve business goals. Prescriptive analytics combines machine learning algorithms with optimization techniques to provide actionable recommendations.

For instance, a logistics company might use prescriptive analytics to determine the most efficient route for delivery trucks based on traffic patterns, fuel costs, and delivery schedules. In finance, prescriptive analytics can suggest portfolio adjustments based on market predictions, risk appetite, and financial goals. AI enhances prescriptive analytics by processing a larger set of variables, evaluating multiple scenarios simultaneously, and selecting the most advantageous strategy.

Prescriptive analytics is particularly valuable in complex decision-making environments where there are multiple potential outcomes. By providing recommendations that maximize efficiency or minimize costs, AI-driven prescriptive analytics helps organizations optimize their operations and enhance overall productivity.

2.2.5 Data Visualization and Business Intelligence Tools

Data visualization is a crucial aspect of data analytics, as it transforms complex data into graphical formats that are easier to understand. Business intelligence (BI) tools use data visualization to present findings through charts, graphs, and dashboards, providing stakeholders with a clear and intuitive way to interpret analytical results. Interactive dashboards allow users to explore data at various levels of detail, from high-level overviews to specific metrics.

AI has revolutionized data visualization by enabling BI tools to generate insights automatically. AI-powered BI systems can create dynamic, real-time visualizations that adjust to new data inputs, providing up-to-date information that supports decision-making. For example, an AI-driven BI dashboard might show a real-time analysis of customer sentiment based on social media data, allowing a company to respond immediately to shifts in customer attitudes.

Moreover, AI enhances BI tools by personalizing the user experience. AI algorithms can identify the specific data points that are most relevant to each user, tailoring the dashboard to individual needs. This customization ensures that each stakeholder receives the insights they need, whether they are in finance, marketing, or operations, thereby fostering a data-driven culture across the organization.

2.2.6 Big Data Integration and Management

With the exponential growth in data volume, velocity, and variety, big data integration has become a critical component of modern data analytics. Big data technologies such as Hadoop and Spark enable businesses to process and analyze massive datasets, uncovering insights that were previously inaccessible. These technologies provide the infrastructure necessary to handle large volumes of heterogeneous data, enabling businesses to tap into vast amounts of information for decision-making(-Farooq, Yuen, et al., 2024; Farooq & Qureshi, 2020; Wang et al., 2021).

AI plays a central role in big data management, helping to handle and process data more efficiently. AI algorithms can quickly analyze unstructured data—such as text, images, and videos—allowing businesses to incorporate diverse data sources into their analytics strategies(Farooq et al., 2025c, 2025a, 2025g). Additionally, machine learning algorithms can detect patterns within big data, revealing insights that drive innovation and strategic planning(Farooq et al., 2025i, 2025j, 2025h, 2025e).

For example, in the healthcare sector, AI-powered big data analytics can process medical records, genomic data, and patient feedback to uncover patterns that support precision medicine and improve patient care. In the retail sector, AI-driven big data tools can analyze customer behavior across online and offline channels, creating a comprehensive view of customer preferences and enhancing personalization.

2.2.7 Transformative Role of AI in the Fundamentals of Data Analytics

AI has fundamentally reshaped the foundations of data analytics, enabling businesses to derive insights with unprecedented speed, accuracy, and depth. By automating data collection, cleansing, and integration, AI has streamlined the preparatory stages of data analytics, ensuring that analysts work with high-quality data from the outset. Machine learning algorithms have transformed statistical and algorithmic analysis, providing powerful tools for identifying trends, relationships, and patterns(Farooq et al., 2025d).

Moreover, AI has extended the capabilities of predictive and prescriptive analytics, allowing organizations to make forward-looking decisions that reduce risk and optimize outcomes. With advancements in deep learning and neural networks, predictive analytics can handle complex, high-dimensional data, providing more accurate and reliable forecasts. Prescriptive analytics, empowered by AI, guides organizations on the best actions to take, fostering proactive strategies rather than reactive responses(Farooq et al., 2025f).

AI-powered data visualization tools, meanwhile, have made it easier for stakeholders to interpret complex data, driving data literacy and enabling a data-driven culture. Big data integration, supported by AI, has expanded the scope of data analytics, allowing businesses to tap into a wider array of data sources for a more holistic view of their operations and market environment(Farooq et al., 2025b).

The transformative impact of AI on data analytics has redefined how organizations approach decision-making in the digital age. From data preparation and cleansing to advanced predictive and prescriptive analytics, AI has enhanced every stage of the data analytics process. By automating routine tasks, identifying patterns, and recommending actions, AI-driven analytics empowers organizations to make strategic, data-driven decisions(Farooq et al., 2025k; Muhammad Farooq, Muhammad Ramzan, 2025).

Furthermore, the integration of AI with big data management tools has opened new avenues for insight generation, allowing businesses to leverage massive datasets that were previously too complex to analyze(Farooq, Buzdar, et al., 2024; Yen et al., 2023). As AI technology continues to evolve, its impact on data analytics is expected to grow, driving innovation, enhancing productivity, and providing organizations with a powerful tool for navigating the complexities of the modern business landscape. The AI-enabled data analytics framework not only optimizes internal operations but also supports sustainable growth by enabling

2.3 TOOLS AND TECHNOLOGIES IN BUSINESS INTELLIGENCE

The foundation of procedures for making decisions based on data is provided by business intelligence technologies. These technologies have a variety of uses, from gathering and storing data to analyzing and visualizing it. Integrating various data sources is the foundation of business intelligence (BI), allowing firms to use the value of both organized and unstructured data (Vecchiarini & Somià, 2023). Unstructured data, which comes from sources like social media and emails, needs sophisticated tools for understanding and analysis, while structured data, which is often found in databases and spreadsheets, is arranged and simple to search (Gornostaeva, 2021).

The introduction of BI technologies that are easy to use has made data analysis more accessible to professionals in a variety of departments, eliminating the need for specialist technical knowledge to access and understand data. Transforming complicated statistics into understandable visual representations has made dashboards and reporting tools essential(Sobocinska, 2021). This not only makes real-time monitoring easier, but it also improves communication by giving stakeholders at all organizational levels easy-to-digest information.

A key component of business intelligence (BI) is data warehousing, which serves as a single location for organizing and managing massive amounts of structured data. This is especially important for businesses where data is created and gathered from several sources. Modern data warehouse architecture is built to maximize query performance and speed up effective data retrieval, enabling businesses to quickly get insights (Chaveesuk et al., 2019).

The possibilities of BI are further enhanced by advanced analytics technologies, like as machine learning and artificial intelligence applications. Predictive analytics is made possible by these technologies, which enables businesses to anticipate trends, spot patterns, and take preventive measures. These cutting-edge solutions provide businesses a competitive advantage as they struggle with the overwhelming amount and complexity of data by automating the analysis process and revealing hidden patterns that would defy conventional analytical techniques(Chhillar & Aguilera, 2022).

With their scalability and flexibility, cloud-based BI solutions have become a revolutionary force for businesses looking to use data without making large infrastructure expenditures. Cloud-based solutions make it easier to collaborate and share data, which promotes a more responsive and flexible approach to business.

2.3: TOOLS AND TECHNOLOGIES IN BUSINESS INTELLIGENCE

Business intelligence (BI) tools and technologies provide the backbone for data-driven decision-making processes, enabling organizations to harness insights from vast volumes of both structured and unstructured data. As businesses strive to stay competitive in the digital era, BI tools have evolved from simple data storage systems to powerful analytics platforms capable of transforming raw data into actionable insights. These tools facilitate the gathering, storing, analyzing, and visualizing of data, creating a comprehensive BI ecosystem that supports strategic decision-making across various organizational levels (Vecchiarini & Somià, 2023).

At the heart of BI is the integration of diverse data sources, which allows companies to leverage information from structured datasets, such as relational databases, and unstructured data, such as social media, emails, and text-based content. Unstructured data, which lacks a defined structure, requires sophisticated tools to process, analyze, and extract meaning, while structured data, often stored in organized formats like spreadsheets, can be easily searched and analyzed (Gornostaeva, 2021). By harmonizing these data sources, BI enables a holistic view of organizational performance, trends, and customer insights, which is crucial for modern businesses to make informed, real-time decisions.

2.3.1 Data Visualization and User-friendly BI Tools

One of the most significant advancements in BI is the development of user-friendly tools that simplify data analysis, making it accessible to non-technical professionals across various departments. In the past, data analysis required specialized technical skills, creating bottlenecks for teams without dedicated data analysts. Modern BI tools, however, have democratized access to data insights by providing intuitive interfaces that require little technical knowledge, empowering users across marketing, finance, HR, and operations to access and interpret data directly. Dashboards and reporting tools, in particular, have become essential in BI due to their ability to transform complex data sets into easily digestible visualizations (Sobocinska, 2021).

These visualization tools offer a variety of chart types, graphs, and interactive features that allow users to customize their data views according to their needs. This capability not only facilitates real-time monitoring of business metrics but also enhances communication within organizations by providing stakeholders at all levels with clear, actionable insights. For example, a sales team can use a dashboard to monitor monthly targets, view performance by region, and adjust strategies based on current data. By breaking down data into visual components, BI tools reduce the cognitive load on users, making it easier to identify trends, outliers, and performance gaps that would otherwise be challenging to discern from raw data alone.

2.3.2 Data Warehousing: The Backbone of BI Infrastructure

A core component of any BI framework is the data warehouse, a centralized repository for storing and managing vast amounts of structured data. Data warehousing is especially critical for large organizations where data is generated from multiple sources, such as transaction systems, CRM software, and ERP applications. The modern data warehouse is designed to handle large volumes of data efficiently, enabling quick data retrieval for analysis and reporting purposes. Data warehouses are optimized for complex query performance, allowing users to obtain insights from massive datasets in seconds rather than hours (Chaveesuk et al., 2019).

The role of a data warehouse is to consolidate data from disparate sources into a single, cohesive platform. This centralization not only simplifies data access for analysts but also ensures that all users within an organization are working from a consistent, unified dataset. Data warehousing architectures, such as star schema and snowflake schema, organize data into structured formats, improving the efficiency of query processes and providing a scalable solution for businesses as their data needs grow. In today's environment, the data warehouse often serves as the core foundation for advanced BI capabilities, including predictive analytics, data mining, and real-time reporting.

2.3.3 Advanced Analytics: AI and Machine Learning in BI

Advanced analytics, powered by artificial intelligence (AI) and machine learning (ML), has dramatically expanded the possibilities within BI, allowing organizations to move from descriptive and diagnostic analytics towards predictive and prescriptive analytics. AI and ML algorithms enable predictive analytics, allowing businesses to forecast trends, identify patterns, and take proactive measures based on anticipated outcomes. These advanced tools automate much of the analysis process, uncovering hidden insights and patterns that may be missed with traditional methods. This gives businesses a distinct competitive advantage, especially in environments where data volume and complexity are constantly growing (Chhillar & Aguilera, 2022).

Machine learning models, such as regression analysis, clustering, and classification, can analyze past data to predict future outcomes, providing valuable insights into customer behavior, product demand, and operational efficiency. For example, in retail, predictive models can analyze past customer purchases and predict future buying trends, allowing stores to stock inventory accordingly. In manufacturing,

AI-driven analytics can predict equipment failures, enabling preventive maintenance that minimizes downtime and increases productivity.

Prescriptive analytics, another benefit of AI, goes beyond prediction by recommending specific actions that align with business goals. For instance, a logistics company might use prescriptive analytics to determine the most efficient delivery routes based on traffic conditions, fuel costs, and delivery timelines. By using AI-driven advanced analytics, organizations not only gain insights into what is likely to happen but also receive actionable recommendations for optimizing their operations.

2.3.4 Cloud-based BI Solutions: Scalability and Flexibility

Cloud-based BI solutions have emerged as a revolutionary force, enabling businesses of all sizes to leverage data insights without making substantial investments in on-premises infrastructure. Traditional BI systems often require costly hardware and maintenance, creating barriers for smaller organizations to adopt data-driven strategies. In contrast, cloud-based BI offers a scalable, flexible, and cost-effective alternative, allowing organizations to expand their BI capabilities as their data needs grow.

One of the key advantages of cloud-based BI is its ability to facilitate collaboration and data sharing, supporting a more responsive and adaptable approach to BI. For example, team members across different departments or geographic locations can access the same data and insights, ensuring that decisions are based on consistent information. This capability has proven invaluable in remote work environments, where teams need real-time access to data from anywhere. Moreover, cloud-based solutions provide robust data security and compliance features, ensuring that sensitive data is protected while meeting regulatory requirements.

Popular cloud-based BI platforms, such as Microsoft Power BI, Google Data Studio, and Tableau Online, offer advanced analytics and visualization capabilities on a subscription basis, making them accessible to businesses without extensive IT resources. Additionally, these platforms are equipped with artificial intelligence and machine learning features, allowing users to perform advanced analytics without requiring in-depth technical knowledge.

2.3.5 Data Integration and Unstructured Data Processing

A crucial aspect of modern BI is the integration of structured and unstructured data from multiple sources. Structured data, commonly found in relational databases and spreadsheets, is organized and easy to search. However, unstructured data, such as social media posts, customer reviews, and emails, lacks a predefined format and presents challenges in analysis. Despite these challenges, unstructured data holds immense value, as it often contains insights into customer sentiment, brand perception, and market trends (Gornostaeva, 2021).

BI tools equipped with natural language processing (NLP) and text analytics capabilities enable businesses to analyze unstructured data effectively. NLP algorithms can process and categorize text-based data, converting it into a structured format that can be analyzed alongside traditional datasets. For example, a company might use NLP to analyze customer feedback on social media, identifying common themes and sentiment related to its products. By combining structured and unstructured data, organizations gain a more comprehensive view of their operations and customer base, allowing for a holistic approach to decision-making.

Data integration tools also play a vital role in BI by merging data from various sources into a unified view. Platforms like Apache Kafka and Talend facilitate data streaming and integration, ensuring that BI systems receive up-to-date information for real-time analysis. These tools enable organizations to combine internal and external data sources, such as CRM systems, ERP applications, and social media feeds, creating a comprehensive dataset that supports more accurate and insightful analysis.

2.3.6 Real-time Analytics and BI

Real-time analytics has become a critical component of BI, especially in fast-paced industries where quick decision-making is essential. Unlike traditional BI, which often relies on historical data, real-time BI provides insights based on the latest data available. This enables organizations to monitor key performance indicators (KPIs) in real-time and respond promptly to changes in the business environment.

Real-time analytics is particularly valuable in sectors such as e-commerce, where customer behavior can change rapidly. For instance, an online retailer might use real-time analytics to monitor website traffic, sales conversions, and inventory levels during a promotion. If a product is selling faster than expected, the retailer can adjust pricing or stock levels immediately, maximizing sales and minimizing stockouts. In finance, real-time analytics allows institutions to detect fraudulent activities by monitoring transaction patterns and flagging anomalies as they occur.

The integration of real-time data with BI tools requires robust data streaming solutions and scalable infrastructure. Technologies like Apache Kafka, AWS Kinesis, and Google BigQuery support real-time data processing, enabling BI platforms to deliver insights as new data becomes available. This capability allows organizations to operate with agility, adapting their strategies to evolving conditions and making data-driven decisions on the fly.

2.3.7 The Future of BI: AI, Automation, and Augmented Analytics

The future of BI lies in the continued integration of artificial intelligence, automation, and augmented analytics. As BI tools evolve, they are becoming more autonomous, capable of performing complex analyses and generating insights with minimal human intervention. This shift towards automation is transforming BI from a reactive tool into a proactive system that anticipates business needs and recommends actions.

AI and machine learning will continue to play a significant role in the evolution of BI, driving advancements in predictive and prescriptive analytics. Augmented analytics, which combines AI and natural language processing, allows BI platforms to interpret data in natural language, making it easier for non-technical users to interact with data and receive insights. For example, a marketing team could ask a BI tool, "What were the top-performing campaigns last quarter?" and receive an instant, data-backed response.

Automation will also enhance data preparation, integration, and analysis processes, freeing up time for analysts to focus on strategic tasks. In a fully automated BI environment, systems will autonomously gather data, identify trends, and alert users to potential risks or opportunities. This proactive approach to BI will enable businesses to stay ahead of the competition by making timely, data-driven decisions.

The landscape of business intelligence is continually evolving, driven by advancements in tools and technologies that make data analysis more accessible, accurate, and actionable. From data warehousing and advanced analytics to cloud-based solutions and real-time BI, each component of the BI ecosystem plays a critical role in supporting data-driven decision-making. By leveraging these tools, organizations can unlock the full potential of their data, transforming it into a strategic asset that drives growth, innovation, and operational efficiency. As BI technology continues to advance, businesses will gain even greater capabilities for predictive insights, automation, and real-time analytics, positioning BI as an indispensable element of modern business strategy.

2.4 PREDICTIVE ANALYTICS AND DATA VISUALIZATION

Predictive analytics is the analysis of past data and forecasting of future events via the use of statistical algorithms and machine learning methods. Organizations may make wise choices that lead to commercial success by using sophisticated analytics to find patterns, trends, and possible hazards. This method offers a proactive technique for foreseeing and reacting to changes in the market, consumer behavior, and other crucial elements, going beyond typical business intelligence(De Andrade & Tumelero, 2022).

The potential of predictive analytics to reduce risks is one of its main benefits. Organizations may detect future hazards and take proactive efforts to address them by studying historical data. This is especially helpful in sectors like finance, where maintaining financial stability depends on anticipating market movements and spotting possible hazards. Predictive analytics also helps to increase overall operational performance, increase efficiency, and optimize procedures (Álvarez, 2023).

Data visualization is essential for converting complex datasets into visually appealing and simple-to-understand representations. Effective visualization becomes crucial for decision-makers to swiftly understand information and make wise decisions as the amount and complexity of data increase. Charts, graphs, and dashboards are examples of visualizations that provide a clear and simple means of conveying information, promoting improved communication and cooperation across various teams within a business. A potent synergy is produced when data visualization and predictive analytics are combined (Poscic, 2021). Forecasts and insights are produced by predictive models; these results are then presented in an understandable manner via visualization tools. This combination helps stakeholders at different organizational levels get insights more effectively and supports data-driven decision-making.

These two are essential for becoming competitive in the field of business intelligence. Businesses may find new possibilities, improve consumer experiences, and optimize marketing efforts by using predictive analytics. Then, data visualization is used to turn the intricate analytical findings into aesthetically appealing representations that decision-makers can quickly understand (Maggi & Marrella, 2021).

The development of user-friendly tools and technology has made predictive analytics and data visualization more accessible to workers in a variety of sectors, removing the need for specific technical knowledge to use data. An organizational culture where workers at all levels can actively contribute to and profit from data-driven insights is fostered by this democratization.

Predictive analytics and data visualization are two essential pillars in the modern landscape of data-driven decision-making. Predictive analytics involves analyzing historical data and forecasting future outcomes using statistical algorithms and machine learning techniques. By identifying patterns, trends, and potential risks, predictive analytics enables organizations to make informed choices, paving the way for business success through proactive strategies (De Andrade & Tumelero, 2022). This approach not only enhances traditional business intelligence but also helps organizations anticipate market changes, understand consumer behavior, and address operational challenges. Paired with data visualization, which converts complex datasets into easily understandable visual formats, predictive analytics becomes even more powerful, offering decision-makers clear and actionable insights. Together, these tools enable organizations to embrace a culture of data-driven insights and agility in their strategies.

2.4.1 The Power of Predictive Analytics: Proactive Strategy and Risk Mitigation

Predictive analytics goes beyond traditional data analysis by providing forecasts that help organizations act proactively rather than reactively. This shift towards predictive insights allows companies to anticipate events such as changes in consumer behavior, market fluctuations, and potential risks, enabling them to respond with agility and strategic foresight. The backbone of predictive analytics lies in statistical algorithms and machine learning models, which analyze historical data to identify patterns that would be difficult or impossible to detect manually.

One of the primary benefits of predictive analytics is its ability to mitigate risk. In sectors like finance, risk assessment is critical for maintaining stability. Financial institutions utilize predictive analytics to anticipate market movements, detect potential downturns, and identify factors that could impact profitability. For example, by analyzing historical stock market data, machine learning algorithms can identify indicators of market volatility, allowing investment firms to adjust their portfolios proactively. The ability to predict financial trends, customer defaults, and fraudulent transactions plays a crucial role in maintaining organizational stability and trust (Álvarez, 2023).

Predictive analytics is also invaluable in supply chain management, where it can optimize inventory and logistics. Retailers, for instance, analyze past sales data, seasonal trends, and even weather forecasts to predict product demand, which helps them prevent stockouts and overstock situations. In healthcare, predictive models analyze patient records, demographic data, and medical histories to forecast patient health outcomes, enabling personalized treatment plans and efficient allocation of resources. Predictive analytics, therefore, helps enhance operational efficiency and promotes resource optimization across various industries.

2.4.2 Key Techniques in Predictive Analytics

Predictive analytics relies on several statistical and machine learning techniques to generate accurate forecasts. Some of the most common methods include regression analysis, classification, clustering, and time series analysis. Each method has unique capabilities and applications:

Regression Analysis: This technique is used to predict continuous outcomes by modeling the relationship between dependent and independent variables. In finance, for example, regression analysis can help predict stock prices or economic indicators based on historical trends and external variables such as interest rates and inflation.

Classification: Classification algorithms, such as decision trees, support vector machines, and neural networks, are employed to categorize data points into predefined groups. For instance, banks use classification to identify potential loan defaulters based on customer credit histories and demographic information.

Clustering: Clustering groups similar data points based on common characteristics. Retailers use clustering to segment customers according to purchasing behavior, enabling targeted marketing strategies that enhance customer engagement.

Time Series Analysis: Time series models, such as ARIMA (Auto-Regressive Integrated Moving Average), predict future values based on sequential data. Time series analysis is widely used for sales forecasting, financial planning, and inventory management, where historical data is a strong indicator of future trends.

Each technique provides a different perspective on data, and predictive analytics models often combine multiple methods to deliver robust and accurate forecasts. Machine learning, particularly deep learning, has further enhanced the predictive capabilities of these models, making it possible to analyze large volumes of data and identify complex, non-linear patterns that traditional methods may overlook.

2.4.3 Data Visualization: Converting Complexity into Clarity

Data visualization is the art of transforming raw data and complex analytics into graphical representations, making information accessible and interpretable for decision-makers. As data grows in volume and complexity, effective visualization becomes crucial for enabling rapid understanding and strategic decision-making. By converting data into charts, graphs, dashboards, and other visual formats, data visualization helps stakeholders identify patterns, trends, and anomalies that might otherwise be obscured within dense datasets (Poscic, 2021).

Visualization tools play a central role in communicating information across teams, breaking down data silos, and fostering a collaborative environment where data insights are shared and understood by all. Visualizations can be customized to reflect different aspects of data, from high-level summaries to detailed breakdowns. For example, a marketing team might use a dashboard displaying customer engagement metrics to understand the effectiveness of recent campaigns, while an operations team monitors production metrics in real-time to identify bottlenecks and optimize efficiency.

Data visualization not only makes it easier for stakeholders to interpret information but also supports strategic planning and performance tracking. Dashboards allow organizations to set and track key performance indicators (KPIs) in real-time, providing a clear picture of organizational health. Heat maps, scatter plots, and line graphs, among other visualization types, highlight trends and outliers, facilitating quick, informed decision-making. In essence, data visualization bridges the gap between data and action, enabling a data-driven culture within organizations.

2.4.4 The Synergy of Predictive Analytics and Data Visualization

When combined, predictive analytics and data visualization create a powerful synergy that enhances data-driven decision-making at every level of an organization. Predictive models generate forecasts and insights, which data visualization tools then present in an intuitive, easily digestible format. This combination not only simplifies complex analytics but also empowers stakeholders to make informed decisions quickly and confidently.

The integration of predictive analytics with visualization is particularly valuable for creating scenario-based analysis, where organizations can visualize the impact of different variables on future outcomes. For example, a retail company might use predictive analytics to forecast demand for different product categories, with the results visualized in a dashboard that shows expected sales figures, potential stock shortages, and profit margins for each scenario. This allows decision-makers to explore various "what-if" scenarios and select the best course of action based on predicted outcomes.

In finance, visualization can highlight trends in stock price predictions or market volatility, providing investors with a visual representation of potential risks and rewards. Similarly, in healthcare, predictive analytics might forecast patient admission rates based on historical data, with visualizations displaying projected resource needs and staffing requirements. By combining predictive insights with visual representation, organizations are better equipped to act on insights and navigate complex decision-making landscapes.

2.4.5 Use Cases and Industry Applications

Predictive analytics and data visualization find applications across numerous industries, each leveraging these tools to address unique challenges and opportunities.

Retail

Predictive analytics helps retailers forecast demand, optimize inventory, and target marketing efforts. For instance, machine learning models analyze past sales data to predict future demand, helping retailers stock the right products in the right quantities. Visualization dashboards display real-time sales data and inventory levels, allowing managers to adjust strategies dynamically.

Finance

Financial institutions use predictive models to forecast economic trends, assess credit risk, and detect fraud. For example, banks employ regression and classification models to identify high-risk borrowers. Data visualization tools display financial metrics and risk assessments, providing a clear view of an institution's risk exposure and financial health.

Healthcare

Predictive analytics supports personalized medicine, resource allocation, and disease outbreak prediction. Hospitals analyze patient records to forecast admission rates and allocate resources efficiently. Visualization tools help healthcare providers interpret patient data, identify trends in health outcomes, and communicate findings to patients and other stakeholders.

Manufacturing

In manufacturing, predictive models anticipate equipment failures and optimize production schedules. For example, predictive maintenance models analyze sensor data from machinery to detect signs of wear and prevent breakdowns. Visualization dashboards provide a real-time overview of production metrics, equipment status, and maintenance schedules, enhancing operational efficiency.

Marketing

Predictive analytics enables marketers to forecast customer behavior, optimize ad targeting, and personalize campaigns. Machine learning algorithms segment audiences based on past behaviors, allowing for targeted advertising that increases engagement. Visualization tools help marketers track campaign performance, analyze customer feedback, and adjust strategies based on real-time data.

Each of these applications demonstrates the transformative impact of predictive analytics and data visualization, empowering organizations to make data-driven decisions and respond effectively to changing conditions.

2.4.6 Accessibility and Democratization of Predictive Analytics and Data Visualization

Advances in user-friendly tools and technologies have made predictive analytics and data visualization accessible to a broader audience within organizations. In the past, these tools required specialized technical knowledge, limiting their use to data scientists and analysts. Today, however, intuitive interfaces, automated analytics features, and drag-and-drop functionality enable non-technical users to work with data, fostering a culture of inclusivity and democratization.

This accessibility has significant implications for organizational culture, as employees at all levels can actively participate in data-driven decision-making. With the right tools, employees across departments—from marketing to HR to finance—can generate insights, interpret data, and contribute to the organization's strategic goals. For example, a sales manager with no formal analytics training can use a dashboard to analyze sales trends, forecast future revenue, and make data-backed decisions for their team. By empowering non-technical users to engage with data, companies can harness diverse perspectives and drive innovation from within.

Cloud-based BI platforms, such as Tableau, Power BI, and Google Data Studio, have played a critical role in this democratization by providing accessible, flexible, and scalable solutions. These platforms often include built-in machine learning algorithms, automated analytics, and customizable visualization templates, enabling users to explore data without requiring coding or advanced technical skills.

2.4.7 The Future of Predictive Analytics and Data Visualization

promises even greater integration, intelligence, and autonomy. Emerging technologies such as artificial intelligence (AI) and augmented analytics are poised to revolutionize both fields, enabling organizations to gain deeper insights and act more swiftly on data-driven recommendations.

AI-driven predictive analytics will continue to evolve, with algorithms that are capable of learning and improving from new data autonomously. This self-learning capability will enable predictive models to become more accurate over time, providing organizations with continuously refined insights. Additionally, augmented analytics, which combines AI, machine learning, and natural language processing, will allow users to interact with data using natural language queries, making predictive analytics and visualization even more accessible.

In terms of visualization, the trend toward immersive data experiences, such as augmented and virtual reality (AR/VR), will enable users to explore data in multidimensional spaces, enhancing understanding and engagement. For instance, a marketing team might use VR to navigate customer journey maps in a 3D space, identifying pain points and opportunities for improvement. These advancements will further empower organizations to embrace data-driven strategies and foster innovation in a rapidly evolving digital landscape.

Predictive analytics and data visualization are transformative tools that enable organizations to navigate uncertainty, optimize performance, and drive strategic decision-making. Predictive analytics provides the foresight needed to anticipate changes, manage risks, and seize opportunities, while data visualization translates complex analytics into actionable insights for stakeholders at all levels. Together, they foster a proactive, data-driven culture, empowering organizations to respond swiftly and effectively to evolving conditions. As tools and technologies continue to advance, predictive analytics and data visualization will become increasingly accessible, intelligent, and indispensable in shaping the future of business intelligence.

2.5 BIG DATA MANAGEMENT

Big Data offers organizations a distinct set of possibilities and problems because of its volume, velocity, diversity, and veracity. To guarantee the best possible use of the massive amount of information created every day, advanced management systems are needed(Ganesh & Kalpana, 2022). To store, handle, and analyze Big Data in this environment, businesses use a wide range of technologies and processes, with a focus on preserving data integrity and quality.

Two key elements in the Big Data Management environment are data warehouses and data lakes. In order to facilitate effective retrieval and analysis, structured data from several sources is centrally stored in data warehouses. However, data lakes provide a more versatile storage option by accommodating a variety of data kinds, including unstructured and structured data. The particular requirements and goals of the company frequently determine which of these two strategies should be used (Rustholkarhu et al., 2022).

Processing and managing massive datasets requires the use of distributed computing frameworks like Apache Hadoop and Apache Spark. By enabling parallel processing, these frameworks let firms manage massive amounts of data more effectively than they could with older systems. Furthermore, cloud-based solutions have become more popular because they provide scalable and affordable infrastructure for processing and storing large amounts of data. Security and data governance become the two most important factors in the Big Data Management environment. To guarantee data quality, regulatory compliance, and security breach prevention, organizations need to set up strong rules and frameworks. Encryption procedures, access restrictions, and routine audits are put into place to ensure the data's integrity and confidentiality(Chen et al., 2022).

Advanced analytics approaches must be integrated as enterprises traverse the challenges of Big Data Management. The enormous databases are analyzed using machine learning algorithms and artificial intelligence models to uncover patterns, forecast future trends, and glean insightful information. Big Data and advanced analytics work hand in hand to enable firms to make data-driven choices that spur innovation and create competitive advantages.

The rise of Big Data has transformed how organizations approach information management, presenting unique opportunities and challenges driven by its volume, velocity, variety, and veracity (Ganesh & Kalpana, 2022). To harness the massive influx of data generated daily, businesses require advanced systems to store, process, and analyze data effectively. Big Data Management encompasses a suite of technologies, frameworks, and processes aimed at handling these massive datasets with a focus on data integrity, quality, and security. Organizations must navigate complex data environments, choosing the appropriate infrastructure and tools to turn raw data into actionable insights while maintaining robust security and governance standards.

2.5.1 The Four Vs of Big Data and Their Impact on Management

The characteristics of Big Data, often referred to as the four Vs, encapsulate the challenges of managing such vast amounts of information:

Volume: Big Data's sheer size is unprecedented, and traditional databases cannot efficiently handle the vast quantities of data generated every day. This requires specialized storage solutions that can expand as needed to accommodate growing data volumes.

Velocity: Data is generated and collected at unprecedented speeds. Real-time data streaming is crucial in sectors such as finance and e-commerce, where timely analysis can affect decision-making and operational efficiency.

Variety: Big Data comes in many formats, including structured data (like databases), semi-structured data (like JSON files), and unstructured data (like social media posts). The diversity in data types presents challenges in storage, retrieval, and analysis.

Veracity: The accuracy and trustworthiness of data can vary, especially with data sources like social media or customer reviews. Ensuring data quality and accuracy is essential for making sound business decisions.

These four characteristics make Big Data Management a complex but essential field, as organizations must ensure they have the right tools and processes to capture, store, process, and analyze these massive and varied datasets.

2.5.2 Data Warehouses and Data Lakes: Centralized Storage for Big Data

Data warehouses and data lakes are two central components of Big Data infrastructure, each serving distinct purposes in data storage and analysis.

Data Warehouses: Designed for structured data, data warehouses are optimized for fast querying and reporting. They serve as a centralized repository where data from multiple sources is stored in a structured format, making it easy to analyze and retrieve. Data warehouses support business intelligence (BI) activities by enabling fast, accurate insights from historical data. However, they are less flexible in handling unstructured data, which limits their applicability in some Big Data scenarios (Rusthollkarhu et al., 2022).

Data Lakes: In contrast, data lakes provide more flexible storage solutions, allowing organizations to store structured, semi-structured, and unstructured data in its raw form. Data lakes accommodate a broader range of data types, making them ideal for organizations that require scalability and the ability to analyze diverse datasets. Data lakes are particularly useful for data science and machine learning applications, as they allow data scientists to pull raw data directly from the source and perform custom transformations.

The decision to implement a data warehouse or data lake—or a combination of both—depends on an organization's specific needs. For instance, if a business primarily relies on structured data for BI reports, a data warehouse might suffice. However, if the organization requires flexibility to store raw, unprocessed data and conduct exploratory analysis, a data lake might be a better fit. As organizations increasingly handle both structured and unstructured data, hybrid data architectures that integrate data lakes and warehouses are becoming more common.

2.5.3 Distributed Computing Frameworks: Apache Hadoop and Apache Spark

Handling the sheer volume and complexity of Big Data requires significant computational power, which traditional systems often cannot provide. Distributed computing frameworks like Apache Hadoop and Apache Spark have become essential for Big Data Management by enabling organizations to process data across multiple nodes in parallel.

Apache Hadoop: Hadoop was one of the first frameworks developed to handle large-scale data processing by distributing data across clusters. It uses a distributed file system (HDFS) that allows data to be stored and accessed across multiple servers. Hadoop's MapReduce programming model enables parallel processing of large datasets, making it efficient for batch processing and analysis. Despite its scalability, Hadoop's reliance on disk storage can slow down real-time data processing.

Apache Spark: Spark builds on Hadoop's distributed computing capabilities but improves upon it with in-memory processing, making it faster and more suitable for real-time analytics. Spark supports a wide range of tasks, from data transformation and machine learning to graph processing and stream processing. Spark's versatility makes it a popular choice for organizations that require a comprehensive framework for both batch and real-time data processing.

These frameworks allow organizations to process massive datasets at speeds that were previously impossible, enabling advanced analytics and decision-making in real-time. For example, in the retail industry, Spark can analyze customer data in real-time to offer personalized recommendations based on current browsing behavior. In healthcare, Hadoop enables the processing of large volumes of patient data to improve diagnostic accuracy and treatment plans.

2.5.4 Cloud-based Solutions: Scalability and Cost-efficiency

Cloud computing has revolutionized Big Data Management by providing scalable and cost-effective solutions that allow organizations to store and process vast datasets without significant upfront infrastructure investments. Major cloud providers like Amazon Web Services (AWS), Google Cloud Platform (GCP), and Microsoft Azure offer a variety of services tailored to Big Data, including data storage, processing, and machine learning capabilities.

Scalability: Cloud platforms allow organizations to scale their storage and processing resources according to demand. This elasticity is particularly valuable for businesses with fluctuating data needs, as they can increase or decrease their cloud resources as needed.

Cost-efficiency: Cloud-based Big Data solutions reduce the need for organizations to invest in physical infrastructure, lowering costs. Organizations can pay only for the resources they use, making it easier to manage budgets and avoid overspending.

Collaboration and Accessibility: Cloud platforms facilitate collaboration by allowing teams to access data from any location, supporting remote work and cross-departmental data sharing. This accessibility has become increasingly important as organizations embrace digital transformation.

For instance, a financial institution can use a cloud-based data lake to store massive amounts of transaction data and apply real-time analytics to detect fraudulent patterns. Similarly, a media company can leverage cloud infrastructure to process video streaming data, analyzing viewership patterns to inform content recommendations.

2.5.5 Security and Data Governance: Ensuring Compliance and Data Integrity

With the vast volumes of data collected, security and governance are paramount in Big Data Management. Organizations must protect sensitive information, adhere to regulatory standards, and maintain data quality. Effective security and governance frameworks address several key areas:

Data Security: Big Data environments are vulnerable to breaches and cyberattacks due to the high value of the data they contain. To mitigate these risks, organizations implement encryption protocols, access controls, and secure authentication methods. Regular audits and vulnerability assessments further ensure data integrity and security.

Data Governance: Proper governance ensures that data remains accurate, consistent, and compliant with regulatory standards. Data governance involves setting up rules for data ownership, data access, and data lifecycle management. For example, under regulations like the GDPR, organizations must follow strict guidelines for data collection, storage, and usage, making governance an essential aspect of Big Data Management (L. J. Chen et al., 2022).

Compliance: Organizations must comply with legal and regulatory requirements to avoid penalties and maintain customer trust. Regulations such as GDPR in Europe and CCPA in California impose strict guidelines on data collection, usage, and storage, requiring organizations to establish compliant practices.

Implementing these security and governance measures is essential not only for regulatory compliance but also for maintaining customer trust. Companies that prioritize data integrity and security can better leverage Big Data as a strategic asset, avoiding reputational damage and regulatory penalties.

2.5.6 Advanced Analytics: Leveraging AI and Machine Learning in Big Data Management

As organizations navigate the complexities of Big Data, integrating advanced analytics is essential to extract actionable insights. Machine learning (ML) and artificial intelligence (AI) play a pivotal role in Big Data Management by enabling automated analysis, pattern recognition, and predictive modeling. These technologies empower organizations to uncover insights that drive innovation and provide a competitive edge.

Machine Learning Models: ML algorithms are capable of identifying patterns and relationships within large datasets, allowing businesses to make predictions based on historical data. In retail, for example, ML models analyze customer purchase behavior to forecast future buying trends. In healthcare, ML can predict patient outcomes based on historical data, supporting personalized treatment plans.

Artificial Intelligence: AI techniques, such as deep learning, are particularly useful in Big Data environments for tasks such as image recognition, natural language processing, and anomaly detection. AI-driven analytics automate data processing tasks, enabling organizations to handle complex datasets without requiring extensive manual intervention.

Predictive and Prescriptive Analytics: Big Data and advanced analytics work hand in hand to offer predictive insights that inform business strategy. Predictive models analyze historical data to forecast trends, while prescriptive analytics recommends specific actions based on those predictions. For instance, in supply chain management, predictive models forecast demand based on past sales data, and prescriptive analytics suggests optimal stock levels to meet that demand.

The integration of Big Data with AI and ML allows organizations to make data-driven decisions that drive efficiency, innovation, and growth. By automating data processing, AI-powered analytics also reduces the workload on data teams, freeing up time for strategic initiatives.

2.5.7 The Future of Big Data Management: Trends and Innovations

The landscape of Big Data Management is continually evolving, with emerging technologies and trends that promise to redefine the field. Some of the most anticipated developments include:

Edge Computing: As organizations gather data from IoT devices, edge computing will play a key role in processing data closer to its source

This approach reduces latency and bandwidth usage, enabling real-time data analysis in environments like smart cities and autonomous vehicles.

Blockchain for Data Security: Blockchain technology offers a decentralized approach to data security, providing a transparent and tamper-proof record of transactions. In Big Data environments, blockchain could improve data traceability and integrity, enhancing security and compliance.

Quantum Computing: Quantum computing has the potential to revolutionize Big Data analysis by solving complex calculations faster than classical computers. As this technology matures, it could enable breakthroughs in areas like cryptography, optimization, and AI.

Augmented Analytics: Augmented analytics combines AI, machine learning, and natural language processing to automate data preparation, analysis, and visualization. This trend makes analytics accessible to non-technical users, allowing organizations to leverage Big Data without extensive technical expertise.

These trends highlight the dynamic nature of Big Data Management and its potential to transform industries. As these technologies become mainstream, organizations will be able to harness the full potential of Big Data, creating new opportunities for innovation and growth.

Big Data Management is a complex yet vital discipline that enables organizations to harness the power of vast datasets to drive innovation, improve decision-making, and maintain a competitive edge. Through a combination of data storage solutions, distributed computing frameworks, cloud-based infrastructure, and advanced analytics, organizations can turn Big Data into a strategic asset. Security, governance, and emerging technologies like AI and blockchain further enhance the Big Data Management environment, ensuring data quality, compliance, and protection.

As organizations continue to navigate the challenges of Big Data, the integration of advanced technologies and forward-looking trends will be crucial for success. The future of Big Data Management lies in automation, real-time processing, and accessibility, providing a foundation for data-driven innovation in an increasingly digital world.

The rise of Big Data has transformed how organizations approach information management, presenting unique opportunities and challenges driven by its volume, velocity, variety, and veracity (Ganesh & Kalpana, 2022). To harness the massive influx of data generated daily, businesses require advanced systems to store, process, and analyze data effectively. Big Data Management encompasses a suite of technologies, frameworks, and processes aimed at handling these massive datasets with a focus on data integrity, quality, and security. Organizations must navigate complex data environments, choosing the appropriate infrastructure and tools to turn raw data into actionable insights while maintaining robust security and governance standards.

2.6 CASE STUDIES ON ANALYTICS DRIVING BUSINESS SUCCESS

The Netflix case study is a powerful illustration of the revolutionary potential of analytics. As the industry leader in streaming, Netflix has improved its content recommendation algorithms by using data analytics. Through the examination of user watching habits, inclinations, and engagement indicators, Netflix has effectively tailored content suggestions for its members. In addition to increasing user happiness, this hyper-personalized strategy is essential for keeping subscribers and fostering client loyalty(Santana & Díaz-Fernández, 2023). Netflix's analytics-driven approach has been successful, as shown by the company's significant increase in subscribers and market leadership.

The massive online retailer Amazon uses data analytics extensively to streamline business processes and improve consumer satisfaction. The recommendation engine on Amazon makes personalized product recommendations based on an analysis of user browsing and purchase activity. This data-driven strategy promotes long-term connections by increasing customer happiness and driving sales simultaneously(Ekinci & Bilginer-Özsaatçi, 2023).

Let's move on to the healthcare industry, where IBM Watson Health offers yet another interesting case study. Predictive analytics is a tool that IBM Watson Health uses to evaluate enormous volumes of medical data and help medical practitioners make choices. IBM Watson Health expedites medical research and enables individualized treatment plans by combining data from many sources, including as clinical trials, patient information, and medical literature. With its ability to improve diagnostic accuracy, optimize treatment plans, and ultimately save lives, this analytics-driven strategy has the potential to completely transform the healthcare industry.

Starbucks has used data analytics to improve customer experience and store placement efficiency in the retail space. By conducting a thorough examination of demographic information, foot traffic trends, and customer behavior, Starbucks carefully chooses new shop sites and customizes its product line to suit regional tastes. Starbucks has seen continuous consumer engagement and worldwide growth as a result of its data-driven strategy(Grassi & Vallati, 2021).

The use of statistics in professional basketball by the NBA franchise, the Golden State Warriors, demonstrates that the sports business is not immune to the analytics revolution. The Warriors used cutting-edge analytics to improve player recruiting choices, boost game strategy, and maximize player performance. The team's success was largely due to their data-driven strategy, which helped them win several titles and set a new standard for the use of analytics in professional sports.

Data analytics has revolutionized various industries by providing insights that drive strategic decisions, optimize processes, and enhance customer satisfaction. The following case studies showcase how leading organizations across diverse sectors—streaming, retail, healthcare, and sports—have harnessed the power of analytics to achieve remarkable business success.

2.6.1 Netflix: Revolutionizing Content Recommendations with Data Analytics

Netflix is a prime example of how data analytics can transform a business model, especially in the digital entertainment industry. As a leader in streaming, Netflix has built a powerful content recommendation system that significantly enhances the viewer experience. Using data analytics, Netflix examines extensive user data, including viewing habits, preferred genres, watch times, and engagement metrics. By leveraging this information, Netflix has created a hyper-personalized recommendation engine that suggests content specifically tailored to individual preferences (Santana & Díaz-Fernández, 2023).

The recommendation engine is powered by machine learning algorithms that continuously improve as they process new user data. For example, if a viewer regularly watches romantic comedies, the algorithm will prioritize similar genres. This personalization extends beyond genres and delves into specific viewing patterns, such as the types of shows users binge-watch versus those they watch episodically. The outcome is a tailored content feed that keeps users engaged, enhances satisfaction, and drives loyalty. The company's data-driven approach has resulted in substantial increases in user retention rates and subscriber growth, cementing Netflix's position as a market leader in the streaming industry.

Beyond user satisfaction, data analytics also guides Netflix's content creation strategy. The platform uses insights from viewing habits and engagement data to identify which types of content resonate most with its audience. This has led to data-driven investments in original programming, such as “Stranger Things” and “The Crown,” which are tailored to audience preferences and have proven to be extremely successful. By basing content creation on analytics, Netflix reduces the risks associated with content production, ensuring that it delivers shows and movies that are likely to succeed.

2.6.2 Amazon: Enhancing Customer Satisfaction Through Data-Driven Recommendations

Amazon, one of the world's largest online retailers, extensively utilizes data analytics to streamline operations and improve the customer experience. The backbone of Amazon's data-driven strategy is its recommendation engine, which analyzes user browsing behavior, purchase history, and even wish lists to make personalized product recommendations. By offering highly relevant product suggestions, Amazon's recommendation system drives sales and fosters customer satisfaction, creating a seamless shopping experience that builds customer loyalty (Ekinci & Bilginer-Özsaatçi, 2023).

Amazon's data analytics capabilities go beyond product recommendations. The company uses analytics to optimize its supply chain and logistics, ensuring that products are delivered quickly and efficiently. By analyzing historical sales data and consumer demand, Amazon can predict which products will be in high demand and adjust its inventory levels accordingly. This proactive approach helps Amazon reduce stockouts and manage its extensive warehouse network, resulting in operational efficiency and improved delivery times.

Additionally, Amazon's predictive analytics are instrumental in pricing strategies. The platform uses algorithms to adjust prices based on demand, competition, and customer behavior. This dynamic pricing ensures that Amazon remains competitive while maximizing profitability. Amazon's analytics-driven approach has allowed the company to enhance customer satisfaction, streamline operations, and drive consistent growth, making it a benchmark for data-driven success in the retail sector.

2.6.3 IBM Watson Health: Transforming Healthcare with Predictive Analytics

In the healthcare industry, IBM Watson Health stands out for its innovative use of predictive analytics to assist medical professionals in making more informed decisions. By analyzing vast volumes of medical data, IBM Watson Health provides insights that can improve diagnostic accuracy and optimize treatment plans. The platform integrates data from a variety of sources, including patient records, clinical trials, and medical literature, to support personalized healthcare (De Andrade & Tumelero, 2022).

One of the key benefits of IBM Watson Health's analytics approach is its ability to process unstructured data from medical research, case studies, and historical patient information. This analysis identifies correlations and patterns that might otherwise go unnoticed, enabling healthcare providers to develop more effective treatment plans. For instance, by analyzing patient demographics, genetic data, and medical histories, IBM Watson Health can predict the likelihood of patients developing certain conditions, allowing for earlier interventions.

IBM Watson Health has also been instrumental in accelerating medical research by identifying promising drug candidates and treatment options. Its predictive models assist researchers in analyzing complex datasets, speeding up the discovery process for new therapies. By providing insights into patient outcomes, risk factors, and treatment efficacy, IBM Watson Health empowers healthcare providers to make data-driven decisions that improve patient care and save lives.

2.6.4 Starbucks: Using Data to Enhance Customer Experience and Optimize Store Locations

In the retail space, Starbucks exemplifies the successful application of data analytics to enhance customer experience and strategic decision-making. Starbucks uses data to understand customer behavior, predict trends, and optimize store locations. By analyzing demographic data, foot traffic patterns, and customer purchase behavior, Starbucks is able to select optimal locations for new stores and customize product offerings based on regional preferences (Grassi & Vallati, 2021).

Starbucks' data-driven approach includes the use of loyalty program data to personalize customer interactions. The Starbucks Rewards program captures a wealth of customer data, including purchase frequency, favorite products, and preferred store locations. By analyzing this data, Starbucks provides tailored promotions, product recommendations, and offers that resonate with individual customers. This personalized approach fosters customer loyalty and encourages repeat visits, contributing to Starbucks' continued growth and brand loyalty.

Data analytics also informs Starbucks' inventory management, helping the company stock products based on demand patterns. For instance, if a specific drink is popular during the summer, Starbucks ensures that stores in warmer regions are well-stocked with the ingredients needed to meet demand. This data-driven inventory strategy minimizes waste, optimizes resource allocation, and ensures that customers can access their favorite products whenever they visit.

2.6.5 Golden State Warriors: Leveraging Analytics for Competitive Advantage in Professional Sports

In the sports industry, the NBA franchise Golden State Warriors exemplifies how analytics can be used to gain a competitive edge. The Warriors have embraced advanced analytics to make data-driven decisions that influence player recruitment, game strategies, and performance optimization. By analyzing player statistics, game data, and even tracking player movement on the court, the Warriors developed a unique approach to team building and gameplay that contributed to their success and multiple championship titles.

Data analytics has been instrumental in the Warriors' player recruitment strategy. Instead of relying solely on traditional scouting methods, the team uses analytics to assess player performance metrics, identify potential recruits, and predict how well a player would fit into their system. For example, by analyzing shooting efficiency, defensive capabilities, and endurance, the team can determine which players are most likely to succeed within their high-paced playing style.

During games, the Warriors use analytics to refine their strategies. By examining shot success rates from different positions on the court, the team adjusts its offensive and defensive plays to maximize scoring opportunities and minimize defensive weaknesses. This data-driven approach has transformed professional basketball by demonstrating how analytics can improve player performance, enhance game strategies, and ultimately contribute to winning championships.

2.6.6 Walmart: Optimizing Inventory and Enhancing Customer Experience with Big Data

Walmart, one of the largest retail chains globally, uses Big Data analytics extensively to optimize its inventory, streamline supply chain operations, and enhance the customer experience. With millions of transactions daily, Walmart captures an enormous amount of data, which it analyzes to understand purchasing patterns, manage inventory levels, and forecast demand. Walmart's data-driven approach helps ensure that popular products are always in stock, improving customer satisfaction and driving sales.

One example of Walmart's analytics-driven strategy is its use of predictive analytics to anticipate demand for certain products based on seasonal trends, regional preferences, and external factors such as weather. For instance, during hurricane season, Walmart can analyze historical data to predict spikes in demand for emergency supplies, ensuring that stores in affected areas are well-stocked. This proactive approach enables Walmart to provide customers with the products they need when they need them, enhancing both the customer experience and operational efficiency.

Additionally, Walmart leverages analytics for targeted marketing and personalized promotions. By analyzing customer data, Walmart tailors its advertising and promotions to individual preferences, increasing the effectiveness of its marketing efforts. For example, a customer who frequently purchases baby products might receive promotions on related items, such as diapers or baby food. This targeted approach not only drives sales but also strengthens customer loyalty.

2.6.7 Tesla: Pioneering Data-Driven Innovation in the Automotive Industry

Tesla stands out in the automotive industry for its use of data analytics to drive innovation and improve vehicle performance. Tesla vehicles are equipped with sensors that collect data on various aspects of performance, including battery efficiency, driving habits, and environmental conditions. This data is transmitted back to Tesla, where it is analyzed to identify patterns and optimize vehicle performance through software updates.

One of Tesla's most notable uses of analytics is in the development of its Autopilot feature, which relies on machine learning algorithms to process vast amounts of data from on-road experiences. Tesla vehicles collect data on driving scenarios, which is used to improve the self-driving algorithms and enhance safety. As more vehicles are driven, Tesla's analytics models become increasingly accurate, enabling continuous improvement in Autopilot performance.

Tesla also uses data analytics for predictive maintenance. By monitoring vehicle performance data in real-time, Tesla can identify potential issues before they become serious problems, allowing for proactive maintenance. This predictive approach not only enhances the customer experience but also extends the lifespan of Tesla vehicles, making data-driven analytics a core component of the company's value proposition.

These case studies underscore the transformative power of analytics across diverse industries. Netflix, Amazon, IBM Watson Health, Starbucks, the Golden State Warriors, Walmart, and Tesla have all leveraged data analytics to optimize operations, enhance customer satisfaction, and drive innovation. From hyper-personalized recommendations to predictive maintenance

and performance optimization, analytics enables these organizations to make data-driven decisions that foster growth and sustain a competitive advantage. As analytics technology continues to evolve, more organizations are likely to adopt data-driven approaches, transforming industries and reshaping business success.

2.7 CHAPTER CONCLUSION

In conclusion, this chapter has provided a comprehensive overview of data analytics and business intelligence, covering their fundamentals, tools and technologies, predictive analytics, data visualization, big data management, and case studies illustrating their impact on driving business success. Data analytics, the systematic analysis of raw data to extract patterns and insights, is fundamental for businesses seeking a competitive advantage in the digital era. It involves gathering, preparing, and analyzing data using statistical methods and algorithms, with the goal of transforming data into actionable insights that drive productivity, innovation, and process optimization. Through predictive analytics, organizations can anticipate future trends and make proactive decisions based on historical data, reducing risks and improving operational performance. Business intelligence serves as the overarching framework that facilitates the integration of data analytics into organizational processes. It provides stakeholders with user-friendly dashboards and reports that condense complex information into easily understandable forms, enabling informed decision-making at all levels of the organization. The synergy between business intelligence and data analytics is evident across various industries, including manufacturing, retail, healthcare, and finance, where they contribute to risk mitigation, personalized services, supply chain optimization, and market prediction. The chapter also explored the tools and technologies underpinning business intelligence, such as data warehousing, data visualization, cloud-based solutions, and advanced analytics. These technologies have made data analysis more accessible to professionals across different departments, enabling real-time monitoring, improved communication, and data-driven decision-making. Additionally, big data management presents both opportunities and challenges for organizations, requiring scalable infrastructure, distributed computing frameworks, and robust security measures to effectively handle and analyze vast amounts of data. Case studies of companies like Netflix, Amazon, IBM Watson Health, Starbucks, and the Golden State Warriors illustrate the transformative power of analytics in driving business success. From personalized content recommendations to optimized store placement and player performance enhancement, these examples showcase how data-driven strategies can lead to increased customer satisfaction, revenue growth, and competitive advantage. In summary, data analytics and business intelligence are indispensable tools for organizations looking to thrive in today's data-driven world. By leveraging data effectively, businesses can uncover valuable insights, anticipate market trends, and make informed decisions that drive innovation and foster long-term success. As technology continues to evolve, organizations must continue to adapt and invest in analytics capabilities to remain competitive in the digital landscape.

REFERENCES

Al Karim, R., Rabiul, M. K., Ahamed, T., Karim, D. N., & Mehzabeen, M. (2024). Integrating Green Entrepreneurial Orientation, Green Information Systems, and Management Support with Green Supply Chain Management to Foster Firms' Environmental Performance. *Sustainability (Basel)*, *16*(12), 4921. DOI: 10.3390/su16124921

Álvarez, J. J. G. (2023). Fintech and Artificial Intelligence: A strategic alliance in the financing of third sector entities. *REVESCO Revista de Estudios Cooperativos*, *145*(145). Advance online publication. DOI: 10.5209/reve.92553

Chaveesuk, S., Khalid, B., & Chaiyasoonthorn, W. (2019). Emergence of new business environment with big data and artificial intelligence. In *ACM International Conference Proceeding Series* (Issue 9th International Conference on Information Communication and Management (ICICM), pp. 181–185). DOI: 10.1145/3357419.3357441

Chen, L. J., Jiang, M. Q., Jia, F., & Liu, G. Q. (2022). Artificial intelligence adoption in business-to-business marketing: Toward a conceptual framework. *Journal of Business and Industrial Marketing*, *37*(5), 1025–1044. DOI: 10.1108/JBIM-09-2020-0448

Chhillar, D., & Aguilera, R. V. (2022). An Eye for Artificial Intelligence: Insights Into the Governance of Artificial Intelligence and Vision for Future Research. *Business & Society*, *61*(5), 1197–1241. DOI: 10.1177/00076503221080959

De Andrade, I. M., & Tumelero, C. (2022). Increasing customer service efficiency through artificial intelligence chatbot. *REGE-REVISTA DE GESTAO*, *29*(3), 238–251. DOI: 10.1108/REGE-07-2021-0120

Ekinci, G., & Bilginer-Özsaatçi, F. G. (2023). Bibliometric Analysis of Publications in Artificial Intelligence and Marketing. [WE - Emerging Sources Citation Index] [ESCI]. *Sosyoekonomi*, *31*(56), 369–388. DOI: 10.17233/sosyoekonomi.2023.02.17

Farooq, M., Buzdar, H. Q., Yen, Y. Y., & Bakhsh, A. (2024). Integrating AI in Sustainable Writing: An Empirical Investigation of the Technology Acceptance Model in Asian Social Sciences. *Journal of Logistics. Informatics and Service Science*, *11*(3), 324–338. DOI: 10.33168/JLISS.2024.0321

Farooq, M., & Qureshi, Q. A. (2020). Practical Approach of Environmental Awareness to Broadening Community Participation: A Case Study of Pindad (Persero). *Journal of Management Practices. Humanities and Social Sciences*, *4*(1). Advance online publication. DOI: 10.33152/jmphss-4.2.1

Farooq, M., & Ramzan, M. Y. Y. Y. (2025). AI in Management. In *Transformative Impacts of AI in Management* (1st ed., pp. 1–44). IGI Global. DOI: 10.4018/979-8-3693-4322-7.ch001

Farooq, M., Ramzan, M., & Yen, Y. Y. (2025a). AI in Consumer Behavior Management. In *Transformative Impacts of AI in Management* (pp. 281–294). IGI Global., DOI: 10.4018/979-8-3693-4322-7.ch011

Farooq, M., Ramzan, M., & Yen, Y. Y. (2025b). AI in Customer Service, HR, and Administration. In *Transformative Impacts of AI in Management* (pp. 45–70). IGI Global. DOI: 10.4018/979-8-3693-4322-7.ch002

Farooq, M., Ramzan, M., & Yen, Y. Y. (2025c). AI in Quality Management. In *Transformative Impacts of AI in Management* (pp. 295–312). IGI Global., DOI: 10.4018/979-8-3693-4322-7.ch012

Farooq, M., Ramzan, M., & Yen, Y. Y. (2025d). Artificial Intelligence and Customer Experiences. In *Transformative Impacts of AI in Management* (pp. 95–114). IGI Global., DOI: 10.4018/979-8-3693-4322-7.ch004

Farooq, M., Ramzan, M., & Yen, Y. Y. (2025e). Artificial Intelligence in Administration Sciences. In *Transformative Impacts of AI in Management* (pp. 115–156). IGI Global., DOI: 10.4018/979-8-3693-4322-7.ch005

Farooq, M., Ramzan, M., & Yen, Y. Y. (2025f). Artificial Intelligence in Business and Law. In *Transformative Impacts of AI in Management* (pp. 71–94). IGI Global., DOI: 10.4018/979-8-3693-4322-7.ch003

Farooq, M., Ramzan, M., & Yen, Y. Y. (2025g). Artificial Intelligence in Ethical Business Decision Making. In *Transformative Impacts of AI in Management* (pp. 265–280). IGI Global., DOI: 10.4018/979-8-3693-4322-7.ch010

Farooq, M., Ramzan, M., & Yen, Y. Y. (2025h). Exploring the Impact of Artificial Intelligence on Brand Management. In *Transformative Impacts of AI in Management* (pp. 157–188). IGI Global., DOI: 10.4018/979-8-3693-4322-7.ch006

Farooq, M., Ramzan, M., & Yen, Y. Y. (2025i). Exploring the Impact of Ethical Leadership and Employee Engagement on Knowledge Sharing Attitudes in the Asian Digital Economy. In *Transformative Impacts of AI in Management* (pp. 241–264). IGI Global., DOI: 10.4018/979-8-3693-4322-7.ch009

Farooq, M., Ramzan, M., & Yen, Y. Y. (2025j). Transformative Impact of AI in Education Management. In *Transformative Impacts of AI in Management* (pp. 189–216). IGI Global., DOI: 10.4018/979-8-3693-4322-7.ch007

Farooq, M., Ramzan, M., & Yen, Y. Y. (2025k). *Transformative Impacts of AI in Management*. IGI Global., DOI: 10.4018/979-8-3693-4322-7

Farooq, M., Yuen, Y. Y., & Buzdar, H. Q. (2024). Exploring the Research Landscape of Artificial Intelligence Integration with Business Management: A Bibliometric Analysis from 1994-2023. *Journal of Logistics. Informatics and Service Science*, (April). Advance online publication. DOI: 10.33168/JLISS.2024.0410

Ganesh, D., & Kalpana, P. (2022). Future of artificial intelligence and its influence on supply chain risk management - A systematic review. *Computers & Industrial Engineering*, *169*, 108206. Advance online publication. DOI: 10.1016/j.cie.2022.108206

Gornostaeva, Z. V. (2021). The Ratio of Staff and Artificial Intelligence in Modern Entrepreneurship: The Specifics of Small and Medium-Sized Businesses. In E. G. Popkova, V. N. Ostrovskaya, & A. V Bogoviz (Eds.), *SOCIO-ECONOMIC SYSTEMS, VOL. 2: Paradigms for the Future* (Vol. 314, pp. 137–144). WE - Book Citation Index – Social Sciences & Humanities (BKCI-SSH) WE - Book Citation Index – Science (BKCI-S)DOI: 10.1007/978-3-030-56433-9_16

Grassi, A., & Vallati, M. (2021). AN EXPLORATORY STUDY ON THE USE OF ARTIFICIAL INTELLIGENCE TO INITIATE LEGAL UNDERSTANDING FOR BUSINESS DEVELOPMENT. *JOURNAL OF APPLIED LOGICS-IFCOLOG JOURNAL OF LOGICS AND THEIR APPLICATIONS*, *8*(4), 1065-1082 WE-Emerging Sources Citation Index (E. Huang, H., Peng, Z. C., Wu, H. T., & Xie, Q. H. (2020). A big data analysis on the five dimensions of emergency management information in the early stage of COVID-19 in China. *JOURNAL OF CHINESE GOVERNANCE*, *5*(2), 213–233. DOI: 10.1080/23812346.2020.1744923

León-Romero, L. P., Aguilar-Fernández, M., Luque-Sendra, A., Zamora-Polo, F., & Francisco-Márquez, M. (2024). Characterization of the information system integrated to the construction project management systems. *Heliyon*, *10*(11), e31886. Advance online publication. DOI: 10.1016/j.heliyon.2024.e31886 PMID: 38841493

Li, Q., & Wu, G. (2021). ERP System in the Logistics Information Management System of Supply Chain Enterprises. *Mobile Information Systems*, *2021*, 1–11. Advance online publication. DOI: 10.1155/2021/7423717

Maggi, F. M., & Marrella, A. (2021). Preface to the Special Issue on Artificial Intelligence for Business Process Management 2019. *Journal on Data Semantics*, *10*(1–2), 1–2. DOI: 10.1007/s13740-021-00131-0

Munodawafa, R. T., & Johl, S. K. (2022). Design and Development of an Eco-Innovation Management Information System to Accelerate Firms' Digital Transformation Strategy. [WE - Science Citation Index Expanded] [SCI-EXPANDED]. *IEEE Access : Practical Innovations, Open Solutions, 10*, 37796–37810. DOI: 10.1109/ACCESS.2022.3163248

Niesler, A. (2020). Adaptability Revised: Process-Aware Information System in Modern Organization Management. In K. S. Soliman (Ed.), *EDUCATION EXCELLENCE AND INNOVATION MANAGEMENT: A 2025 VISION TO SUSTAIN ECONOMIC DEVELOPMENT DURING GLOBAL CHALLENGES* (Issues 35th International-Business-Information-Management-Association Conference (IBIMA), pp. 16488-16496 WE-Conference Proceedings Citation).

Poscic, A. (2021). Is There a Need To Regulate Artificial Intelligence in the European Union: Reasons for and Against. [WE - Emerging Sources Citation Index] [ESCI]. *Zbornik Pravnog Fakulteta Sveucilista u Rijeci, 42*(2), 385–404. DOI: 10.30925/zpfsr.42.2.7

Ram, J., & Zhang, Z. (2022). Examining the needs to adopt big data analytics in B2B organizations: Development of propositions and model of needs. *Journal of Business and Industrial Marketing, 37*(4), 790–809. DOI: 10.1108/JBIM-10-2020-0464

Rusthollkarhu, S., Toukola, S., Aarikka-Stenroos, L., & Mahlamaki, T. (2022). Managing B2B customer journeys in digital era: Four management activities with artificial intelligence-empowered tools. *Industrial Marketing Management, 104*, 241–257. DOI: 10.1016/j.indmarman.2022.04.014

Santana, M., & Díaz-Fernández, M. (2023). Competencies for the artificial intelligence age: Visualisation of the state of the art and future perspectives. *Review of Managerial Science, 17*(6), 1971–2004. DOI: 10.1007/s11846-022-00613-w

Sobocinska, M. (2021). Artificial Intelligence and Human Talent in Decision Making in the Sphere of Marketing in an Enterprise. [WE - Emerging Sources Citation Index] [ESCI]. *PROBLEMY ZARZADZANIA-MANAGEMENT ISSUES, 19*(1), 65–75. DOI: 10.7172/1644-9584.91.5

Vecchiarini, M., & Somià, T. (2023). Redefining entrepreneurship education in the age of artificial intelligence: An explorative analysis. *International Journal of Management Education, 21*(3), 100879. Advance online publication. DOI: 10.1016/j.ijme.2023.100879

Wang, Y., Lin, J., Osman, Z., Farooq, M., & Raju, V. (2021). Transformational leadership and employee performance in international commercial banking industry in Malaysia: The role of self-efficacy as a mediator under BRI. *Journal of Chinese Human Resource Management*, *12*(2), 25–36. DOI: 10.47297/wspchrmWSP2040-800503.20211202

Wang, Y., Xue, W., & Zhang, A. (2023). Application of Big Data Technology in Enterprise Information Security Management and Risk Assessment. *Journal of Global Information Management*, *31*(3), 1–16. Advance online publication. DOI: 10.4018/JGIM.324465

Yen, Y. Y., Wen, L. J., Ramasamy, S., & Farooq, M. (2023). Sustainable petrol subsidy program in Malaysia. *Asian Development Policy Review*, *12*(1), 1–9. DOI: 10.55493/5008.v12i1.4948

Zhang, H., Zang, Z., Zhu, H., Uddin, M. I., & Amin, M. A. (2022). Big data-assisted social media analytics for business model for business decision making system competitive analysis. *Information Processing & Management*, *59*(1), 102762. Advance online publication. DOI: 10.1016/j.ipm.2021.102762

Chapter 3
Transformative Impacts of AI in Information Systems for Strategic Advantage

ABSTRACT

With the rise of information systems (IS), firms may now benefit from a strategic edge that cuts beyond conventional operational lines (Farooq & Qureshi, 2020; Y. Wang et al., 2021). A paradigm shift is represented by information systems for strategic advantage, when using data and technology effectively becomes essential to the success of a business, (Behera et al., 2023). These systems include a variety of components hardware, software, networks, and people to enable smooth information exchange and decision-making, (Farooq et al., 2024).

3.1 CHAPTER INTRODUCTION

Strategic advantage via information systems is centered on the clever use of information for competitive positioning rather than just technical competence(Cebulla et al., 2023). By using these technologies, organizations may collect, process, and analyze data to get deep insights into customer behavior, market dynamics, and industry trends(Farooq et al., 2025c, 2025a). Businesses are better equipped to make quick choices and allocate resources efficiently when relevant information is readily

DOI: 10.4018/979-8-3373-0513-4.ch003

available in real time. This improves overall operational efficiency (Chenyang et al., 2024; Zhai & Chen, 2024).

Information systems provide flexibility and responsiveness to changing market circumstances by acting as innovation catalysts (Chatzimichailidou et al., 2024; Xie et al., 2024). These technologies' core components—cloud computing, big data analytics, and artificial intelligence—push businesses toward a future where success is determined by flexibility and foresight(Okada et al., 2024). Businesses must strategically integrate information systems to not only survive but also thrive in a competitive and constantly changing environment as they traverse the complexities of a data-driven age(Karim et al., 2024).

Figure 1. Mind map of information systems and strategic advantage

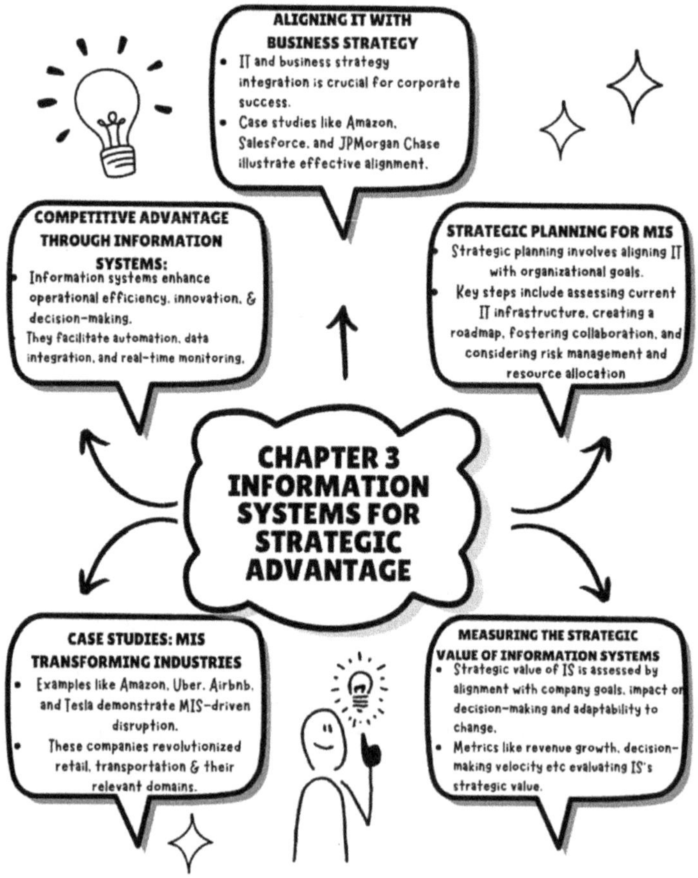

3.2 ALIGNING IT WITH BUSINESS STRATEGY

In today's corporate environment, integrating information technology (IT) with business strategy is essential. The growing dependence of firms on technology to propel their operations and accomplish strategic objectives has made the synchronization of IT with business strategy important for triumph (Chang, 2012). By ensuring that technology investments complement and advance the overarching corporate goals, this synergy improves productivity, creativity, and competitive advantage(Y. Wang et al., 2023; Zhidong, 2023).

Amazon is a prominent case study that shows how alignment may be effective. The e-commerce behemoth has continuously shown how to seamlessly integrate IT with business strategy, allowing the firm to grow into a major force in the world economy(Godoy et al., 2023; Gupta & Panigrahi, 2023). Amazon's dedication to prioritizing its customers is evident in its IT infrastructure, which is engineered to optimize the user experience. With its advanced logistical systems and tailored suggestions driven by sophisticated algorithms, Amazon's IT strategy supports its corporate objective of providing unmatched customer pleasure (Kar et al., 2021).

Salesforce, a well-known platform for customer relationship management, offers yet another striking illustration of IT business alignment(Dalloul et al., 2023; Na & Shon, 2022). Salesforce deliberately focuses on giving companies the tools they need to establish and nurture solid client relationships(Gödeke et al., 2020). Its cloud-based CRM systems provide insightful data on consumer behavior in addition to streamlining internal procedures. Because of this synergy, Salesforce has been able to establish itself as a major player in the software-as-a-service (SaaS) sector and show how an effective IT strategy can directly impact business performance (Z. Huang, 2022; Li et al., 2022).

JPMorgan Chase is a notable illustration of successful IT business alignment in the banking industry. The massive financial company has continuously made investments in state-of-the-art technology to improve its offerings, boost operational effectiveness, and keep ahead of market trends (Pereira et al., 2022; X. Zhang, 2022). Because of JPMorgan Chase's dedication to integrating IT with its business strategy, cutting-edge technologies like blockchain applications, AI-driven risk management systems, and mobile banking apps have been made possible(L. Huang, 2022; Iliescu, 2022). These technical developments help the bank maintain its position as a market leader and remain competitive overall while also satisfying the changing requirements of its clientele (H. P. Fu et al., 2023).

In the digital age, the alignment of information technology (IT) with business strategy has emerged as a critical component of corporate success. As organizations increasingly rely on technology to drive operations and achieve strategic objectives, the integration of IT into business strategy becomes imperative (Chang, 2012). Proper alignment ensures that technology investments are not only operationally relevant but also strategically beneficial, enhancing productivity, innovation, and competitive advantage(Guo & Shuai, 2022; Runge et al., 2022; G. Wang et al., 2022).

One compelling example of successful IT-business alignment is **Amazon**, the global e-commerce leader. Amazon exemplifies how IT alignment with business strategy can transform an organization. The company's technological infrastructure, including its advanced logistics systems and recommendation algorithms, is designed to optimize the customer experience(S. Fu & Xu, 2022; R. Liu & Wang, 2022). Amazon's IT strategy directly supports its corporate goal of enhancing customer satisfaction by offering personalized services, efficient delivery, and seamless online interactions(Song, 2022; Tian et al., 2022). Through these innovations, Amazon has managed to position itself as a powerhouse in global commerce, demonstrating how IT alignment can lead to sustainable growth and market leadership (Kar et al., 2021).

Salesforce also showcases effective IT alignment in its customer relationship management (CRM) platform, which emphasizes customer engagement and satisfaction(Lian, 2022; Liang & Wang, 2022). Salesforce's IT infrastructure focuses on cloud-based solutions that streamline CRM processes, offer real-time customer insights, and provide integrated platforms for communication and data analysis(W. Liu & Wei, 2022; Shi et al., 2022). By aligning its IT capabilities with its business goal of enabling businesses to build strong client relationships, Salesforce has established itself as a leader in the Software-as-a-Service (SaaS) sector (Gödeke et al., 2020). This alignment has proven critical for Salesforce's sustained competitive advantage and its ability to meet evolving customer needs (Kamenska et al., 2022; Y. Liu, 2022).

Another example is **JPMorgan Chase**, a leading financial institution that has effectively aligned IT with business strategy to enhance operational efficiency and customer experience(Y. Wang, 2022; Xiaobao et al., 2022). By investing in cutting-edge technologies such as blockchain, AI-driven risk management systems, and user-friendly mobile banking applications, JPMorgan Chase remains at the forefront of the banking industry. Its IT strategy aligns with its business objectives by improving risk assessment, streamlining transactions, and enhancing customer engagement through digital platforms(Haiying, 2022; Y. Zhang, 2022). JPMorgan's integration of IT with its business goals has enabled it to maintain a leadership position in financial services while adapting to changing market demands (Fu et al., 2023).

3.3 COMPETITIVE ADVANTAGE THROUGH INFORMATION SYSTEMS

In today's competitive landscape, information systems (IS) are pivotal to developing and sustaining competitive advantage(Jian, 2022; Khan et al., 2022). A competitive advantage arises from a unique set of resources and capabilities that allow an organization to outperform its competitors. By leveraging IS to enhance operational efficiency, drive innovation, and enable informed decision-making, organizations can maintain a distinct advantage in their respective industries (Valter et al., 2017).

Operational efficiency is a cornerstone of competitive advantage. Information systems enable organizations to automate processes, integrate data, and monitor operations in real-time(Shin & Choi, 2022; C. Zhang et al., 2022). This reduces errors, increases productivity, and minimizes costs, resulting in faster service delivery, enhanced customer satisfaction, and greater flexibility to respond to market changes(Xie & Luo, 2022; Zekun et al., 2022). For example, automated supply chain management systems help retailers track inventory levels, optimize order processing, and reduce stockouts, directly enhancing customer satisfaction and operational performance(Chen, 2021; Y. Wang et al., 2021).

Information systems also foster **innovation** by providing a platform for data-driven insights and collaboration. Knowledge-sharing systems and collaborative tools allow cross-functional teams to work together seamlessly, promoting a culture of creativity and innovation(Jin et al., 2021; Xuelei et al., 2021). As a result, organizations that can quickly innovate and adapt to changing market dynamics are better positioned to stay ahead of competitors (Karimova, 2022).

Another critical aspect of IS in competitive advantage is **strategic decision-making**. Information systems facilitate timely access to relevant information, empowering executives to make informed and strategic decisions(Farooq et al., 2025c, 2025a, 2025g). Business intelligence tools, analytics, and data visualization platforms transform raw data into actionable insights, supporting decisions based on current market trends, customer behavior, and operational performance(Farooq et al., 2025i, 2025j, 2025h, 2025e). This data-driven approach allows organizations to predict market trends, seize new opportunities, and effectively navigate challenges (Thayyib et al., 2023).

The digital era has placed a significant emphasis on **customer experience** as a differentiating factor(Farooq et al., 2025d, 2025f, 2025b). Information systems enable personalized marketing, efficient customer service, and the development of customer-centric initiatives. By understanding customer preferences and behaviors, organizations can tailor their offerings to meet individual needs, gaining a competitive edge through enhanced customer satisfaction and loyalty.

3.4 STRATEGIC PLANNING FOR MIS

Strategic planning for Management Information Systems (MIS) involves aligning an organization's technology infrastructure and resources with its broader strategic objectives. The process begins with an in-depth assessment of the current IT infrastructure, capabilities, and future needs, ensuring that the MIS framework supports productivity, innovation, and competitive advantage (Birchall & Kehler, 2023).

One of the key elements of MIS strategic planning is the development of a **roadmap** that outlines specific actions and initiatives for aligning IT with business strategy. This roadmap considers factors such as organizational capabilities, industry standards, and technological advancements. It acts as a guide for decision-makers, facilitating coordination and communication across different organizational units. For instance, a retail organization may prioritize e-commerce and digital customer engagement as part of its MIS roadmap, allocating resources to build user-friendly platforms, enhance data analytics capabilities, and support mobile commerce.

Continuous assessment of the organization's information needs and technological environment is essential for adapting the MIS strategy. This evaluation helps identify emerging opportunities or challenges, enabling the organization to adjust its strategy proactively. With the rapid pace of technological advancements, businesses must remain flexible and responsive to leverage MIS for competitive advantage.

Effective strategic planning for MIS also requires **collaboration** between business leaders and IT experts. A mutual understanding of organizational goals and technological limitations ensures that IT projects align with business needs. For example, executives may prioritize digital transformation, while IT teams ensure that the necessary infrastructure is in place to support these initiatives. This collaborative approach ensures that MIS investments are relevant, agile, and capable of adapting to future business needs.

Strategic planning for MIS also encompasses risk management to mitigate potential disruptions and prepare for unexpected scenarios. Organizations must establish contingency plans to minimize the impact of unforeseen events on MIS functionality. Additionally, resource allocation for both financial and human capital is integral to the strategic planning process, ensuring that the organization can maintain and scale its MIS infrastructure to meet current and future business needs.

3.5 CASE STUDIES: MIS TRANSFORMING INDUSTRIES

Management Information Systems (MIS) have driven transformative change across various industries, enabling organizations to enhance efficiency, improve customer experience, and disrupt traditional business models.

Amazon is a prime example of MIS-driven transformation in the retail sector. Founded by Jeff Bezos in 1994, Amazon has leveraged sophisticated MIS to revolutionize online shopping. Its recommendation algorithms, advanced inventory management systems, and streamlined supply chain processes have set new standards for operational efficiency and customer satisfaction. Through these systems, Amazon has redefined the e-commerce landscape, offering a seamless and personalized shopping experience that caters to individual preferences. This MIS-driven approach has positioned Amazon as a dominant player in global retail, showcasing how effectively implemented MIS can enhance competitiveness (Baek & Lee, 2021).

Uber disrupted the traditional taxi industry by building a platform driven by MIS. Uber's app connects drivers and passengers while dynamically adjusting routes and pricing based on complex MIS algorithms. This system benefits customers by offering convenience, affordability, and transparency while providing drivers with flexible income opportunities. Uber's MIS-enabled platform not only transformed the transportation industry but also paved the way for the broader gig economy. Uber's success demonstrates the disruptive potential of MIS and its ability to reshape entire industries.

Airbnb leveraged MIS to create a global platform for short-term rentals, changing the way people experience travel and lodging. The platform connects travelers with hosts, offering a wide range of accommodation options and allowing for safe transactions and personalized recommendations. By using MIS to streamline booking, enhance security, and tailor suggestions, Airbnb has revolutionized the hospitality industry. This case highlights the strategic significance of MIS in creating innovative business models that challenge established norms.

Tesla, under the leadership of Elon Musk, has transformed the automotive industry through its innovative use of MIS. Tesla's electric vehicles (EVs) are equipped with sophisticated information systems, including sensors, autonomous driving capabilities, and over-the-air software updates. This integration of MIS has positioned Tesla at the forefront of automotive innovation, demonstrating the impact of MIS on traditionally mechanical industries. Tesla's commitment to technology-driven transformation has influenced other automakers to adopt digital innovations, reshaping the automotive landscape.

These case studies underscore the transformative impact of MIS across industries, from retail and transportation to hospitality and automotive. MIS has not only driven operational efficiencies but also enabled disruptive innovations, setting new standards for customer experience and redefining industry norms.

3.6 MEASURING THE STRATEGIC VALUE OF INFORMATION SYSTEMS

Measuring the strategic value of information systems (IS) is essential for organizations seeking long-term success. This evaluation goes beyond traditional metrics and considers the impact of IS on decision-making, business processes, and overall performance. Assessing IS value involves several dimensions and measurement approaches.

Alignment with Business Goals: The primary measure of IS strategic value is its alignment with organizational objectives. Effective IS enables organizations to achieve operational efficiency, enhance customer satisfaction, and drive innovation in line with broader corporate strategies. Key metrics, such as revenue growth, cost savings, and return on investment (ROI), are used to assess how well IS complements and advances organizational goals. For instance, an e-commerce company might measure IS effectiveness through increased online sales and improved customer retention rates.

Decision-Making Impact: Another crucial dimension of IS value is its influence on strategic decision-making. Information systems provide decision-makers with timely and relevant data, empowering them to make informed choices. Metrics such as decision speed, accuracy, and the quality of insights delivered by IS can gauge its impact on decision-making. For instance, a financial institution may evaluate IS effectiveness by tracking the speed and accuracy of risk assessments, which directly influence investment decisions.

Flexibility and Scalability: The adaptability of IS to meet changing business needs is another indicator of its strategic value. Organizations assess the scalability and flexibility of their IS infrastructure to ensure it can support future growth and respond to market changes. Metrics related to system responsiveness, scalability, and agility are critical for evaluating long-term IS value. A manufacturing company, for instance, might measure IS effectiveness by its ability to scale production operations in response to shifts in demand.

Competitive Advantage: One of the most significant indicators of IS strategic value is its contribution to competitive advantage. IS that enables unique capabilities, enhances customer experiences, and creates barriers to entry for competitors adds substantial value to an organization's strategy. Metrics such as market share, customer loyalty, and brand positioning are used to assess IS-driven competitive advantages. For example, a tech company may evaluate IS success through its ability to retain a loyal customer base and maintain a leading market position.

In conclusion, information systems provide measurable strategic value by aligning with business goals, enhancing decision-making, ensuring flexibility, and supporting competitive advantage. These metrics help organizations quantify the impact of IS investments and guide future technology decisions.

3.7 CHAPTER CONCLUSION

In conclusion, this chapter has delved into the pivotal role of information systems (IS) in driving strategic advantage for businesses in the modern digital landscape. With the advent of information systems, firms now have the capability to leverage data and technology strategically, going beyond traditional operational boundaries to gain a competitive edge. By effectively utilizing components such as hardware, software, networks, and human resources, organizations can facilitate seamless information exchange and decision-making processes.

Strategic advantage through information systems entails harnessing information for competitive positioning rather than merely focusing on technical competence. Through the collection, processing, and analysis of data, organizations can gain deep insights into customer behavior, market dynamics, and industry trends, enabling them to make informed decisions and allocate resources efficiently. Moreover, information systems foster flexibility and responsiveness to changing market conditions, acting as catalysts for innovation and driving businesses towards a future where success is contingent upon adaptability and foresight.

Aligning IT with business strategy is paramount in today's corporate environment, as technology plays an increasingly integral role in propelling operations and achieving strategic objectives. Case studies of industry leaders like Amazon, Salesforce, and JPMorgan Chase illustrate the effectiveness of seamlessly integrating IT with business strategy to drive growth, enhance customer satisfaction, and maintain competitive advantage.

Competitive advantage through information systems is predicated on improving operational efficiency, accelerating innovation, and facilitating well-informed decision-making. By automating processes, integrating data, and enabling real-time monitoring, information systems contribute to higher productivity, increased customer satisfaction, and cost savings. Furthermore, strategic decision-making is enhanced through the transformation of raw data into actionable insights via business intelligence tools and analytics platforms.

Strategic planning for Management Information Systems (MIS) involves aligning IT initiatives with business goals and continuously evaluating the organization's information requirements and technological environment. Collaboration between business executives and IT specialists is essential to ensure that information systems remain flexible and responsive to evolving business needs. Additionally, strategic value measurement of IS involves assessing its alignment with company goals, influence on decision-making processes, adaptability to changing demands, and contribution to competitive advantage.

Case studies of disruptive innovators like Amazon, Uber, Airbnb, and Tesla underscore the transformative power of MIS in reshaping industries and redefining consumer expectations. These examples highlight the need for organizations to consistently innovate and adapt in the digital era, leveraging MIS strategically to gain a competitive edge and drive industry-wide change.

In summary, the strategic value of information systems lies in their ability to align with business objectives, enhance decision-making processes, adapt to changing demands, and drive competitive advantage. By strategically integrating IT with business strategy and continuously measuring its impact, organizations can position themselves for long-term success in the dynamic and rapidly evolving digital landscape.

REFERENCES

Al Karim, R., Rabiul, M. K., Ahamed, T., Karim, D. N., & Mehzabeen, M. (2024). Integrating Green Entrepreneurial Orientation, Green Information Systems, and Management Support with Green Supply Chain Management to Foster Firms' Environmental Performance. *Sustainability (Basel), 16*(12), 4921. DOI: 10.3390/su16124921

Behera, R. K., Bala, P. K., & Rana, N. P. (2023). Creation of sustainable growth with explainable artificial intelligence: An empirical insight from consumer packaged goods retailers. *Journal of Cleaner Production, 399*, 136605. Advance online publication. DOI: 10.1016/j.jclepro.2023.136605

Cebulla, A., Szpak, Z., & Knight, G. (2023). Preparing to work with artificial intelligence: Assessing WHS when using AI in the workplace. *International Journal of Workplace Health Management, 16*(4), 294–312. DOI: 10.1108/IJWHM-09-2022-0141

Chang, A. C. (2012). Primary Prevention of Sudden Cardiac Death of the Young Athlete: The Controversy About the Screening Electrocardiogram and Its Innovative Artificial Intelligence Solution. [WE - Science Citation Index Expanded] [SCI-EXPANDED]. *Pediatric Cardiology, 33*(3), 428–433. DOI: 10.1007/s00246-012-0244-5 PMID: 22327231

Chatzimichailidou, M., Whitcher, T., & Suzic, N. (2024). Complementarity and Compatibility of Systems Integration and Building Information Management. *IEEE Systems Journal, 18*(2), 1198–1207. DOI: 10.1109/JSYST.2024.3387064

Chen, Y. (2021). Optimization of Clinical Nursing Management System Based on Data Mining (Retracted Article). *Complexity, 2021*. Advance online publication. DOI: 10.1155/2021/2110154

Chenyang, X., Piao, W., Zilun, L., Qing, L., & Yadong, K. (2024). Research on Science and Technology Management Information Security Guarantee System. *Journal of Information Security Research, 10*(7), 675–681.

Dalloul, M. H. M., binti Ibrahim, Z., & Urus, S. T. (2023). Financial Crises Management in Light of Accounting Information Systems Success: Investigating Direct and Indirect Influences. *Sustainability (Basel), 15*(10), 8131. Advance online publication. DOI: 10.3390/su15108131

Farooq, M., & Qureshi, Q. A. (2020). Practical Approach of Environmental Awareness to Broadening Community Participation: A Case Study of Pindad (Persero). *Journal of Management Practices. Humanities and Social Sciences*, *4*(1). Advance online publication. DOI: 10.33152/jmphss-4.2.1

Farooq, M., Ramzan, M., & Yen, Y. Y. (2025a). AI in Consumer Behavior Management. In *Transformative Impacts of AI in Management* (pp. 281–294). IGI Global., DOI: 10.4018/979-8-3693-4322-7.ch011

Farooq, M., Ramzan, M., & Yen, Y. Y. (2025b). AI in Customer Service, HR, and Administration. In *Transformative Impacts of AI in Management* (pp. 45–70). IGI Global. DOI: 10.4018/979-8-3693-4322-7.ch002

Farooq, M., Ramzan, M., & Yen, Y. Y. (2025c). AI in Quality Management. In *Transformative Impacts of AI in Management* (pp. 295–312). IGI Global., DOI: 10.4018/979-8-3693-4322-7.ch012

Farooq, M., Ramzan, M., & Yen, Y. Y. (2025d). Artificial Intelligence and Customer Experiences. In *Transformative Impacts of AI in Management* (pp. 95–114). IGI Global., DOI: 10.4018/979-8-3693-4322-7.ch004

Farooq, M., Ramzan, M., & Yen, Y. Y. (2025e). Artificial Intelligence in Administration Sciences. In *Transformative Impacts of AI in Management* (pp. 115–156). IGI Global., DOI: 10.4018/979-8-3693-4322-7.ch005

Farooq, M., Ramzan, M., & Yen, Y. Y. (2025f). Artificial Intelligence in Business and Law. In *Transformative Impacts of AI in Management* (pp. 71–94). IGI Global., DOI: 10.4018/979-8-3693-4322-7.ch003

Farooq, M., Ramzan, M., & Yen, Y. Y. (2025g). Artificial Intelligence in Ethical Business Decision Making. In *Transformative Impacts of AI in Management* (pp. 265–280). IGI Global., DOI: 10.4018/979-8-3693-4322-7.ch010

Farooq, M., Ramzan, M., & Yen, Y. Y. (2025h). Exploring the Impact of Artificial Intelligence on Brand Management. In *Transformative Impacts of AI in Management* (pp. 157–188). IGI Global., DOI: 10.4018/979-8-3693-4322-7.ch006

Farooq, M., Ramzan, M., & Yen, Y. Y. (2025i). Exploring the Impact of Ethical Leadership and Employee Engagement on Knowledge Sharing Attitudes in the Asian Digital Economy. In *Transformative Impacts of AI in Management* (pp. 241–264). IGI Global., DOI: 10.4018/979-8-3693-4322-7.ch009

Farooq, M., Ramzan, M., & Yen, Y. Y. (2025j). Transformative Impact of AI in Education Management. In *Transformative Impacts of AI in Management* (pp. 189–216). IGI Global., DOI: 10.4018/979-8-3693-4322-7.ch007

Farooq, M., Yuen, Y. Y., & Buzdar, H. Q. (2024). Exploring the Research Landscape of Artificial Intelligence Integration with Business Management: A Bibliometric Analysis from 1994-2023. *Journal of Logistics. Informatics and Service Science*, (April). Advance online publication. DOI: 10.33168/JLISS.2024.0410

Fu, H. P., Chang, T. H., Lin, S. W., Teng, Y. H., & Huang, Y. Z. (2023). Evaluation and adoption of artificial intelligence in the retail industry. *International Journal of Retail & Distribution Management*, *51*(6), 773–790. DOI: 10.1108/IJRDM-12-2021-0610

Fu, S., & Xu, B. (2022). Facial Expression Recognition and Beauty Health Management Based on Image Feature Analysis. *Mobile Information Systems*, *2022*, 1–11. Advance online publication. DOI: 10.1155/2022/4336840

Gödeke, J., Muensterer, O., & Rohleder, S. (2020). Artificial intelligence in pediatric surgery Present and future. *Der Chirurg*, *91*(3), 222–228. DOI: 10.1007/s00104-019-01051-3 PMID: 31654102

Godoy, M. P., Rusu, C., Hatibovic, F., Granollers, T., & Ugalde, J. (2023). Addressing Information Consumer Experience through a User-Centered Information Management System in a Chilean University. *Sustainability (Basel)*, *15*(22), 15998. Advance online publication. DOI: 10.3390/su152215998

Guo, B., & Shuai, L. (2022). Research on Object-oriented Data Model Technology in Tourism Information Management. In S. F. ElZoghdy & M. K. Mohiddin (Eds.), *THIRD INTERNATIONAL CONFERENCE ON ELECTRONICS AND COMMUNICATION; NETWORK AND COMPUTER TECHNOLOGY (ECNCT 2021)* (Vol. 12167, Issues 3rd International Conference on Electronics and Communication; Network and Computer Technology (ECNCT) CL-Xiamen. DOI: 10.1117/12.2629214

Gupta, B. B., & Panigrahi, P. K. (2023). Analysis of the Role of Global Information Management in Advanced Decision Support Systems (DSS) for Sustainable Development. *Journal of Global Information Management*, *31*(1), 1–13. Advance online publication. DOI: 10.4018/JGIM.320185

Haiying, J. (2022). Conceptual model construction of building information management system based on BIM architecture. *Soft Computing*, *26*(16), 7925–7931. DOI: 10.1007/s00500-022-06851-0

Huang, L. (2022). Research and Application of Business Law Information Management System Based on Big Data. *Journal of Sensors*, *2022*, 1–12. Advance online publication. DOI: 10.1155/2022/5885451

Huang, Z. (2022). Integrated Management System of Instrument and Equipment in University Financial Media Laboratory Based on Hybrid Cloud Architecture. In S. Liu & X. Ma (Eds.), *ADVANCED HYBRID INFORMATION PROCESSING, PT I* (Vol. 416, Issues 5th EAI International Conference on Advanced Hybrid Information Processing (ADHIP), pp. 587–600). DOI: 10.1007/978-3-030-94551-0_46

Iliescu, D. (2022). Some Considerations on Conceptual Modeling for a Laboratory Information Management System. In D. Popescu, L. Barbulescu, E. Popescu, M. Roman, & D. Sendrescu (Eds.), *2022 23RD INTERNATIONAL CARPATHIAN CONTROL CONFERENCE (ICCC)* (Issues 23rd International Carpathian Control Conference (ICCC) CL-Sinaia, pp. 19–24). DOI: 10.1109/ICCC54292.2022.9805898

Jian, L. (2022). Design of enterprise human resources decision support system based on data mining. *Soft Computing*, *26*(20), 10571–10580. DOI: 10.1007/s00500-021-06659-4

Jin, Y., Zhao, J., Yu, W., Li, H., Liu, B., Sun, Y., Zheng, Y., He, C., Duan, S., & IOP. (2021). Research on Image Data Management System of Power Transmission Project Based on Geographic Information. In *2020 ASIA CONFERENCE ON GEOLOGICAL RESEARCH AND ENVIRONMENTAL TECHNOLOGY* (Vol. 632, Issue Asia Conference on Geological Research and Environmental Technology (GRET). DOI: 10.1088/1755-1315/632/4/042038

Kamenska, L., Moiseenko, V., Shendryk, V., Kamenskyi, S., & Shendryk, S. (2022). Implementation of Distributed Information Systems in Solving Problems of Energy Consumption Monitoring. In I. Karabegovic, A. Kovacevic, & S. Mandzuka (Eds.), *NEW TECHNOLOGIES, DEVELOPMENT AND APPLICATION V* (Vol. 472, Issue International Conference on New Technologies, pp. 758–767). DOI: 10.1007/978-3-031-05230-9_90

Kar, S., Kar, A. K., & Gupta, M. P. (2021). Modeling Drivers and Barriers of Artificial Intelligence Adoption: Insights from a Strategic Management Perspective. *Intelligent Systems in Accounting, Finance & Management*, *28*(4), 217–238. DOI: 10.1002/isaf.1503

Khan, M. S., Khan, M., Bughio, M., Talpur, B. D., Kim, I. S., & Seo, J. (2022). An Integrated HBIM Framework for the Management of Heritage Buildings. *Buildings (Basel, Switzerland)*, *12*(7), 964. Advance online publication. DOI: 10.3390/buildings12070964

Li, X., Wang, L., & Fang, L. (2022). Optimal Design of an Information Management System for Government: A Bridge between Government and Citizens. *Mathematical Problems in Engineering*, *2022*, 1–10. Advance online publication. DOI: 10.1155/2022/3127858

Lian, J. (2022). Optimization of Music Teaching Management System for College Students Based on Similarity Distribution Method (Retracted Article). *Mathematical Problems in Engineering*, *2022*, 1–11. Advance online publication. DOI: 10.1155/2022/6444554

Liang, C., & Wang, C. (2022). Coding structure of highway engineering information model. In *Shenzhen Daxue Xuebao (Ligong Ban)/Journal of Shenzhen University Science and Engineering* (Vol. 39, Issue 4, pp. 424–431). DOI: 10.3724/SP.J.1249.2022.04424

Liu, R., & Wang, L. (2022). Information Resource Sharing Based on University Dance Big Data Management and Utilization System Design. *Mathematical Problems in Engineering*, *2022*, 1–9. Advance online publication. DOI: 10.1155/2022/4325984

Liu, W., & Wei, S. (2022). Design and Management of Comprehensive Art Student Information Database from the Perspective of Internet plus Education (Retracted Article). *Security and Communication Networks*, *2022*, 1–9. Advance online publication. DOI: 10.1155/2022/6494404

Liu, Y. (2022). Design of Financial Information Management System and IoT Application Based on Fuzzy Comprehensive Evaluation (Retracted Article). *Wireless Communications and Mobile Computing*, *2022*, 1–11. Advance online publication. DOI: 10.1155/2022/2483306

Na, S.-H., & Shon, T.-S. (2022). A Study on the Development of Information Security Management System Using RMF. *Journal of Digital Contents Society*, *23*(5), 977–983. DOI: 10.9728/dcs.2022.23.5.977

Okada, K., Sugimoto, K., Wada, S., Konishi, S., Manabe, S., Matsumura, Y., & Takeda, T. (2024). Development of the Clinical Specimen Information Management System for Multicenter Clinical Studies. In J. Bichel-Findlay, P. Otero, P. Scott, & E. Huesing (Eds.), *MEDINFO 2023 - THE FUTURE IS ACCESSIBLE* (Vol. 310, Issues 19th World Congress on Medical and Health Informatics (MEDINFO), pp. 119–123). DOI: 10.3233/SHTI230939

Pereira, J., Varajao, J., & Takagi, N. (2022). Evaluation of Information Systems Project Success - Insights from Practitioners. *Information Systems Management*, *39*(2), 138–155. DOI: 10.1080/10580530.2021.1887982

Runge, M., Reiche, L. T., Niemann, K. H., & Fay, A. (2022). Universal energy information model for industrial communication. In *IEEE International Conference on Emerging Technologies and Factory Automation, ETFA* (Vols. 2022-Septe, Issue IEEE 27th International Conference on Emerging Technologies and Factory Automation (ETFA) CL-Stuttgart, GERMANY PU-IEEE PI-NEW YORK PA-345 E 47TH ST, NEW YORK, NY 10017 USA). DOI: 10.1109/ETFA52439.2022.9921557

Shi, Y., Ying, J., Shi, D., & Yan, J. (2022). Service-Oriented Modeling for Blockchain-Enabled Supply Chain Quality Information Systems. *Security and Communication Networks, 2022*, 1–16. Advance online publication. DOI: 10.1155/2022/1987933

Shin, J., & Choi, B. (2022). Design and Implementation of Quality Information Management System for Modular Construction Factory. *Buildings (Basel, Switzerland), 12*(5), 654. Advance online publication. DOI: 10.3390/buildings12050654

Song, Q. (2022). Design and Application of Land Resource Management System Based on Internet of Things. *Wireless Communications and Mobile Computing, 2022*, 1–14. Advance online publication. DOI: 10.1155/2022/2726673

Tian, J., Liu, Y., Yang, M., Sun, R., & Zheng, X. (2022). Blockchain Information Sharing Mechanism Based on Embedded System in Project Management System (Retracted Article). *Computational Intelligence and Neuroscience, 2022*, 1–13. Advance online publication. DOI: 10.1155/2022/1835626 PMID: 35965759

Wang, G., Li, D., Ge, J., & Wang, T. (2022). Medical informatization of management system for admission office under convolutional neural network. *Expert Systems: International Journal of Knowledge Engineering and Neural Networks, 39*(3), e12780. Advance online publication. DOI: 10.1111/exsy.12780

Wang, Y. (2022). Optimization of the Music Teaching Management System Based on Emotion Recognition. *Computational Intelligence and Neuroscience, 2022*, 1–9. Advance online publication. DOI: 10.1155/2022/4568041 PMID: 35586091

Wang, Y., Lin, J., Osman, Z., Farooq, M., & Raju, V. (2021). Transformational leadership and employee performance in international commercial banking industry in Malaysia: The role of self-efficacy as a mediator under BRI. *Journal of Chinese Human Resource Management, 12*(2), 25–36. DOI: 10.47297/wspchrmWSP2040-800503.20211202

Wang, Y., Xue, W., & Zhang, A. (2023). Application of Big Data Technology in Enterprise Information Security Management and Risk Assessment. *Journal of Global Information Management, 31*(3), 1–16. Advance online publication. DOI: 10.4018/JGIM.324465

Xiaobao, L., Shumin, L., & Kunyan, L. (2022). Establishment and application of hospital clinical trial management information system for improving clinical trial quality. *Chinese Journal of New Drugs and Clinical Remedies*, *41*(3), 146–150.

Xie, J., Jablonski, M., Smith, J., & Navedo, A. (2024). A Graphical Interface to Support Low-Flow Volatile Anesthesia: Implications for Patient Safety, Teaching, and Design of Anesthesia Information Management Systems. *Journal of Medical Systems*, *48*(1), 36. Advance online publication. DOI: 10.1007/s10916-024-02055-1 PMID: 38532235

Xie, J., & Luo, W. (2022). General Surgery Clinical Information Management System Based on Intelligent Data Management (Retracted Article). *Computational Intelligence and Neuroscience*, *2022*, 1–11. Advance online publication. DOI: 10.1155/2022/8601164 PMID: 35958777

Xuelei, L., Enjing, L., Yuetian, L., Kai, H., Yongyi, Z., & Kexin, L. (2021). Research on Function Optimization of University Laboratory Security Access System Information System Based on Environmental Monitoring Laboratory. In *Environmental Monitoring in China* (Vol. 37, Issue 1, pp. 23–28).

Zekun, W., Yakun, Z., Xuteng, Z., Wenzhe, T., & Maoshan, Q. (2022). Information management of water conservancy project partnering. *Qinghua Daxue Xuebao. Ziran Kexue Ban*, *62*(8), 1351–1356.

Zhai, Q., & Chen, X. (2024). Design and application of optical communication technology based on machine learning algorithms in physical education teaching information management system. *Optical and Quantum Electronics*, *56*(1), 111. Advance online publication. DOI: 10.1007/s11082-023-05717-5

Zhang, C., Xu, X., Duan, L., & Liu, S. (2022). Research on Information Assets Security Management of Electric Power Enterprise Based on Cloud Edge Collaboration Technology. In *2022 4th International Conference on Smart Power and Internet Energy Systems, SPIES 2022* (Issues 4th International Conference on Smart Power and Internet Energy Systems (SPIES) CL-Beijing, pp. 2266–2270). DOI: 10.1109/SPIES55999.2022.10082089

Zhang, X. (2022). Design and Implementation of Management Information System Based on Network Environment. In D. Zhou & Z. Y. Du (Eds.), *Lecture Notes in Electrical Engineering: Vol. 827 LNEE* (Issue International Conference on Information Technology and Industrial Engineering CL-Wuhan, pp. 1076–1080). DOI: 10.1007/978-981-16-8052-6_147

Zhang, Y. (2022). Development Strategy of College Sports Information Management System Using Data Mining in Mobile Internet Environment (Retracted Article). *Journal of Environmental and Public Health, 2022*. Advance online publication. DOI: 10.1155/2022/3895555 PMID: 36159766

Zhidong, L. (2023). Construction of management mechanism model of soil and water conservation information system. In *Science of Soil and Water Conservation* (Vol. 21, Issue 5, pp. 106–110).

Chapter 4
Transformative Impacts of AI in Emerging Technologies in Business

ABSTRACT

The incorporation of developing technology is now a revolutionary force that is changing how businesses operate as a whole. Technology advancements like blockchain, Internet of Things (IoT), and artificial intelligence (AI) are causing a paradigm change in the way businesses operate. Artificial intelligence has enabled organizations to improve customer experiences, streamline operations, and make strategic choices with previously unheard-of accuracy (Khan et al., 2023). It does this by analyzing large datasets and drawing well informed conclusions. Traditional ideas of trust and transparency have been completely transformed by blockchain technology, which is known for being decentralized and secure. This is especially true in the context of financial transactions and supply chain management.

4.1 CHAPTER INTRODUCTION

In the meanwhile, a smooth, networked environment has been established by the Internet of Things, allowing gadgets to interact and communicate on their own. Because of this connectedness, processes have become more efficient and cost-effective, from predictive maintenance to inventory management. The fields of product creation, consumer interaction, and staff training are all changing as a result of augmented and virtual reality (Munoko et al., 2020).

The combination of these new technologies promises operational efficiencies and opens up new avenues for innovation as businesses navigate this technologically driven era. This will pave the way for a future in which being able to adapt to these

DOI: 10.4018/979-8-3373-0513-4.ch004

advancements will be synonymous with long-term success in the cutthroat global marketplace.

Figure 1. Mind map of emerging technologies in business

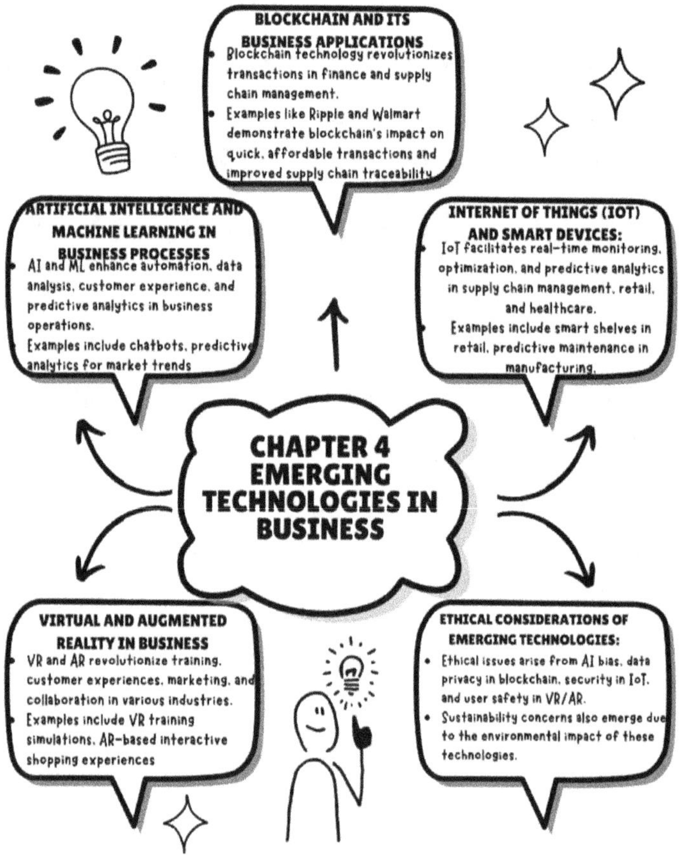

4.2 BLOCKCHAIN AND ITS BUSINESS APPLICATIONS

Blockchain technology has become a disruptive force that will affect many different businesses. Fundamentally, blockchain is a distributed, decentralized ledger system that guarantees data security, immutability, and transparency. Its uses are not limited to cryptocurrencies; it is increasingly having an influence on other business procedures (Kuzior et al., 2023).

Blockchain has completely changed the way that transactions are carried out in the financial industry. Ripple, a blockchain based payment system that enables quick and affordable cross-border transactions, is one such example (Putra Rahmadhan et al., 2023; Rafi-ul-shan & Ahmed, 2023). Conventional banking methods can include complicated procedures and middlemen, which causes delays and higher expenses. With its blockchain technology, ripple speeds up these transactions and lowers costs (Ullah et al., 2021).

Another area where blockchain is having a big influence is supply chain management. One of the biggest retailers in the world, Walmart, has improved food product traceability by using blockchain technology(Borowski & Khurana, 2019; Keshkar et al., 2019). Walmart guarantees more accountability and transparency by tracking each stage of the supply chain on a blockchain. In the event of a product recall, the business may promptly determine which goods are impacted and remove them, reducing customer harm and averting any emergencies.

Smart contracts, which are self-executing agreements with the conditions of the deal encoded directly into the code, are an effective use of blockchain technology. These smart contracts may be created on the decentralized Ethereum platform. The insurance sector is one real-world example, where smart contracts are used to automate the processing of claims. The contract reduces processing time and administrative cost by automatically executing the agreed upon compensation when predetermined circumstances. (such a weather event or aircraft delay) are satisfied.

Blockchain has an influence on the healthcare industry as well, helping with interoperability and data security concerns. Through the blockchain-based platform Medical Chain, patients can safely manage and exchange their medical data. In addition to giving people more control over their health data, this promotes smooth information sharing between healthcare professionals, enabling more informed and effective decision-making.

Blockchain technology has also been used to digital rights management and intellectual property. Within the music business, musicians often deal with issues of fair pay and copyright infringement. Blockchain technology helps platforms like My copy Rights and Ujo Music to manage and safeguard artists' intellectual property, guaranteeing an equitable and transparent royalty's distribution.

Figure 2. Applications of blockchain

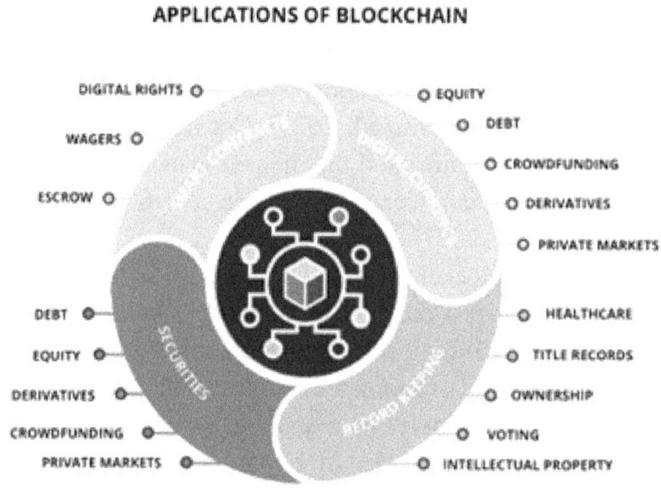

Blockchain technology, with its decentralized and immutable structure, has transformed numerous industries by offering unparalleled transparency, security, and efficiency. Initially developed as the backbone of cryptocurrencies, blockchain has since demonstrated far-reaching potential in sectors like finance, healthcare, supply chain management, insurance, and digital rights management (Kuzior et al., 2023). Now, with the integration of Artificial Intelligence (AI), blockchain's applications are expanding further, harnessing the capabilities of AI to enhance data analytics, automate processes, and provide greater insights. This chapter delves into blockchain's transformative impact across business applications, highlighting its integration with AI for even more powerful outcomes.

4.2.1 Blockchain and AI in the Financial Industry: Streamlining Transactions

In the financial industry, blockchain has introduced unprecedented efficiency by eliminating intermediaries in transactions, reducing costs, and enhancing security. Traditional banking systems often involve multiple intermediaries in cross-border payments, resulting in higher fees and slower processing times. Blockchain, however, allows for direct, peer-to-peer transactions, speeding up processes and reducing costs significantly. One example is Ripple, a blockchain-based payment system that facilitates quick and affordable cross-border transactions. Ripple uses its own distributed ledger to enable real-time global payments, bypassing traditional banking networks and cutting down processing times from days to seconds (N. Ullah et al., 2021).

The combination of blockchain and AI is particularly transformative for financial analytics and fraud prevention. AI algorithms can analyze blockchain transactions in real time, detecting unusual patterns that may indicate fraudulent activities or money laundering(Farooq et al., 2022). These AI-powered fraud detection systems can scan through vast volumes of data to identify suspicious behaviors, flagging them instantly and protecting both individuals and institutions from financial crimes.

Moreover, Decentralized Finance (DeFi) has emerged as a promising development within the blockchain and AI landscape. DeFi aims to create an alternative, decentralized financial system by allowing users to lend, borrow, and trade assets without traditional banking intermediaries(Abid et al., 2021). AI enhances DeFi platforms by optimizing loan approval processes, calculating creditworthiness, and analyzing risks with greater accuracy. For instance, AI can assess borrower profiles based on multiple variables, such as transaction history and behavior patterns, to provide more secure lending processes(Kaklauskas et al., 2021). Through AI-enhanced blockchain technology, DeFi platforms are increasingly able to democratize financial services, providing access to a broader range of users globally.

4.2.2 Blockchain and AI in Supply Chain Management: Enhancing Transparency and Efficiency

Blockchain's immutable ledger capabilities have proven revolutionary in supply chain management, where transparency and traceability are essential(Flynn et al., 2021; Kale et al., 2019). The technology enables every step of the supply chain to be recorded, from production to delivery, ensuring that all stakeholders have a clear view of product origins and handling. A prime example is Walmart's blockchain system, which tracks food products to improve traceability(Farooq, 2019; Huang et al., 2022; Liu, 2020). By using blockchain, Walmart can quickly identify the source of a product in case of a recall, reducing the potential for harm to consumers and promoting accountability among suppliers.

AI further enhances these capabilities by automating decision-making processes and analyzing data for insights. For example, AI can predict potential delays in the supply chain by analyzing external factors, such as weather patterns and traffic data, enabling companies to plan better(Al-Tit et al., 2022). Machine learning models can also assess supply chain data to identify inefficiencies or bottlenecks, recommending optimizations in real time. Through predictive analytics, AI improves inventory management by forecasting demand and helping companies avoid stockouts or overstock situations.

Combining blockchain's transparency with AI's analytical power transforms supply chain management, enabling companies to reduce waste, ensure compliance, and improve responsiveness. By integrating blockchain and AI, organizations can leverage data-driven insights for continuous improvement, aligning their supply chain strategies with sustainability and customer satisfaction goals.

4.2.3 Smart Contracts: Automating Agreements with AI-Enhanced Blockchain

Smart contracts are one of the most powerful applications of blockchain, as they automate the execution of agreements when predefined conditions are met. These contracts, often built on platforms like Ethereum, eliminate the need for intermediaries in contractual agreements, reducing administrative costs and enhancing trust between parties(Farooq et al., 2025i, 2025f). In the insurance industry, for example, smart contracts automate the processing of claims, executing payments when specified conditions, such as flight delays or weather events, are verified. By removing the need for manual verification and intermediaries, smart contracts streamline claim processing, benefiting both insurers and clients (Farooq et al., 2025j, 2025d, 2025b).

The addition of AI to smart contracts unlocks even more potential. AI algorithms can dynamically adjust contract terms based on external data inputs, making contracts adaptive to changing circumstances(Farooq et al., 2025a, 2025g, 2025c). For instance, in a flight insurance contract, AI could use weather forecasting models to assess risk levels and adjust coverage parameters in real time. Moreover, AI-enhanced smart contracts in supply chain finance can track goods automatically and release payments when products reach specific checkpoints, increasing financial transparency and reducing disputes.

AI also strengthens contract analysis and verification. Machine learning models can be trained to detect anomalies or inconsistencies in contract data, helping to prevent fraud and ensuring that all contractual obligations are met(Farooq et al., 2025h, 2025e; Xie et al., 2024). Through blockchain and AI, smart contracts become more efficient, reliable, and capable of adapting to complex business environments, opening up new possibilities for automated, trustworthy agreements across industries.

4.2.4 Blockchain and AI in Healthcare: Securing Data and Enhancing Patient Care

The healthcare industry faces significant challenges related to data security, interoperability, and patient privacy. Traditional healthcare systems are often siloed and vulnerable to data breaches, leading to inefficiencies and compromised patient care(Chatzimichailidou et al., 2024; Chenyang et al., 2024). Blockchain, with its secure, decentralized data storage, offers a solution to these challenges by allowing health records to be stored in an immutable ledger, accessible only with patient consent(Zhai & Chen, 2024).

One blockchain-based platform, **Medical Chain**, enables patients to manage and share their medical records securely, giving them control over their health data. Through MedicalChain, patients can decide who accesses their information, enhancing data privacy while facilitating data sharing among healthcare providers. This system improves collaboration between healthcare professionals, leading to better-informed and timely decision-making.

AI further enhances these blockchain capabilities by analyzing patient data for patterns, helping physicians make better diagnostic and treatment decisions. For example, machine learning algorithms can analyze patient histories, lab results, and genetic data to predict potential health risks, allowing for early intervention. AI's predictive capabilities are also useful in managing chronic diseases, where monitoring and early detection are critical.

Blockchain and AI also address the issue of clinical trial data integrity. By recording trial data on an immutable blockchain, researchers ensure transparency and prevent tampering, fostering trust in medical research outcomes. AI analyzes trial data for insights into treatment efficacy and side effects, enabling more accurate results and faster drug development. Through blockchain and AI, healthcare systems become more secure, efficient, and capable of delivering personalized patient care.

4.2.5 Digital Rights Management and Intellectual Property Protection

In the digital era, issues surrounding digital rights management (DRM) and intellectual property (IP) protection have become more pressing. Content creators and artists often face challenges related to copyright infringement, unauthorized distribution, and lack of fair compensation. Blockchain's ability to record ownership and transfer rights in a transparent, tamper-proof manner provides a solution to these problems, ensuring that creators maintain control over their work.

For instance, blockchain platforms like Mycelia and Ujo Music empower musicians to manage their intellectual property and receive fair royalties for their work. These platforms allow artists to publish their music on the blockchain, where every purchase and streaming event is recorded, guaranteeing transparent and direct compensation. This approach eliminates the need for intermediaries such as record labels, enabling artists to interact directly with fans and ensuring fair distribution of royalties.

Blockchain and AI are also transforming the art industry through non-fungible tokens (NFTs). NFTs are unique digital assets stored on the blockchain, representing ownership of a specific digital or physical item. By minting their artwork as NFTs, artists can authenticate their work, track ownership, and receive royalties from secondary sales. AI-powered platforms help identify and verify the originality of digital art, ensuring that creators receive recognition and compensation even when their work is resold.

In addition to creative industries, blockchain and AI safeguard intellectual property in fields like biotechnology and software development. By recording patents, research findings, and software code on the blockchain, companies create a verifiable, time-stamped record of ownership, protecting their IP from infringement. AI algorithms can assist by monitoring digital assets for unauthorized usage, sending alerts if suspicious activities are detected. This combination of blockchain and AI helps companies preserve the value of their intellectual assets, fostering innovation and fair compensation for creators.

4.2.6 Blockchain and AI in Government: Enhancing Transparency and Public Trust

Governments worldwide are beginning to recognize the benefits of blockchain and AI in public administration, as these technologies offer greater transparency, accountability, and efficiency. By recording public records, transactions, and voting results on the blockchain, governments can prevent fraud, reduce corruption, and build public trust.

For instance, blockchain-based voting systems enable secure and transparent elections by recording every vote on an immutable ledger. This ensures that election results cannot be altered, reducing concerns of electoral fraud. In this context, AI can assist by analyzing voting patterns to detect anomalies, ensuring the integrity of democratic processes.

Blockchain also improves public administration through transparent land registry systems. In many countries, property disputes arise from unclear ownership records and bureaucratic inefficiencies. Blockchain-based land registries provide a transparent and tamper-proof record of property ownership, making it easier to verify ownership and transfer property rights. AI can analyze land registry data to identify patterns in ownership changes and detect fraudulent transactions.

Additionally, AI and blockchain improve public **welfare programs** by ensuring that funds reach the intended recipients. For example, a blockchain-based welfare system could verify beneficiary eligibility in real-time, preventing fraudulent claims and ensuring that public funds are distributed fairly. AI can predict which welfare programs are most effective, allowing governments to allocate resources more efficiently. Through blockchain and AI, governments can enhance service delivery, increase transparency, and build stronger public trust.

4.2.7 Future Potential and Challenges of Blockchain and AI Integration

The integration of blockchain and AI has the potential to reshape industries and redefine business practices, but it also presents challenges. One major challenge is scalability: as blockchain networks grow, processing and storing data on a distributed ledger can become resource-intensive, slowing down transactions and increasing costs. AI can help alleviate this by predicting network congestion and optimizing transaction pathways, but ongoing technological advancements are needed to ensure that blockchain and AI systems remain scalable.

Interoperability between different blockchain platforms is another challenge, as businesses need to collaborate across networks with varying protocols and standards. AI can assist by analyzing network interactions and facilitating data exchange between blockchains, but a unified standard for interoperability remains necessary.

Privacy is another concern, especially as AI processes large volumes of sensitive data on blockchain networks. While blockchain provides data security, the transparency of public blockchains can conflict with privacy requirements. Advanced AI algorithms for data anonymization and secure multi-party computation are being developed to address these concerns, but privacy will remain a complex issue as these technologies evolve.

The integration of blockchain and AI offers transformative potential across numerous industries, creating a new paradigm of efficiency, transparency, and security. In finance, blockchain and AI streamline cross-border payments and enhance fraud detection. In supply chains, these technologies enable transparency and improve operational efficiency. Blockchain's ability to secure health records and AI's data analytics capabilities are transforming healthcare, while digital rights management and intellectual property protection safeguard creative work and foster fair compensation for artists. Government applications demonstrate how blockchain and AI can increase transparency and trust in public administration.

Despite the challenges, the synergies between blockchain and AI hold immense promise, laying the foundation for innovative business models and new standards for trust and accountability. As technology continues to advance, blockchain and AI will play an increasingly pivotal role in shaping the future of business, government, and society at large.

4.3 ARTIFICIAL INTELLIGENCE AND MACHINE LEARNING IN BUSINESS PROCESSES

Emerging as game-changing technologies, artificial intelligence (AI) and machine learning (ML) are changing how business activities are conducted in a variety of sectors. An innovative, efficient, and data-driven age of decision-making has begun with the incorporation of AI and ML into company processes(Danish & Senjyu, 2023).

Artificial intellect (AI) is the imitation of human intellect in computers, allowing them to carry out activities like voice recognition, planning, problem solving, and learning that normally need human intelligence. As a branch of artificial intelligence, machine learning uses statistical models and algorithms to help computers learn from data and experience to execute tasks more effectively (Farooq, Bakhsh, et al., 2023).

Automation is one of the main uses of AI and ML in business operations. Automation has made it possible to free up human resources for more strategic and creative projects by automating repetitive and rule-based processes that were previously laborious and prone to mistakes. Businesses are now operating more efficiently and are saving money as a result of this.

Algorithms using AI and ML are skilled at sifting through massive datasets to find insightful information. These technologies may be used by businesses to produce data driven forecasts and trends that will help them make well informed choices. AI, for instance, may evaluate consumer behavior and preferences in marketing to provide customized suggestions that improve customer happiness and boost revenue(Farooq, Hafsa Qadir, et al., 2023).

Chatbots and virtual assistants driven by AI are already standard features. These apps improve the entire customer experience by responding to inquiries from customers quickly and effectively. Since AI algorithms are always learning and adapting, these virtual assistants will eventually become more skilled at managing complicated interactions.

Another area where AI and ML excel in corporate operations is predictive analytics. These technologies use past data analysis to predict future patterns, which helps businesses prepare for changes in the market, manage inventories more efficiently, and make strategic choices that offer them a competitive advantage.

Risk management and fraud detection have also benefited greatly from the widespread use of AI and ML. For example, financial organizations use sophisticated algorithms to spot trends that point to fraud in order to reduce risks and preserve the integrity of their financial systems.

AI and ML have also helped collaborative technologies, which have enhanced cooperation and communication inside businesses. Artificial intelligence (AI)-enabled virtual collaboration solutions improve productivity by automating repetitive operations, managing documents, and suggesting content. While there is no denying the advantages of AI and ML in corporate operations, proper implementation and ethical concerns are essential. It is essential to tackle problems like algorithmic prejudice, data privacy, and employment displacement to guarantee that new technologies have a constructive impact o### 4.3 Artificial Intelligence and Machine Learning in Business Processes

Artificial intelligence (AI) and machine learning (ML) are transforming the way businesses operate, creating a more efficient, innovative, and data-driven environment across industries. The integration of AI and ML into business processes marks a new era in decision-making, enabling organizations to harness data insights, streamline operations, and enhance customer experiences (Danish & Senjyu, 2023). This chapter explores how AI and ML are being implemented in various business functions, from automation to predictive analytics, customer service, risk management, and collaborative technologies, as well as the ethical considerations that accompany their deployment.

4.3.1 The Foundation of AI and ML in Business

Artificial intelligence, broadly defined as the simulation of human intelligence by machines, allows computers to perform tasks such as voice recognition, problem-solving, planning, and learning, which typically require human intervention. Machine learning, a subset of AI, uses statistical models and algorithms to enable computers to learn from data and improve their performance over time without explicit programming (Farooq, Bakhsh, et al., 2023). By analyzing data patterns, ML algorithms can make predictions, recognize complex patterns, and automate decision-making processes, providing businesses with actionable insights that fuel growth and competitiveness.

The application of AI and ML in business processes is wide-ranging and has proven beneficial across industries. Businesses leverage these technologies to automate routine tasks, gain insights from big data, make data-driven decisions, and personalize customer interactions. Companies can enhance productivity, optimize resources, and improve operational efficiency by aligning AI and ML capabilities with their strategic objectives.

4.3.2 Automation: Transforming Business Efficiency

One of the most impactful applications of AI and ML in business is automation, particularly in handling repetitive and rule-based tasks. Automation not only increases efficiency but also reduces human errors, freeing employees to focus on more strategic, creative, and value-driven activities. For example, robotic process automation (RPA), an AI-driven automation tool, can manage routine tasks such as data entry, invoice processing, and report generation.

In **human resources (HR),** AI-powered automation is streamlining tasks such as resume screening and candidate assessments. AI algorithms can analyze thousands of resumes to identify top candidates based on predefined criteria, expediting the recruitment process and enabling HR teams to focus on relationship-building and strategic hiring. Similarly, in **finance**, automation is applied to manage financial reporting, accounts payable, and transaction reconciliation. By automating these tasks, finance departments can improve accuracy and reduce the risk of financial discrepancies.

AI-driven automation also plays a crucial role in **inventory management** within the retail and manufacturing sectors. Through real-time inventory tracking and demand forecasting, AI systems help companies maintain optimal stock levels, reducing storage costs and minimizing stockouts or overstock situations. With AI and ML, businesses can manage resources more effectively, streamline workflows, and reduce operational costs, creating a substantial competitive edge.

4.3.3 Data Analysis and Decision-Making: Harnessing AI and ML for Insights

AI and ML algorithms excel at analyzing vast datasets to uncover patterns, trends, and actionable insights that can guide strategic decision-making. By employing predictive and prescriptive analytics, businesses can make informed decisions based on data-driven insights, enhancing both operational and financial outcomes.

In **marketing**, AI-driven analytics provides valuable insights into customer behavior and preferences, enabling companies to create highly targeted campaigns and personalized experiences. By analyzing past purchase data, browsing patterns, and demographic information, AI models can generate recommendations tailored to individual customers, enhancing satisfaction and boosting sales (Farooq, Hafsa Qadir, et al., 2023). Additionally, AI-powered analytics enable marketers to assess campaign performance in real time, allowing for agile adjustments that maximize return on investment (ROI).

AI also empowers sales teams to forecast demand more accurately, track customer engagement, and identify cross-selling and upselling opportunities. By segmenting customer data and using predictive modeling, sales teams can focus on leads with the highest conversion potential, optimizing their strategies and improving sales efficiency.

Moreover, in the supply chain sector, AI and ML provide predictive insights that enhance demand forecasting, supplier performance, and logistics planning. By analyzing historical and real-time data, AI models can predict demand spikes, optimize delivery routes, and recommend inventory adjustments. This capability reduces waste, minimizes costs, and ensures that products are available when and where they are needed, resulting in an optimized supply chain that supports overall business goals.

4.3.4 Enhancing Customer Experience with AI-Powered Chatbots and Virtual Assistants

AI-driven chatbots and virtual assistants have become essential tools for improving customer experience across various industries. These applications provide fast, personalized, and efficient responses to customer inquiries, enhancing engagement and satisfaction. Unlike traditional customer service agents, AI-powered chatbots can handle multiple customer interactions simultaneously, reducing response times and ensuring that customers receive timely support.

For example, in **e-commerce**, chatbots can assist customers by answering product-related questions, providing personalized product recommendations, and guiding them through the purchasing process. By leveraging natural language processing (NLP), these bots can understand and respond to customer queries in a conversational manner, enhancing the shopping experience.

AI-driven virtual assistants are also increasingly common in **banking and finance**. Banks use virtual assistants to assist customers with tasks such as checking account balances, making transactions, and setting up payment reminders. These assistants not only improve convenience for customers but also reduce operational costs by handling routine queries that would otherwise require human agents.

As AI algorithms learn from past interactions, chatbots and virtual assistants become more adept at handling complex queries, providing accurate information, and even predicting customer needs. The continuous learning and adaptation capabilities of these AI-powered tools make them invaluable assets in delivering consistent, high-quality customer service.

4.3.5 Predictive Analytics: Preparing for the Future with Data-Driven Forecasts

Predictive analytics is another area where AI and ML have significantly improved business processes. By analyzing historical data, predictive models can forecast future trends, helping businesses to anticipate market shifts, optimize inventory, and make strategic decisions that provide a competitive advantage. Predictive analytics empowers companies to stay agile, respond to customer demands, and reduce risks.

In **retail**, predictive analytics is used to forecast demand for specific products based on factors such as seasonality, consumer preferences, and economic conditions. This enables retailers to optimize inventory levels, minimize waste, and ensure that popular products are available during peak demand periods. Similarly, in **manufacturing**, predictive models forecast production needs and identify potential equipment failures before they occur, allowing companies to schedule preventive maintenance and avoid costly downtime.

Predictive analytics is also transforming **human resources** by identifying trends in employee performance, attrition, and engagement. By analyzing workforce data, HR departments can predict which employees are at risk of leaving, allowing managers to take proactive steps to improve retention. Furthermore, predictive models can identify skill gaps, helping organizations plan future training and hiring needs effectively.

4.3.6 Risk Management and Fraud Detection: Safeguarding Business Integrity

AI and ML play a pivotal role in enhancing risk management and fraud detection, especially in sectors like finance and insurance. Traditional methods of identifying fraud and assessing risks are often time-consuming and prone to human error. By using machine learning algorithms, businesses can automate these processes, detecting anomalies and identifying high-risk transactions in real time.

In **banking,** AI-driven fraud detection systems analyze transaction patterns to flag suspicious activities, such as unauthorized transactions or account takeovers. Machine learning algorithms can identify subtle patterns that human analysts might miss, providing a higher level of security and reducing the likelihood of fraudulent transactions. For instance, AI can detect unusual spending patterns or login behaviors, alerting the bank to potential security breaches and enabling swift response.

Similarly, in the **insurance industry,** AI-powered risk assessment models analyze claims data to identify fraudulent claims, improving overall efficiency and reducing costs. These models can identify inconsistencies, such as repeated claims for similar injuries, and cross-reference data across multiple sources to verify claims. By enhancing risk assessment, AI and ML help insurance companies protect their financial integrity and offer fair pricing for their services.

4.3.7 Enhancing Collaboration and Communication with AI-Driven Technologies

AI and ML are also revolutionizing collaborative technologies, fostering improved communication and cooperation within organizations. AI-driven tools facilitate efficient document management, automate repetitive tasks, and suggest relevant content for collaborative projects, increasing productivity and enabling teams to work seamlessly, regardless of location.

Virtual collaboration tools powered by AI offer real-time transcription, language translation, and summarization features, making it easier for teams to communicate effectively. For example, **Microsoft Teams** and **Zoom** incorporate AI to provide automated meeting transcriptions and real-time translation services, which are invaluable for global teams working across different languages

AI also enhances knowledge-sharing platforms, enabling employees to access and share information more effectively. Machine learning algorithms can recommend relevant documents or resources based on project requirements, ensuring that team members have access to the latest information. This increases efficiency by reducing the time spent searching for information and facilitates better decision-making within teams.

4.3.8 Ethical Considerations in AI and ML Implementation

While AI and ML offer numerous benefits in business processes, their implementation also raises ethical concerns that organizations must address. Key issues include algorithmic bias, data privacy, and potential job displacement. As AI and ML technologies become more integral to business operations, it is essential to implement these systems responsibly to ensure they have a positive impact on both society and business.

Algorithmic Bias: AI systems are only as unbiased as the data they are trained on. If an AI model is trained on biased data, it may produce unfair outcomes, such as favoring certain demographic groups over others in hiring or lending decisions. Businesses must ensure that their AI models are trained on diverse datasets and periodically audited for fairness and transparency to prevent discriminatory outcomes

Data Privacy: AI and ML systems rely on vast amounts of data, raising concerns about data privacy and security. Organizations must comply with data protection regulations, such as GDPR and CCPA, to ensure that customer data is handled responsibly. Implementing strong data governance policies and encryption techniques can help protect user data and maintain trust with customers.

Job Displacement: Automation through AI and ML can lead to job displacement in certain roles, particularly those involving routine and repetitive tasks. To address this, businesses should focus on reskilling and upskilling their workforce, preparing employees for roles that require human intelligence, creativity, and emotional intelligence. Rather than replacing human workers, AI should be viewed as a tool for enhancing human capabilities and supporting employee growth.

The transformative impact of AI and ML on business processes is evident across sectors. These technologies are not only enhancing efficiency and productivity but also enabling businesses to make data-driven decisions, personalize customer experiences, manage risks, and improve collaboration. As AI and ML continue to evolve, their applications in business will expand, creating new opportunities for innovation and competitive advantage.

However, successful implementation requires a careful balance between leveraging technology and addressing ethical concerns. Organizations must prioritize transparency, fairness, and data privacy to maximize the positive impact of AI and ML on business and society. By integrating AI responsibly, businesses can create a sustainable framework that fosters growth, resilience, and ethical advancement in the digital age society.

4.4 INTERNET OF THINGS (IOT) AND SMART DEVICES

With the seamless communication and data sharing between connected physical items, the Internet of Things (IoT) has evolved as a paradigm-shifting technology. The operations, shipping, customer service, and product development aspects of company have all been profoundly influenced by this networked ecosystem of smart gadgets.

IoT refers to the process of turning commonplace items into smart devices by integrating sensors, actuators, and communication technology. Real-time monitoring, analysis, and control are made possible by these technologies' ability to gather, send, and receive data. The consequences for corporate procedures are significant, providing chances for innovation, better decision-making, and increased productivity. Supply chain management and operational optimization are two of the main uses of IoT in business. Realtime data on performance, maintenance requirements, and inventory levels is provided via sensors integrated into industrial equipment, automobiles, and warehouses. This enables companies to save expenses related to human monitoring and maintenance, simplify operations, and decrease downtime.

IoT is essential to the retail industry's goal of delivering a customized and engaging shopping experience. Retailers can manage inventory levels, assess client preferences, and send tailored promotions with the help of smart shelves, RFID tags, and beacons. This helps firms maximize their inventory and sales methods in addition to increasing client happiness. The idea of "smart cities," which improve urban life via networked gadgets and sensors, has also been transformed by IoT. The use of IoT technology enables waste management strategies, intelligent traffic management systems, and energy-efficient infrastructure. Companies that operate in urban areas may take advantage of these developments to increase sustainability and help create smart, effective cities. IoT has opened the door for predictive analytics, smart medical equipment, and remote patient monitoring in the healthcare sector. Sensor-equipped wearables may monitor vital indicators and instantly provide data to medical specialists, allowing for proactive and individualized treatment plans.

Even though IoT has a lot to offer corporate operations, there are still issues that need to be resolved, such security and privacy issues. Strong cybersecurity measures are necessary to protect against possible threats and illegal access to the massive volume of data created by networked devices.

The Internet of Things (IoT) has emerged as a transformative technology that enables seamless communication and data sharing between interconnected physical objects. By embedding sensors, actuators, and communication technology in everyday items, IoT turns these objects into smart devices capable of collecting, transmitting, and receiving data. This technology has reshaped various aspects of business operations, from supply chain management to customer service and product development, providing unprecedented opportunities for innovation, enhanced decision-making, and improved efficiency.

This chapter explores the significant impact of IoT on business processes, including its applications in supply chain management, retail, urban infrastructure, and healthcare, along with challenges associated with privacy and security.

4.4.1 Transforming Everyday Objects into Smart Devices

At its core, IoT involves converting traditional items into smart devices that can interact with each other and with centralized systems. IoT-enabled devices use sensors to collect data, transmit it to other devices or platforms, and receive commands for further action. This interconnected ecosystem creates an environment where physical objects—ranging from household items to industrial machinery—can communicate and respond to real-time data, leading to more efficient and optimized processes.

For instance, a coffee machine with IoT capabilities might track the user's preferences and make personalized suggestions. In the industrial sector, IoT sensors on machinery can monitor performance and detect early signs of malfunction, allowing timely maintenance and reducing costly downtime. This ability to transform static objects into dynamic, interactive tools has given businesses unprecedented insight into their operations and enhanced their capability to make data-driven decisions.

4.4.2 IoT in Supply Chain Management and Operational Optimization

One of the most significant applications of IoT in business is in **supply chain management** and **operational optimization** . By embedding IoT sensors in equipment, vehicles, and warehouses, companies gain real-time visibility into every stage of their supply chain. These sensors provide live data on equipment performance, maintenance requirements, and inventory levels, enabling companies to streamline operations, reduce costs, and improve productivity.

In **manufacturing,** IoT sensors monitor machinery health and performance, helping predict maintenance needs before a breakdown occurs. Known as predictive maintenance, this approach minimizes downtime by addressing potential issues proactively rather than reactively. For example, a factory with IoT-enabled machinery can identify when a part is close to wearing out and schedule maintenance before it fails, thus avoiding interruptions to the production process.

In **logistics**, IoT plays a vital role by tracking vehicles and optimizing routes in real time. Sensors in delivery trucks can provide data on location, traffic conditions, and even vehicle health, allowing logistics managers to adjust routes for efficiency and reduce fuel costs. IoT also enables precise **inventory management** through smart shelves and automated warehouses that track stock levels and automate reordering processes when inventory is low, ensuring that products are always available when needed. By leveraging IoT, companies can respond dynamically to changes in demand, minimizing delays and improving customer satisfaction.

4.4.3 Personalizing Retail with IoT

In the retail sector, IoT technology has revolutionized the shopping experience by allowing businesses to provide personalized and interactive customer engagement. IoT-enabled devices such as smart shelves, RFID tags, and beacons help retailers manage inventory, track customer behavior, and deliver tailored promotions.

Smart shelves are equipped with sensors that monitor product levels and automatically update inventory counts. When stock is low, the system alerts store managers, ensuring timely restocking and reducing the risk of empty shelves. This capability not only enhances the shopping experience by keeping products readily available but also improves inventory management by preventing overstock and stockouts.

Beacons are small, wireless devices that connect to customers' smartphones via Bluetooth. Retailers use beacons to deliver personalized offers and recommendations directly to shoppers' devices as they browse the store. For example, a customer walking past a section of winter clothing might receive a promotion on jackets or accessories. This level of personalization enhances the customer experience, increases engagement, and drives sales by providing relevant and timely offers.

Additionally, IoT-enabled RFID tags allow retailers to track items in real-time, reducing losses due to theft or misplacement. By tracking each item from manufacturer to sales floor, RFID technology ensures a seamless flow of products and enables retailers to analyze shopping patterns and preferences. This data helps businesses optimize store layouts, tailor product assortments, and develop marketing strategies that cater to customer needs.

4.4.4 IoT in Smart Cities: Enhancing Urban Life

The concept of smart cities relies heavily on IoT technology, as interconnected devices and sensors are used to improve urban infrastructure, increase efficiency, and enhance quality of life for residents. Cities around the world are implementing IoT solutions to address challenges related to traffic management, waste disposal, energy consumption, and environmental sustainability.

Traffic management is a primary focus in smart cities, where IoT-enabled traffic lights, cameras, and sensors collect real-time data on road conditions and vehicle flow. By analyzing this data, city authorities can adjust traffic signals, prevent congestion, and optimize transportation routes. This approach reduces traffic delays, lowers emissions, and improves public safety.

IoT also contributes to smart waste management by optimizing the collection and disposal of waste. Sensors installed in garbage bins provide data on fill levels, enabling waste management companies to plan efficient routes and prevent overflowing bins. This results in reduced collection costs and a cleaner environment, benefiting both the community and city services.

Energy efficiency is another area where IoT has made a significant impact in smart cities. IoT sensors monitor and adjust lighting, heating, and ventilation systems in public buildings based on occupancy and weather conditions. For instance, streetlights equipped with sensors can dim automatically when no activity is detected, reducing energy consumption and costs. Businesses located in smart cities can also benefit from this infrastructure by incorporating sustainable practices and leveraging IoT to minimize their environmental footprint.

4.4.5 IoT in Healthcare: Revolutionizing Patient Care

The healthcare industry has seen considerable advancements due to IoT, particularly in areas like patient monitoring, predictive analytics, and remote care. IoT-enabled wearable devices and smart medical equipment have opened up new possibilities for improving patient outcomes and making healthcare more accessible.

Wearable devices, such as fitness trackers and smartwatches, collect real-time data on vital signs like heart rate, blood pressure, and physical activity. This information is transmitted to healthcare providers, enabling them to monitor patients remotely and detect health issues early. For example, patients with chronic conditions, such as diabetes or hypertension, can use wearable devices to track their health and share data with their doctors, allowing for more personalized care.

IoT also enables remote patient monitoring, which has become especially relevant in managing healthcare for elderly or remote populations. Patients can receive timely healthcare without visiting a facility, reducing hospital readmissions and lowering the strain on healthcare resources. For instance, an IoT-enabled glucometer can record blood sugar levels and alert caregivers if readings fall outside safe ranges, allowing for immediate intervention.

In hospitals, smart medical equipment connected to the IoT helps streamline workflows and improve patient care. IoT-enabled devices can track the usage of medical equipment, manage inventory of medications, and monitor environmental conditions, ensuring that critical resources are always available when needed. Moreover, IoT enhances clinical efficiency by providing real-time data to healthcare providers, facilitating quicker and more accurate decision-making

4.4.6 Security and Privacy Challenges in IoT

While IoT offers numerous benefits to businesses and society, it also presents significant security and privacy challenges. With billions of devices connected to the IoT network, ensuring the security of data and preventing unauthorized access are critical concerns. As IoT devices collect and transmit vast amounts of sensitive data, such as personal health information and financial records, they become attractive targets for cybercriminals.

Data security in IoT involves protecting information from breaches, unauthorized access, and tampering. Without robust security measures, IoT devices are vulnerable to hacking, which could lead to data leaks or manipulation of connected systems. For instance, a hacker could potentially take control of a smart device in a manufacturing facility, disrupting production and causing financial losses. Strong encryption, authentication protocols, and regular software updates are necessary to mitigate these risks and protect IoT devices from external threats.

Privacy is another significant concern, as IoT devices often collect personal data that can be misused if not adequately protected. IoT devices used in healthcare, for example, gather sensitive information about patients' health, and unauthorized access to this data could result in severe privacy violations. Businesses must adhere to data protection regulations, such as the GDPR, and implement stringent privacy policies to ensure that user data is handled responsibly and ethically.

Moreover, the sheer volume of data generated by IoT devices raises questions about data ownership and consent. Individuals and businesses need to know who has access to their data and how it is used. Transparent data policies, clear terms of service, and opt-in consent models are essential to building trust and ensuring responsible use of IoT data.

4.4.7 Future Prospects and Challenges of IoT in Business

The future of IoT in business holds immense potential as technology continues to evolve and address current limitations. Integrating IoT with other technologies, such as AI and blockchain, can enhance its capabilities and applications across industries.

AI integration can help IoT devices analyze data more effectively, allowing businesses to gain insights and automate decision-making processes. For example, AI-powered analytics can detect patterns in IoT data, enabling predictive maintenance and personalized customer experiences. Similarly, **blockchain technology** can improve data security by providing a decentralized, tamper-proof ledger for recording IoT data, reducing the risk of data breaches and unauthorized access.

Despite these advancements, there are still challenges to be addressed, particularly in terms of scalability and interoperability. As IoT networks grow, managing the large volumes of data and ensuring seamless connectivity across diverse devices become more complex. Industry standards and protocols are essential for achieving interoperability, allowing different IoT devices to communicate effectively regardless of the manufacturer or platform.

Another challenge lies in the regulatory landscape. As IoT becomes more pervasive, regulatory bodies may introduce stricter policies to address privacy and security concerns. Businesses must stay informed about regulatory developments and adapt their practices to remain compliant. This proactive approach will ensure that companies can continue to leverage IoT effectively while safeguarding user data and meeting legal requirements.

The Internet of Things has redefined the way businesses operate by connecting everyday objects and enabling real-time data exchange across systems. IoT has transformed supply chain management, personalized retail experiences, optimized urban infrastructure, revolutionized healthcare, and presented numerous other applications that improve efficiency, innovation, and customer satisfaction. However, the widespread adoption of IoT brings forth challenges in data security and privacy that require careful consideration and proactive measures.

As IoT technology advances, its integration with AI, blockchain, and other emerging technologies will unlock even greater potential, allowing businesses to innovate further and improve their decision-making capabilities. By addressing scalability, interoperability, and regulatory challenges, businesses can continue to harness the power of IoT while safeguarding user privacy and security. In doing so, IoT will continue to serve as a cornerstone of digital transformation, empowering businesses to thrive in an increasingly connected world.

4.5 VIRTUAL AND AUGMENTED REALITY IN BUSINESS

Virtual and augmented reality, or VR and AR, are emerging as game-changing technologies that might completely change a number of business-related processes. These immersive technologies provide one-of-a-kind experiences that transcend conventional limits, opening up new possibilities for interaction, dialogue, and problem-solving. VR and AR are being used more and more in the business world to improve decision-making, customer experiences, and productivity in a variety of industries.

Virtual reality, which is defined by computer-generated simulations that submerge viewers in a three-dimensional world, has been used in virtual meetings, staff training, and product development. Training programs are one of the most prominent areas where virtual reality is making major progress. VR is used by the aviation, healthcare, and industrial sectors to provide risk-free, realistic training environments for staff members. This lowers the expenses related to conventional training techniques while simultaneously improving skill development.

Augmented reality enhances the user's experience of their surroundings by superimposing digital information over the actual world. AR interfaces allow personnel to obtain realtime information and direction in domains like maintenance and repair, where AR has found practical uses. AR is used in retail to provide consumers customized and interactive shopping experiences, letting them see things in their own environments before deciding what to buy.

Collaboration might be redefined by incorporating VR and AR into corporate operations. Through the use of virtual reality (VR) technology, participants in virtual meetings may have immersive talks that transcend geographical boundaries and create a feeling of presence even in situations when they are physically apart. This improves team cohesiveness and cooperation worldwide in addition to improving communication.

Because VR and AR provide new and interesting methods to present goods and services, they are having an impact on marketing techniques. Companies may use augmented reality (AR) apps to let consumers see things in their own settings or build virtual showrooms. This interactive strategy draws customers in and improves their entire experience, which might increase sales and brand loyalty.

As these immersive technologies develop further, companies are looking at creative methods to use AR and VR for analytics and data visualization. Through the use of immersive data experiences, decision-makers may investigate intricate information in three dimensions, leading to a more profound comprehension of patterns and trends. Better strategic planning and more informed decision-making may result from this.

Despite the significant commercial advantages that VR and AR have to offer, issues with device pricing, user acceptance, and data privacy must be resolved. Because VR and AR equipment may be expensive initially, smaller firms may find it difficult to embrace these technologies. Building confidence and promoting broad adoption also requires making sure interfaces are easy to use and resolving privacy and data security issues.

Virtual reality (VR) and augmented reality (AR) are rapidly emerging as transformative technologies with the potential to revolutionize business processes across a range of industries. VR and AR technologies provide immersive experiences that blur the boundaries between the digital and physical worlds, opening new avenues for interaction, communication, and problem-solving. By enhancing decision-making, improving customer experiences, and boosting productivity, VR and AR are reshaping the way businesses operate and engage with their audiences. This chapter explores the applications of VR and AR in training, product development, collaboration, marketing, data visualization, and more, along with the challenges and future potential of these immersive technologies.

4.5.1 Virtual Reality in Business: Immersive Training, Meetings, and Product Development

Virtual reality creates fully immersive, computer-generated simulations that transport users into three-dimensional worlds. This technology has found significant applications in business, particularly in areas where realistic simulations and spatial understanding are critical.

One of the most prominent applications of VR in business is in **employee training**. Industries like aviation, healthcare, and manufacturing have adopted VR-based training programs to create realistic, risk-free environments where employees can learn and practice skills without the dangers associated with real-world scenarios. For example, VR simulators in aviation allow pilots to train for complex flight conditions and emergency situations in a controlled, virtual environment. Similarly, VR training programs in healthcare enable medical professionals to practice surgeries and procedures without putting patients at risk. These VR-based simulations not only enhance skill development but also reduce the costs and logistical challenges associated with traditional training.

In **manufacturing and industrial sectors**, VR is used to train workers on machinery and equipment operation, safety protocols, and maintenance procedures. VR simulations enable workers to interact with digital replicas of machinery, familiarizing themselves with complex systems before operating them in real-life situations. This reduces on-the-job risks, accelerates learning, and improves overall workforce competency.

Beyond training, VR has also transformed **virtual meetings and collaboration** by creating immersive environments that replicate face-to-face interactions. In VR-based meetings, participants can experience a sense of presence and spatial awareness, making virtual interactions feel more like in-person ones. Unlike traditional video conferencing, VR meetings allow participants to visualize spatial arrangements, engage with 3D objects, and collaborate more naturally. This capability is particularly beneficial for global teams, as it enhances team cohesion and communication across distances.

Product development is another area where VR is making a significant impact. Engineers, designers, and product developers use VR to create and visualize prototypes in three dimensions before they are physically produced. This enables teams to identify design flaws, make improvements, and gather feedback early in the development process, reducing production costs and time to market. For instance, automakers use VR to design vehicles, allowing designers to experiment with shapes, materials, and interior layouts virtually. By facilitating a more iterative and flexible design process, VR helps companies innovate more effectively and produce high-quality products.

4.5.2 Augmented Reality in Business: Enhancing Real-World Interactions

Augmented reality enhances users' perception of their surroundings by overlaying digital information onto the physical world. AR technology has become particularly valuable in industries where real-time information is crucial for decision-making and operational efficiency.

One prominent application of AR is in **maintenance and repair**. AR interfaces provide technicians with step-by-step instructions and real-time data while they work on equipment, reducing errors and improving efficiency. For example, a technician working on a complex piece of machinery can use an AR headset to view digital overlays that identify parts, display maintenance histories, and guide them through repair procedures. This hands-free access to information minimizes disruptions and allows technicians to complete tasks more quickly and accurately.

In retail, AR is reshaping the customer experience by enabling shoppers to visualize products in their own environments before making purchasing decisions. For example, furniture retailers like IKEA offer AR apps that allow customers to place virtual furniture in their homes to see how it fits and looks in their space. Similarly, cosmetics brands use AR to let customers "try on" makeup virtually, helping them choose products that match their preferences and appearance. This personalized, interactive approach increases customer engagement, reduces the likelihood of returns, and enhances the overall shopping experience.

AR-powered marketing is another significant application. AR-based apps and advertisements allow businesses to create engaging and interactive experiences for consumers. For example, brands can use AR to create virtual showrooms where customers can explore products as if they were physically present. This approach not only captures attention but also deepens the customer's connection to the brand. By immersing customers in the brand experience, AR-based marketing can drive higher sales and foster long-term loyalty.

4.5.3 VR and AR in Marketing and Customer Experience: Engaging and Interactive Interactions

As VR and AR technologies continue to evolve, they are opening new possibilities for businesses to enhance their marketing strategies and create immersive customer experiences. By leveraging VR and AR, companies can present products and services in innovative ways that capture attention and leave a lasting impression.

In **real estate**, VR has transformed property tours by enabling prospective buyers to explore homes virtually. With VR headsets, potential buyers can walk through properties, view different layouts, and experience the space as if they were physically present. This capability has proven especially valuable for remote buyers and during times when in-person visits are not possible. Virtual property tours save time and resources, while also providing a convenient way for buyers to explore multiple properties.

In **tourism and hospitality**, VR allows users to experience destinations virtually, helping them make informed decisions about their travel plans. For instance, hotels and travel agencies offer VR tours of accommodations, tourist attractions, and recreational activities, allowing potential customers to "preview" their vacation before booking. This immersive marketing approach increases customer confidence and encourages bookings by providing a realistic sense of what the experience will be like.

AR has similarly transformed retail marketing by enabling interactive product visualization. Brands can use AR to create in-app experiences that allow customers to "place" products in their homes or "try on" items before purchasing. This immersive approach not only enhances customer satisfaction but also increases conversion rates by reducing hesitation and building confidence in the purchasing decision.

4.5.4 Data Visualization and Analytics with VR and AR: Enhancing Decision-Making

The integration of VR and AR into data visualization and analytics offers new ways for businesses to interpret complex data and make informed decisions. Traditional data visualization tools, such as charts and graphs, are limited to two dimensions, which can make it difficult to analyze multidimensional data sets effectively. VR and AR overcome this limitation by presenting data in an immersive, three-dimensional environment, allowing decision-makers to explore data from multiple perspectives.

VR data visualization tools enable users to manipulate and interact with data in a 3D space. For example, a company analyzing sales data can use VR to visualize geographic sales trends, customer demographics, and purchasing patterns in a virtual space. This approach allows decision-makers to identify trends and relationships that may not be apparent in 2D visualizations. By immersing users in the data, VR helps them gain deeper insights, which can lead to more effective strategic planning and data-driven decisions.

AR in data visualization can be used to overlay data onto the physical environment, providing real-time insights in specific contexts. For example, in a manufacturing plant, managers can use AR to view production metrics and machine performance data in real-time, superimposed onto the physical equipment. This allows them to monitor operations, identify inefficiencies, and make adjustments without leaving the production floor. By providing contextual data in real time, AR improves situational awareness and enables faster decision-making.

VR and AR data visualization tools are especially valuable for collaborative analysis, as they allow multiple users to interact with data simultaneously. In a virtual environment, teams can explore data, share insights, and discuss strategies, making data analysis a more collaborative and interactive process.

4.5.5 Collaboration and Remote Work with VR and AR: Redefining Team Interactions

The rise of remote work has accelerated the adoption of VR and AR technologies for virtual collaboration and teamwork. By creating immersive environments where employees can interact as if they were in the same room, VR and AR overcome the limitations of traditional remote work tools and enhance team dynamics.

In virtual meetings, VR enables participants to join a simulated conference room where they can interact with 3D objects, use whiteboards, and view presentations in a shared virtual space. This creates a sense of presence and engagement that is often lacking in video conferencing. Companies like Spatial and AltspaceVR offer VR platforms designed for team collaboration, where users can participate in brainstorming sessions, workshops, and team-building activities. This immersive approach strengthens team cohesion, fosters creativity, and improves communication in remote work environments.

AR also enhances remote work by allowing employees to access information and receive guidance from experts in real time. For example, in a remote support scenario, a technician can use an AR headset to receive instructions from an expert who views the same environment through a camera feed. The expert can draw on the screen, highlight specific parts, and provide real-time guidance, enabling the technician to complete tasks efficiently. This capability has proven valuable in fields like field service, maintenance, and healthcare, where remote assistance is essential.

4.5.6 Challenges of Implementing VR and AR in Business

While VR and AR offer numerous benefits, their adoption in business also presents challenges related to cost, user experience, and data privacy.

Device Costs: VR and AR devices can be expensive, with high-quality headsets and hardware often priced beyond the budgets of small and medium-sized businesses. This initial investment can be a barrier to adoption, especially for companies that are uncertain about the ROI of VR and AR applications. As technology advances and production costs decrease, however, it is expected that VR and AR devices will become more affordable, making these technologies accessible to a broader range of businesses.

User Acceptance: Ensuring a smooth user experience is essential for the successful implementation of VR and AR in business. Users may face challenges related to motion sickness, device weight, and ease of use, which can limit their ability to engage with these technologies fully. Designing intuitive interfaces and reducing hardware limitations are crucial for driving user adoption and creating positive VR and AR experiences.

Data Privacy and Security: VR and AR applications collect significant amounts of user data, including location, movement patterns, and potentially sensitive information. This raises concerns about data privacy and security, as unauthorized access to this data could compromise user privacy. Businesses must implement strong data protection measures and comply with privacy regulations to protect user information and build trust in VR and AR applications.

Virtual and augmented reality have the potential to revolutionize various aspects of business by providing immersive, interactive experiences that enhance training, collaboration, marketing, and decision-making. As these technologies evolve, businesses are exploring creative ways to use VR and AR for product development, customer engagement, data visualization, and remote work. By integrating VR and AR into business processes, companies can improve efficiency, drive innovation, and create more meaningful connections with customers and employees.

However, the successful adoption of VR and AR requires addressing challenges related to cost, user experience, and data privacy. By investing in user-friendly interfaces, protecting data privacy, and fostering a culture of innovation, businesses can harness the power of VR and AR to transform their operations and achieve a competitive advantage in the digital landscape. As technology advances, VR and AR are expected to become essential tools for businesses seeking to thrive in an increasingly immersive and connected world.

4.6 ETHICAL CONSIDERATIONS OF EMERGING TECHNOLOGIES

The ethical implications of developing technologies are receiving more and more attention. The incorporation of cutting-edge technologies like blockchain, IoT, VR, AR, and artificial intelligence (AI) presents ethical issues that need to be carefully considered and implemented responsibly. To guarantee that new technologies advance society, it is crucial to tackle ethical issues while pursuing innovation.

The proper use of AI and machine learning algorithms is one of the main ethical issues. As these technologies advance in sophistication, issues with discrimination, prejudice, and transparency surface. Crucial issues include ensuring AI systems are equitable and avoiding unforeseen outcomes like algorithmic prejudice. Aims are being made to create moral norms and rules for AI development with an emphasis on responsibility, inclusion, and openness.

The decentralized and open nature of blockchain technology raises ethical questions about data ownership and privacy. Blockchain improves security and lowers the possibility of data tampering, yet user privacy is a problem due to transaction openness. Establishing a harmonious equilibrium between openness and confidentiality is crucial in cultivating confidence in blockchain implementations across diverse sectors, such as banking, logistics, and medical field.

Concerns about data security and monitoring are brought up by the growth of IoT devices and the networked nature of smart gadgets. As more technologies gather and share data, safeguarding people's privacy becomes critical. To solve ethical issues related to IoT, it is essential to establish strong security standards, acquire informed permission for data collecting, and adopt encryption methods.

Ethical issues are brought up by virtual and augmented reality, especially when it comes to user permission, content filtering, and possible effects on mental health. Companies that employ VR and AR technology have to put user safety first and make sure that immersive experiences are created ethically. Enforcing rules for the production and use of material might lessen moral dilemmas and enhance user satisfaction.

Emerging technologies' effects on the environment are also ethically relevant. The environmental impact of these technologies is influenced by the energy use of blockchain networks, the production procedures for AI hardware, and the electronic trash left behind from defunct electronics. In order to reduce the ecological effect of developing technologies, sustainability must be prioritized throughout their development and implementation.

4.7 CHAPTER CONCLUSION

In conclusion, Chapter 4 has explored the transformative impact of emerging technologies on various aspects of business operations, ushering in a new era of innovation and efficiency. The integration of cutting-edge technologies such as blockchain, artificial intelligence (AI), machine learning (ML), the Internet of Things (IoT), and virtual/augmented reality (VR/AR) is reshaping traditional business paradigms and driving unprecedented levels of productivity and creativity.

Blockchain technology has emerged as a disruptive force, revolutionizing industries such as finance, supply chain management, healthcare, and intellectual property management. Its decentralized and transparent nature ensures data security and immutability, paving the way for more efficient and accountable business processes. Smart contracts, supply chain traceability, and data management are just a few examples of how blockchain is being leveraged to streamline operations and enhance trust in business transactions.

Artificial intelligence and machine learning are revolutionizing decision-making processes and operational efficiency across various sectors. From automation of repetitive tasks to predictive analytics and risk management, AI and ML technologies are enabling businesses to unlock valuable insights from large datasets and make data-driven decisions with unparalleled accuracy. Moreover, virtual assistants, chatbots, and collaborative technologies powered by AI are enhancing customer experiences and improving internal communication and collaboration.

The Internet of Things (IoT) is creating a connected ecosystem of smart devices that is revolutionizing industries such as manufacturing, retail, healthcare, and transportation. Real-time monitoring, predictive maintenance, and personalized customer experiences are just a few examples of how IoT is driving operational optimization and innovation in business processes. However, challenges such as security and privacy must be addressed to ensure the responsible and ethical implementation of IoT technologies.

Virtual and augmented reality (VR/AR) technologies are redefining how businesses interact with customers, train employees, and visualize data. From immersive training simulations to interactive marketing experiences, VR/AR technologies are enhancing engagement, improving decision-making, and driving innovation across industries. However, ethical considerations such as user privacy and content filtering must be addressed to mitigate potential risks associated with these immersive technologies.

Finally, as businesses embrace emerging technologies to gain a competitive edge and drive innovation, it is crucial to prioritize ethical considerations and responsible implementation. Addressing issues such as algorithmic bias, data privacy, environmental impact, and user safety is essential to ensure that these technologies benefit society as a whole. By adopting ethical frameworks and standards, businesses can harness the transformative power of emerging technologies while mitigating potential risks and maximizing positive outcomes for stakeholders.

REFERENCES

Abid, N., Ikram, M., Wu, J., & Ferasso, M. (2021). Towards environmental sustainability: Exploring the nexus among ISO 14001, governance indicators and green economy in Pakistan. *Sustainable Production and Consumption*, *27*, 653–666. DOI: 10.1016/j.spc.2021.01.024

Al-Tit, A. A., Al-Ayed, S., Alhammadi, A., Hunitie, M., Alsarayreh, A., & Albassam, W. (2022). The Impact of Employee Development Practices on Human Capital and Social Capital: The Mediating Contribution of Knowledge Management. *Journal of Open Innovation*, *8*(4), 218. Advance online publication. DOI: 10.3390/joitmc8040218

Borowski, J., & Khurana, B. S. (2019). Technology Transformation: Reinvent the Network and Change the Way of Working, Now! In *Future Telco* (pp. 359–369). DOI: 10.1007/978-3-319-77724-5_32

Chatzimichailidou, M., Whitcher, T., & Suzic, N. (2024). Complementarity and Compatibility of Systems Integration and Building Information Management. *IEEE Systems Journal*, *18*(2), 1198–1207. DOI: 10.1109/JSYST.2024.3387064

Chenyang, X., Piao, W., Zilun, L., Qing, L., & Yadong, K. (2024). Research on Science and Technology Management Information Security Guarantee System. *Journal of Information Security Research*, *10*(7), 675–681.

Danish, M. S. S., & Senjyu, T. (2023). AI-Enabled Energy Policy for a Sustainable Future. *Sustainability (Basel)*, *15*(9), 7643. Advance online publication. DOI: 10.3390/su15097643

Dhillon, M. K., Rafi-Ul-Shan, P. M., Amar, H., Sher, F., & Ahmed, S.Rafi-ul-shan. (2023). Flexible Green Supply Chain Management in Emerging Economies : A Systematic Literature Review. *Global Journal of Flexible Systems Managment*, *24*(1), 1–28. DOI: 10.1007/s40171-022-00321-0 PMID: 37519431

Farooq, M. (2019). Emerging sciences in Social Sciences : An overview, A Research Agenda. *Global Journal of Emerging Sciences*, *1*(October), 183–197.

Farooq, M., Bakhsh, A., Hafsa Qadir, B., & Warda, N. (2023). Digital Empowerment: Freedom of Expression Beyond 5G and 6G Networks in Developing Countries. *Pakistan Journal of Social Sciences*, *43*(4), 569–584. DOI: 10.5281/zenodo.10448484

Farooq, M., Cheng, J., Khan, N. U., Saufi, R. A., Kanwal, N., & Bazkiaei, H. A. (2022). Sustainable Waste Management Companies with Innovative Smart Solutions: A Systematic Review and Conceptual Model. *Sustainability (Basel)*, *14*(20), 13146. Advance online publication. DOI: 10.3390/su142013146

Farooq, M., Hafsa Qadir, B., & Saeed, M. (2023, December). AI-Enhanced Social Sciences: A Systematic Literature Review and Bibliographic Analysis of Web of Science Published Research Papers. *Pakistan Journal of Society* [PJSEL]. *Education and Language*, *10*, 1–2.

Farooq, M., Ramzan, M., & Yen, Y. Y. (2025a). AI in Consumer Behavior Management. In *Transformative Impacts of AI in Management* (pp. 281–294). IGI Global., DOI: 10.4018/979-8-3693-4322-7.ch011

Farooq, M., Ramzan, M., & Yen, Y. Y. (2025b). AI in Customer Service, HR, and Administration. In *Transformative Impacts of AI in Management* (pp. 45–70). IGI Global. DOI: 10.4018/979-8-3693-4322-7.ch002

Farooq, M., Ramzan, M., & Yen, Y. Y. (2025c). AI in Quality Management. In *Transformative Impacts of AI in Management* (pp. 295–312). IGI Global., DOI: 10.4018/979-8-3693-4322-7.ch012

Farooq, M., Ramzan, M., & Yen, Y. Y. (2025d). Artificial Intelligence and Customer Experiences. In *Transformative Impacts of AI in Management* (pp. 95–114). IGI Global., DOI: 10.4018/979-8-3693-4322-7.ch004

Farooq, M., Ramzan, M., & Yen, Y. Y. (2025e). Artificial Intelligence in Administration Sciences. In *Transformative Impacts of AI in Management* (pp. 115–156). IGI Global., DOI: 10.4018/979-8-3693-4322-7.ch005

Farooq, M., Ramzan, M., & Yen, Y. Y. (2025f). Artificial Intelligence in Business and Law. In *Transformative Impacts of AI in Management* (pp. 71–94). IGI Global., DOI: 10.4018/979-8-3693-4322-7.ch003

Farooq, M., Ramzan, M., & Yen, Y. Y. (2025g). Artificial Intelligence in Ethical Business Decision Making. In *Transformative Impacts of AI in Management* (pp. 265–280). IGI Global., DOI: 10.4018/979-8-3693-4322-7.ch010

Farooq, M., Ramzan, M., & Yen, Y. Y. (2025h). Exploring the Impact of Artificial Intelligence on Brand Management. In *Transformative Impacts of AI in Management* (pp. 157–188). IGI Global., DOI: 10.4018/979-8-3693-4322-7.ch006

Farooq, M., Ramzan, M., & Yen, Y. Y. (2025i). Exploring the Impact of Ethical Leadership and Employee Engagement on Knowledge Sharing Attitudes in the Asian Digital Economy. In *Transformative Impacts of AI in Management* (pp. 241–264). IGI Global., DOI: 10.4018/979-8-3693-4322-7.ch009

Farooq, M., Ramzan, M., & Yen, Y. Y. (2025j). Transformative Impact of AI in Education Management. In *Transformative Impacts of AI in Management* (pp. 189–216). IGI Global., DOI: 10.4018/979-8-3693-4322-7.ch007

Flynn, B., Cantor, D., Pagell, M., Dooley, K. J., & Azadegan, A. (2021). From the Editors: Introduction to Managing Supply Chains Beyond Covid-19 - Preparing for the Next Global Mega-Disruption. *Journal of Supply Chain Management, 57*(1), 3–6. DOI: 10.1111/jscm.12254

Huang, T. C., Wang, Y. J., & Lai, H. M. (2022). What Drives Internet Entrepreneurial Intention to Use Technology Products? An Investigation of Technology Product Imagination Disposition, Social Support, and Motivation. *Frontiers in Psychology, 13*(March), 1–13. DOI: 10.3389/fpsyg.2022.829256 PMID: 35369240

Kaklauskas, A., Lepkova, N., Raslanas, S., Vetloviene, I., Milevicius, V., & Sepliakov, J. (2021). COVID-19 and green housing: A review of relevant literature. In *Energies* (Vol. 14, Issue 8). DOI: 10.3390/en14082072

Kale, E., Aknar, A., & Başar, Ö. (2019). Absorptive capacity and firm performance: The mediating role of strategic agility. *International Journal of Hospitality Management, 78*(September), 276–283. DOI: 10.1016/j.ijhm.2018.09.010

Keshkar, S., Lawrence, I., Dodds, M., Morris, E., Mahoney, T., Heisey, K., Addesa, F., Hedlund, D. P., Dickson, G., Ghasemi, H., Faruq, A., Naylor, M., & Santomier, J.Jr. (2019). The role of culture in sports sponsorship: An update. *Annals of Applied Sport Science, 7*(1), 57–81. DOI: 10.29252/aassjournal.7.1.57

Khan, S., Khan, H. U., Nazir, S., Albahooth, B., & Arif, M. (2023). Users Sentiment Analysis Using Artificial Intelligence-Based FinTech Data Fusion in Financial Organizations. *Mobile Networks and Applications*. Advance online publication. DOI: 10.1007/s11036-023-02246-z

Kuzior, A., Sira, M., & Brozek, P. (2023). Use of Artificial Intelligence in Terms of Open Innovation Process and Management. [WE - Science Citation Index Expanded] [SCI-EXPANDED] [WE - Social Science Citation Index] [SSCI]. *Sustainability (Basel), 15*(9), 7205. Advance online publication. DOI: 10.3390/su15097205

Liu, K. (2020). Chinese consumer finance: A primer. *Frontiers of Business Research in China, 14*(1), 9. Advance online publication. DOI: 10.1186/s11782-020-00077-3

Munoko, I., Brown-Liburd, H. L., & Vasarhelyi, M. (2020). The Ethical Implications of Using Artificial Intelligence in Auditing. *Journal of Business Ethics*, *167*(2), 209–234. DOI: 10.1007/s10551-019-04407-1

Putra Rahmadhan, M. A. W., Sensuse, D. I., & Suryono, R. R. (2023). Trends and Applications of Gamification in E-Commerce: A Systematic Literature Review. *Journal of Information Systems Engineering and Business Intelligence*, *9*(1), 28–37. DOI: 10.20473/jisebi.9.1.28-37

Ullah, N., Al-rahmi, W. M., & Alkhalifah, A. (2021). Predictors for distributed ledger technology adoption: Integrating tree traditional adoption theories for manufacturing and service operations. [WE - Emerging Sources Citation Index] [ESCI]. *Production & Manufacturing Research*, *9*(1), 178–205. DOI: 10.1080/21693277.2021.1976963

Xie, J., Jablonski, M., Smith, J., & Navedo, A. (2024). A Graphical Interface to Support Low-Flow Volatile Anesthesia: Implications for Patient Safety, Teaching, and Design of Anesthesia Information Management Systems. *Journal of Medical Systems*, *48*(1), 36. Advance online publication. DOI: 10.1007/s10916-024-02055-1 PMID: 38532235

Zhai, Q., & Chen, X. (2024). Design and application of optical communication technology based on machine learning algorithms in physical education teaching information management system. *Optical and Quantum Electronics*, *56*(1), 111. Advance online publication. DOI: 10.1007/s11082-023-05717-5

Chapter 5
Transformative Impacts of AI Cybersecurity and Risk Management

ABSTRACT

Risk management and cybersecurity have become essential elements in defending companies against the ubiquitous hazards found in the digital sphere. The multidimensional field of cybersecurity involves protecting digital systems, networks, and data against hostile attacks using a wide range of technologies, procedures, and practices (Bistron & Piotrowski, 2021). The primary goal of cybersecurity is to reduce the risks arising from the constantly changing threat environment (AL-Dosari & Fetais, 2023; Gaglo et al., 2022; Trescakova, 2020). In the digital realm, risk management entails locating, evaluating, and ranking any risks and weaknesses (Mugari et al., 2023). It's a dynamic, continuing process that demands regular attention to detail and adjustment to new dangers in the cyberspace.

5.1 CHAPTER INTRODUCTION

The growing dependence of organizations on linked digital ecosystems has made the cooperation of cybersecurity and risk management essential. In order to preserve operational efficiency and provide strong defenses against cyber threats, organizations need to strike a careful balance(Kioskli et al., 2023; J. K. Lee et al., 2018; Mugari et al., 2023). Modern technology is linked, which emphasizes the need

DOI: 10.4018/979-8-3373-0513-4.ch005

of a comprehensive strategy that smoothly incorporates cybersecurity measures into company risk management plans (Bhatia & Alojail, 2022).

The successful fusion of cybersecurity and risk management becomes not only a strategic need but also a vital component of the survival and adaptability of organizations in the digital age in this complex tango between protection and functioning.

Figure 1. Mind map of cybersecurity and risk management

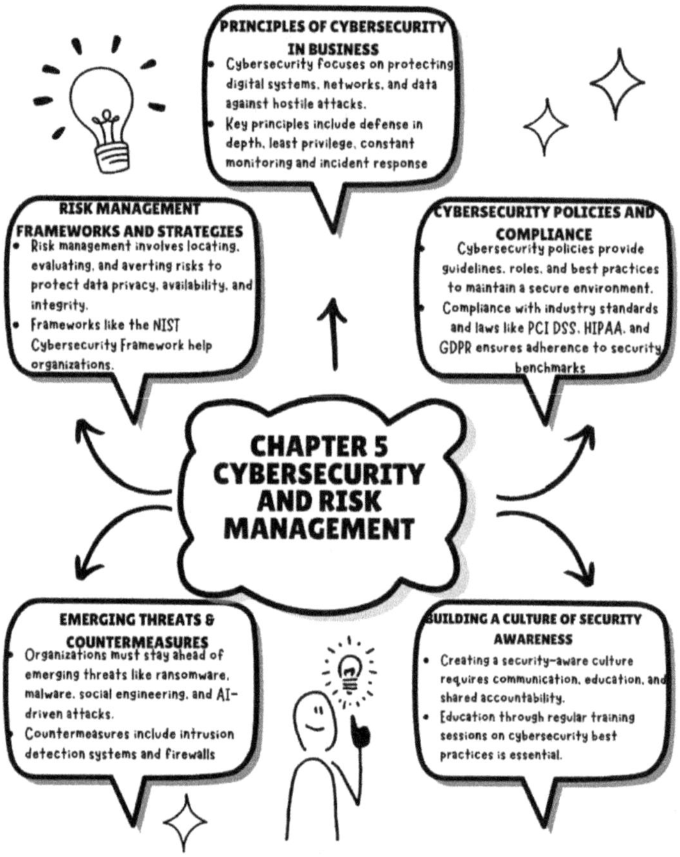

5.2 PRINCIPLES OF CYBERSECURITY IN BUSINESS

Implementing safeguards against hostile activity, illegal access, and data breaches is known as cybersecurity. The first principles centers on the idea of defense in depth, highlighting the need of many security tiers to establish a strong defensive system (G. Lee, 2019). To build a thorough defensive barrier, this strategy entails implementing a variety of firewalls, encryption, intrusion detection systems, and other security measures (Méndez-Suárez et al., 2023).

It is essential to follow the concept of least privilege in order to restrict access to sensitive information to those who need it in order to fulfill their particular duties(Annarelli & Palombi, 2021; Pham & Xiong, 2021). Organizations may improve overall security posture by reducing the likelihood of insider threats and illegal access by limiting permissions based on job duties (G. Lee, 2019).

Constant observation and evaluation is another fundamental tenet. Businesses need to take the initiative in a world where cyber dangers are always changing(Conger, 2020; Ghobakhloo & Iranmanesh, 2021; Popescu et al., 2021). Organizations may decrease the probability of successful cyberattacks by rapidly identifying and addressing vulnerabilities via routine monitoring of networks, systems, and applications. Equally important is the idea of incident reaction and recovery. Since no system is 100% secure, companies need to be ready to react to security problems quickly and efficiently. By creating a thorough incident response plan and practicing often, a company may minimize downtime and data loss by effectively containing and mitigating the effects of a cyberattack.

The need of safe architecture and design is highlighted by interconnected systems and the growing dependence on cloud services(Abu Othman et al., 2021; Berbecaru & Lioy, 2022; Miller & Brugan, 2021). It is essential for businesses to integrate security concerns into the core architecture of their technology systems, making sure that security is taken into account throughout the application and system design phases(Chehri & Zimmermann, 2021).

In cybersecurity, user awareness and education are crucial. The idea behind user training is that staff should get continual education in order to foster a culture of alertness (Asif et al., 2023; Bathla et al., 2022; Jaloliddin, 2023; Mhlanga, 2020). Topics like password best practices, social engineering attack threats, and phishing awareness should all be included in training programs.

One important idea for protecting data when it's in transit or at rest is encryption. Businesses may add an extra degree of protection to their digital assets by preventing unwanted access to critical information by using strong encryption methods (Bracarense et al., 2022).

In today's digital landscape, cybersecurity has become a cornerstone of business operations, protecting organizations against hostile activities, unauthorized access, and data breaches (Farooq et al., 2025i, 2025f, 2025j). Key cybersecurity principles, such as defense-in-depth, least privilege, and secure system architecture, form the foundation of an effective security strategy(Farooq et al., 2025d, 2025b; Muhammad Farooq, Muhammad Ramzan, 2025). With the rise of sophisticated cyber threats, organizations are turning to Artificial Intelligence (AI) to enhance traditional cybersecurity frameworks. AI's capabilities in detecting, predicting, and responding to cyber threats provide businesses with a more proactive and adaptive approach to securing their digital assets(Farooq et al., 2025a, 2025g). This chapter explores these core principles of cybersecurity in business, as well as the transformative role of AI in strengthening these defenses.

5.2.1 Defense-in-Depth: Layered Security with AI

The principle of defense-in-depth emphasizes the importance of implementing multiple layers of security measures to establish a robust defense system. This approach requires deploying a variety of cybersecurity tools, such as firewalls, encryption, intrusion detection systems (IDS), and security information and event management (SIEM) systems, to create multiple barriers that cybercriminals must breach to gain unauthorized access (Lee, 2019). AI further enhances this multi-layered defense by providing real-time threat analysis, anomaly detection, and predictive capabilities(Farooq et al., 2025k).

AI-powered firewalls are capable of dynamically adjusting their rules based on detected threats and patterns, making it harder for attackers to bypass them. Traditional firewalls rely on predefined rules and signatures, which can leave them vulnerable to new or evolving threats. By contrast, AI-driven firewalls learn from past incidents and continuously adapt their defenses, providing a more robust barrier against cyber threats.

In addition to firewalls, AI-based intrusion detection systems (IDS) play a crucial role in defense-in-depth. These systems use machine learning to analyze network traffic and identify unusual patterns that may indicate malicious activity. For example, an AI-enhanced IDS can detect subtle signs of a distributed denial-of-service (DDoS) attack, phishing attempts, or malware infiltration. By leveraging AI, IDS tools can quickly identify and alert security teams to potential threats, allowing for timely responses and reducing the risk of a breach.

5.2.2 Principle of Least Privilege: Limiting Access with AI-Based Identity Management

The principle of least privilege (PoLP) is a fundamental cybersecurity concept that restricts access to sensitive information and resources to only those employees who need it to perform their job functions. By minimizing the number of people with access to critical data, organizations can reduce the risk of insider threats and unauthorized access (Lee, 2019). AI enhances PoLP by automating identity and access management (IAM) processes, ensuring that access privileges are assigned, managed, and monitored with precision.

AI-based IAM systems use behavioral analytics to monitor user activity and flag any deviations from normal behavior. For instance, if an employee suddenly accesses files outside of their usual work hours or attempts to retrieve data that does not align with their job role, the system can trigger an alert or temporarily restrict access until the activity is verified(Farooq et al., 2025c, 2025h). This approach minimizes the chances of internal misuse and helps identify potential insider threats before they result in significant damage.

Additionally, AI-driven IAM platforms can use adaptive access control, which adjusts access privileges based on real-time risk assessments. This dynamic approach to access control allows organizations to provide employees with the appropriate level of access based on contextual factors, such as their location, device, and recent behavior(Farooq, Buzdar, et al., 2024; Farooq et al., 2025e). For example, an employee accessing sensitive information from an unfamiliar IP address might be prompted to complete additional authentication steps before gaining access. Through AI, organizations can implement a more granular and responsive approach to access control, further enhancing security.

5.2.3 Constant Monitoring and Vulnerability Assessment: AI-Powered Threat Detection

In the ever-evolving landscape of cyber threats, constant monitoring and vulnerability assessment are crucial principles for proactive cybersecurity. Organizations must continuously monitor networks, systems, and applications to detect vulnerabilities and identify potential attack vectors(Farooq, Hafsa Qadir, et al., 2023; Farooq, Yuen, et al., 2024). AI significantly enhances this process by providing real-time monitoring, predictive threat analysis, and rapid response capabilities.

AI-powered threat detection systems analyze vast amounts of data from network traffic, user activity, and system logs to identify anomalies and potential threats (Farooq, Bakhsh, et al., 2023; Yen et al., 2023). Machine learning algorithms trained on historical cyber-attack data can recognize patterns associated with malware, phishing, or ransomware attacks, allowing organizations to respond to threats before they escalate. For instance, if AI detects an unusual spike in network traffic that resembles a DDoS attack, it can alert security teams and initiate automated defense mechanisms, such as rate limiting or traffic filtering(Farooq et al., 2022b).

AI can also improve the vulnerability assessment process by identifying weak points in an organization's infrastructure. Traditional vulnerability assessments often rely on periodic scans and manual reviews, which may miss emerging threats(Farooq et al., 2022a). AI systems, however, continuously analyze software and system configurations, detecting vulnerabilities as they arise and prioritizing them based on their potential impact(Buzdar & Farooq, 2020; Farooq & Qureshi, 2020). For example, if AI identifies an outdated software component with known vulnerabilities, it can alert the IT team and recommend updates, ensuring that systems remain secure and resilient.

5.2.4 Incident Response and Recovery: AI-Driven Automation for Rapid Response

Despite an organization's best efforts, cyber incidents are sometimes inevitable, making incident response and recovery critical aspects of cybersecurity(Farooq et al., 2020; Wang et al., 2021). An effective incident response plan (IRP) enables companies to react quickly to security incidents, contain the damage, and minimize data loss. With AI-driven automation, incident response and recovery processes can become faster, more accurate, and more efficient.

AI plays a key role in automating incident response tasks, such as isolating compromised systems, blocking malicious IP addresses, and executing predefined actions to contain a breach(Farooq, Khalil-Ur-Rehman, et al., 2019; Farooq, Rehman, et al., 2019). For example, if AI detects signs of a ransomware attack, it can automatically disconnect affected systems from the network, preventing the spread of malware and protecting other assets. This rapid response minimizes downtime and allows security teams to focus on investigating the root cause(Farooq & Raju, 2019a, 2019d; Ghulam et al., 2019).

Furthermore, AI-based incident recovery systems assist organizations in restoring compromised systems to a secure state. After an attack, AI can automate data recovery processes, verify the integrity of backups, and ensure that systems are free from residual threats. AI also aids in the post-incident analysis by identifying the attack vectors, vulnerabilities exploited, and weaknesses in the security posture. By analyzing this information, organizations can strengthen their defenses and reduce the risk of future incidents.

5.2.5 Secure Architecture and Design: AI-Enhanced Security Frameworks

With the increasing interconnectivity of systems and the rise of cloud services, secure architecture and design are essential for building resilient digital infrastructures. This principle involves embedding security considerations into the core architecture of an organization's IT systems, ensuring that security is prioritized during the design, development, and deployment stages (Chehri & Zimmermann, 2021).

AI supports secure architecture by helping organizations identify potential design flaws, enforce best practices, and proactively manage security risks.

For example, AI-driven security testing tools use machine learning to conduct vulnerability assessments and penetration testing on applications, networks, and cloud environments. These tools simulate various attack scenarios, revealing weaknesses in system architecture and recommending mitigation measures. By integrating AI into security testing, companies can detect and address potential threats before they reach production, ensuring a more secure system design.

AI also enables dynamic security management by continuously evaluating the security posture of cloud and on-premise systems. As organizations deploy new applications or modify existing ones, AI-powered platforms assess the potential security impact of these changes. If AI identifies a misconfiguration that could expose sensitive data, it alerts administrators, ensuring that security remains a top priority(Farooq, Muhammad, et al., 2019; Farooq & Raju, 2019b, 2019c). Through AI-enhanced architecture, businesses can build adaptive, resilient security frameworks that can adjust to emerging threats and evolving technologies.

5.2.6 User Awareness and Education: AI-Supported Training Programs

In cybersecurity, user awareness and education are essential to prevent human errors that can lead to breaches. As the first line of defense, employees must be well-informed about potential threats, safe practices, and the importance of cybersecurity in their roles. AI can play a supportive role in enhancing user training by personalizing educational content and identifying knowledge gaps.

AI-based training platforms use adaptive learning to create customized cybersecurity training for employees. These systems assess individual learning styles, track performance on quizzes and simulated phishing tests, and adjust content to address specific weaknesses. For example, if an employee repeatedly fails phishing simulations, the AI platform may assign additional training on identifying phishing emails. By personalizing the training experience, AI can ensure that each employee develops a comprehensive understanding of cybersecurity risks and best practices.

In addition to training, AI-powered phishing detection tools can assist employees in identifying potential threats. For instance, AI systems embedded in email platforms can scan incoming messages for signs of phishing, such as suspicious links, spoofed sender addresses, or unusual language patterns. When AI detects a potential phishing attempt, it can flag the email and notify the recipient, reducing the risk of human error and enhancing overall security.

5.2.7 Encryption: AI for Enhanced Data Protection

Encryption is a critical principle for securing sensitive data both in transit and at rest. By converting information into an unreadable format, encryption protects data from unauthorized access and interception. However, as cybercriminals develop more sophisticated methods to bypass encryption, organizations are increasingly turning to AI to enhance data protection.

AI assists in automating encryption processes, ensuring that data is encrypted based on predefined policies and compliance requirements. For example, AI can detect sensitive information in files, emails, or databases and apply encryption automatically, reducing the likelihood of human error. This capability ensures that all critical data is encrypted according to organizational policies, protecting it from unauthorized access and compliance violations.

AI also enhances encryption key management by generating, storing, and rotating encryption keys securely. Key management is often a complex and error-prone task, as lost or mismanaged keys can result in data loss or security breaches. AI-based key management systems automate key rotation and provide secure storage, reducing the risk of keys being compromised. Through AI-enhanced encryption, businesses can add an extra layer of protection to their digital assets, safeguarding critical information from cyber threats.

5.2.8 The Role of Artificial Intelligence in Future Cybersecurity

As cyber threats continue to evolve, AI's role in cybersecurity will become even more significant. Future advancements in AI could enable predictive cybersecurity, where AI algorithms anticipate cyber threats before they materialize. By analyzing global cyber-attack data, network traffic, and organizational vulnerabilities, AI can predict emerging threats, allowing businesses to proactively strengthen their defenses.

In addition, AI-based autonomous response systems may soon be capable of fully automated incident response, where AI not only detects threats but also takes corrective actions without human intervention. For example, in the case of a malware infection, an autonomous AI system could isolate the affected devices, remove the malware, and restore system integrity without any manual input. This level of automation could enable organizations to respond to cyber threats instantly, reducing the risk of widespread damage.

Moreover, the combination of AI with other emerging technologies, such as blockchain, could further enhance cybersecurity. Blockchain's decentralized and tamper-proof nature, combined with AI's predictive capabilities, offers the potential for more secure data storage and improved identity verification. For instance,

AI algorithms could verify blockchain transactions in real time, identifying any anomalies or fraudulent activities immediately.

The principles of cybersecurity, including defense-in-depth, least privilege, constant monitoring, incident response, and secure architecture, are essential for protecting businesses against cyber threats. AI is reshaping these principles, providing enhanced monitoring, predictive capabilities, automated incident response, and personalized user training. By leveraging AI, businesses can not only strengthen their cybersecurity defenses but also adopt a more proactive and adaptive approach to managing digital risks.

However, as organizations integrate AI into their cybersecurity strategies, they must address challenges such as data privacy, algorithmic transparency, and ethical considerations. Ensuring responsible AI use in cybersecurity will be crucial for building trust, protecting digital assets, and navigating the increasingly complex landscape of cyber threats. As technology advances, AI will continue to play a pivotal role in shaping the future of cybersecurity, empowering businesses to safeguard their operations and thrive in the digital age.

5.3 RISK MANAGEMENT FRAMEWORKS AND STRATEGIES

Organizations are always facing new and emerging threats that have the potential to steal confidential information, interfere with business processes, and harm their brand. In order to successfully traverse this difficult terrain, companies need to have thorough risk management frameworks and procedures. In cybersecurity, risk management is locating, evaluating, and averting any risks to protect the privacy, availability, and integrity of vital data assets (Kharchenko et al., 2020).

The National Institute of Standards and Technology (NIST) Cybersecurity Framework is a well-known framework that is often used in cybersecurity risk management. An organization's cybersecurity posture may be managed and improved in an organized manner with the help of this framework. Identify, Protect, Detect, Respond, and Recover are its five main tasks. Businesses may build a systematic and risk-based strategy to cybersecurity by aligning with these functions.

Threat, vulnerability, and asset identification is a critical component of cybersecurity risk management. In order to detect possible flaws, organizations must do extensive asset inventories, evaluate threats to ascertain the probability and effect of prospective occurrences, and assess vulnerabilities. Making educated judgments about risk reduction starts with this knowledge.

Risks must be recognized, and then their potential effect must be evaluated. This entails assessing the possibility that a threat may exploit a vulnerability and the consequences. Organizations may more effectively allocate resources and prioritize cybersecurity initiatives with the use of risk assessments. Businesses may improve their overall security posture by concentrating on fixing the most significant vulnerabilities first by classifying threats according to their severity.

The use of risk mitigation techniques is essential for controlling cybersecurity threats. These tactics include putting controls and precautions in place to lessen the possibility and effect of hazards that have been recognized. Implementing intrusion detection systems, firewalls, encryption, and routine security awareness training for staff members are a few examples. Maintaining an effective defense against cyberattacks and adapting to emerging threats need frequent security measure upgrades and ongoing monitoring (Abbasi & Rahmani, 2023).

5.4 CYBERSECURITY POLICIES AND COMPLIANCE

The key to protecting an organization's digital assets is developing and executing strong rules. Cybersecurity policies provide a structure for outlining guidelines, roles, and best practices that direct staff members and other stakeholders in maintaining a secure environment. Furthermore, it is essential for firms to comply with industry standards and laws in order to guarantee that they meet established security benchmarks and legal obligations.

Developing successful cybersecurity policy requires a multifaceted strategy. First and foremost, in order to identify possible risks and weaknesses unique to their operations, firms must carry out a comprehensive risk assessment. The foundation for creating policies that handle the particular risks and difficulties the business faces comes from this evaluation. Policies need to address things like personnel training, incident response, data security, and access control (Bhatt & Sandhu, 2020).

For example, access control rules specify who inside an organization has access to what systems and data. Organizations may reduce the possible harm that unauthorized access may create by putting the least privilege into practice. Data protection policies provide instructions for the management, archiving, and sharing of private data, guaranteeing the security of sensitive information. Policies for incident response are essential for reducing the effects of security events. These guidelines provide a methodical way to locate, contain, eliminate, recover from, and absorb lessons from cybersecurity events. Establishing a clear and comprehensive incident response strategy enables companies to minimize disruptions, lessen harm, and enhance their overall ability to fend against cyberattacks (Khan et al., 2020).

Awareness and training programs for employees are essential parts of cybersecurity strategies. Employers need to make sure that staff members are aware of the most recent cybersecurity risks, recommended procedures, and their part in maintaining a safe workplace. To create a workforce that is aware of cybersecurity, regular training sessions, simulated phishing exercises, and awareness campaigns are helpful. In the linked corporate world of today, adherence to industry norms and laws is crucial. Organizations may be required to follow standards like the Payment Card business Data Security Standard (PCI DSS), Health Insurance Portability and Accountability Act (HIPAA), or General Data Protection Regulation (GDPR) depending on their business. In addition to assisting in avoiding legal repercussions, compliance shows a dedication to cybersecurity best practices.

5.5 EMERGING THREATS AND COUNTERMEASURES

It is critical for firms looking to safeguard sensitive data and preserve operational integrity to remain ahead of new threats. Cybercriminals who are creative and skilled are always attacking the digital sphere, taking advantage of holes in systems and networks. A strong cybersecurity plan must take into account these risks and put appropriate remedies in place (Lu & Ning, 2020).

Emerging threats may come in many different forms, such as ransomware, sophisticated malware, social engineering scams, and zero-day vulnerabilities. The increasing use of artificial intelligence (AI) in cyberattacks, where threat actors use machine learning algorithms to adapt and get beyond conventional security measures, is one major cause for worry. Furthermore, as linked devices develop potentially exploitable vulnerabilities, the Internet of Things' (IoT) spread creates new attack surfaces (Ogbuke et al., 2023).

Organizations must implement a multi-layered defensive strategy to address these threats. To defend against malware and unauthorized access, it is essential to implement intrusion detection systems, firewalls, and comprehensive endpoint security. Software may be kept up to date and patched on a regular basis to help reduce the risks associated with known vulnerabilities and the possibility of successful assaults. Threat information is essential for being up to date on the most recent cyber threats. Through proactive monitoring of industry-specific trends and collaboration with cybersecurity groups, firms may effectively mitigate new threats by adapting their security measures. Rapid identification and reaction to any security events are made possible by ongoing network traffic monitoring and analysis, user behavior analysis, and system log analysis (Almufarreh & Arshad, 2023).

Working together within the cybersecurity ecosystem is essential to creating successful defenses. By exchanging threat information, industry colleagues, governmental organizations, and security vendors may improve collective understanding and fortify the cybersecurity posture as a whole. Organizations may adjust their strategy to changing threats and benefit from one other's experiences when there is open communication (Wiemer et al., 2023).

A thorough cybersecurity plan must include personnel education and awareness in addition to technology protections. Phishing and other social engineering attacks take advantage of human weaknesses. Employee awareness and reporting training may dramatically lower the chance that an assault will be successful.

There is always room for improvement when it comes to cybersecurity countermeasures. Organizations may detect security infrastructure gaps and mitigate possible threats by regularly conducting penetration tests and vulnerability assessments. By taking a proactive approach to cybersecurity, companies can make sure that they are actively bolstering their defenses in addition to being reactive to new threats.

5.6 BUILDING A CULTURE OF SECURITY AWARENESS

Although technology is essential for protecting digital assets, creating a security-aware culture inside a business is just as vital. Workers are often the first to defend a company from cyberattacks, and their knowledge of security procedures greatly strengthens the company's overall resilience. Creating and maintaining a security-aware culture calls for an all-encompassing strategy that incorporates communication, education, and a feeling of shared accountability.

A key component of fostering security awareness is education. Regular training on cybersecurity best practices, such as how to spot phishing efforts, make safe passwords, and manage sensitive data, should be provided to staff members. Real-world examples are used in interactive and captivating training sessions to emphasize the possible repercussions of security violations.

For security awareness to be reinforced, communication is essential. It is important for organizations to keep lines of communication open in order to exchange best practices, notify the public about emerging dangers, and update their cybersecurity policy. Employee participation in the organization's security initiatives is encouraged and a feeling of openness is fostered via regular communication.

Putting in place a strong security policy is essential to developing a culture that values security. All workers should be able to access clear, straightforward policies. They need to describe proper data management techniques, authorized technology usage, and how to report security problems. Policies should be reviewed and updated often to guarantee their continued applicability in the face of changing organizational structures and increasing cyber threats. Employee participation in security procedures gives them the ability to actively contribute to the organization's protection. Promoting a common sense of accountability fosters a group commitment to cybersecurity. Workers should be free to report security problems without fear of retaliation, encouraging teamwork among coworkers as they all contribute to keeping the workplace safe.

The significance of security awareness is increased when security-conscious conduct is acknowledged and rewarded. Employee appreciation initiatives, including praising those who see and report possible dangers, provide a positive feedback loop and inspire others to become involved in the organization's security initiatives.

The dedication of the leadership is essential to creating a security-aware culture. Managers and executives should set an example by actively engaging in training programs and exhibiting a commitment to cybersecurity concepts. When executives place a high priority on security, it communicates to staff members the organization's commitment to safeguarding its resources and information.

Programs for raising security awareness may be evaluated for efficacy and areas for development via regular surveys and evaluations. Employee feedback enables firms to customize their efforts to target particular issues or difficulties, guaranteeing that the security culture stays flexible and adaptable to the changing landscape of threats.

5.7 CHAPTER CONCLUSION

In conclusion, Chapter 5 has delved into the critical realm of cybersecurity and risk management, emphasizing their indispensable roles in safeguarding businesses against the ever-evolving threats present in the digital landscape. The fusion of cybersecurity and risk management has become essential for organizations striving to maintain operational efficiency while effectively mitigating cyber risks.

The chapter began by highlighting the fundamental principles of cybersecurity in business, emphasizing the importance of defense in depth, least privilege, continuous monitoring, incident response, and secure architecture design. By adopting these principles, organizations can establish robust defensive measures to protect their digital assets and sensitive information from cyber threats.

Moreover, the chapter discussed various risk management frameworks and strategies, with a focus on the National Institute of Standards and Technology (NIST) Cybersecurity Framework. By identifying threats, vulnerabilities, and assets, conducting risk assessments, and implementing risk mitigation techniques, organizations can systematically manage cybersecurity risks and enhance their overall security posture.

Cybersecurity policies and compliance were also emphasized as crucial components of effective cybersecurity practices. By developing comprehensive policies, addressing access control, data protection, incident response, and compliance with industry standards and regulations, organizations can establish clear guidelines and best practices to safeguard their digital infrastructure.

Furthermore, the chapter addressed emerging threats and countermeasures, underscoring the importance of staying ahead of new and evolving cyber threats. By implementing a multi-layered defensive strategy, leveraging threat intelligence, collaborating within the cybersecurity ecosystem, and fostering a culture of security awareness, organizations can effectively mitigate emerging threats and enhance their cyber resilience.

Lastly, the chapter emphasized the importance of building a culture of security awareness within organizations. Through education, communication, strong security policies, employee participation, leadership commitment, and continuous evaluation, organizations can cultivate a security-aware culture that empowers employees to actively contribute to cybersecurity efforts and mitigate risks effectively.

In essence, the chapter underscored the interconnected nature of cybersecurity and risk management, highlighting the need for organizations to adopt a holistic approach to cybersecurity to navigate the complex landscape of cyber threats and safeguard their digital assets in the digital age.

REFERENCES

Abbasi, S., & Rahmani, A. M. (2023). Artificial Intelligence and Software Modeling Approaches in Autonomous Vehicles for Safety Management: A Systematic Review. *Information (Basel)*, *14*(10), 555. Advance online publication. DOI: 10.3390/info14100555

Abu Othman, N. A., Norman, A. A., & Mat Kiah, M. L. (2021). Information System Audit for Mobile Device Security Assessment. In *2021 3rd International Cyber Resilience Conference, CRC 2021* (Issue 3rd International Cyber Resilience Conference (CRC), pp. 50–55). DOI: 10.1109/CRC50527.2021.9392468

AL-Dosari, K., & Fetais, N. (2023). Risk-Management Framework and Information-Security Systems for Small and Medium Enterprises (SMEs): A Meta-Analysis Approach. [WE - Science Citation Index Expanded] [SCI-EXPANDED]. *Electronics (Basel)*, *12*(17), 3629. Advance online publication. DOI: 10.3390/electronics12173629

Almufarreh, A., & Arshad, M. (2023). Promising Emerging Technologies for Teaching and Learning: Recent Developments and Future Challenges. *Sustainability (Basel)*, *15*(8), 6917. Advance online publication. DOI: 10.3390/su15086917

Annarelli, A., & Palombi, G. (2021). Digitalization Capabilities for Sustainable Cyber Resilience: A Conceptual Framework. [WE - Science Citation Index Expanded] [SCI-EXPANDED] [WE - Social Science Citation Index] [SSCI]. *Sustainability (Basel)*, *13*(23), 13065. Advance online publication. DOI: 10.3390/su132313065

Asif, R., Hassan, S. R., & Parr, G. (2023). Integrating a Blockchain-Based Governance Framework for Responsible AI. [WE - Emerging Sources Citation Index] [ESCI]. *Future Internet*, *15*(3), 97. Advance online publication. DOI: 10.3390/fi15030097

Bathla, G., Bhadane, K., Singh, R. K., Kumar, R., Aluvalu, R., Krishnamurthi, R., Kumar, A., Thakur, R. N., & Basheer, S. (2022). Autonomous Vehicles and Intelligent Automation: Applications, Challenges, and Opportunities. [WE - Science Citation Index Expanded] [SCI-EXPANDED]. *Mobile Information Systems*, *2022*, 1–36. Advance online publication. DOI: 10.1155/2022/7632892

Berbecaru, D. G., & Lioy, A. (2022). Attack Strategies and Countermeasures in Transport-Based Time Synchronization Solutions. In D. Camacho, D. Rosaci, G. M. L. Sarne, & M. Versaci (Eds.), *Studies in Computational Intelligence* (Vol. 1026, Issue 14th International Symposium on Intelligent Distributed Computing (IDC), pp. 203–213). DOI: 10.1007/978-3-030-96627-0_19

Bhatia, S., & Alojail, M. (2022). A Novel Approach for Deciphering Big Data Value Using Dark Data. [WE - Science Citation Index Expanded] [SCI-EXPANDED]. *Intelligent Automation & Soft Computing, 33*(2), 1261–1271. DOI: 10.32604/iasc.2022.023501

Bhatt, S., & Sandhu, R. (2020). Convergent Access Control to Enable Secure Smart Communities. In *Proceedings - 2020 2nd IEEE International Conference on Trust, Privacy and Security in Intelligent Systems and Applications, TPS-ISA 2020* (Issues 2nd IEEE International Conference on Trust, Privacy and Security in Intelligent Systems and Applications (TPS-ISA), pp. 148–156). DOI: 10.1109/TPS-ISA50397.2020.00029

Bistron, M., & Piotrowski, Z. (2021). Artificial Intelligence Applications in Military Systems and Their Influence on Sense of Security of Citizens. *Electronics (Basel), 10*(7), 871. DOI: 10.3390/electronics10070871

Bracarense, N., Bawack, R. E., Wamba, S. F., & Carillo, K. D. A. (2022). Artificial Intelligence and Sustainability: A Bibliometric Analysis and Future Research Directions. [WE - Emerging Sources Citation Index] [ESCI]. *PACIFIC ASIA JOURNAL OF THE ASSOCIATION FOR INFORMATION SYSTEMS, 14*(2), 136–159. DOI: 10.17705/1pais.14209

Buzdar, A. Q., & Farooq, M. (2020). Memorization of Quran through Mobile Application in the Era of Transformative Marketing. [PJSS]. *Pakistan Journal of Social Sciences, 40*(2), 689–698.

Chehri, A., & Zimmermann, A. (2021). 5G Assisted Smart Manufacturing and Industrial Automation. In C. Leitner, W. Ganz, D. Satterfield, & C. Bassano (Eds.), *ADVANCES IN THE HUMAN SIDE OF SERVICE ENGINEERING (AHFE 2021)* (Vol. 266, Issue 12th International Conference on Applied Human Factors and Ergonomics (AHFE) / AHFE Virtual Conference on The Human Side of Service Engineering, pp. 385–393). WE - Conference Proceedings Citation Index - Science (CPCI-S)DOI: 10.1007/978-3-030-80840-2_44

Conger, S. (2020). The Impact of the COVID-19 Pandemic on Information Systems Management. *Information Systems Management, 37*(4), 327–331. DOI: 10.1080/10580530.2020.1820636

Farooq, M., Bakhsh, A., Hafsa Qadir, B., & Warda, N. (2023). Digital Empowerment: Freedom of Expression Beyond 5G and 6G Networks in Developing Countries. *Pakistan Journal of Social Sciences, 43*(4), 569–584. DOI: 10.5281/zenodo.10448484

Farooq, M., Buzdar, H. Q., Yen, Y. Y., & Bakhsh, A. (2024). Integrating AI in Sustainable Writing: An Empirical Investigation of the Technology Acceptance Model in Asian Social Sciences. *Journal of Logistics. Informatics and Service Science*, *11*(3), 324–338. DOI: 10.33168/JLISS.2024.0321

Farooq, M., Cheng, J., Khan, N. U., Saufi, R. A., Kanwal, N., & Bazkiaei, H. A. (2022a). Sustainable Waste Management Companies with Innovative Smart Solutions: A Systematic Review and Conceptual Model. *Sustainability (Basel)*, *14*(20), 13146. Advance online publication. DOI: 10.3390/su142013146

Farooq, M., Cheng, J., Khan, N. U., Saufi, R. A., Kanwal, N., & Bazkiaei, H. A. (2022b). Sustainable Waste Management Companies with Innovative Smart Solutions: A Systematic Review and Conceptual Model. *Sustainability (Basel)*, *14*(20), 13146. DOI: 10.3390/su142013146

Farooq, M., Hafsa Qadir, B., & Saeed, M. (2023, December). AI-Enhanced Social Sciences: A Systematic Literature Review and Bibliographic Analysis of Web of Science Published Research Papers. *Pakistan Journal of Society* [PJSEL]. *Education and Language*, *10*, 1–2.

Farooq, M., Khalil-Ur-Rehman, F., Abdurrahaman, D. T., Younas, W., Sajjad, S., & Zreen, A. (2019). SERVICE QUALITY ANALYSIS OF PRIVATE UNIVERSITIES LIBRARIES IN MALAYSIA IN THE ERA OF TRANSFORMATIVE MARKETING. *International Journal of Qualitative Research*, *13*(2), 269–284. DOI: 10.24874/IJQR13.02-02

Farooq, M., Muhammad, S., Raju, V., Kalimuthu, K. R., & Qadir, A. (2019). Measuring and Comparing the Desired and Actual Service Quality of Pakistan International Airline. *The Journal of Social Sciences Research*, *52*(52), 484–490. DOI: 10.32861/jssr.52.484.490

Farooq, M., & Qureshi, Q. A. (2020). Practical Approach of Environmental Awareness to Broadening Community Participation: A Case Study of Pindad (Persero). *Journal of Management Practices. Humanities and Social Sciences*, *4*(1). Advance online publication. DOI: 10.33152/jmphss-4.2.1

Farooq, M., & Raju, V. (2019a). Impact of Over-the-Top (OTT) Services on the Telecom Companies in the Era of Transformative Marketing. *Global Journal of Flexible Systems Managment*, *20*(2), 177–188. DOI: 10.1007/s40171-019-00209-6

Farooq, M., & Raju, V. (2019b). Want to Stay the Market Leader in the Era of Transformative Marketing? Keep the Customers Satisfied! *Global Journal of Flexible Systems Management*. DOI: 10.1007/s40171-019-00213-w

Farooq, M., & Raju, V. (2019c). Impact of Over-the-Top (OTT) Services on the Telecom Companies in the Era of Transformative Marketing. *Global Journal of Flexible Systems Managment, 20*(2), 177–188. DOI: 10.1007/s40171-019-00209-6

Farooq, M., & Raju, V. (2019d). Want to Stay the Market Leader in the Era of Transformative Marketing? Keep the Customers Satisfied! *Global Journal of Flexible Systems Managment, 20*(3), 257–266. DOI: 10.1007/s40171-019-00213-w

Farooq, M., & Ramzan, M. Y. Y. Y. (2025). AI in Management. In *Transformative Impacts of AI in Management* (1st ed., pp. 1–44). IGI Global. DOI: 10.4018/979-8-3693-4322-7.ch001

Farooq, M., Ramzan, M., & Yen, Y. Y. (2025a). AI in Consumer Behavior Management. In *Transformative Impacts of AI in Management* (pp. 281–294). IGI Global., DOI: 10.4018/979-8-3693-4322-7.ch011

Farooq, M., Ramzan, M., & Yen, Y. Y. (2025b). AI in Customer Service, HR, and Administration. In *Transformative Impacts of AI in Management* (pp. 45–70). IGI Global. DOI: 10.4018/979-8-3693-4322-7.ch002

Farooq, M., Ramzan, M., & Yen, Y. Y. (2025c). AI in Quality Management. In *Transformative Impacts of AI in Management* (pp. 295–312). IGI Global., DOI: 10.4018/979-8-3693-4322-7.ch012

Farooq, M., Ramzan, M., & Yen, Y. Y. (2025d). Artificial Intelligence and Customer Experiences. In *Transformative Impacts of AI in Management* (pp. 95–114). IGI Global., DOI: 10.4018/979-8-3693-4322-7.ch004

Farooq, M., Ramzan, M., & Yen, Y. Y. (2025e). Artificial Intelligence in Administration Sciences. In *Transformative Impacts of AI in Management* (pp. 115–156). IGI Global., DOI: 10.4018/979-8-3693-4322-7.ch005

Farooq, M., Ramzan, M., & Yen, Y. Y. (2025f). Artificial Intelligence in Business and Law. In *Transformative Impacts of AI in Management* (pp. 71–94). IGI Global., DOI: 10.4018/979-8-3693-4322-7.ch003

Farooq, M., Ramzan, M., & Yen, Y. Y. (2025g). Artificial Intelligence in Ethical Business Decision Making. In *Transformative Impacts of AI in Management* (pp. 265–280). IGI Global., DOI: 10.4018/979-8-3693-4322-7.ch010

Farooq, M., Ramzan, M., & Yen, Y. Y. (2025h). Exploring the Impact of Artificial Intelligence on Brand Management. In *Transformative Impacts of AI in Management* (pp. 157–188). IGI Global., DOI: 10.4018/979-8-3693-4322-7.ch006

Farooq, M., Ramzan, M., & Yen, Y. Y. (2025i). Exploring the Impact of Ethical Leadership and Employee Engagement on Knowledge Sharing Attitudes in the Asian Digital Economy. In *Transformative Impacts of AI in Management* (pp. 241–264). IGI Global., DOI: 10.4018/979-8-3693-4322-7.ch009

Farooq, M., Ramzan, M., & Yen, Y. Y. (2025j). Transformative Impact of AI in Education Management. In *Transformative Impacts of AI in Management* (pp. 189–216). IGI Global., DOI: 10.4018/979-8-3693-4322-7.ch007

Farooq, M., Ramzan, M., & Yen, Y. Y. (2025k). *Transformative Impacts of AI in Management*. IGI Global., DOI: 10.4018/979-8-3693-4322-7

Farooq, M., Rehman, F. K. U., Younas, W., Raju, V., Ahmed, Q. M., & Ali, M. (2019). Investigating Relationship between Net Promoter Score and Company Performance: A Longitudinal Study. *Global Journal of Emerging Sciences*, *1*(1), 1–10. https://www.gjoes.org/wp-content/uploads/2019/04/1-1.pdf

Farooq, M., Saeed, M., Ali, W., & Javid, R. (2020). Online Buying and Customer Satisfaction in the Era of Transformative Marketing. *City University Research Journal*, *10*(2), 274–288.

Farooq, M., Yuen, Y. Y., & Buzdar, H. Q. (2024). Exploring the Research Landscape of Artificial Intelligence Integration with Business Management: A Bibliometric Analysis from 1994-2023. *Journal of Logistics. Informatics and Service Science*, (April). Advance online publication. DOI: 10.33168/JLISS.2024.0410

Gaglo, K., Degboe, B. M., Kossingou, G. M., & Ouya, S. (2022). Proposal of conversational chatbots for educational remediation in the context of covid-19. In *International Conference on Advanced Communication Technology, ICACT* (Vols. 2022-Febru, Issues 24th International Conference on Advanced Communication Technology (ICACT)-Artificial Intelligence Technologies toward Cybersecurity, pp. 354–358). DOI: 10.23919/ICACT53585.2022.9728860

Ghobakhloo, M., & Iranmanesh, M. (2021). Digital transformation success under Industry 4.0: A strategic guideline for manufacturing SMEs. [WE - Science Citation Index Expanded] [SCI-EXPANDED] [WE - Social Science Citation Index] [SSCI]. *Journal of Manufacturing Technology Management*, *32*(8), 1533–1556. DOI: 10.1108/JMTM-11-2020-0455

Ghulam, W. A., Ali, W., Ali, S., Khan, M. M., Khan, R. N., & Farooq, M. (2019). Investigating factors influencing brain drain of citizens of Azad Kashmir Pakistan. *Journal of Social Sciences Research*, *5*(3), 782–788. Advance online publication. DOI: 10.32861/jssr.53.782.788

Jaloliddin, R. (2023). Digitalization in Global Trade: Opportunities and Challenges for Investment. *GLOBAL TRADE AND CUSTOMS JOURNAL, 18*(10), 391-395 WE-Emerging Sources Citation Index (ESC. Khan, L. U., Yaqoob, I., Imran, M., Han, Z., & Hong, C. S. (2020). 6G Wireless Systems: A Vision, Architectural Elements, and Future Directions. *IEEE Access : Practical Innovations, Open Solutions, 8*, 147029–147044. DOI: 10.1109/ACCESS.2020.3015289

Kharchenko, V., Illiashenko, O., Morozova, O., Sokolov, S., & IEEE. (2020). Combination of Digital Twin and Artificial Intelligence in Manufacturing Using Industrial IoT. In *2020 IEEE 11TH INTERNATIONAL CONFERENCE ON DEPENDABLE SYSTEMS, SERVICES AND TECHNOLOGIES (DESSERT): IOT, BIG DATA AND AI FOR A SAFE & SECURE WORLD AND INDUSTRY 4.0* (Issue IEEE 11th International Conference on Dependable Systems, Services and Technologies (DESSERT)-IoT, Big Data and AI for a Safe & Secure World and Industry 4.0, pp. 196–201). WE - Conference Proceedings Citation Index - Science (CPCI-S)DOI: 10.1109/DESSERT50317.2020.9125038

Kioskli, K., Papastergiou, S., & IEEE. (2023). A Swarm Artificial Intelligence Approach for Effective Treatment of Chronic Conditions. In *2023 19TH INTERNATIONAL CONFERENCE ON THE DESIGN OF RELIABLE COMMUNICATION NETWORKS, DRCN* (Issue 19th International Conference on the Design of Reliable Communication Networks (DRCN)). WE - Conference Proceedings Citation Index - Science (CPCI-S)DOI: 10.1109/DRCN57075.2023.10108128

Lee, G. (2019). What roles should the government play in fostering the advancement of the internet of things? *Telecommunications Policy*, *43*(5), 434–444. Advance online publication. DOI: 10.1016/j.telpol.2018.12.002

Lee, J. K., Cho, D., & Lim, G. G. (2018). Design and validation of the bright internet. *Journal of the Association for Information Systems*, *19*(2), 63–85. DOI: 10.17705/jais1.00484

Lu, Y., & Ning, X. (2020). A vision of 6G–5G's successor. *Journal of Management Analytics*, *7*(3), 301–320. DOI: 10.1080/23270012.2020.1802622

Méndez-Suárez, M., de Obesso, M. D., Márquez, O. C., & Palacios, C. M. (2023). Why Do Companies Employ Prohibited Unethical Artificial Intelligence Practices? *IEEE Transactions on Engineering Management*. Advance online publication. DOI: 10.1109/TEM.2023.3258686

Mhlanga, D. (2020). Industry 4.0 in Finance: The Impact of Artificial Intelligence (AI) on Digital Financial Inclusion. [WE - Emerging Sources Citation Index] [ESCI]. *INTERNATIONAL JOURNAL OF FINANCIAL STUDIES, 8*(3), 45. Advance online publication. DOI: 10.3390/ijfs8030045

Miller, S. W., & Brugan, J. M. (2021). Technological trends: A focus on citizen security. [WE - Emerging Sources Citation Index] [ESCI]. *Ingeniería Solidaria, 17*(1), 1–28. DOI: 10.16925/2357-6014.2021.01.02

Mugari, I., Kunambura, M., Obioha, E. E., & Gopo, N. R. (2023). *Trends, impacts and responses to cybercrime in the Zimbabwean retail sector.* SAFER COMMUNITIES., DOI: 10.1108/SC-03-2023-0011

Ogbuke, N., Yusuf, Y. Y., Gunasekaran, A., Colton, N., & Kovvuri, D. (2023). Data-driven technologies for global healthcare practices and COVID-19: Opportunities and challenges. *Annals of Operations Research.* Advance online publication. DOI: 10.1007/s10479-023-05462-8

Pham, M., & Xiong, K. (2021). A survey on security attacks and defense techniques for connected and autonomous vehicles. *Computers & Security, 109*, 102269. Advance online publication. DOI: 10.1016/j.cose.2021.102269

Popescu, T. M., Popescu, A. M., & Prostean, G. (2021). Leaders' perspectives on iot security risk management strategies in surveyed organizations relative to iotsrm2. *Applied Sciences (Basel, Switzerland), 11*(19), 9206. Advance online publication. DOI: 10.3390/app11199206

Trescakova, D. (2020). DIGITAL TRANSFORMATION OF BUSINESS ENTITIES UNDER THE CURRENT CONDITIONS REALITY OR UTOPIA? In D. Duic, T. Petrasevic, & A. Novokmet (Eds.), *EU 2020 - LESSONS FROM THE PAST AND SOLUTIONS FOR THE FUTURE* (Vol. 4, Issue International Scientific Conference on Lessons from the Past and Solutions for the Future (EU), pp. 798-814 WE-Conference Proceedings Citation Inde).

Wang, Y., Lin, J., Osman, Z., Farooq, M., & Raju, V. (2021). Transformational leadership and employee performance in international commercial banking industry in Malaysia: The role of self-efficacy as a mediator under BRI. *Journal of Chinese Human Resource Management, 12*(2), 25–36. DOI: 10.47297/wspchrmWSP2040-800503.20211202

Wiemer, H., Schneider, D., Lang, V., Conrad, F., Mälzer, M., Boos, E., Feldhoff, K., Drowatzky, L., & Ihlenfeldt, S. (2023). Need for UAI–Anatomy of the Paradigm of Usable Artificial Intelligence for Domain-Specific AI Applicability. *Multimodal Technologies and Interaction*, *7*(3), 27. Advance online publication. DOI: 10.3390/mti7030027

Yen, Y. Y., Wen, L. J., Ramasamy, S., & Farooq, M. (2023). Sustainable petrol subsidy program in Malaysia. *Asian Development Policy Review*, *12*(1), 1–9. DOI: 10.55493/5008.v12i1.4948

Chapter 6
Transformative Impacts of AI in Enterprise Resource Planning (ERP) Systems

ABSTRACT

ERP (enterprise resource planning) solutions are the foundation of contemporary organizational effectiveness, combining many corporate operations into a streamlined and unified framework with ease (Dziembek, 2021; Tao et al., 2021). These all-inclusive software programs transform the way businesses handle their resources by providing a unified method for handling vital operations like finance, HR, supply chain, and CRM (Bhatia & Alojail, 2022). A complex infrastructure that enables real-time data interchange across departments is at the core of ERP systems. Because of this interconnection, stakeholders have a more comprehensive understanding of the organization's activities, which improves cooperation and decision-making. ERP solutions promote data accuracy and lower mistake risk by replacing disjointed historical systems with a single database (Mulyani et al., 2017; Shao et al., 2017). They provide companies the ability to quickly adjust to changing market conditions, promoting competitiveness and agility (Zhang et al., 2023).

6.1 CHAPTER INTRODUCTION

ERP systems guarantee data consistency and integrity while meeting the specialized requirements of various departments via modules designed for certain tasks. Workflows are optimized by this integration, reducing duplication and increasing output (Abusalim, 2023; Dong & IEEE, 2021; Vihari & Yadav, 2021). ERP solu-

DOI: 10.4018/979-8-3373-0513-4.ch006

tions assist businesses in navigating the intricacies of today's business environment, stimulating growth and operational excellence, by automating repetitive operations and allowing data-driven insights. ERP systems are essentially the cornerstone of organizational coherence, providing a strong basis for long-term success in the dynamic world of business (Wen et al., 2023).

Figure 1. Enterprise Resource Planning (ERP) systems

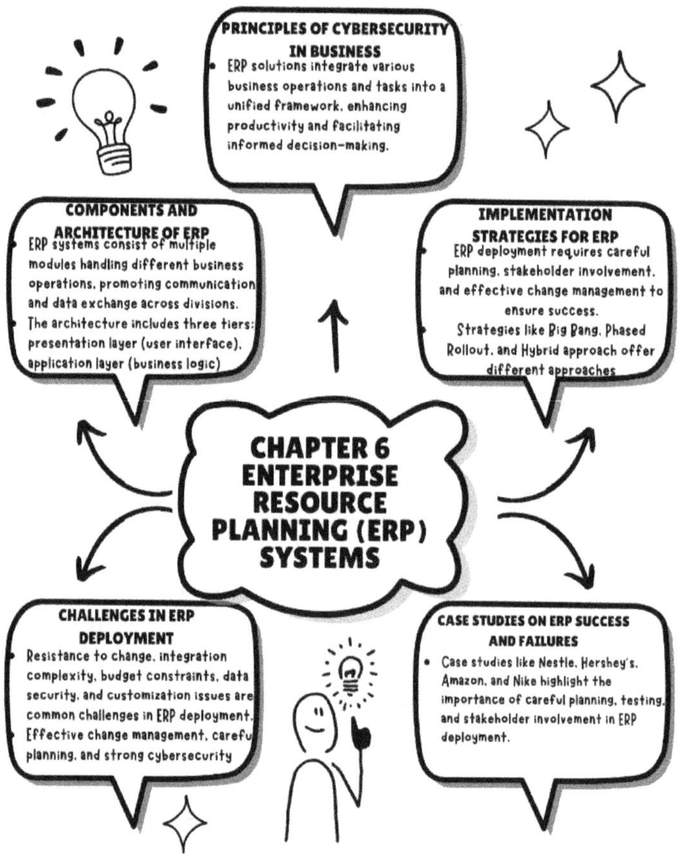

6.2 OVERVIEW OF ERP SYSTEMS

ERP systems are all-inclusive software programs created to make it easier for different business operations and tasks to be integrated across a company (Khan et al., 2023). Enhancing productivity, making the most use of available resources, and offering Realtime insights to support well-informed decision-making are the main objectives. These solutions promote unity and cooperation across many divisions within an organization, marking a change from conventional siloed methods to data administration(Vihari & Yadav, 2021).

ERP systems include a broad range of company functions, including supply chain management, customer relationship management, finance, and human resources, among others(Aasi et al., 2022). ERP systems facilitate smooth data transfer and departmental collaboration by combining various tasks into a single platform. By encouraging a comprehensive understanding of their processes, this integrated approach enables businesses to function more cogently (Dong & IEEE, 2021).

ERP systems' modular nature is one of its key characteristics; it enables businesses to choose certain modules that are customized to meet their individual requirements. This adaptability guarantees that companies may put ERP systems into place that meet the unique demands of their industry and operational quirks(El Hairech & Lyhyaoui, 2022; Zhao & Tu, 2021). ERP systems are hence flexible frameworks that meet a range of organizational needs rather than being one-size-fits-all solutions (Dziembek, 2021).

All organizational data is stored in a centralized database, which is a common feature of ERP system architectures. The ERP system relies heavily on this database to keep data current and easily available across the whole company. A user interface is another feature of the design that enables users at different levels to engage with the system and get pertinent information according to their roles and responsibilities(Camarrone & Van Hulle, 2019; Li & Wu, 2021; Lin, 2019).

A crucial component of ERP design is integration, which effectively connects various departments and modules. Achieving the appropriate degree of synergy and preventing data contradictions depend on this integration. In order to ensure seamless information flow across the whole organizational landscape, ERP systems often use technologies like Application Programming Interfaces (APIs) to allow compatibility with other software programs and external systems (Abdymanapov et al., 2021).

To achieve a smooth transition, ERP system deployment requires a planned and staged strategy. Companies need to carefully plan the deployment, taking into account elements like the extent of the implementation, the need for customization, and the degree to which staff members are prepared to adjust to the new system. Stages including system selection, setup, data transfer, testing, and training are often included in the installation process(Erpyleva, 2023; Mader et al., 2023; Onal et al., 2022).

ERP deployment techniques differ according to the size of the firm, the sector, and the particular needs. A Big Bang strategy is used by certain businesses, in which the complete system is built all at once. Some would rather build out the system gradually, adding new modules one at a time. Every strategy includes benefits and drawbacks, and the decision is based on things like how complicated the organization's procedures are and how much disruption you can handle while things are changing (Tao et al., 2021).

ERP adoption will always provide challenges, and in order to guarantee a seamless transition, enterprises must avoid common pitfalls. Employee aversion to change, problems with data transfer, integration difficulties, and the need for intensive training are typical obstacles(Astuty et al., 2022; Kuzdowicz, 2021). To overcome these obstacles and guarantee the ERP implementation's success, careful planning, clear communication, and a dedication to quickly resolving problems are necessary.

6.3 KEY COMPONENTS AND ARCHITECTURE OF ERP

Multiple linked modules that handle different business operations make up an ERP system. These classes cover a variety of topics, such as manufacturing, supply chain management, finance, human resources, and customer relationship management(Carlan & Vanelslander, 2021; El-Kefraoui et al., 2023). Every module focuses on a certain facet of the company, facilitating smooth communication and exchange of data across various divisions. Eliminating data silos and fostering an integrated perspective of the whole company process depend on this integration(Song & Hu, 2023).

Three tiers make up the display, application, and data tiers of an ERP system's architecture. The user interface that facilitates user interaction with the system is known as the presentation layer. This offers a user-friendly experience for staff members at all levels and may be a desktop program or web-based interface(Farooq, Khalil-Ur-Rehman, et al., 2019; Farooq et al., 2022b). Process automation and business logic are stored at the application layer. It guarantees seamless data transfer between various components and promotes instantaneous communication(Farooq, Hafsa Qadir, et al., 2023; Yen et al., 2023). The massive volumes of data produced by the system must be stored and managed by the data layer, on the other hand. A centralized database that underpins the whole ERP system is often the foundation of this layer(Guo et al., 2022).

The deployment types of ERP systems may be categorized as on-premise, cloud-based, or hybrid. With on-premise ERP systems, the program is installed and managed inside on the organization's servers(Farooq et al., 2022a; Farooq, Kalimuthu, et al., 2019; Farooq, Rehman, et al., 2019). However, cloud-based ERP is dependent on distant servers that are housed by a different company. More accessibility, scalability, and flexibility are provided by this architecture, especially for companies with varied and scattered activities(Farooq, 2019; Farooq, Ali, et al., 2019; Naseer et al., 2019). By combining aspects of onpremise and cloud-based models, hybrid ERP systems enable businesses to take advantage of both strategies' advantages.

ERP architecture must prioritize interoperability. A seamless information flow depends on the ERP system's capacity to interface with other systems and already installed software applications(Farooq et al., 2025i, 2025f, 2025j). This guarantees that information from several sources including third-party apps and legacy systems—can be integrated into the ERP system, offering a thorough and precise picture of the business's activities.

Another essential element of ERP systems is customization. Businesses often have distinctive business procedures that call for customized solutions. ERP solutions need to permit customization without sacrificing the integrity of the system or its capacity to accept upgrades(Farooq, Buzdar, et al., 2024; Farooq et al., 2025d). By doing this, the organization's overall efficiency and effectiveness are increased since the ERP system is guaranteed to be in line with its unique demands and processes (Farooq et al., 2025b, 2025a; Muhammad Farooq, Muhammad Ramzan, 2025).

6.4 IMPLEMENTATION STRATEGIES FOR ERP

An enterprise resource planning (ERP) system's deployment is a complicated and diverse process that calls for careful planning, strategic thinking, and a thorough grasp of organizational demands. Implementing ERP successfully is dependent on a number of variables, such as the selected approach, stakeholder participation, and efficient change management (Krupitzer & Stein, 2021).

The "Big Bang" method of ERP installation is one such tactic. Using this approach, the ERP system is deployed across the whole company at once(Farooq et al., 2025g, 2025k, 2025c). This method is distinguished by a quick switchover from the old ERP system to the new one, but at the expense of a large initial investment and thorough staff training. Because the Big Bang technique is implemented simultaneously across all departments, it has more risks even while it provides fast integration and removes the need to maintain parallel systems.

The ERP system is gradually implemented department by department or module by module under the "Phased Rollout" plan. By using this method, companies may lower the total risk of implementation by testing and optimizing each module before going on to the next. Because of its gradual approach and ability to let firms fix problems as they come up, phased rollout is often preferred(Farooq et al., 2020, 2025h, 2025e). It also facilitates an easier transition for workers. But it may lead to extended periods of cohabitation with older systems, which might cause problems with integration (M. Wang et al., 2021).

A hybrid strategy incorporates aspects of the Phased Rollout and Big Bang approaches. With this technique, enterprises may deploy certain modules or features all at once, while implementing others gradually. Because of the flexibility this technique offers, firms may decide which features are most important to execute right once and manage the risks involved in rolling out less important features gradually.

Involving stakeholders is essential to the success of ERP deployment. Key stakeholders, such as department heads, end users, and executives, must be included at every stage of the process. Their involvement aids in the definition of needs, guarantees alignment with corporate objectives, and cultivates an employee feeling of ownership (Farooq, Bakhsh, et al., 2023; Farooq & Raju, 2019d; Ghulam et al., 2019). To reduce opposition and ensure a seamless adoption of the new ERP system, it is essential to implement change management efforts and provide enough training to staff prior to the changeover.

Another crucial component of implementing ERP is data transfer. Businesses need to make sure that data is accurately transferred from old ERP systems to the new ones (Buzdar & Farooq, 2020; Farooq, Muhammad, et al., 2019; Farooq & Raju, 2019a). To preserve correctness and integrity, this procedure entails converting, verifying, and cleaning the data. To avoid interruptions and data inconsistencies throughout the transfer, a strong data migration strategy that incorporates backup plans and contingency measures is essential.

Throughout the deployment phase, regular monitoring and communication are essential. Having open lines of communication makes it easier to handle problems, manage expectations, and update all parties on developments. By enabling firms to quickly detect and resolve problems, continuous monitoring guarantees that the ERP system is in line with changing business requirements.

6.5 CHALLENGES IN ERP DEPLOYMENT

The organization's aversion to change is a significant obstacle to the implementation of ERP. A major change in current workflows and procedures is often necessary when implementing an ERP system. Workers may be reluctant to accept new technology because they worry about having their daily routines disrupted and even losing their jobs. Organizations need to make investments in thorough change management plans to solve this. Effective communication, training initiatives, and cultivating an environment that values innovation and ongoing development are a few of them. Another big obstacle to ERP implementation is integration complexity(Farooq, Yuen, et al., 2024; Farooq & Raju, 2019b, 2019c). A lot of businesses use a disorganized collection of outdated systems that could not perform well with the brand-new ERP program. Errors, data discrepancies, and information flow delays may result from this. Organizations may manage these difficulties by using middleware to bridge gaps, data migration techniques, and thorough system integration design. Implementing changes gradually and tackling integration issues one step at a time might also be helpful(Vogt & Hollenstein, 2021).

Budgetary restrictions and cost overruns are two more frequent issues that arise with ERP implementation. It is possible for organizations to underestimate the total cost of ownership, which includes ongoing maintenance costs, hardware, software licensing, and consultancy fees(Farooq & Qureshi, 2020; Y. Wang et al., 2021). Organizations should create realistic budgets, carry out thorough financial evaluations, and closely consider the total cost of ownership throughout the course of the system's lifespan in order to control expenses efficiently. Additionally, firms may adjust to changing demands without incurring prohibitive expenditures by choosing an ERP system that is adaptable and expandable.

In today's digital world, privacy and data security are crucial issues. Since ERP systems often concentrate sensitive company information, cybercriminals find them to be appealing targets. For the protection of their ERP systems and the data they manage, organizations need strong cybersecurity measures like encryption, access limits, and frequent security assessments. It's also essential to follow data privacy laws to stay out of trouble with the law and keep customers' confidence.

Organizations trying to modify ERP systems to match certain business processes may run into customization issues. Customization might improve the fit of the system, it can also result in more complexity, longer implementation times, and challenges during system updates. Achieving the ideal balance between personalization and uniformity is crucial. Businesses should carefully assess the special needs that they have and give top priority to setups that follow industry best practices.

One major cause of ERP adoption difficulty is vendor-related concerns. Companies may run into problems choosing a vendor, negotiating a contract, and providing postimplementation assistance. To lessen these difficulties, careful consideration of all relevant factors throughout the vendor selection process, unambiguous contractual terms, and continuous contact with the vendor are crucial. Building a solid working relationship with the ERP provider will help ensure a more seamless adoption process and effective problem-solving when difficulties emerge.

6.6 CASE STUDIES ON ERP SUCCESS AND FAILURES

Within the corporate environment, there have been success stories and cautionary tales around the deployment of Enterprise Resource Planning (ERP) systems. Analyzing case studies yields important information about the elements that make ERP successful as well as the traps that might cause failures. One excellent example of an enterprise-wide change that has been effective is Nestle's deployment of ERP. Nestle chose an ERP system to improve visibility and simplify operations after encountering difficulties with heterogeneous systems across its international operations. The business used a step-by-step strategy, implementing its plan in a particular area as a prototype before going worldwide. Nestle gave change management a priority, made significant training program investments, and actively included staff members in the shift (Akbari & Hopkins, 2022). Improved productivity, instant access to data, and a large drop in operating expenses were the outcome, demonstrating the benefits of a well-managed ERP deployment.

The deployment of Hershey's ERP serves as a lesson in how hasty deployment and poor planning may have disastrous results. Just before the critical Halloween season, Hershey's introduced an ERP system in an effort to modernize its distribution and supply chain operations. The hasty installation caused major revenue loss, supply delays, and operational interruptions. The failure was ascribed to poor staff training, a deficiency in backup plans, and inadequate testing. The Hershey's ERP debacle highlights how crucial careful design, testing, and timing of installation are to prevent dire outcomes (Mithas et al., 2022).

The effective ERP deployment that Amazon had in place was essential to the company's capacity to grow quickly and effectively oversee its enormous operations. Overcoming obstacles Amazon put in place a strong ERP system in order to handle its increasing worldwide reach and growing product selection. In order to minimize disruption, the firm used a modular strategy and integrated ERP component progressively. Strong emphasis on scalability, continual improvement, and using ERP data for strategic decision making have been linked to Amazon's success. For long-term success, the instance emphasizes how crucial it is to match ERP systems with organizational development goals(Abrokwah-Larbi & Awuku-Larbi, 2023).

The early 2000s ERP implementation misstep by Nike serves as a lesson on the difficulties of integrating technology with business procedures. In an effort to increase efficiency, the firm made a significant investment in an ERP system for supply chain management. Unfortunately, the deployment resulted in longer lead times, a significant drop in income, and interruptions in order fulfillment. Inadequate testing, a lack of system integration, and a disregard for end-user demands were cited as the reasons for Nike's failure. This scenario highlights that in order to minimize ERP deployment difficulties, careful planning, testing, and verification of alignment with current processes are essential.

6.7 CHAPTER CONCLUSION

In conclusion, Chapter 6 has provided a comprehensive overview of Enterprise Resource Planning (ERP) systems, emphasizing their crucial role in enhancing organizational effectiveness and streamlining business operations. ERP solutions serve as the backbone of modern organizational management by integrating various functions such as finance, HR, supply chain, and CRM into a unified platform, thereby promoting data accuracy, collaboration, and informed decision-making.

The chapter began by outlining the fundamental principles and objectives of ERP systems, highlighting their ability to facilitate real-time data exchange, improve workflow efficiency, and adapt to changing market conditions. ERP systems offer modular flexibility, allowing organizations to customize their solutions to meet specific business requirements while maintaining data consistency and integrity through centralized databases.

Moreover, the chapter discussed the key components and architecture of ERP systems, including the presentation, application, and data tiers, as well as deployment options such as on-premise, cloud-based, and hybrid models. Interoperability and customization were emphasized as essential features of ERP architecture, enabling seamless integration with other systems and tailored solutions to meet organizational needs.

Implementation strategies for ERP systems were also examined, including the "Big Bang," phased rollout, and hybrid approaches, each with its own benefits and challenges. Stakeholder involvement, change management, and data migration were identified as critical factors for successful ERP deployment, along with continuous monitoring and communication to address issues and adapt to changing requirements.

Furthermore, the chapter highlighted common challenges in ERP deployment, such as resistance to change, integration complexity, budgetary constraints, data security concerns, customization issues, and vendor-related issues. Case studies of ERP success stories and failures, including Nestle, Hershey's, Amazon, and Nike, provided valuable insights into the factors that contribute to successful ERP implementation and the pitfalls to avoid.

In essence, Chapter 6 underscored the importance of careful planning, strategic decision-making, stakeholder engagement, and effective change management in ensuring the success of ERP systems. By understanding the principles, components, challenges, and best practices associated with ERP deployment, organizations can leverage these powerful tools to enhance operational efficiency, drive growth, and achieve long-term success in today's competitive business landscape.

REFERENCES

Aasi, P., Gråhns, E., Geijer, R., & Rusu, L. (2022). Organizational Aspects in Achieving a Successful Digital Transformation: Case of an ERP System Change. In M. Themistocleous & M. Papadaki (Eds.), *Lecture Notes in Business Information Processing: Vol. 437 LNBIP* (Issues 18th European, Mediterranean, and Middle Eastern Conference on Information Systems (EMCIS), pp. 653–666). DOI: 10.1007/978-3-030-95947-0_46

Abdymanapov, S. A., Muratbekov, M., Altynbek, S., & Barlybayev, A. (2021). Fuzzy Expert System of Information Security Risk Assessment on the Example of Analysis Learning Management Systems. [WE - Science Citation Index Expanded] [SCI-EXPANDED]. *IEEE Access : Practical Innovations, Open Solutions, 9*, 156556–156565. DOI: 10.1109/ACCESS.2021.3129488

Abrokwah-Larbi, K., & Awuku-Larbi, Y. (2023). The impact of artificial intelligence in marketing on the performance of business organizations: evidence from SMEs in an emerging economy. *Journal of Entrepreneurship in Emerging Economies*. DOI: 10.1108/JEEE-07-2022-0207

Abusalim, A. (2023). Coloniality and social sciences research: ERPP realities and border thinking in the Arab world. *English for Specific Purposes, 70*, 210–223. DOI: 10.1016/j.esp.2023.01.002

Akbari, M., & Hopkins, J. L. (2022). Digital technologies as enablers of supply chain sustainability in an emerging economy. *Operations Management Research : Advancing Practice Through Research, 15*(3–4), 689–710. DOI: 10.1007/s12063-021-00226-8

Astuty, W., Pratama, I., Basir, I., & Harahap, J. P. R. (2022). DOES ENTERPRISE RESOURCE PLANNING LEAD TO THE QUALITY OF THE MANAGEMENT ACCOUNTING INFORMATION SYSTEM? [WE - Emerging Sources Citation Index] [ESCI]. *POLISH JOURNAL OF MANAGEMENT STUDIES, 25*(2), 93–107. DOI: 10.17512/pjms.2022.25.2.06

Bhatia, S., & Alojail, M. (2022). A Novel Approach for Deciphering Big Data Value Using Dark Data. [WE - Science Citation Index Expanded] [SCI-EXPANDED]. *Intelligent Automation & Soft Computing, 33*(2), 1261–1271. DOI: 10.32604/iasc.2022.023501

Buzdar, A. Q., & Farooq, M. (2020). Memorization of Quran through Mobile Application in the Era of Transformative Marketing. [PJSS]. *Pakistan Journal of Social Sciences, 40*(2), 689–698.

Camarrone, F., & Van Hulle, M. M. (2019). Measuring brand association strength with EEG: A single-trial N400 ERP study. *PLoS One*, *14*(6), e0217125. Advance online publication. DOI: 10.1371/journal.pone.0217125 PMID: 31181083

Carlan, V., & Vanelslander, T. (2021). Economic Aspects of Introducing Artificial Intelligence Solutions in Logistics and Port Sectors: The Data Entry Case. [WE - Emerging Sources Citation Index] [ESCI]. *FRONTIERS IN FUTURE TRANSPORTATION*, *2*, 710330. Advance online publication. DOI: 10.3389/ffutr.2021.710330

Dong, A. L., & IEEE. (2021). ERP and Artificial Intelligence based Smart Financial Information System Data Analysis Framework. In *PROCEEDINGS OF THE 6TH INTERNATIONAL CONFERENCE ON INVENTIVE COMPUTATION TECHNOLOGIES (ICICT 2021)* (Issue 6th International Conference on Inventive Computation Technologies (ICICT), pp. 845–848). WE - Conference Proceedings Citation Index - Science (CPCI-S)DOI: 10.1109/ICICT50816.2021.9358659

Dziembek, D. (2021). Integrated ERP-Class Management Information Systems - Evolution, Current State and Development Directions. [WE - Emerging Sources Citation Index] [ESCI]. *PROBLEMY ZARZADZANIA-MANAGEMENT ISSUES*, *19*(3), 187–210. DOI: 10.7172/1644-9584.93.10

El Hairech, O., & Lyhyaoui, A. (2022). The New Generation of ERP in the Era of Artificial Intelligence and Industry 4.0. In J. Kacprzyk, V. E. Balas, & M. Ezziyyani (Eds.), *ADVANCED INTELLIGENT SYSTEMS FOR SUSTAINABLE DEVELOPMENT (AI2SD'2020), VOL 1* (Vol. 1417, Issue 3rd International Conference on Advanced Intelligent Systems for Sustainable Development (AI2SD), pp. 1086–1094). WE - Conference Proceedings Citation Index - Science (CPCI-S) DOI: 10.1007/978-3-030-90633-7_96

El-Kefraoui, C., Do, U., Miller, A., Kouyoumdjian, A., Cui, D. V., Khorasani, E., Landry, T., Amar-Zifkin, A., Lee, L. W. C., Feldman, L. S., & Fiore, J. F.Jr. (2023). Impact of enhanced recovery pathways on patient-reported outcomes after abdominal surgery: A systematic review. *Surgical Endoscopy*, *37*(10), 8043–8056. Advance online publication. DOI: 10.1007/s00464-023-10289-2 PMID: 37474828

Erpyleva, S. (2023). Protest Event, Political Culture, and Biography: Post-protest Local Activism in Russia. *American Journal of Cultural Sociology*. Advance online publication. DOI: 10.1057/s41290-023-00194-5

Farooq, M. (2019). Emerging sciences in Social Sciences : An overview, A Research Agenda. *Global Journal of Emerging Sciences*, *1*(October), 183–197.

Farooq, M., Ali, W., Younas, W., Khalil-Ur-rehman, F., & Qurashi, Q. A. (2019). the Era of Transformative Marketing: Service Quality of Mobile App Based Taxi Services in Kuala Lumpur. *Proceedings on Engineering Sciences*, *1*(2), 49–58. DOI: 10.24874/PES01.02.006

Farooq, M., Bakhsh, A., Hafsa Qadir, B., & Warda, N. (2023). Digital Empowerment: Freedom of Expression Beyond 5G and 6G Networks in Developing Countries. *Pakistan Journal of Social Sciences*, *43*(4), 569–584. DOI: 10.5281/zenodo.10448484

Farooq, M., Buzdar, H. Q., Yen, Y. Y., & Bakhsh, A. (2024). Integrating AI in Sustainable Writing: An Empirical Investigation of the Technology Acceptance Model in Asian Social Sciences. *Journal of Logistics. Informatics and Service Science*, *11*(3), 324–338. DOI: 10.33168/JLISS.2024.0321

Farooq, M., Cheng, J., Khan, N. U., Saufi, R. A., Kanwal, N., & Bazkiaei, H. A. (2022a). Sustainable Waste Management Companies with Innovative Smart Solutions: A Systematic Review and Conceptual Model. *Sustainability (Basel)*, *14*(20), 13146. Advance online publication. DOI: 10.3390/su142013146

Farooq, M., Cheng, J., Khan, N. U., Saufi, R. A., Kanwal, N., & Bazkiaei, H. A. (2022b). Sustainable Waste Management Companies with Innovative Smart Solutions: A Systematic Review and Conceptual Model. *Sustainability (Basel)*, *14*(20), 13146. DOI: 10.3390/su142013146

Farooq, M., Hafsa Qadir, B., & Saeed, M. (2023, December). AI-Enhanced Social Sciences: A Systematic Literature Review and Bibliographic Analysis of Web of Science Published Research Papers. *Pakistan Journal of Society* [PJSEL]. *Education and Language*, *10*, 1–2.

Farooq, M., Kalimuthu, R., & Reza, M. H. (2019). Measuring and Comparing Brand Equity of Malaysian Banks in the Era of Transformative Marketing. *Global Journal of Emerging Sciences*, *1*(June), 96–102.

Farooq, M., Khalil-Ur-Rehman, F., Abdurrahaman, D. T., Younas, W., Sajjad, S., & Zreen, A. (2019). SERVICE QUALITY ANALYSIS OF PRIVATE UNIVERSITIES LIBRARIES IN MALAYSIA IN THE ERA OF TRANSFORMATIVE MARKETING. *International Journal of Qualitative Research*, *13*(2), 269–284. DOI: 10.24874/IJQR13.02-02

Farooq, M., Muhammad, S., Raju, V., Kalimuthu, K. R., & Qadir, A. (2019). Measuring and Comparing the Desired and Actual Service Quality of Pakistan International Airline. *The Journal of Social Sciences Research*, *52*(52), 484–490. DOI: 10.32861/jssr.52.484.490

Farooq, M., & Qureshi, Q. A. (2020). Practical Approach of Environmental Awareness to Broadening Community Participation: A Case Study of Pindad (Persero). *Journal of Management Practices. Humanities and Social Sciences*, *4*(1). Advance online publication. DOI: 10.33152/jmphss-4.2.1

Farooq, M., & Raju, V. (2019a). Impact of Over-the-Top (OTT) Services on the Telecom Companies in the Era of Transformative Marketing. *Global Journal of Flexible Systems Managment*, *20*(2), 177–188. DOI: 10.1007/s40171-019-00209-6

Farooq, M., & Raju, V. (2019b). Want to Stay the Market Leader in the Era of Transformative Marketing? Keep the Customers Satisfied! *Global Journal of Flexible Systems Management*. DOI: 10.1007/s40171-019-00213-w

Farooq, M., & Raju, V. (2019c). Impact of Over-the-Top (OTT) Services on the Telecom Companies in the Era of Transformative Marketing. *Global Journal of Flexible Systems Managment*, *20*(2), 177–188. DOI: 10.1007/s40171-019-00209-6

Farooq, M., & Raju, V. (2019d). Want to Stay the Market Leader in the Era of Transformative Marketing? Keep the Customers Satisfied! *Global Journal of Flexible Systems Managment*, *20*(3), 257–266. DOI: 10.1007/s40171-019-00213-w

Farooq, M., & Ramzan, M. Y. Y. Y. (2025). AI in Management. In *Transformative Impacts of AI in Management* (1st ed., pp. 1–44). IGI Global. DOI: 10.4018/979-8-3693-4322-7.ch001

Farooq, M., Ramzan, M., & Yen, Y. Y. (2025a). AI in Consumer Behavior Management. In *Transformative Impacts of AI in Management* (pp. 281–294). IGI Global., DOI: 10.4018/979-8-3693-4322-7.ch011

Farooq, M., Ramzan, M., & Yen, Y. Y. (2025b). AI in Customer Service, HR, and Administration. In *Transformative Impacts of AI in Management* (pp. 45–70). IGI Global. DOI: 10.4018/979-8-3693-4322-7.ch002

Farooq, M., Ramzan, M., & Yen, Y. Y. (2025c). AI in Quality Management. In *Transformative Impacts of AI in Management* (pp. 295–312). IGI Global., DOI: 10.4018/979-8-3693-4322-7.ch012

Farooq, M., Ramzan, M., & Yen, Y. Y. (2025d). Artificial Intelligence and Customer Experiences. In *Transformative Impacts of AI in Management* (pp. 95–114). IGI Global., DOI: 10.4018/979-8-3693-4322-7.ch004

Farooq, M., Ramzan, M., & Yen, Y. Y. (2025e). Artificial Intelligence in Administration Sciences. In *Transformative Impacts of AI in Management* (pp. 115–156). IGI Global., DOI: 10.4018/979-8-3693-4322-7.ch005

Farooq, M., Ramzan, M., & Yen, Y. Y. (2025f). Artificial Intelligence in Business and Law. In *Transformative Impacts of AI in Management* (pp. 71–94). IGI Global., DOI: 10.4018/979-8-3693-4322-7.ch003

Farooq, M., Ramzan, M., & Yen, Y. Y. (2025g). Artificial Intelligence in Ethical Business Decision Making. In *Transformative Impacts of AI in Management* (pp. 265–280). IGI Global., DOI: 10.4018/979-8-3693-4322-7.ch010

Farooq, M., Ramzan, M., & Yen, Y. Y. (2025h). Exploring the Impact of Artificial Intelligence on Brand Management. In *Transformative Impacts of AI in Management* (pp. 157–188). IGI Global., DOI: 10.4018/979-8-3693-4322-7.ch006

Farooq, M., Ramzan, M., & Yen, Y. Y. (2025i). Exploring the Impact of Ethical Leadership and Employee Engagement on Knowledge Sharing Attitudes in the Asian Digital Economy. In *Transformative Impacts of AI in Management* (pp. 241–264). IGI Global., DOI: 10.4018/979-8-3693-4322-7.ch009

Farooq, M., Ramzan, M., & Yen, Y. Y. (2025j). Transformative Impact of AI in Education Management. In *Transformative Impacts of AI in Management* (pp. 189–216). IGI Global., DOI: 10.4018/979-8-3693-4322-7.ch007

Farooq, M., Ramzan, M., & Yen, Y. Y. (2025k). *Transformative Impacts of AI in Management*. IGI Global., DOI: 10.4018/979-8-3693-4322-7

Farooq, M., Rehman, F. K. U., Younas, W., Raju, V., Ahmed, Q. M., & Ali, M. (2019). Investigating Relationship between Net Promoter Score and Company Performance: A Longitudinal Study. *Global Journal of Emerging Sciences*, *1*(1), 1–10. https://www.gjoes.org/wp-content/uploads/2019/04/1-1.pdf

Farooq, M., Saeed, M., Ali, W., & Javid, R. (2020). Online Buying and Customer Satisfaction in the Era of Transformative Marketing. *City University Research Journal*, *10*(2), 274–288.

Farooq, M., Yuen, Y. Y., & Buzdar, H. Q. (2024). Exploring the Research Landscape of Artificial Intelligence Integration with Business Management: A Bibliometric Analysis from 1994-2023. *Journal of Logistics. Informatics and Service Science*, (April). Advance online publication. DOI: 10.33168/JLISS.2024.0410

Ghulam, W. A., Ali, W., Ali, S., Khan, M. M., Khan, R. N., & Farooq, M. (2019). Investigating factors influencing brain drain of citizens of Azad Kashmir Pakistan. *Journal of Social Sciences Research*, *5*(3), 782–788. Advance online publication. DOI: 10.32861/jssr.53.782.788

Guo, F., Tang, B., & Tang, M. (2022). Joint optimization of delay and cost for microservice composition in mobile edge computing. *World Wide Web (Bussum), 25*(5), 2019–2047. DOI: 10.1007/s11280-022-01017-2

Khan, M. A., Khan, A. Z., Ali, M. I., & Mahmood, F. (2023). The role of post-implementation strategies for projects of enterprise information systems in enhancing management system: A case study approach. [WE - Emerging Sources Citation Index] [ESCI]. *Human Systems Management, 42*(2), 247–256. DOI: 10.3233/HSM-220061

Krupitzer, C., & Stein, A. (2021). Food Informatics-Review of the Current State-of-the-Art, Revised Definition, and Classification into the Research Landscape. [WE - Science Citation Index Expanded] [SCI-EXPANDED]. *Foods, 10*(11), 2889. Advance online publication. DOI: 10.3390/foods10112889 PMID: 34829170

Kuzdowicz, P. (2021). A Management Information System for Incremental Reporting in an Enterprise. In A. GarciaPerez & L. Simkin (Eds.), *PROCEEDINGS OF THE 22ND EUROPEAN CONFERENCE ON KNOWLEDGE MANAGEMENT (ECKM 2021)* (Issue 22nd European Conference on Knowledge Management (ECKM), pp. 467–475). https://doi.org/ WE - Conference Proceedings Citation Index - Social Science & Humanities (CPCI-SSH)DOI: 10.34190/EKM.21.121

Li, Q., & Wu, G. (2021). ERP System in the Logistics Information Management System of Supply Chain Enterprises. *Mobile Information Systems, 2021*, 1–11. Advance online publication. DOI: 10.1155/2021/7423717

Lin, P. (2019). Design and Implementation of Financial Accounting Information Management System of Shipping Companies Based on ERP. *Journal of Coastal Research, 94*(sp1), 470–474. DOI: 10.2112/SI94-093.1

Mader, A., Dertien, E., Weda, J., & van Erp, J. (2023). Tinkering with social touch technology. [WE - Emerging Sources Citation Index] [ESCI]. *Frontiers of Computer Science, 5*, 848023. Advance online publication. DOI: 10.3389/fcomp.2023.848023

Mithas, S., Chen, Z. L., Saldanha, T. J. V., & Silveira, A. D. (2022). How will artificial intelligence and Industry 4.0 emerging technologies transform operations management? *Production and Operations Management, 31*(12), 4475–4487. DOI: 10.1111/poms.13864

Mulyani, S., Putra, D., Sukmadilaga, C., & Rozak, Y. (2017). The empirical testing for the effect of organizational commitment and leadership style on the implementation success of Enterprise Resource Planning (ERP) systems and its implications on the quality of accounting information (survey on state-owned enterprises in Bandung, West Java, Indonesia). In Proceedings of the 29th International Business Information Management Association Conference-Education Excellence and Innovation Management through Vision 2020: From Regional Development Sustainability to Global Economic Growth (pp. 807-822).

Naseer, M., Farooq, M., Younas, W., & Raju, V. (2019). Antecedents of employee retention in the pharmaceutical industry of Pakistan. *Journal of Social Sciences Research, 5*(3), 656–664. Advance online publication. DOI: 10.32861/jssr.53.655.664

Onal, C., Nur Demiral, A., Atalar, B., Yalman, D., Dagoglu, N., Hurmuz, P., Erpolat, P., Akyurek, S., Karabulut Gul, S., Berber, T., Cem Guler, O., Umay, C., Sert, F., Karahacioglu, E., Duru Birgi, S., Yaprak, G., & Kaytan Saglam, E. (2022). National Multi-Center Observational Retrospective Study to Understand Treatment Patterns and Outcomes for Stage III Non-Small Cell Lung Cancer Patients in Turkey: Turkish Society for Radiation Oncology Study, STONE Trial. *UHOD: Uluslararasi Hematoloji-Onkoloji Dergisi, 32*(1), 23–34. DOI: 10.4999/uhod.225876

Shao, Z., Feng, Y. Q., & Hu, Q. (2017). Impact of top management leadership styles on ERP assimilation and the role of organizational learning. [WE - Science Citation Index Expanded] [SCI-EXPANDED] [WE - Social Science Citation Index] [SSCI]. *Information & Management, 54*(7), 902–919. DOI: 10.1016/j.im.2017.01.005

Song, R. L., & Hu, H. (2023). Impact of green technology innovation based on IoT and industrial supply chain on the promotion of enterprise digital economy. [WE - Science Citation Index Expanded] [SCI-EXPANDED]. *PeerJ. Computer Science, 9*, e1416. Advance online publication. DOI: 10.7717/peerj-cs.1416 PMID: 37346566

Tao, Z., Si Jun, B., & Xi Bai, R. (2021). Research on marketing management system based on independent ERP and business BI using fuzzy TOPSIS. *Journal of Intelligent & Fuzzy Systems, 40*(4), 8247–8255. DOI: 10.3233/JIFS-189647

Vihari, N. S., & Yadav, M. (2021). Effect of Change Agent Leadership Style on Successful ERP Implementation and Firm Performance: Empirical Evidence. [WE - Emerging Sources Citation Index] [ESCI]. *International Journal of Information System Modeling and Design, 12*(4), 42–57. Advance online publication. DOI: 10.4018/IJISMD.288555

Vogt, F., & Hollenstein, L. (2021). Exploring digital transformation through pretend play in kindergarten. [WE - Social Science Citation Index] [SSCI]. *British Journal of Educational Technology*, *52*(6), 2130–2144. DOI: 10.1111/bjet.13142

Wang, M., Zuo, X., & Zhu, T. (2021). Blockchain in 5G and 6G networks. In Huang, H., Wang, L., Wu, Y., & Choo, K. K. R. (Eds.), *Blockchains for Network Security: Principles, technologies and applications* (Vol. 29)., DOI: 10.1049/PBPC029E_ch6

Wang, Y., Lin, J., Osman, Z., Farooq, M., & Raju, V. (2021). Transformational leadership and employee performance in international commercial banking industry in Malaysia: The role of self-efficacy as a mediator under BRI. *Journal of Chinese Human Resource Management*, *12*(2), 25–36. DOI: 10.47297/wspchrmWSP2040-800503.20211202

Wen, C., Liu, W., He, Z., & Liu, C. (2023). Research on emergency management of global public health emergencies driven by digital technology: A bibliometric analysis. *Frontiers in Public Health*, *10*, 1100401. Advance online publication. DOI: 10.3389/fpubh.2022.1100401 PMID: 36711394

Yen, Y. Y., Wen, L. J., Ramasamy, S., & Farooq, M. (2023). Sustainable petrol subsidy program in Malaysia. *Asian Development Policy Review*, *12*(1), 1–9. DOI: 10.55493/5008.v12i1.4948

Zhang, L. J., Zhu, X. Y., & Ma, J. F. (2023). A study of ensemble feature selection and adversarial training for malicious user detection. *China Communications*, *20*(10), 212–229. Advance online publication. DOI: 10.23919/JCC.ea.2021-0512.202302

Zhao, B., & Tu, C. (2021). Research and Development of Inventory Management and Human Resource Management in ERP. *Wireless Communications and Mobile Computing*, *2021*(1), 3132062. Advance online publication. DOI: 10.1155/2021/3132062

Chapter 7
Transformative Impacts of AI in Future Trends in Management Information Systems Beyond AI

ABSTRACT

The dynamic momentum of the Management Information Systems (MIS) trajectory is providing a look into future developments that have the potential to completely transform organizational management (Farooq et al., 2025c, 2025a). The smooth integration of machine learning (ML) and artificial intelligence (AI) algorithms inside MIS frameworks is one prominent trend (Farooq et al., 2024; León-Romero et al., 2024). Through the analysis of large datasets, the extraction of insights, and the remarkably accurate prediction of future events, these technologies improve decision-making processes (Jayasuriya & Sims, 2023). Businesses are depending more and more on data driven initiatives, therefore AI-powered MIS is essential for promoting competitiveness and agility.

7.1 CHAPTER INTRODUCTION

Cloud computing's widespread use is revolutionizing management information systems (MIS) by providing resources with ubiquitous access and allowing real-time collaboration amongst teams that are geographically separated. The move to cloud-

DOI: 10.4018/979-8-3373-0513-4.ch007

based MIS solutions meets the needs of contemporary businesses by streamlining operations, reducing infrastructure costs, and improving scalability (Muir et al., 2023).

The introduction of blockchain technology offers unmatched data management security and transparency. MIS can guarantee the integrity and immutability of crucial information by using decentralized ledgers, hence reducing potential risks.

Figure 1. Mind map of future trends in management systems

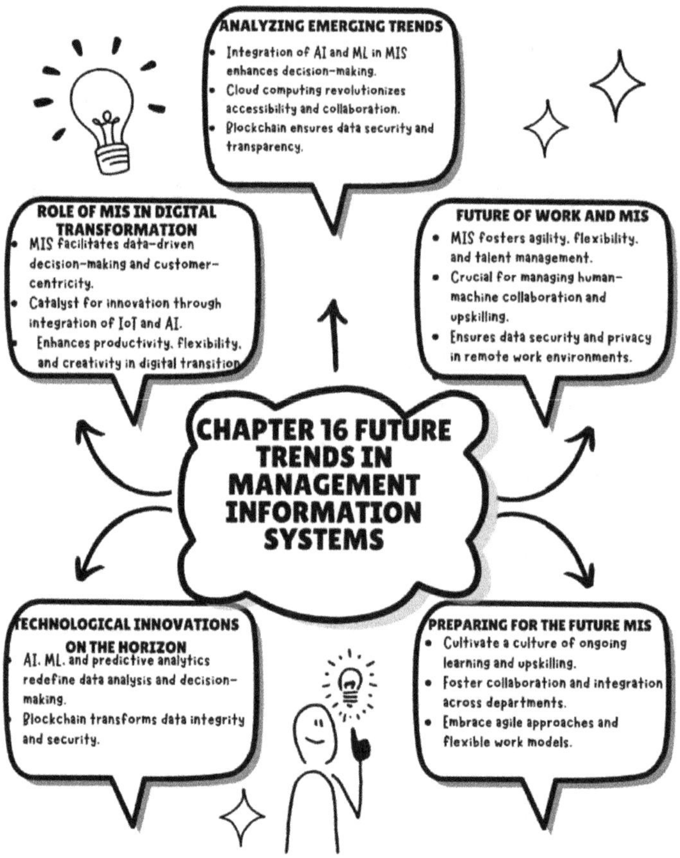

7.2 ANALYZING EMERGING TRENDS IN MIS

The growing use of business intelligence and data analytics in MIS is one of the major developments. Businesses are using sophisticated analytics technologies to glean valuable insights from massive data sets. This change makes it possible for managers and executives to make well-informed decisions since they can now base their plans on data-driven, real-time information (S. Ahmad et al., 2022; Nawaz et al., 2022). The predictive power of MIS is further improved by the integration of machine learning (ML) and artificial intelligence (AI) algorithms, which enables businesses to identify patterns and take proactive action(dos Santos & Molina, 2023).

Another significant innovation that is changing MIS is cloud computing. Using cloud-based MIS solutions makes it possible to have more accessibility, scalability, and flexibility. Data may now be stored and accessed by organizations from any location, encouraging cooperation and optimizing procedures (Z. Ahmad et al., 2020; Nawaz et al., 2022; Ramzan et al., 2021). Additionally, the cloud makes it easier to integrate systems with one another, which promotes a more cohesive and effective MIS environment (Yadav et al., 2023).

The incorporation of strong security measures into MIS frameworks has been prompted by the growing concerns about cybersecurity(Chenyang et al., 2024; Zhai & Chen, 2024). Organizations are spending more on sophisticated security procedures to protect sensitive data as data breaches and cyberattacks get more complex. This includes multi-factor authentication, encryption, and ongoing monitoring to quickly identify and address any possible threats(Ahmed et al., 2020; Ramzan et al., 2019).

MIS is undergoing a paradigm change because to the Internet of Things (IoT), which connects gadgets and sensors to collect data in real time. Organizations are able to monitor and control a variety of areas of their operations, from customer interactions to supply chain logistics, thanks to this networked network of devices. In addition to improving operational effectiveness, IoT integration in MIS creates new opportunities for innovation and corporate growth(Chatzimichailidou et al., 2024; Karim et al., 2024; Okada et al., 2024; Xie et al., 2024).

Blockchain technology's decentralization is also impacting MIS trends. By ensuring safe and transparent transactions, blockchain technology eliminates the need for middlemen and boosts confidence in data transfers. In order to establish unchangeable, tamper-proof records, organizations are investigating the possibilities of blockchain in MIS, especially in areas like supply chain management and financial transactions.

User experience (UX) is becoming more and more important while designing MIS. With the increasing integration of technology into regular company activities, the emphasis is now on developing user-friendly interfaces and intuitive workflows. In addition to increasing productivity, a good user experience encourages user adoption and acceptance of MIS inside businesses(Gupta & Panigrahi, 2023; Wang et al., 2023; Zhidong, 2023).

7.3 ROLE OF MIS IN DIGITAL TRANSFORMATION

Using technology to improve productivity, flexibility, and creativity is known as digital transformation. By offering an organized framework for gathering, evaluating, and sharing information within an organization, MIS makes this process easier. The smooth integration of various systems and processes, promoting interoperability and dismantling silos that impede cooperation, is one of the main roles of MIS in digital transformation(Agarwal, 2023).

MIS enables businesses to fully use business information and data analytics. MIS facilitates data-driven decision-making by enabling the extraction of meaningful insights from large datasets using sophisticated analytics techniques. This improves operational effectiveness and helps companies to foresee future changes in the market, consumer preferences, and possible hazards(Dalloul et al., 2023; Godoy et al., 2023; Na & Shon, 2022).

The function of MIS in the context of digital transformation goes beyond internal operations to include customer interaction and experience(Z. Huang, 2022; X. Li et al., 2022; Zhang, 2022). One of the main tenets of digital transformation is customer-centricity, and MIS helps businesses to comprehend and react to client demands instantly. Organizations may acquire a competitive advantage in the digital market by personalizing interactions, streamlining communication, and establishing enduring partnerships by integrating consumer data across several touchpoints (Xu et al., 2023).

When a business is going through a digital transition, MIS serves as a catalyst for innovation. It offers a venue for testing and deploying cutting-edge technologies including Internet of Things (IoT), machine learning, and artificial intelligence. Organizations may use MIS to track these technologies' performance, evaluate their effects, and decide whether to scale up or improve their implementation(L. Huang, 2022; Iliescu, 2022; Pereira et al., 2022).

7.4 FUTURE OF WORK AND MIS

The workforce is changing, workers' expectations are rising, and technology developments are all contributing to a significant shift of the future of work. Management Information Systems (MIS) become a crucial facilitator in this dynamic environment, influencing how businesses organize, oversee, and maximize their labor force (H. Li et al., 2019).

MIS goes beyond its conventional function of information management and reporting in the context of the future of work. It turns into a tactical instrument that synchronizes corporate objectives with employee talents and expectations. With gig economies, remote work, and varied talent pools becoming the norm, MIS is essential to facilitating effective communication, teamwork, and production across geographically distributed teams (Özköse et al., 2023).

The focus on agility and flexibility is one of the main features of the workplace of the future. This is made possible by MIS, which offers real-time information on project milestones, worker performance, and general organizational indicators(B. Guo & Shuai, 2022; Lee, 2022; Runge et al., 2022). This enables companies to deploy workers and improve their skills more efficiently, respond swiftly to changing market circumstances, and make well-informed choices about resource allocation.

The function of MIS in the modern workplace encompasses employee experience and talent management. It helps with talent identification and nurturing, skill alignment with company objectives, and the creation of individualized development plans. Furthermore, via encouraging cooperation, clear communication, and a continual feedback culture, MIS helps to create a healthy work atmosphere. MIS plays a crucial role in managing the human-machine cooperation that is occurring in the workplace as automation and artificial intelligence proliferate. It assists businesses in finding automation possibilities, streamlining processes, and striking a balance between machine and human skills (Aliman & Kester, 2020).

Additionally, MIS is essential to upskilling and reskilling programs, guaranteeing that workers have the abilities needed to prosper in a workplace that is becoming more automated and digital.

Future employment will need a high level of security and data privacy due to the growing popularity of remote work and the greater dependence on digital platforms. MIS takes on the role of data protection guardian, putting strong cybersecurity safeguards in place and making sure that data protection laws are followed. This is essential for preserving stakeholder and employee trust as well as for protecting organizational assets(X. Li, 2021; Thorpe et al., 2021; Zhigang, 2021).

7.5 TECHNOLOGICAL INNOVATIONS ON THE HORIZON

Keeping up with technology advancements is essential for businesses looking to remain competitive. Looking forward, we see a number of innovative technologies that have the potential to completely transform how companies run and use MIS(Z. Guo et al., 2021; Kuzovkova et al., 2021). The increasing use of machine learning

(ML) and artificial intelligence (AI) is one such advancement. These technologies have the potential to completely change how data is analyzed, how decisions are made, and how effective MIS is as a whole (Deglaire et al., 2023).

Applications of AI and ML in MIS go beyond work automation. They let businesses to extract useful information from huge databases, facilitating well-informed decision-making(Doutcheva, 2021; Gang et al., 2021). A key role is expected for predictive analytics, a subset of artificial intelligence. Predictive models may be used by organizations to anticipate trends, spot possible hazards, and allocate resources as efficiently as possible. MIS will depend more and more on AI algorithms as they develop to improve data security, optimize workflows, and provide individualized user experiences(Han et al., 2021; Junru et al., 2021).

Another disruptive technology that is going to change MIS is blockchain. Blockchain, which is well-known for being safe and decentralized, has the power to completely transform data openness and integrity. Blockchain may be used in the field of MIS to produce records that are unchangeable and impervious to tampering, guaranteeing the accuracy of the data. This invention is especially important for sectors like banking and healthcare where data quality is critical(Farooq et al., 2025h, 2025i, 2025g). By incorporating blockchain technology into MIS frameworks, the dangers of data modification and illegal access may be reduced, promoting dependability and confidence.(Farooq et al., 2025e, 2025d, 2025f)

It is anticipated that the introduction of 5G technology would spur improvements in MIS infrastructure. 5G's high-speed, low-latency capabilities will make it possible to process data in real time and have continuous communication(Farooq et al., 2024, 2025b; León-Romero et al., 2024). This plays a crucial role in improving the effectiveness of MIS systems, especially in situations when instantaneous data transmission is essential. It is anticipated that when 5G becomes more widely used, MIS systems will be able to manage bigger data loads, speed up device connectivity, and provide new opportunities for remote and mobile work settings(Chenyang et al., 2024; Xie et al., 2024; Zhai & Chen, 2024).

The field of quantum computing is young, yet it has enormous potential to transform data processing. Though it is still in its early stages, MIS systems might analyze and understand complex information tenfold faster thanks to the capabilities of quantum computing(Farooq et al., 2019; Farooq & Raju, 2019a, 2019b). This exponential increase in processing power may open up previously unheard-of possibilities for data-intensive jobs, improving MIS's ability to handle complex situations and spurring innovation in a range of sectors.

7.6 PREPARING FOR THE FUTURE: STRATEGIES AND BEST PRACTICES

Building a culture of ongoing learning is essential to be ready for MIS in the future. Organizations that want to upskill their personnel must invest in training programs given the speed at which technology is advancing. By doing this, employers may make sure that staff members have the skills and knowledge needed to properly use evolving technology. Establishing a learning-focused atmosphere enables firms to develop a workforce that is flexible and responsive to the changing field of management information systems (Roberson, 2020).

Future-proofing MIS initiatives need collaboration and integration. Businesses can encourage cross-functional cooperation between IT, data analytics, and business divisions by dismantling organizational silos (Gul et al., 2021; Sajjad et al., 2013) . By using an integrated strategy, it is ensured that MIS systems are in line with corporate objectives and that data-driven insights are efficiently applied across departments. The creation of thorough MIS frameworks and the smooth deployment of new technologies are further facilitated by collaboration. Developing strategic alliances with IT suppliers and business leaders is essential to be ready for MIS's future. Through strategic partnerships with forward-thinking solution providers, companies may get access to state-of-the-art technology and insights. Through these relationships, firms may adopt state-of-the-art solutions, remain abreast of technology developments, and get advice on how to effectively optimize MIS for particular industry requirements(Martin & Murphy, 2017).

Agile approaches provide a flexible framework that can be adjusted to meet evolving MIS needs. Organizations may design and improve MIS systems iteratively and stay flexible in response to changing business requirements and technical improvements by adopting agile approaches. In addition to allowing for speedier reaction times to new trends, agile approaches help firms remain ahead of the curve in the everchanging field of management information systems (MIS). Remote and hybrid work models are also becoming more and more common. In order to facilitate smooth cooperation and communication among geographically dispersed teams, organizations must embrace flexible work arrangements and make use of MIS. Coordination tools, virtual communication tools, and cloud-based MIS solutions are all crucial for creating a flexible and robust foundation for the workplace of the future.

Sustainability should be given top priority in MIS strategy for enterprises. Eco-friendly practice integration into MIS frameworks becomes more important as environmental concerns gain traction. This entails using sustainable technology, cutting energy use, and improving data center operations. In addition to supporting environmental stewardship, sustainable MIS practices also conform to changing legal and cultural norms.

7.7 CHAPTER CONCLUSION

Overall, the future of Management Information Systems (MIS) is expected to gain significant speed, providing insights into upcoming advancements that might fundamentally transform how organisations are managed. The incorporation of machine learning (ML) and artificial intelligence (AI) algorithms into MIS frameworks is a notable development that enables data-driven decision-making and enhances competitiveness and agility.

The extensive use of cloud computing is transforming management information systems (MIS) by offering universal access to resources and facilitating immediate communication among teams located in different geographical areas. This, in turn, simplifies operations, decreases infrastructure expenses, and improves scalability. Moreover, the implementation of blockchain technology guarantees unparalleled security and transparency in data management, effectively protecting the integrity of vital information and minimising potential dangers.

Examining developing patterns in Management Information Systems (MIS) indicates an increasing dependence on business intelligence, data analytics, and predictive modelling. This enables organisations to make informed decisions by utilising up-to-date information. The use of Internet of Things (IoT) technology improves the efficiency of operations and opens up new possibilities for creativity and expansion inside a company. Furthermore, the significance of user experience (UX) is increasing, underscoring the requirement for interfaces that are easy for users to use and processes that are intuitive, in order to improve productivity and promote user acceptance.

Within the framework of digital transformation, Management Information Systems (MIS) are crucial for enhancing productivity, adaptability, and customer satisfaction. MIS empowers organisations to make informed decisions based on data and ensures that different systems can work together effectively, allowing organisations to adjust to market changes and fulfil the increasing needs of customers. In addition, Management Information Systems (MIS) plays a crucial role in driving innovation by facilitating the experimentation and implementation of advanced technologies like the Internet of Things (IoT) and Artificial Intelligence (AI).

As we consider the future of work, the field of Management Information Systems (MIS) becomes essential in handling the changing dynamics of the workforce. MIS is crucial for facilitating efficient communication, collaboration, and talent management among teams that are spread out across different locations. Additionally, it promotes collaboration between humans and machines, ensuring a harmonious integration of automation and artificial intelligence with human capabilities. Furthermore, Management Information Systems (MIS) play a vital role in enhancing and updating training programmes, guaranteeing that employees possess the essential abilities to excel in an ever-evolving digital work environment.

The imminent technological advancements, including the growing use of artificial intelligence (AI) and machine learning (ML), blockchain technology, 5G, and quantum computing, possess the capability to revolutionise management information systems (MIS) and stimulate organisational creativity. Organisations need to use continuous learning, collaboration, and agile methods to ensure the long-term success of their Management Information Systems (MIS) projects and stay competitive in a quickly changing environment. Furthermore, it is crucial to prioritise sustainability in the MIS strategy in order to ensure alignment with environmental concerns and regulatory obligations, as well as to promote the adoption of eco-friendly practices.

By adopting new technologies, promoting cooperation, and prioritizing sustainability, organisations may fully utilise Management Information Systems (MIS) to stimulate innovation, adaptability, and expansion in the era of digitalization.

REFERENCES

Agarwal, A. (2023). AI adoption by human resource management: A study of its antecedents and impact on HR system effectiveness. *Foresight, 25*(1), 67–81. DOI: 10.1108/FS-10-2021-0199

Ahmad, S., Qureshi, I. U., Ramzan, M., & Rehman, S. U. (2022). Research Elite of Pakistan: Profile and Determinants of Productivity and Impact. *Publishing Research Quarterly, 38*(2), 263–280. DOI: 10.1007/s12109-022-09874-5

Ahmad, Z., Tariq, M., Chaudhry, M. S., & Ramzan, M. (2020). Parent's role in promoting reading habits among children: an empirical examination. *Library Philosophy and Practice*, 1–21.

Ahmed, S., Ramzan, M., Sheikh, A., & Ali, A. (2020). Impact of students personality traits on social networking sites usage, benefits and risks. *Global Knowledge, Memory and Communication, 70*(6–7), 518–537. DOI: 10.1108/GKMC-04-2020-0048

Al Karim, R., Rabiul, M. K., Ahamed, T., Karim, D. N., & Mehzabeen, M. (2024). Integrating Green Entrepreneurial Orientation, Green Information Systems, and Management Support with Green Supply Chain Management to Foster Firms' Environmental Performance. *Sustainability (Basel), 16*(12), 4921. DOI: 10.3390/su16124921

Aliman, N. M., & Kester, L. (2020). Facing immersive "post-truth" in aivr? *Philosophies, 5*(4), 45. Advance online publication. DOI: 10.3390/philosophies5040045

Chatzimichailidou, M., Whitcher, T., & Suzic, N. (2024). Complementarity and Compatibility of Systems Integration and Building Information Management. *IEEE Systems Journal, 18*(2), 1198–1207. DOI: 10.1109/JSYST.2024.3387064

Chenyang, X., Piao, W., Zilun, L., Qing, L., & Yadong, K. (2024). Research on Science and Technology Management Information Security Guarantee System. *Journal of Information Security Research, 10*(7), 675–681.

Dalloul, M. H. M., binti Ibrahim, Z., & Urus, S. T. (2023). Financial Crises Management in Light of Accounting Information Systems Success: Investigating Direct and Indirect Influences. *Sustainability (Basel), 15*(10), 8131. Advance online publication. DOI: 10.3390/su15108131

Deglaire, A., Lee, J., Lanotte, L., Croguennec, T., Le Floch-Fouere, C., Jeantet, R., Berkova, N., Pedrono, F., Le Loir, Y., Dupont, D., Gesan-Guiziou, G., & Even, S. (2023). Towards more biomimetic and sustainable infant formula: Challenges and future opportunities. *Trends in Food Science & Technology*, *137*, 109–123. DOI: 10.1016/j.tifs.2023.05.010

dos Santos, J. C., & Molina, L. G. (2023). Repertory memory and its interrelationships with knowledge management in organizational environments. *ENCONTROS BIBLI-REVISTA ELETRONICA DE BIBLIOTECONOMIA E* [WE - Emerging Sources Citation Index] [ESCI]. *Ciência da Informação*, *28*. Advance online publication. DOI: 10.5007/1518-2924.2023.e89762

Doutcheva, N. Z.-. (2021). *Information Management of Family Caregivers of Children with Medical Complexity*.

Farooq, M., Khalil-Ur-Rehman, F., Abdurrahaman, D. T., Younas, W., Sajjad, S., & Zreen, A. (2019). SERVICE QUALITY ANALYSIS OF PRIVATE UNIVERSITIES LIBRARIES IN MALAYSIA IN THE ERA OF TRANSFORMATIVE MARKETING. *International Journal of Qualitative Research*, *13*(2), 269–284. DOI: 10.24874/IJQR13.02-02

Farooq, M., & Raju, V. (2019a). Want to Stay the Market Leader in the Era of Transformative Marketing? Keep the Customers Satisfied! *Global Journal of Flexible Systems Management*. DOI: 10.1007/s40171-019-00213-w

Farooq, M., & Raju, V. (2019b). Impact of Over-the-Top (OTT) Services on the Telecom Companies in the Era of Transformative Marketing. *Global Journal of Flexible Systems Managment*, *20*(2), 177–188. DOI: 10.1007/s40171-019-00209-6

Farooq, M., Ramzan, M., & Yen, Y. Y. (2025a). AI in Consumer Behavior Management. In *Transformative Impacts of AI in Management* (pp. 281–294). IGI Global., DOI: 10.4018/979-8-3693-4322-7.ch011

Farooq, M., Ramzan, M., & Yen, Y. Y. (2025b). AI in Customer Service, HR, and Administration. In *Transformative Impacts of AI in Management* (pp. 45–70). IGI Global. DOI: 10.4018/979-8-3693-4322-7.ch002

Farooq, M., Ramzan, M., & Yen, Y. Y. (2025c). AI in Quality Management. In *Transformative Impacts of AI in Management* (pp. 295–312). IGI Global., DOI: 10.4018/979-8-3693-4322-7.ch012

Farooq, M., Ramzan, M., & Yen, Y. Y. (2025d). Artificial Intelligence and Customer Experiences. In *Transformative Impacts of AI in Management* (pp. 95–114). IGI Global., DOI: 10.4018/979-8-3693-4322-7.ch004

Farooq, M., Ramzan, M., & Yen, Y. Y. (2025e). Artificial Intelligence in Administration Sciences. In *Transformative Impacts of AI in Management* (pp. 115–156). IGI Global., DOI: 10.4018/979-8-3693-4322-7.ch005

Farooq, M., Ramzan, M., & Yen, Y. Y. (2025f). Artificial Intelligence in Business and Law. In *Transformative Impacts of AI in Management* (pp. 71–94). IGI Global., DOI: 10.4018/979-8-3693-4322-7.ch003

Farooq, M., Ramzan, M., & Yen, Y. Y. (2025g). Exploring the Impact of Artificial Intelligence on Brand Management. In *Transformative Impacts of AI in Management* (pp. 157–188). IGI Global., DOI: 10.4018/979-8-3693-4322-7.ch006

Farooq, M., Ramzan, M., & Yen, Y. Y. (2025h). Exploring the Impact of Ethical Leadership and Employee Engagement on Knowledge Sharing Attitudes in the Asian Digital Economy. In *Transformative Impacts of AI in Management* (pp. 241–264). IGI Global., DOI: 10.4018/979-8-3693-4322-7.ch009

Farooq, M., Ramzan, M., & Yen, Y. Y. (2025i). Transformative Impact of AI in Education Management. In *Transformative Impacts of AI in Management* (pp. 189–216). IGI Global., DOI: 10.4018/979-8-3693-4322-7.ch007

Farooq, M., Yuen, Y. Y., & Buzdar, H. Q. (2024). Exploring the Research Landscape of Artificial Intelligence Integration with Business Management: A Bibliometric Analysis from 1994-2023. *Journal of Logistics. Informatics and Service Science*, (April). Advance online publication. DOI: 10.33168/JLISS.2024.0410

Gang, S., Xiaoming, W., Junfeng, W., Shufang, L., Zhuowen, L., & Wang, X. (2021). Analysis of the information management system in the manufacturing process of cigarette enterprises using fuzzy AHP. *Journal of Intelligent & Fuzzy Systems*, *40*(4), 8257–8267. DOI: 10.3233/JIFS-189648

Godoy, M. P., Rusu, C., Hatibovic, F., Granollers, T., & Ugalde, J. (2023). Addressing Information Consumer Experience through a User-Centered Information Management System in a Chilean University. *Sustainability (Basel)*, *15*(22), 15998. Advance online publication. DOI: 10.3390/su152215998

Gul, A., Kazmi, S. J. H., Irfan, M., Zaidi, S. M., & Jan, B. (2021). Forecasting micro area broadband demand using urban land use planning tools in Karachi, Pakistan: A GIS perspective. *GeoJournal*. Advance online publication. DOI: 10.1007/s10708-021-10514-2

Guo, B., & Shuai, L. (2022, March). Research on object-oriented data model technology in tourism information management. In Third International Conference on Electronics and Communication; Network and Computer Technology (ECNCT 2021) (Vol. 12167, pp. 392-397). SPIE.

Guo, Z., Zhang, X., Gao, Y., Hao, W., Zhang, S., & Du, X. (2021). Design of Information Management System for Large Modular Manned Spacecraft. In *Proceedings of the 16th IEEE Conference on Industrial Electronics and Applications, ICIEA 2021* (Issues 16th IEEE Conference on Industrial Electronics and Applications (ICIEA) CL-Chengdu, PEOPLES R CHINA PU-IEEE PI-NEW YORK PA-345 E 47TH ST, NEW YORK, NY 10017 USA, pp. 655–659). DOI: 10.1109/ICIEA51954.2021.9516303

Gupta, B. B., & Panigrahi, P. K. (2023). Analysis of the Role of Global Information Management in Advanced Decision Support Systems (DSS) for Sustainable Development. *Journal of Global Information Management, 31*(1), 1–13. Advance online publication. DOI: 10.4018/JGIM.320185

Han, Y., Lei, Y., Bao, Z., & Zhou, Q. (2021). Research and Implementation of Mobile Internet Management Optimization and Intelligent Information System Based on Smart Decision. *Computational Intelligence and Neuroscience, 2021*(1), 5144568. Advance online publication. DOI: 10.1155/2021/5144568 PMID: 34925490

Huang, L. (2022). Research and Application of Business Law Information Management System Based on Big Data. *Journal of Sensors, 2022*, 1–12. Advance online publication. DOI: 10.1155/2022/5885451

Huang, Z. (2022). Integrated Management System of Instrument and Equipment in University Financial Media Laboratory Based on Hybrid Cloud Architecture. In S. Liu & X. Ma (Eds.), *ADVANCED HYBRID INFORMATION PROCESSING, PT I* (Vol. 416, Issues 5th EAI International Conference on Advanced Hybrid Information Processing (ADHIP) pp. 587–600). DOI: 10.1007/978-3-030-94551-0_46

Iliescu, D. (2022). Some Considerations on Conceptual Modeling for a Laboratory Information Management System. In D. Popescu, L. Barbulescu, E. Popescu, M. Roman, & D. Sendrescu (Eds.), *2022 23RD INTERNATIONAL CARPATHIAN CONTROL CONFERENCE (ICCC)* (Issues 23rd International Carpathian Control Conference (ICCC) CL-Sinaia, pp. 19–24). DOI: 10.1109/ICCC54292.2022.9805898

Jayasuriya, D. D., & Sims, A. (2023). From the abacus to enterprise resource planning: Is blockchain the next big accounting tool? *Accounting, Auditing & Accountability Journal, 36*(1), 24–62. DOI: 10.1108/AAAJ-08-2020-4718

Junru, Z., Bo, Y., Yanfeng, G., Jian, X., & Dingding, L. (2021). Research Status and Prospects of Intelligent Monitoring Technology and Information Management System for Tunnel Engineering. *Chinese Journal of Underground Space and Engineering*, *17*(2), 567–579.

Kuzovkova, T. A., Saliutina, T. Y., & Sharavova, O. I. (2021). The impact of digital platforms on the business management information system. In *2021 Systems of Signal Synchronization, Generating and Processing in Telecommunications, SYNCHROINFO 2021 - Conference Proceedings* (Issue Conference on Systems of Signal Synchronization, Generating and Processing in Telecommunications (SYNCHROINFO) CL-Svetlogorsk. DOI: 10.1109/SYNCHROINFO51390.2021.9488330

Lee, S. (2022). A Study on the Improvement Model of Administrative Information Dataset Records Management Environment: Focused on the Dataset of Picture Archiving and Communication System. *Journal of Korean Society of Archives and Records Management*, *22*(2), 51–73. DOI: 10.14404/JKSARM.2022.22.2.051

León-Romero, L. P., Aguilar-Fernández, M., Luque-Sendra, A., Zamora-Polo, F., & Francisco-Márquez, M. (2024). Characterization of the information system integrated to the construction project management systems. *Heliyon*, *10*(11), e31886. Advance online publication. DOI: 10.1016/j.heliyon.2024.e31886 PMID: 38841493

Li, H., Fang, Y., Lim, K. H., & Wang, Y. (2019). PLATFORM-BASED FUNCTION REPERTOIRE, REPUTATION, AND SALES PERFORMANCE OF E-MARKETPLACE SELLERS. *Management Information Systems Quarterly*, *43*(1), 207–236. http://10.0.98.212/MISQ/2019/14201. DOI: 10.25300/MISQ/2019/14201

Li, X. (2021). Design and Implementation of Project Cost Management Information System Based on Web. In *Proceedings - 2021 6th International Conference on Smart Grid and Electrical Automation, ICSGEA 2021* (Issues 6th International Conference on Smart Grid and Electrical Automation (ICSGEA) CL-Kunming, pp. 288–292). DOI: 10.1109/ICSGEA53208.2021.00070

Li, X., Wang, L., & Fang, L. (2022). Optimal Design of an Information Management System for Government: A Bridge between Government and Citizens. *Mathematical Problems in Engineering*, *2022*, 1–10. Advance online publication. DOI: 10.1155/2022/3127858

Martin, K. D., & Murphy, P. E. (2017). The role of data privacy in marketing. *Journal of the Academy of Marketing Science*, *45*(2), 135–155. DOI: 10.1007/s11747-016-0495-4

Muir, A. M., Bernhardt, J. R., Boucher, N. W., Cvitanovic, C., Dettmers, J. M., Gaden, M., Hinderer, J. L. M., Locke, B., Robinson, K. F., Siefkes, M. J., Young, N., & Cooke, S. J. (2023). Confronting a post-pandemic new-normal-threats and opportunities to trust-based relationships in natural resource science and management. *Journal of Environmental Management, 330*, 117140. Advance online publication. DOI: 10.1016/j.jenvman.2022.117140 PMID: 36603252

Na, S.-H., & Shon, T.-S. (2022). A Study on the Development of Information Security Management System Using RMF. *Journal of Digital Contents Society*, *23*(5), 977–983. DOI: 10.9728/dcs.2022.23.5.977

Nawaz, R., Bin-Naeem, S., & Ramzan, M. (2022). *Relationship between Awareness and Use of Digital Information Resources among University Students of Southern Punjab*. Library Philosophy & Practice.

Okada, K., Sugimoto, K., Wada, S., Konishi, S., Manabe, S., Matsumura, Y., & Takeda, T. (2024). Development of the Clinical Specimen Information Management System for Multicenter Clinical Studies. In J. Bichel-Findlay, P. Otero, P. Scott, & E. Huesing (Eds.), *MEDINFO 2023 - THE FUTURE IS ACCESSIBLE* (Vol. 310, Issues 19th World Congress on Medical and Health Informatics (MEDINFO) CL-Sydney, pp. 119–123). DOI: 10.3233/SHTI230939

Özköse, H., Ozyurt, O., & Ayaz, A. (2023). Management Information Systems Research: A Topic Modeling Based Bibliometric Analysis. *Journal of Computer Information Systems*, *63*(5), 1166–1182. DOI: 10.1080/08874417.2022.2132429

Pereira, J., Varajao, J., & Takagi, N. (2022). Evaluation of Information Systems Project Success - Insights from Practitioners. *Information Systems Management*, *39*(2), 138–155. DOI: 10.1080/10580530.2021.1887982

Ramzan, M., Ahmad, D., & Asif, M. (2019). Dynamics of WhatsApp Usage by University Students. *Pakistan Library & Information Science Journal, 50*(2), 2–6. https://search.ebscohost.com/login.aspx?direct=true&db=lxh&AN=136486307&site=eds-live&authtype=ip,uid

Ramzan, M., Asif, M., & Ahmad, S. (2021). Librarians' attitudes towards application of information technology in academic libraries in Pakistan. In *Information Research* (Vol. 26, Issue 1). Citeseer. DOI: 10.47989/irpaper887

Roberson, D. N. (2020). *Still Living at Home : Learning Resilience*. DOI: 10.24966/PMRD-8670/100042

Runge, M., Reiche, L. T., Niemann, K. H., & Fay, A. (2022). Universal energy information model for industrial communication. In *IEEE International Conference on Emerging Technologies and Factory Automation, ETFA* (Vols. 2022-Septe, Issue IEEE 27th International Conference on Emerging Technologies and Factory Automation (ETFA) CL-Stuttgart. DOI: 10.1109/ETFA52439.2022.9921557

Sajjad, A., Ghazanfar, H., & Ramzan, M. (2013). Impact of motivation on employee turnover in telecom sector of Pakistan. *Journal of Business Studies Quarterly*, *5*(1), 76.

Thorpe, D., Aghili, N., van Neuren, C., & IEEE. (2021). Managing Sustainable Asset Networks using Advanced Information Systems. In *2021 INTERNATIONAL CONFERENCE ON MAINTENANCE AND INTELLIGENT ASSET MANAGEMENT (ICMIAM)* (Issue International Conference on Maintenance and Intelligent Asset Management (ICMIAM) CL-Ballarat. DOI: 10.1109/ICMIAM54662.2021.9715219

Wang, Y., Xue, W., & Zhang, A. (2023). Application of Big Data Technology in Enterprise Information Security Management and Risk Assessment. *Journal of Global Information Management*, *31*(3), 1–16. Advance online publication. DOI: 10.4018/JGIM.324465

Xie, J., Jablonski, M., Smith, J., & Navedo, A. (2024). A Graphical Interface to Support Low-Flow Volatile Anesthesia: Implications for Patient Safety, Teaching, and Design of Anesthesia Information Management Systems. *Journal of Medical Systems*, *48*(1), 36. Advance online publication. DOI: 10.1007/s10916-024-02055-1 PMID: 38532235

Xu, R. Y., Chen, H. L., & Zhao, J. L. (2023). SocioLink: Leveraging Relational Information in Knowledge Graphs for Startup Recommendations. [WE - Science Citation Index Expanded] [SCI-EXPANDED] [WE - Social Science Citation Index] [SSCI]. *Journal of Management Information Systems*, *40*(2), 655–682. DOI: 10.1080/07421222.2023.2196771

Yadav, R. S., Kaya, S. K., Pant, A., & Tiwari, A. (2023). AI-enabled human capital management (HCM) software adoption using full consistency method (FUCOM): Evidence from banking industry. *Global Knowledge, Memory and Communication*. Advance online publication. DOI: 10.1108/GKMC-04-2023-0128

Zhai, Q., & Chen, X. (2024). Design and application of optical communication technology based on machine learning algorithms in physical education teaching information management system. *Optical and Quantum Electronics*, *56*(1), 111. Advance online publication. DOI: 10.1007/s11082-023-05717-5

Zhang, X. (2022). Design and Implementation of Management Information System Based on Network Environment. In D. Zhou & Z. Y. Du (Eds.), *Lecture Notes in Electrical Engineering: Vol. 827 LNEE* (Issue International Conference on Information Technology and Industrial Engineering CL-Wuhan, pp. 1076–1080). DOI: 10.1007/978-981-16-8052-6_147

Zhidong, L. (2023). Construction of management mechanism model of soil and water conservation information system. In *Science of Soil and Water Conservation* (Vol. 21, Issue 5, pp. 106–110).

Zhigang, W. (2021). Research on the Framework of Library Management System Based on Internet of Things. In *Proceedings - 2021 13th International Conference on Measuring Technology and Mechatronics Automation, ICMTMA 2021* (Issues 13th International Conference on Measuring Technology and Mechatronics Automation (ICMTMA) CL-Beihai, pp. 384–388). DOI: 10.1109/ICMTMA52658.2021.00089

Chapter 8
Transformative Impacts of AI in Customer Relationship Management (CRM) Systems

ABSTRACT

Systems for managing customer relationships (CRM) are advanced technologies that have the potential to completely change how companies communicate with their customers (Carlan & Vanelslander, 2021). The careful administration of client data, which promotes a thorough knowledge of unique preferences, behaviors, and interactions, is at the heart of these systems. CRM systems function as the digital hub, facilitating the smooth integration of marketing, sales, and customer support initiatives to provide a cohesive and effective operational setting (Chatterjee, Ghosh, et al., 2020a; Holloway et al., 2019).

CHAPTER INTRODUCTION

By offering a comprehensive perspective of customer experience, these solutions help firms build and maintain long-term connections with their clients. Every interaction, from the first point of contact to the post-purchase assistance, is painstakingly documented and examined(AL-Rubaiee et al., 2018; Chatterjee et al., 2021; Sorayaei et al., 2013). Customized communication is made possible by the central

DOI: 10.4018/979-8-3373-0513-4.ch008

data hub, which enables companies to adjust their outreach tactics in accordance with the requirements and preferences of certain clients(Ruiz-Palomo et al., 2019).

CRM solutions enable businesses to predict client trends and demands while also streamlining internal procedures(Dułu, 2010; Dutt & Chauhan, 2019). Businesses are able to find development possibilities, allocate resources optimally, and make well-informed choices by using analytics and predictive modeling. CRM solutions essentially reinvent customer interaction, turning it into a responsive and dynamic partnership that goes beyond transactions and promotes brand promotion and loyalty. CRM systems are becoming essential tools in today's business environment, driving businesses toward excellence in customer service and long-term profitability(Arab et al., 2010; Chatterjee, Ghosh, et al., 2020b).

Figure 1. Mind map of customer relationship management

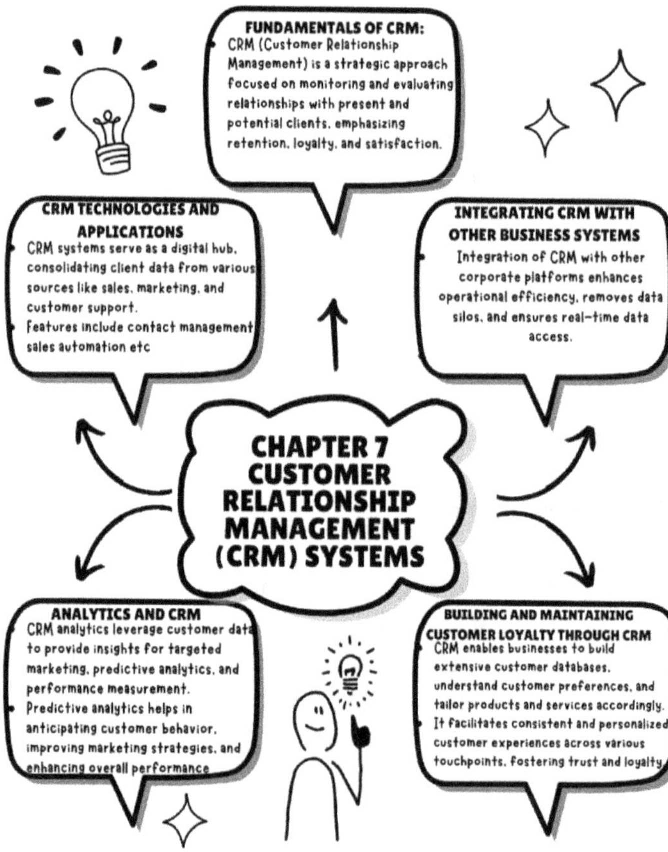

8.2 Fundamentals of CRM

CRM stands for customer relationship management, which is a strategic strategy that companies use to monitor and evaluate their relationships with both present and future clients(C. Kim et al., 2015; Peng, 2014). CRM is fundamentally a holistic mindset that places a high value on customer retention, loyalty, and satisfaction. Understanding the customer journey, establishing deep connections, and using technology to strengthen these bonds are the cornerstones of CRM(Chatterjee et al., 2022; Chatterjee, Nguyen, et al., 2020).

CRM is based on the understanding that customers are people with specific wants and preferences, not just a transactional entity(Kumar et al., 2014; Sharma et al., 2019). This calls for a change in emphasis from customer centric to product-centric initiatives. Businesses may learn more about the behavior, tastes, and expectations of their customers by collecting and evaluating customer data. Every connection with the consumer is made more valuable by using this information as the basis for individualized interactions. The establishment of a consolidated client database is a crucial component of CRM principles(Khanh et al., 2022). By combining data from several touchpoints, this database enables companies to get a comprehensive picture of every client. Organizations may better fulfill the demands of each individual client by customizing their goods, services, and communication thanks to this unified viewpoint. It also makes it easier for clients to switch between several platforms and channels with ease. CRM also stresses how crucial good communication is. Businesses may encourage open contact with consumers by providing clear avenues for feedback and discussion. This not only facilitates rapid resolution of issues but also offers chances for proactive participation. Businesses may create a feeling of exclusivity and give consumers a sense of value and appreciation by using individualized communication (Farooq, Khalil-Ur-Rehman, et al., 2019).

CRM foundations heavily rely on automation. By automating repetitive processes like data input, follow-ups, and lead nurturing, companies can concentrate on establishing genuine relationships. Additionally, automation increases productivity, freeing up teams to devote more time to critical tasks like customer data analysis and engagement strategy optimization (Farooq, Kalimuthu, et al., 2019).

The foundations of CRM go beyond procedures and technology; they also include a change in organizational culture. From the top leadership to the frontline staff, the company's culture must be deeply rooted in customer-centric ideals (Farooq et al., 2025i, 2025f). Because of this cultural congruence, everyone in the company is guaranteed to see the value of client connections and to actively participate in their development.

8.3 CRM Technologies and Applications

The Customer Relationship Management system (CRM system) is a technology of CRM. Consolidating client data from several sources, such as sales, marketing, and customer support, this software serves as a single hub. CRM systems provide businesses the ability to keep an accurate picture of every client, facilitating targeted marketing and individualized interactions (Farooq & Raju, 2019b).

Contact management is a crucial element of CRM technology. Businesses may use this feature to arrange and save client contact information, making it possible for teams to quickly retrieve pertinent information when required (Farooq et al., 2025j, 2025d, 2025b). Effective customer communication and relationship development are based on contact management, which enables prompt and tailored interactions (Farooq et al., 2025a, 2025g; Muhammad Farooq, Muhammad Ramzan, 2025).

Sales automation also heavily relies on CRM solutions. Automation boosts productivity and frees up sales people to concentrate on high-value work by automating sales procedures like lead scoring, opportunity management, and pipeline monitoring (Farooq et al., 2025k, 2025c, 2025h, 2025e). Organizations may increase the overall efficacy of their sales efforts and shorten sales cycles by automating mundane tasks(Farooq, Yuen, et al., 2024; Farooq, Buzdar, et al., 2024).

An additional essential component of CRM systems is marketing automation(-Farooq, Hafsa Qadir, et al., 2023; Yen et al., 2023). Businesses may use this feature to measure client interaction, automate email communication, and build customized marketing campaigns (Farooq et al., 2022b; Farooq, Bakhsh, et al., 2023). Organizations may increase engagement and conversion rates by using marketing automation to target certain client groups with tailored content (Farooq et al., 2022a; Y. Wang et al., 2021).

CRM technology include customer support and service as well (Buzdar & Farooq, 2020; Farooq et al., 2020). CRM systems with integrated customer service solutions help firms effectively handle client comments, complaints, and queries (Farooq, Khalil-Ur-Rehman, et al., 2019; Farooq & Qureshi, 2020). Customer satisfaction levels rise when customer care professionals are able to give more knowledgeable and individualized help thanks to access to past customer data. The development of machine learning (ML) and artificial intelligence (AI) has further transformed CRM systems(Farooq, Kalimuthu, et al., 2019; Farooq, Rehman, et al., 2019). AI powered predictive analytics enables businesses to anticipate consumer behavior, spot patterns, and make data-driven choices. Artificial intelligence (AI)-powered chatbots and virtual assistants improve client interactions by offering prompt, tailored assistance, hence elevating the entire customer experience (Buzdar & Farooq, 2020).

In CRM technology, integration skills are also essential. Coherent data flow across the company is ensured via seamless connectivity with other business systems, including e-commerce platforms and enterprise resource planning (ERP)(Farooq, 2019; Farooq, Ali, et al., 2019). A single approach to client contacts is made possible by this integration, which also improves cross-functional cooperation.

8.4 Integrating CRM with Other Business Systems

A company's contacts with both present and future consumers may be managed using a variety of strategies, including customer relationship management, or CRM(-Farooq & Raju, 2019d; Naseer et al., 2019). Although CRM tools and technologies are essential for improving client connections, their efficacy is much increased when they are smoothly connected with other corporate processes(Farooq & Raju, 2019a; Ghulam et al., 2019). Integration guarantees a comprehensive and cohesive strategy for handling client information, correspondence, and general corporate activities (Farooq et al., 2020).

Operational efficiency is increased and procedures are streamlined via CRM interaction with other corporate platforms. The removal of data silos is one of the main advantages. A consolidated repository of client data is made possible by the integration of CRM with various platforms, including sales tools, marketing automation, and enterprise resource planning (ERP) (Farooq, Muhammad, et al., 2019). Employees no longer have to switch between several platforms, giving them a complete picture of all contacts and transactions with customers (Ahmad et al., 2022).

Integration facilitates upgrades and real-time data access. Timely information is essential for making well-informed choices in a changing corporate environment (Farooq & Raju, 2019b, 2019c). CRM guarantees that the most recent client data is promptly accessible to all relevant departments when it is connected with systems like as order processing or inventory management. The ability to synchronize in real-time facilitates improved teamwork and allows teams to react quickly to requests and questions from customers.

Integration is essential for enhancing the client experience. Client care professionals may see a client's whole history of interactions with them, for example, when data flows seamlessly between CRM and customer support systems. This gives them the ability to serve customers in a tailored and effective manner, which increases customer satisfaction. Additionally, companies may monitor consumer behavior and preferences via interaction with e-commerce platforms, which enables customized marketing campaigns and suggestions (Nawaz et al., 2022).

Integrating CRM with other corporate platforms improves decision-making procedures from a strategic standpoint. Through the integration of client data with financial, sales, and marketing data, companies are able to get a full company performance picture. Through the use of an integrated strategy, businesses may make data-driven decisions that help them predict demand, spot trends, and allocate resources as efficiently as possible.

8.5 Analytics and CRM

Client relationship management (CRM) has made analytics a cornerstone by giving businesses the means to glean valuable insights from massive amounts of client data. Businesses can make more informed choices, improve customer engagement, and propel strategic goals when analytics and CRM work together in harmony (Ogiela et al., 2014; Qiu et al., 2014; Yan et al., 2014).

In CRM analytics, customer data is systematically analyzed to provide insights that may be put to use. By using cutting edge methods like data mining, predictive modeling, and machine learning, this procedure goes beyond conventional reporting. Finding patterns, trends, and correlations in the data is the aim in order to help businesses predict the behavior and preferences of their customers (Guerola-Navarro et al., 2020).

Developing customized and targeted marketing strategies is one of the main benefits of integrating analytics with CRM. Businesses may target certain client categories with their marketing efforts by examining customer interactions, past purchases, and demographic data. This level of targeted accuracy not only raises the efficacy of marketing initiatives but also improves the general consumer experience(Nestor & Ogudo, 2018).

A subset of CRM analytics called predictive analytics is essential for predicting future customer behavior. Businesses may find trends in past data that point to possible consumer behaviors, such probability of churn or purchase choices. Proactive actions are made possible by this foresight, which helps businesses to put plans into place that help them retain consumers, improve their product offerings, and remain ahead of market trends(Denic et al., 2014; Feng, 2014; J. Wang et al., 2014).

CRM analytics helps with performance improvement and measurement. Client satisfaction ratings, conversion rates, and client lifetime value are a few examples of key performance indicators (KPIs) that may be regularly tracked and evaluated. Organizations may pinpoint areas for development, hone consumer interaction tactics, and deploy resources wisely in order to meet corporate goals using this data-driven strategy (Saha et al., 2021).

An additional level of complexity is added to CRM analytics with the integration of machine learning (ML) and artificial intelligence (AI). Large datasets may now be automatically analyzed thanks to these technologies, which can reveal hidden insights that would not be seen using more conventional techniques. The customer experience may be improved overall by using AI-driven data to help forecast consumer preferences, automate repetitive operations, and provide tailored suggestions(Chagas et al., 2020).

8.6 Building and Maintaining Customer Loyalty through CRM

Beyond just making repeat purchases, customer loyalty is a highly sought-after commodity. It includes a consumer's emotional connection, level of trust, and contentment with a brand, all of which contribute to sustained loyalty. CRM is essential to this process because it gives companies the tools and techniques they need to comprehend, interact with, and satisfy their consumers. In a dynamic and demanding business climate, firms may develop, nurture, and sustain client loyalty with successful CRM practices (Ledro et al., 2022).

Building an extensive client database is one of the main ways that CRM promotes loyalty. Businesses may learn about their customers' interests, actions, and purchasing habits by gathering and analyzing customer data. This makes it possible for businesses to customize their goods, services, and marketing initiatives to match the unique requirements and preferences of their clientele. CRM essentially enables companies to provide a tailored and focused customer experience, which is a major factor in increasing client loyalty. CRM solutions make it easier for companies and customers to communicate smoothly(Kaewta & Chutima, 2014; Kammergruber et al., 2014; G. Li & Hou, 2014). A good customer experience is enhanced by prompt and pertinent interactions, such as customized emails, focused promotions, and attentive customer service. Businesses may automate communication procedures and make sure that clients get the appropriate messages at the appropriate time by using CRM technologies. This not only improves customer happiness but also strengthens the bond between the brand and the client, gradually encouraging loyalty(L. Li et al., 2023).

When it comes to retaining customers, consistency is key. CRM facilitates the development of coherent and consistent customer experiences across a range of touchpoints. CRM systems make ensuring that a consumer has a consistent and tailored experience whether they engage with a company inperson, on social media, or online. A feeling of familiarity and dependability is fostered by this consistency, which strengthens the brand's identity and fosters trust, all of which support enduring client loyalty.

The capacity of CRM to quickly detect and resolve customer complaints is another essential component in fostering loyalty. CRM systems help firms find areas for development and identify pain spots by analyzing consumer input. In addition to fixing urgent issues, proactive problem resolution shows a dedication to client satisfaction and fortifies the relationship between the consumer and the business.

This proactive strategy is essential for reducing client attrition and building long-term loyalty.

CRM systems are also essential to loyalty programs, which are intended to encourage and reward loyal consumers.

Businesses may increase the relevance and efficacy of their loyalty programs by customizing them for each individual consumer based on the purchases, preferences, and interaction data they collect. CRM-driven loyalty programs foster a feeling of exclusivity and gratitude in consumers by offering tailored incentives, exclusive deals, or discounts. This encourages customers to stay with the brand.

Building and sustaining client loyalty is greatly aided by analytics, an essential CRM component. Businesses may get profound insights into the behavior, tastes, and trends of their customers by using data analytics solutions. Businesses may predict client demands, refine product offerings, and customize marketing campaigns for optimal effect by using this data-driven strategy. Through strategic and data-driven efforts, CRM analytics enable organizations to make choices that connect with their consumer base and eventually increase customer loyalty.

CHAPTER CONCLUSION

Chapter provides insights into the intricacies of Customer Relationship Management (CRM), highlighting its transformative potential in revolutionizing how companies interact with their customers. At its core, CRM is a strategic approach that focuses on managing and evaluating relationships with both current and prospective clients. The chapter elucidates the fundamentals of CRM, CRM technologies and applications, integrating CRM with other business systems, analytics and CRM, and building and maintaining customer loyalty through CRM.

The chapter begins by emphasizing the importance of CRM as an advanced technology that centralizes client data, facilitating a comprehensive understanding of customer preferences, behaviors, and interactions. By acting as a digital hub, CRM systems seamlessly integrate marketing, sales, and customer support initiatives, thereby fostering long-term connections with customers and enhancing operational efficiency.

Fundamentals of CRM are discussed, highlighting its holistic approach that prioritizes customer retention, loyalty, and satisfaction. Understanding the customer journey, establishing deep connections, leveraging technology, and fostering a customer-centric culture are underscored as key pillars of CRM.

CRM technologies and applications are explored, showcasing how CRM systems serve as a centralized repository for client data from various sources such as sales, marketing, and customer support. Contact management, sales automation, marketing automation, and customer service are highlighted as essential components of CRM systems, alongside the integration skills necessary for seamless connectivity with other business platforms.

Integration of CRM with other business systems is elucidated as crucial for enhancing operational efficiency, streamlining processes, and improving the customer experience. By removing data silos, enabling real-time data access, and improving decision-making procedures, integration ensures a cohesive strategy for managing client information and corporate activities.

REFERENCES

Ahmad, S., Qureshi, I. U., Ramzan, M., & Rehman, S. U. (2022). Research Elite of Pakistan: Profile and Determinants of Productivity and Impact. *Publishing Research Quarterly*, *38*(2), 263–280. DOI: 10.1007/s12109-022-09874-5

AL-Rubaiee, H., Alomar, K., Qiu, R., & Li, D. (2018). Tuning of Customer Relationship Management (CRM) via Customer Experience Management (CEM) using Sentiment Analysis on Aspects Level. *International Journal of Advanced Computer Science and Applications*, *9*(5), 300–312.

Arab, F., Selamat, H., & Zamani, M. (2010). An overview of success factors for CRM. In E. Lau & S. Tseng (Eds.), *Proceedings - 2010 2nd IEEE International Conference on Information and Financial Engineering, ICIFE 2010* (Issues 2nd IEEE International Conference on Information and Financial Engineering (ICIFE) CL-Chongqing, PEOPLES R CHINA PU-IEEE PI-NEW YORK PA-345 E 47TH ST, NEW YORK, NY 10017 USA, pp. 702–705). DOI: 10.1109/ICIFE.2010.5609453

Buzdar, A. Q., & Farooq, M. (2020). Memorization of Quran through Mobile Application in the Era of Transformative Marketing. [PJSS]. *Pakistan Journal of Social Sciences*, *40*(2), 689–698.

Carlan, V., & Vanelslander, T. (2021). Economic Aspects of Introducing Artificial Intelligence Solutions in Logistics and Port Sectors: The Data Entry Case. [WE - Emerging Sources Citation Index] [ESCI]. *FRONTIERS IN FUTURE TRANSPORTATION*, *2*, 710330. Advance online publication. DOI: 10.3389/ffutr.2021.710330

Chagas, B. N. R., Viana, J., Reinhold, O., Lobato, F. M. F., Jacob, A. F. L.Jr, & Alt, R. (2020). A literature review of the current applications of machine learning and their practical implications. [WE - Emerging Sources Citation Index] [ESCI]. *WEB INTELLIGENCE*, *18*(1), 69–83. DOI: 10.3233/WEB-200429

Chatterjee, S., Chaudhuri, R., Vrontis, D., & Basile, G. (2022). Digital transformation and entrepreneurship process in SMEs of India: A moderating role of adoption of AI-CRM capability and strategic planning. *Journal of Strategy and Management*, *15*(3), 416–433. DOI: 10.1108/JSMA-02-2021-0049

Chatterjee, S., Chaudhuri, R., Vrontis, D., Thrassou, A., & Ghosh, S. K. (2021). Adoption of artificial intelligence-integrated CRM systems in agile organizations in India. *Technological Forecasting and Social Change*, *168*, 120783. Advance online publication. DOI: 10.1016/j.techfore.2021.120783

Chatterjee, S., Ghosh, S. K., Chaudhuri, R., & Chaudhuri, S. (2020a). Adoption of AI-integrated CRM system by Indian industry: From security and privacy perspective. *Information and Computer Security*, *29*(1), 1–24. DOI: 10.1108/ICS-02-2019-0029

Chatterjee, S., Ghosh, S. K., Chaudhuri, R., & Chaudhuri, S. (2020b). Adoption of AI-integrated CRM system by Indian industry: From security and privacy perspective. *Information and Computer Security*, *29*(1), 1–24. DOI: 10.1108/ICS-02-2019-0029

Chatterjee, S., Nguyen, B., Ghosh, S. K., Bhattacharjee, K. K., & Chaudhuri, S. (2020). Adoption of artificial intelligence integrated CRM system: An empirical study of Indian organizations. *The Bottom Line (New York, N.Y.)*, *33*(4), 359–375. DOI: 10.1108/BL-08-2020-0057

Denic, N., Moracanin, V., Milic, M., & Nesic, Z. (2014). RISK MANAGEMENT IN INFORMATION SYSTEM PROJECTS. *TEHNICKI VJESNIK-TECHNICAL GAZETTE*, *21*(6), 1239–1242.

Dułu, C. (2010). CRM Processes and the Impact on Business Performance. *Proceedings of the 5th WSEAS International Conference on Economy and Management Transformation, III*(Volume II), 762–767.

Dutt, H., & Chauhan, K. (2019). Using Flexibility in Designing CRM Solution. *Global Journal of Flexible Systems Managment*, *20*(2), 103–116. DOI: 10.1007/s40171-018-0203-y

Farooq, M. (2019). Emerging sciences in Social Sciences : An overview, A Research Agenda. *Global Journal of Emerging Sciences*, *1*(October), 183–197.

Farooq, M., Ali, W., Younas, W., Khalil-Ur-rehman, F., & Qurashi, Q. A. (2019). the Era of Transformative Marketing: Service Quality of Mobile App Based Taxi Services in Kuala Lumpur. *Proceedings on Engineering Sciences*, *1*(2), 49–58. DOI: 10.24874/PES01.02.006

Farooq, M., Bakhsh, A., Hafsa Qadir, B., & Warda, N. (2023). Digital Empowerment: Freedom of Expression Beyond 5G and 6G Networks in Developing Countries. *Pakistan Journal of Social Sciences*, *43*(4), 569–584. DOI: 10.5281/zenodo.10448484

Farooq, M., Buzdar, H. Q., Yen, Y. Y., & Bakhsh, A. (2024). Integrating AI in Sustainable Writing: An Empirical Investigation of the Technology Acceptance Model in Asian Social Sciences. *Journal of Logistics. Informatics and Service Science*, *11*(3), 324–338. DOI: 10.33168/JLISS.2024.0321

Farooq, M., Cheng, J., Khan, N. U., Saufi, R. A., Kanwal, N., & Bazkiaei, H. A. (2022a). Sustainable Waste Management Companies with Innovative Smart Solutions: A Systematic Review and Conceptual Model. *Sustainability (Basel), 14*(20), 13146. Advance online publication. DOI: 10.3390/su142013146

Farooq, M., Cheng, J., Khan, N. U., Saufi, R. A., Kanwal, N., & Bazkiaei, H. A. (2022b). Sustainable Waste Management Companies with Innovative Smart Solutions: A Systematic Review and Conceptual Model. *Sustainability (Basel), 14*(20), 13146. DOI: 10.3390/su142013146

Farooq, M., Hafsa Qadir, B., & Saeed, M. (2023, December). AI-Enhanced Social Sciences: A Systematic Literature Review and Bibliographic Analysis of Web of Science Published Research Papers. *Pakistan Journal of Society* [PJSEL]. *Education and Language, 10*, 1–2.

Farooq, M., Kalimuthu, R., & Reza, M. H. (2019). Measuring and Comparing Brand Equity of Malaysian Banks in the Era of Transformative Marketing. *Global Journal of Emerging Sciences, 1*(June), 96–102.

Farooq, M., Khalil-Ur-Rehman, F., Abdurrahaman, D. T., Younas, W., Sajjad, S., & Zreen, A. (2019). SERVICE QUALITY ANALYSIS OF PRIVATE UNIVERSITIES LIBRARIES IN MALAYSIA IN THE ERA OF TRANSFORMATIVE MARKETING. *International Journal of Qualitative Research, 13*(2), 269–284. DOI: 10.24874/IJQR13.02-02

Farooq, M., Muhammad, S., Raju, V., Kalimuthu, K. R., & Qadir, A. (2019). Measuring and Comparing the Desired and Actual Service Quality of Pakistan International Airline. *The Journal of Social Sciences Research, 52*(52), 484–490. DOI: 10.32861/jssr.52.484.490

Farooq, M., & Qureshi, Q. A. (2020). Practical Approach of Environmental Awareness to Broadening Community Participation: A Case Study of Pindad (Persero). *Journal of Management Practices. Humanities and Social Sciences, 4*(1). Advance online publication. DOI: 10.33152/jmphss-4.2.1

Farooq, M., & Raju, V. (2019a). Impact of Over-the-Top (OTT) Services on the Telecom Companies in the Era of Transformative Marketing. *Global Journal of Flexible Systems Managment, 20*(2), 177–188. DOI: 10.1007/s40171-019-00209-6

Farooq, M., & Raju, V. (2019b). Want to Stay the Market Leader in the Era of Transformative Marketing? Keep the Customers Satisfied! *Global Journal of Flexible Systems Management*. DOI: 10.1007/s40171-019-00213-w

Farooq, M., & Raju, V. (2019c). Impact of Over-the-Top (OTT) Services on the Telecom Companies in the Era of Transformative Marketing. *Global Journal of Flexible Systems Managment, 20*(2), 177–188. DOI: 10.1007/s40171-019-00209-6

Farooq, M., & Raju, V. (2019d). Want to Stay the Market Leader in the Era of Transformative Marketing? Keep the Customers Satisfied! *Global Journal of Flexible Systems Managment, 20*(3), 257–266. DOI: 10.1007/s40171-019-00213-w

Farooq, M., & Ramzan, M. Y. Y. Y. (2025). AI in Management. In *Transformative Impacts of AI in Management* (1st ed., pp. 1–44). IGI Global. DOI: 10.4018/979-8-3693-4322-7.ch001

Farooq, M., Ramzan, M., & Yen, Y. Y. (2025a). AI in Consumer Behavior Management. In *Transformative Impacts of AI in Management* (pp. 281–294). IGI Global., DOI: 10.4018/979-8-3693-4322-7.ch011

Farooq, M., Ramzan, M., & Yen, Y. Y. (2025b). AI in Customer Service, HR, and Administration. In *Transformative Impacts of AI in Management* (pp. 45–70). IGI Global. DOI: 10.4018/979-8-3693-4322-7.ch002

Farooq, M., Ramzan, M., & Yen, Y. Y. (2025c). AI in Quality Management. In *Transformative Impacts of AI in Management* (pp. 295–312). IGI Global., DOI: 10.4018/979-8-3693-4322-7.ch012

Farooq, M., Ramzan, M., & Yen, Y. Y. (2025d). Artificial Intelligence and Customer Experiences. In *Transformative Impacts of AI in Management* (pp. 95–114). IGI Global., DOI: 10.4018/979-8-3693-4322-7.ch004

Farooq, M., Ramzan, M., & Yen, Y. Y. (2025e). Artificial Intelligence in Administration Sciences. In *Transformative Impacts of AI in Management* (pp. 115–156). IGI Global., DOI: 10.4018/979-8-3693-4322-7.ch005

Farooq, M., Ramzan, M., & Yen, Y. Y. (2025f). Artificial Intelligence in Business and Law. In *Transformative Impacts of AI in Management* (pp. 71–94). IGI Global., DOI: 10.4018/979-8-3693-4322-7.ch003

Farooq, M., Ramzan, M., & Yen, Y. Y. (2025g). Artificial Intelligence in Ethical Business Decision Making. In *Transformative Impacts of AI in Management* (pp. 265–280). IGI Global., DOI: 10.4018/979-8-3693-4322-7.ch010

Farooq, M., Ramzan, M., & Yen, Y. Y. (2025h). Exploring the Impact of Artificial Intelligence on Brand Management. In *Transformative Impacts of AI in Management* (pp. 157–188). IGI Global., DOI: 10.4018/979-8-3693-4322-7.ch006

Farooq, M., Ramzan, M., & Yen, Y. Y. (2025i). Exploring the Impact of Ethical Leadership and Employee Engagement on Knowledge Sharing Attitudes in the Asian Digital Economy. In *Transformative Impacts of AI in Management* (pp. 241–264). IGI Global., DOI: 10.4018/979-8-3693-4322-7.ch009

Farooq, M., Ramzan, M., & Yen, Y. Y. (2025j). Transformative Impact of AI in Education Management. In *Transformative Impacts of AI in Management* (pp. 189–216). IGI Global., DOI: 10.4018/979-8-3693-4322-7.ch007

Farooq, M., Ramzan, M., & Yen, Y. Y. (2025k). *Transformative Impacts of AI in Management.* IGI Global., DOI: 10.4018/979-8-3693-4322-7

Farooq, M., Rehman, F. K. U., Younas, W., Raju, V., Ahmed, Q. M., & Ali, M. (2019). Investigating Relationship between Net Promoter Score and Company Performance: A Longitudinal Study. *Global Journal of Emerging Sciences, 1*(1), 1–10. https://www.gjoes.org/wp-content/uploads/2019/04/1-1.pdf

Farooq, M., Saeed, M., Ali, W., & Javid, R. (2020). Online Buying and Customer Satisfaction in the Era of Transformative Marketing. *City University Research Journal, 10*(2), 274–288.

Farooq, M., Yuen, Y. Y., & Buzdar, H. Q. (2024). Exploring the Research Landscape of Artificial Intelligence Integration with Business Management: A Bibliometric Analysis from 1994-2023. *Journal of Logistics. Informatics and Service Science*, (April). Advance online publication. DOI: 10.33168/JLISS.2024.0410

Feng, Z. (2014). The functional framework of tourism resources management information systems. In P. Ren & Z. Du (Eds.), *INFORMATION SCIENCE AND MANAGEMENT ENGINEERING, VOLS 1-3* (Vol. 46, Issue International Conference of Information Science and Management Engineering (ISME) CL-Wuhan, pp. 2283–2287). DOI: 10.2495/ISME20133073

Ghulam, W. A., Ali, W., Ali, S., Khan, M. M., Khan, R. N., & Farooq, M. (2019). Investigating factors influencing brain drain of citizens of Azad Kashmir Pakistan. *Journal of Social Sciences Research*, *5*(3), 782–788. Advance online publication. DOI: 10.32861/jssr.53.782.788

Guerola-Navarro, V., Oltra-Badenes, R., & Gil-Gomez, H. (2020). ANALYSIS OF THE RELATIONSHIP BETWEEN THE DEGREE OF INTRODUCTION OF CRM AND THE BENEFITS OF THE COMPANY THROUGH ORGANIZATIONAL PERFORMANCE AND BUSINESS INNOVATION. *3C EMPRESA, 9*(1), 67–87. https://doi.org/ WE - Emerging Sources Citation Index (ESCI)DOI: 10.17993/3cemp.2020.090147.67-87

Holloway, J., Yuan, X., Ouyang, J., Laird, G., Jackson, V., Arnold, T., Bedolla, M., & Nigam, S. (2019). USING HIGH POWERED ANALYTICS AND CUSTOMER RELATIONSHIP MANAGEMENT (CRM) TOOLS TO PROVIDE A BETTER MEMBER EXPERIENCE: BCBSLA MAKING A DIFFERENCE. *Value in Health, 22*(2), S265–S266. DOI: 10.1016/j.jval.2019.04.1252

Kaewta, S., & Chutima, P. (2014). Improvement of project portfolio management in an information technology consulting company. In F. L. Gaol, J. Webb, & J. Ding (Eds.), *IOP Conference Series: Materials Science and Engineering* (Vol. 58, Issue 1). DOI: 10.1088/1757-899X/58/1/012012

Kammergruber, R., Robold, S., Karliç, J., & Durner, J. (2014). The future of the laboratory information system - What are the requirements for a powerful system for a laboratory data management? *Clinical Chemistry and Laboratory Medicine, 52*(11), e225–e230. DOI: 10.1515/cclm-2014-0276 PMID: 24897404

Khanh, C. N. T., Phong, L., & Cao, K. D. (2022). The impact of organizational factors on E-CRM success implementation. *VINE Journal of Information and Knowledge Management Systems, 52*(4), 612–629. DOI: 10.1108/VJIKMS-05-2020-0096

Kim, C., Lee, I.-S., Wang, T., & Mirusmonov, M. (2015). Evaluating effects of mobile CRM on employees' performance. *Industrial Management & Data Systems, 115*(4), 740–764. DOI: 10.1108/IMDS-08-2014-0245

Kumar, V., Umashankar, N., & Won, J. (2014). CRM metrics and strategies to enhance performance in service industries. In *Handbook of Service Marketing Research*. Issue January., DOI: 10.4337/9780857938855.00015

Ledro, C., Nosella, A., & Vinelli, A. (2022). Artificial intelligence in customer relationship management: Literature review and future research directions. [WE - Social Science Citation Index] [SSCI]. *Journal of Business and Industrial Marketing, 37*(13), 48–63. DOI: 10.1108/JBIM-07-2021-0332

Li, G., & Hou, L. (2014). Power Enterprise Performance Management Information System Development and Research. In K. M. Lee, P. Yarlagadda, & Y. M. Lu (Eds.), *PROGRESS IN MECHATRONICS AND INFORMATION TECHNOLOGY, PTS 1 AND 2* (Vols. 462–463, Issue International Conference on Mechatronics and Information Technology (ICMIT 2013) CL-Guilin, pp. 964–967). https://doi.org/ DOI: 10.4028/www.scientific.net/AMM.462-463.964

Li, L., Lin, J. B., Luo, W. Y., & Luo, X. (2023). INVESTIGATING THE EFFECT OF ARTIFICIAL INTELLIGENCE ON CUSTOMER RELATIONSHIP MANAGEMENT PERFORMANCE IN E-COMMERCE ENTERPRISES. [WE-Social Science Citation Index] [SSCI]. *Journal of Electronic Commerce Research, 24*(1), 68–83.

Naseer, M., Farooq, M., Younas, W., & Raju, V. (2019). Antecedents of employee retention in the pharmaceutical industry of Pakistan. *Journal of Social Sciences Research, 5*(3), 656–664. Advance online publication. DOI: 10.32861/jssr.53.655.664

Nawaz, R., Bin-Naeem, S., & Ramzan, M. (2022). *Relationship between Awareness and Use of Digital Information Resources among University Students of Southern Punjab*. Library Philosophy & Practice.

Nestor, D. M. J., & Ogudo, K. A. (2018). Practical Implementation of Machine Learning and Predictive Analytics in Cellular Network Transactions in Real Time. *2018 International Conference on Advances in Big Data, Computing and Data Communication Systems, IcABCD 2018*. DOI: 10.1109/ICABCD.2018.8465476

Ogiela, M. R., Ogiela, L., & Ogiela, U. (2014). Advanced techniques for computer sharing and management of strategic data. In Linawati, M. S. Mahendra, E. J. Neuhold, A. M. Tjoa, & I. You (Eds.), *Lecture Notes in Computer Science (including subseries Lecture Notes in Artificial Intelligence and Lecture Notes in Bioinformatics): Vol. 8407 LNCS* (Issues 2nd IFIP TC5/8 International Conference on ICT-EurAsia CL-Bali, pp. 521–525). DOI: 10.1007/978-3-642-55032-4_53

Peng, X. (2014). Design and implementation of CRM system based on AMS cloud platform. In W. Jing, X. Ning, & Z. Huiyu (Eds.), *Proceedings - 2014 5th International Conference on Intelligent Systems Design and Engineering Applications, ISDEA 2014* (Vol. 76, Issues 7th International Conference on Education, Management, Information and Mechanical Engineering (EMIM) CL-Shenyang, pp. 330–333). DOI: 10.1109/ISDEA.2014.81

Qiu, L., Wen, J., & Cai, H. (2014). Design and Implementation of A Management Information System of Equipment Based on RFID. In Y. H. Kim & P. Yarlagadda (Eds.), *RESEARCH IN MATERIALS AND MANUFACTURING TECHNOLOGIES, PTS 1-3* (Vols. 835–836, Issues 3rd International Conference on Materials and Products Manufacturing Technology (ICMPMT 2013) CL-Guangzhou, pp. 1031-+). https://doi.org/DOI: 10.4028/www.scientific.net/AMR.834-836.1031

Ruiz-Palomo, D., Diéguez-Soto, J., Duréndez, A., & Santos, J. A. C. (2019). Family Management and Firm Performance in Family SMEs: The Mediating Roles of Management Control Systems and Technological Innovation. *Sustainability (Basel), 11*(14), 3805. DOI: 10.3390/su11143805

Saha, L., Tripathy, H. K., Nayak, S. R., Bhoi, A. K., & Barsocchi, P. (2021). Amalgamation of customer relationship management and data analytics in different business sectors—A systematic literature review. *Sustainability (Basel), 13*(9), 5279. Advance online publication. DOI: 10.3390/su13095279

Sharma, R., Jagtap, U. R., & Mishra, D. P. (2019). Effects of Customer Relationship Management (CRM) Strategies on AverageRevenue per User (ARPU) in the context of Telecommunication Sector. *Pacific Business Review International, 12*(3), 55–61.

Sorayaei, A., Reaz Valiollahi, H., Hossein Zadeh, M., Hossein Ghoryshian, S., & Masoud Dinari, A. (2013). Impact of Customer Relationship Management (CRM) on Marketing Performance: A Case Study in Mellat Bank of Mazandaran Province. *European Online Journal of Natural and Social Sciences*, *2*(3), 2612–2619.

Wang, J., Hu, X., Li, X., & Ding, F. (2014). A Research of Information Management System Based on Data Mining. In D. L. Liu, X. B. Zhu, K. L. Xu, & D. M. Fang (Eds.), *APPLIED SCIENCE, MATERIALS SCIENCE AND INFORMATION TECHNOLOGIES IN INDUSTRY* (Vols. 513–517, Issue International Conference on Advances in Materials Science and Information Technologies in Industry (AMSITI) CL-Xian, pp. 616–619). DOI: 10.4028/www.scientific.net/AMM.513-517.616

Wang, Y., Lin, J., Osman, Z., Farooq, M., & Raju, V. (2021). Transformational leadership and employee performance in international commercial banking industry in Malaysia: The role of self-efficacy as a mediator under BRI. *Journal of Chinese Human Resource Management*, *12*(2), 25–36. DOI: 10.47297/wspchrmWSP2040-800503.20211202

Yan, X., Lin, Z., Zhang, X., & Yang, W. (2014). Design and realization of micro-information system based on Alfresco development tool. In X. Jiang, S. Li, Y. Dai, & Y. Cheng (Eds.), *Proceedings - 2014 International Conference on Information Science, Electronics and Electrical Engineering, ISEEE 2014* (Vol. 3, Issue International Conference on pp. 1604–1608). DOI: 10.1109/InfoSEEE.2014.6946192

Yen, Y. Y., Wen, L. J., Ramasamy, S., & Farooq, M. (2023). Sustainable petrol subsidy program in Malaysia. *Asian Development Policy Review*, *12*(1), 1–9. DOI: 10.55493/5008.v12i1.4948

Chapter 9 Transformative Impacts of AI in Supply Chain Management (SCM) Systems

ABSTRACT

Modern corporate operations rely heavily on supply chain management (SCM) systems, which coordinate a complicated dance of interrelated procedures to guarantee the smooth flow of products and services from production to consumption (Farooq, Yuen, et al., 2024; Verwijmeren, 1998). Supply chain management (SCM) systems are the digital architects of efficiency, painstakingly arranging each link in the chain to maximize resources and save expenses (Dorcak, 2013). A wide range of operations are integrated by these systems, including distribution, logistics, inventory management, production planning, and procurement (L. Wang et al., 2009; Zoubeidi et al., 2014). SCM systems enable businesses to anticipate market needs and adjust to changing conditions by using sophisticated algorithms and real-time data analytics (Xiong et al., 2008a). Their ability to provide transparency across the supply chain makes it easier for manufacturers, distributors, and suppliers to collaborate and communicate effectively (Hart, 2017).

9.1 CHAPTER INTRODUCTION

SCM systems improve visibility and control by using cutting edge technology like machine learning, artificial intelligence, and the Internet of Things (IoT) (Mirarchi et al., 2018; Xiong et al., 2008b). They provide companies the ability to keep tabs on supply chain performance, keep track of inventory levels, and proactively manage

DOI: 10.4018/979-8-3373-0513-4.ch009

risks. SCM systems promote sustainability by reducing waste and increasing resource utilization. They also increase operational efficiency by boosting responsiveness and streamlining operations (Lin & Ghodrati, 2012; Zhong et al., 2010). These systems are essentially the quiet builders that balance the complex global trade symphony, guaranteeing that goods arrive at their destinations on schedule and with accuracy.

Figure 1. Mind map of supply chain management systems

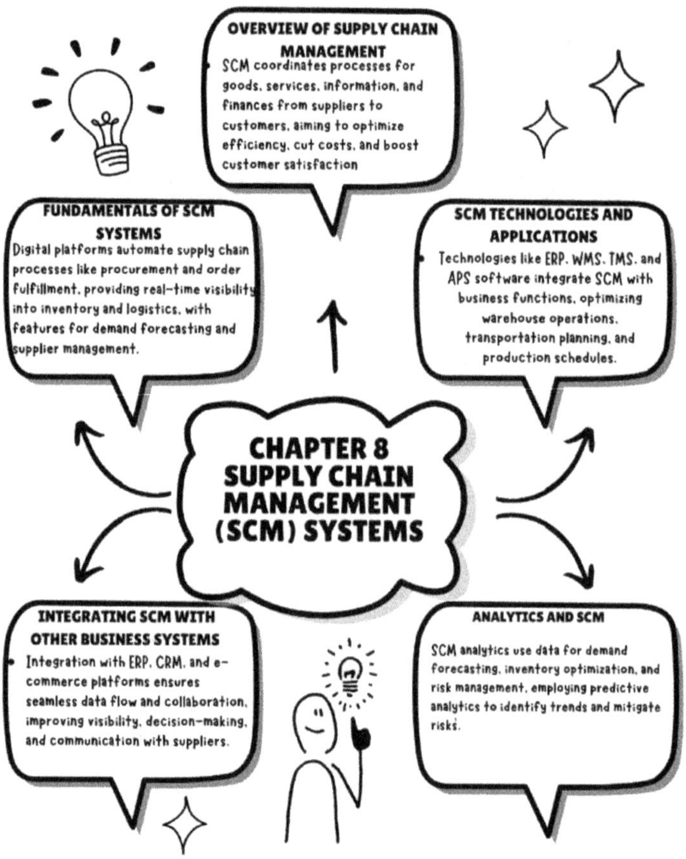

9.2 BASICS OF SUPPLY CHAIN MANAGEMENT

A key component of contemporary corporate operations is supply chain management (SCM), which entails integrating and coordinating a number of procedures to guarantee the smooth movement of products and services from the place of origin to the final customer(Tarigan et al., 2019; Y. Wang & Deng, 2015). It includes a wide variety of tasks, such as manufacturing, distribution, transportation, and customer support, among others. SCM's main objectives are to optimize these procedures, save expenses, boost productivity, and ultimately provide value to clients and companies alike (Flynn et al., 2021).

Strategic planning and administration of all operations pertaining to product procurement, manufacturing, and delivery are included in supply chain management (SCM)(Yinbin & Hongbo, 2009; W. Zhang et al., 2012). In order to provide a smooth flow of products and services, it involves a network of businesses, suppliers, manufacturers, distributors, retailers, and consumers. SCM's reach goes beyond individual businesses; it emphasizes cooperation and coordination across the whole supply chain.(Hawkins, 2017)

Demand forecasting, inventory control, order fulfillment, and logistics are important aspects of supply chain management. Demand forecasting enables businesses to better plan and manage their inventories by assisting them in anticipating client demands (Li et al., 2008; Olson, 2018). By ensuring that goods are accessible when and where they are required, effective inventory management lowers the possibility of stock outs or overstock scenarios. While logistics focuses on the actual physical transfer of items from manufacturing facilities to distribution hubs and, finally, to the end consumer, order fulfillment include processing client orders effectively(Iskanderov & Pautov, 2019; Shah et al., 2002).

SCM relies heavily on the use of technology to improve productivity and optimize workflows. SCM has been completely transformed by the incorporation of cutting-edge technologies like blockchain, Internet of Things, and artificial intelligence (AI)(Shi et al., 2022; Zhao & Zhu, 2011). With the real-time insight these technologies provide into supply chain activities, decision-making becomes easier, responses happen more quickly, and performance is enhanced all around (Park & Koh, 2015; Wenhui et al., 2009).

Artificial intelligence can analyze enormous volumes of data to find patterns and trends, assisting businesses in making better choices(Park & Koh, 2015; Yang & Sun, 2020). Real-time monitoring of commodities throughout the supply chain is made possible by IoT devices like sensors and RFID tags, which improve visibility and lower the possibility of mistakes(Karim et al., 2024; Roy et al., 2012). Blockchain technology lowers the possibility of fraud and mistakes in the supply chain by generating an immutable record of transactions, ensuring transparency and security (Farooq et al., 2025i, 2025f).

An essential part of supply chain management (SCM) is strategic sourcing and procurement, which focuses on finding and choosing suppliers that can provide the most value to the company(Farooq et al., 2025j, 2025d). This entails evaluating elements including price, innovation, quality, and dependability. Organizations may improve their relationships with suppliers, negotiate advantageous terms, and reduce the risks involved in the purchase of products and services by proactively managing the sourcing process (Farooq et al., 2025b, 2025a).

Another crucial component that handles the many uncertainties and possible interruptions that might affect the supply chain is supply chain risk management (Farooq et al., 2025g, 2025c, 2025h). As the world has confronted with recent problems, these risks might include natural catastrophes, geopolitical conflicts, swings in the economy, and even pandemics(Farooq et al., 2025e, 2025k; Muhammad Farooq, Muhammad Ramzan, 2025). In order to maintain supply chain continuity, effective risk management entails detecting possible hazards, creating mitigation methods, and creating backup plans.

9.3 TECHNOLOGIES DRIVING SCM EFFICIENCY

Modern technology integration is now essential for improving supply chain management's (SCM) performance.

Technological advances are essential for increasing overall performance, optimizing resources, and simplifying operations(Farooq, Yuen, et al., 2024; Farooq, Buzdar, et al., 2024). A number of innovative technologies are key to improving SCM effectiveness, challenging conventional wisdom, and opening the door for a more integrated and flexible supply chain (Kokodey et al., 2020).

Internet of Things (IoT) is one of the major technologies that is revolutionizing SCM(Farooq, Bakhsh, et al., 2023; Farooq, Hafsa Qadir, et al., 2023). The Internet of Things (IoT) allows for real-time data gathering and monitoring by embedding sensors and devices at different points in the supply chain. Improved visibility throughout the whole supply chain from production to delivery and distribution is made possible by this interconnectedness (Farooq et al., 2022b; Yen et al., 2023).

Businesses may use IoT to follow the flow of goods, keep an eye on inventory levels, and even evaluate the state of commodities while they are in route. This degree of openness facilitates well-informed decision-making, cutting down on mistakes, delays, and improving inventory control(Farooq et al., 2022a; Y. Wang et al., 2021).

Artificial Intelligence (AI) is a disruptive technology in supply chain management. Applications of artificial intelligence (AI), such predictive analytics and machine learning algorithms, enable businesses to examine enormous volumes of data in order to anticipate demand, spot patterns, and make data driven choices(Farooq et al., 2020; Farooq & Qureshi, 2020). AI can improve inventory control, warehouse management, and route planning, resulting in more productive operations. AI-driven demand forecasting also lowers the risk of overstocking and stock outs by assisting businesses in anticipating market swings (Buzdar & Farooq, 2020; Farooq & Raju, 2019d; Ghulam et al., 2019).

Blockchain technology has shown to be a game-changer for improving supply chain traceability and transparency(Farooq, Muhammad, et al., 2019; Farooq & Raju, 2019a). Blockchain makes it possible to preserve safe, distributed records, generating an auditable, immutable ledger of all transactions. This reduces the possibility of fraud and mistakes while ensuring the accuracy of the information. In supply chains where traceability is essential, like those in the food and pharmaceutical sectors, blockchain technology is very helpful(Farooq & Raju, 2019b, 2019c). It promotes trust and accountability by giving stakeholders and customers real-time insight into the provenance and path of goods(Farooq, Khalil-Ur-Rehman, et al., 2019; Farooq, Rehman, et al., 2019).

SCM is changing as a result of automation and robots, which increase operational efficiency and automate repetitive processes. Automated technologies in distribution centers and warehouses may improve accuracy, shorten lead times, and expedite order fulfillment(Farooq, Kalimuthu, et al., 2019). Order processing, data input, and invoice verification are among the jobs that robotic process automation (RPA) is used for. This allows human resources to be allocated to more strategic and value-added activities(Farooq, Ali, et al., 2019).

Another technology that is transforming supply chain management (SCM) is cloud computing, which offers an adaptable and scalable infrastructure for processing and storing data(Farooq, 2019; Naseer et al., 2019). Stakeholders may collaborate in real-time and access information from any location using cloud-based supply chain management tools. Better coordination and communication between distributors, manufacturers, and suppliers is made possible by this, which eventually raises the supply chain's overall responsiveness.

9.4 STRATEGIC SOURCING AND PROCUREMENT

The process of strategic sourcing is locating, assessing, and choosing suppliers according to a range of factors, including price, quality, dependability, and innovation(Karim et al., 2024; Okada et al., 2024). It takes into account the whole value that a supplier provides to the company, going beyond the conventional cost-centric approach. Through the establishment of strategic alliances, organizations may optimize suppliers' technological prowess, skills, and knowledge to augment the competitiveness of their offerings (VanVactor, 2017).

Efficient procurement tactics are essential for controlling expenses, reducing risks, and guaranteeing a steady flow of products and services. Achieving cost efficiency requires maximizing the procurement process, taking advantage of economies of scale, and negotiating advantageous terms. By diversifying the supplier base, evaluating geopolitical issues, and putting backup plans in place to handle supply chain interruptions, procurement experts also concentrate on risk management(Gupta & Panigrahi, 2023; Y. Wang et al., 2023; Zhidong, 2023).

Strategic sourcing and procurement need a strong foundation in cooperation and relationship management. Fostering open communication, innovation, and continual improvement is facilitated by establishing strong and transparent partnerships with suppliers(Dalloul et al., 2023; Godoy et al., 2023). Organizations may use suppliers' experience, promote product innovation, and adapt to market shifts more skillfully by collaborating closely with them. Better supply chain resilience is also a result of strategic collaborations, as suppliers turn into valuable allies in overcoming obstacles and ambiguities(Z. Huang, 2022; Na & Shon, 2022).

Strategic sourcing and procurement procedures are being modernized in large part because to digital technology. Supplier Relationship Management (SRM) tools, e-Sourcing platforms, and e-Procurement systems simplify processes, increase visibility, and strengthen buyer-supplier cooperation. Procurement teams may concentrate on value adding strategic initiatives by automating repetitive chores like invoice reconciliation and purchase order processing(Li et al., 2022; X. Zhang, 2022).

Sustainability is becoming a more crucial factor in strategic buying and sourcing decisions. Companies are incorporating sustainability standards into the selection and assessment of their suppliers as they become more aware of the effects their supply chain operations have on the environment and society(L. Huang, 2022; Pereira et al., 2022). This satisfies customer desire for items that are both ecologically sustainable and sourced ethically, in addition to being in line with CSR objectives.

Figure 2. ZONG CSR objectives

9.5 SUPPLY CHAIN RISK MANAGEMENT

Supply Chain Risk Management (SCRM) has emerged as a crucial component of contemporary company operations, as enterprises maneuver across an ever-more intricate global terrain. In a world where supply chains are interdependent and susceptible to many kinds of interruptions, maintaining operations and guaranteeing continuity depend heavily on the efficient management of risks(Hussain et al., 2022).

Risks that might affect the supply chain are identified, evaluated, and mitigated as part of supply chain risk management (SCRM). These risks can include a variety of things, including natural catastrophes, geopolitical crises, economic uncertainty, and operational interruptions. The first step in the process is a thorough risk assessment, in which businesses examine every link in their supply chain to find weak areas and possible sources of failure(Korecki & Adamkova, 2018).

The creation of backup plans and risk-reduction techniques is one of the main tenets of SCRM. This entails developing backup suppliers, coming up with alternate sourcing strategies, and building adaptable logistical networks that can handle unanticipated events. Enterprises may enhance their ability to tolerate shocks and disruptions by expanding their supply networks and diversifying their sourcing regions. Technology is essential to increasing the efficacy of SCRM. Businesses are better equipped to anticipate and evaluate possible hazards thanks to advanced analytics, AI, and ML technologies. Large volumes of data, such as market trends, historical patterns, and geopolitical indicators, may be analyzed by these technologies, yielding insightful information for proactive risk management.

Communication and teamwork are crucial for a successful SCRM. A more robust supply chain may be achieved via building trusting relationships with suppliers, exchanging information, and promoting transparency. Together, the two sides will create cooperative risk-reduction plans to make sure their efforts to reduce any interruptions are coordinated. Through continuous observation of key performance indicators (KPIs), businesses may assess how well their risk management tactics are working. This entails having real-time insight throughout the whole supply chain, allowing for prompt reaction to new risks and continuous optimization of mitigation strategies.

9.6 SUSTAINABLE SUPPLY CHAIN PRACTICES

Supply chain operations are being profoundly impacted by the paradigm shift in favor of sustainability that has taken place in the world of business. Because people are becoming more conscious of their social and environmental obligations, sustainable supply chain management, or SSCM, has become a crucial corporate approach. This change aims to implement ethical and environmentally sustainable practices throughout the whole supply chain, going beyond simple regulatory compliance (Alfawaz & Alshehri, 2022).

Sustainability-focused supply chain management (SSCM) entails incorporating sustainable practices into all phases of the supply chain, including product design, sourcing, manufacturing, distribution, and end-of-life disposal. This all-encompassing strategy seeks to reduce the negative effects on the environment, support moral work habits, and provide long-term benefits for all parties concerned.

Responsible sourcing is a crucial component of sustainable supply chain management techniques. This entails choosing suppliers according to their commitment to moral and sustainable business practices, in addition to factors like price and quality. Businesses are keeping a closer eye on the social and environmental performance of their suppliers to make sure they follow applicable laws, employ eco-friendly products, and follow ethical labor practices.

The reduction of carbon footprints throughout the whole supply chain is another essential component. Businesses are using cutting-edge techniques and technology to streamline shipping routes, reduce manufacturing energy use, and provide environmentally friendly packaging options. This not only supports environmental objectives but also lowers costs and improves brand recognition.

Sustainable supply chain techniques are increasingly incorporating the ideas of the circular economy. This entails promoting material reuse, reducing trash output, and developing goods with recycling in mind. In an effort to establish a more sustainable and circular supply chain, businesses are looking at methods to increase product life cycles, decrease single-use packaging, and put in place efficient recycling processes.

Businesses dedicated to openly communicating about their social and environmental effects now routinely report on sustainability. In order to enable stakeholders to evaluate a company's performance in terms of environmental preservation, social responsibility, and ethical business practices, this entails monitoring and publishing essential sustainability measures.

9.7 CHAPTER CONCLUSION

Chapter 8 delves into the intricacies of Supply Chain Management (SCM), emphasizing its critical role in modern corporate operations. SCM serves as the backbone of efficiency, orchestrating a complex web of interconnected processes to ensure the seamless flow of products and services from production to consumption. From strategic planning and administration to leveraging cutting-edge technologies, SCM is essential for optimizing resources, reducing costs, and ultimately providing value to both customers and businesses alike.

Supply Chain Management (SCM) systems act as digital architects of efficiency, meticulously arranging each link in the chain to maximize resources and save costs. By integrating various operations such as distribution, logistics, inventory management, production planning, and procurement, SCM systems enable businesses to anticipate market needs, adjust to changing conditions, and foster collaboration across the supply chain.

Key components of SCM, including demand forecasting, inventory control, logistics, and order fulfillment, are essential for ensuring the smooth flow of products and services. Leveraging technologies such as Internet of Things (IoT), artificial intelligence (AI), and blockchain revolutionizes SCM, enabling real-time data gathering, predictive analytics, and enhanced transparency and traceability throughout the supply chain.

Strategic sourcing and procurement play a crucial role in SCM, focusing on finding suppliers that provide the most value to the company beyond just cost considerations. By fostering strong partnerships, utilizing digital tools, and prioritizing sustainability, organizations can optimize their supply chain operations and mitigate risks effectively.

Supply Chain Risk Management (SCRM) has emerged as a critical aspect of SCM, addressing various risks that may disrupt supply chain operations. Through thorough risk assessment, proactive mitigation strategies, and leveraging advanced technologies, businesses can enhance their resilience and ensure continuity in the face of uncertainties.

Sustainable Supply Chain Practices are increasingly becoming integral to SCM, as businesses strive to incorporate ethical and environmentally sustainable practices into their operations. From responsible sourcing to reducing carbon footprints and embracing circular economy principles, sustainable SCM aims to minimize environmental impact, promote ethical work practices, and deliver long-term benefits for all stakeholders.

REFERENCES

Al Karim, R., Rabiul, M. K., Ahamed, T., Karim, D. N., & Mehzabeen, M. (2024). Integrating Green Entrepreneurial Orientation, Green Information Systems, and Management Support with Green Supply Chain Management to Foster Firms' Environmental Performance. *Sustainability (Basel), 16*(12), 4921. DOI: 10.3390/su16124921

Alfawaz, K. M., & Alshehri, A. A. (2022). Applying Artificial Intelligence in Supply Chain Management. [WE - Emerging Sources Citation Index] [ESCI]. *COMMUNICATIONS IN MATHEMATICS AND APPLICATIONS, 13*(1), 367–377. DOI: 10.26713/cma.v13i1.1976

Buzdar, A. Q., & Farooq, M. (2020). Memorization of Quran through Mobile Application in the Era of Transformative Marketing. [PJSS]. *Pakistan Journal of Social Sciences, 40*(2), 689–698.

Dalloul, M. H. M., binti Ibrahim, Z., & Urus, S. T. (2023). Financial Crises Management in Light of Accounting Information Systems Success: Investigating Direct and Indirect Influences. *Sustainability (Basel), 15*(10), 8131. Advance online publication. DOI: 10.3390/su15108131

Dorcak, D. (2013). The logistics information system in production company. In I. Petras, I. Podlubny, J. Kacur, A. Nawrocka, & B. Sapinski (Eds.), *Proceedings of the 2013 14th International Carpathian Control Conference, ICCC 2013* (Issues 14th International Carpathian Control Conference (ICCC) CL-Rytro, POLAND PU-IEEE PI-NEW YORK PA-345 E 47TH ST, NEW YORK, NY 10017 USA, pp. 44–48). DOI: 10.1109/CarpathianCC.2013.6560508

Farooq, M. (2019). Emerging sciences in Social Sciences : An overview, A Research Agenda. *Global Journal of Emerging Sciences, 1*(October), 183–197.

Farooq, M., Ali, W., Younas, W., Khalil-Ur-rehman, F., & Qurashi, Q. A. (2019). the Era of Transformative Marketing: Service Quality of Mobile App Based Taxi Services in Kuala Lumpur. *Proceedings on Engineering Sciences, 1*(2), 49–58. DOI: 10.24874/PES01.02.006

Farooq, M., Bakhsh, A., Hafsa Qadir, B., & Warda, N. (2023). Digital Empowerment: Freedom of Expression Beyond 5G and 6G Networks in Developing Countries. *Pakistan Journal of Social Sciences, 43*(4), 569–584. DOI: 10.5281/zenodo.10448484

Farooq, M., Buzdar, H. Q., Yen, Y. Y., & Bakhsh, A. (2024). Integrating AI in Sustainable Writing: An Empirical Investigation of the Technology Acceptance Model in Asian Social Sciences. *Journal of Logistics. Informatics and Service Science, 11*(3), 324–338. DOI: 10.33168/JLISS.2024.0321

Farooq, M., Cheng, J., Khan, N. U., Saufi, R. A., Kanwal, N., & Bazkiaei, H. A. (2022a). Sustainable Waste Management Companies with Innovative Smart Solutions: A Systematic Review and Conceptual Model. *Sustainability (Basel), 14*(20), 13146. Advance online publication. DOI: 10.3390/su142013146

Farooq, M., Cheng, J., Khan, N. U., Saufi, R. A., Kanwal, N., & Bazkiaei, H. A. (2022b). Sustainable Waste Management Companies with Innovative Smart Solutions: A Systematic Review and Conceptual Model. *Sustainability (Basel), 14*(20), 13146. DOI: 10.3390/su142013146

Farooq, M., Hafsa Qadir, B., & Saeed, M. (2023, December). AI-Enhanced Social Sciences: A Systematic Literature Review and Bibliographic Analysis of Web of Science Published Research Papers. *Pakistan Journal of Society* [PJSEL]. *Education and Language, 10*, 1–2.

Farooq, M., Kalimuthu, R., & Reza, M. H. (2019). Measuring and Comparing Brand Equity of Malaysian Banks in the Era of Transformative Marketing. *Global Journal of Emerging Sciences, 1*(June), 96–102.

Farooq, M., Khalil-Ur-Rehman, F., Abdurrahaman, D. T., Younas, W., Sajjad, S., & Zreen, A. (2019). SERVICE QUALITY ANALYSIS OF PRIVATE UNIVERSITIES LIBRARIES IN MALAYSIA IN THE ERA OF TRANSFORMATIVE MARKETING. *International Journal of Qualitative Research, 13*(2), 269–284. DOI: 10.24874/IJQR13.02-02

Farooq, M., Muhammad, S., Raju, V., Kalimuthu, K. R., & Qadir, A. (2019). Measuring and Comparing the Desired and Actual Service Quality of Pakistan International Airline. *The Journal of Social Sciences Research, 52*(52), 484–490. DOI: 10.32861/jssr.52.484.490

Farooq, M., & Qureshi, Q. A. (2020). Practical Approach of Environmental Awareness to Broadening Community Participation: A Case Study of Pindad (Persero). *Journal of Management Practices. Humanities and Social Sciences, 4*(1). Advance online publication. DOI: 10.33152/jmphss-4.2.1

Farooq, M., & Raju, V. (2019a). Impact of Over-the-Top (OTT) Services on the Telecom Companies in the Era of Transformative Marketing. *Global Journal of Flexible Systems Managment, 20*(2), 177–188. DOI: 10.1007/s40171-019-00209-6

Farooq, M., & Raju, V. (2019b). Want to Stay the Market Leader in the Era of Transformative Marketing? Keep the Customers Satisfied! *Global Journal of Flexible Systems Management*. DOI: 10.1007/s40171-019-00213-w

Farooq, M., & Raju, V. (2019c). Impact of Over-the-Top (OTT) Services on the Telecom Companies in the Era of Transformative Marketing. *Global Journal of Flexible Systems Managment*, *20*(2), 177–188. DOI: 10.1007/s40171-019-00209-6

Farooq, M., & Raju, V. (2019d). Want to Stay the Market Leader in the Era of Transformative Marketing? Keep the Customers Satisfied! *Global Journal of Flexible Systems Managment*, *20*(3), 257–266. DOI: 10.1007/s40171-019-00213-w

Farooq, M., & Ramzan, M. Y. Y. Y. (2025). AI in Management. In *Transformative Impacts of AI in Management* (1st ed., pp. 1–44). IGI Global. DOI: 10.4018/979-8-3693-4322-7.ch001

Farooq, M., Ramzan, M., & Yen, Y. Y. (2025a). AI in Consumer Behavior Management. In *Transformative Impacts of AI in Management* (pp. 281–294). IGI Global., DOI: 10.4018/979-8-3693-4322-7.ch011

Farooq, M., Ramzan, M., & Yen, Y. Y. (2025b). AI in Customer Service, HR, and Administration. In *Transformative Impacts of AI in Management* (pp. 45–70). IGI Global. DOI: 10.4018/979-8-3693-4322-7.ch002

Farooq, M., Ramzan, M., & Yen, Y. Y. (2025c). AI in Quality Management. In *Transformative Impacts of AI in Management* (pp. 295–312). IGI Global., DOI: 10.4018/979-8-3693-4322-7.ch012

Farooq, M., Ramzan, M., & Yen, Y. Y. (2025d). Artificial Intelligence and Customer Experiences. In *Transformative Impacts of AI in Management* (pp. 95–114). IGI Global., DOI: 10.4018/979-8-3693-4322-7.ch004

Farooq, M., Ramzan, M., & Yen, Y. Y. (2025e). Artificial Intelligence in Administration Sciences. In *Transformative Impacts of AI in Management* (pp. 115–156). IGI Global., DOI: 10.4018/979-8-3693-4322-7.ch005

Farooq, M., Ramzan, M., & Yen, Y. Y. (2025f). Artificial Intelligence in Business and Law. In *Transformative Impacts of AI in Management* (pp. 71–94). IGI Global., DOI: 10.4018/979-8-3693-4322-7.ch003

Farooq, M., Ramzan, M., & Yen, Y. Y. (2025g). Artificial Intelligence in Ethical Business Decision Making. In *Transformative Impacts of AI in Management* (pp. 265–280). IGI Global., DOI: 10.4018/979-8-3693-4322-7.ch010

Farooq, M., Ramzan, M., & Yen, Y. Y. (2025h). Exploring the Impact of Artificial Intelligence on Brand Management. In *Transformative Impacts of AI in Management* (pp. 157–188). IGI Global., DOI: 10.4018/979-8-3693-4322-7.ch006

Farooq, M., Ramzan, M., & Yen, Y. Y. (2025i). Exploring the Impact of Ethical Leadership and Employee Engagement on Knowledge Sharing Attitudes in the Asian Digital Economy. In *Transformative Impacts of AI in Management* (pp. 241–264). IGI Global., DOI: 10.4018/979-8-3693-4322-7.ch009

Farooq, M., Ramzan, M., & Yen, Y. Y. (2025j). Transformative Impact of AI in Education Management. In *Transformative Impacts of AI in Management* (pp. 189–216). IGI Global., DOI: 10.4018/979-8-3693-4322-7.ch007

Farooq, M., Ramzan, M., & Yen, Y. Y. (2025k). *Transformative Impacts of AI in Management*. IGI Global., DOI: 10.4018/979-8-3693-4322-7

Farooq, M., Rehman, F. K. U., Younas, W., Raju, V., Ahmed, Q. M., & Ali, M. (2019). Investigating Relationship between Net Promoter Score and Company Performance: A Longitudinal Study. *Global Journal of Emerging Sciences*, *1*(1), 1–10. https://www.gjoes.org/wp-content/uploads/2019/04/1-1.pdf

Farooq, M., Saeed, M., Ali, W., & Javid, R. (2020). Online Buying and Customer Satisfaction in the Era of Transformative Marketing. *City University Research Journal*, *10*(2), 274–288.

Farooq, M., Yuen, Y. Y., & Buzdar, H. Q. (2024). Exploring the Research Landscape of Artificial Intelligence Integration with Business Management: A Bibliometric Analysis from 1994-2023. *Journal of Logistics. Informatics and Service Science*, (April). Advance online publication. DOI: 10.33168/JLISS.2024.0410

Flynn, B., Cantor, D., Pagell, M., Dooley, K. J., & Azadegan, A. (2021). From the Editors: Introduction to Managing Supply Chains Beyond Covid-19 - Preparing for the Next Global Mega-Disruption. In *Journal of Supply Chain Management* (Vol. 57, Issue 1). DOI: 10.1111/jscm.12254

Ghulam, W. A., Ali, W., Ali, S., Khan, M. M., Khan, R. N., & Farooq, M. (2019). Investigating factors influencing brain drain of citizens of Azad Kashmir Pakistan. *Journal of Social Sciences Research*, *5*(3), 782–788. Advance online publication. DOI: 10.32861/jssr.53.782.788

Godoy, M. P., Rusu, C., Hatibovic, F., Granollers, T., & Ugalde, J. (2023). Addressing Information Consumer Experience through a User-Centered Information Management System in a Chilean University. *Sustainability (Basel)*, *15*(22), 15998. Advance online publication. DOI: 10.3390/su152215998

Gupta, B. B., & Panigrahi, P. K. (2023). Analysis of the Role of Global Information Management in Advanced Decision Support Systems (DSS) for Sustainable Development. *Journal of Global Information Management, 31*(1), 1–13. Advance online publication. DOI: 10.4018/JGIM.320185

Hart, M. (2017). The design of integrated logistics management system of an industrial company. In O. Stopka (Ed.), *MATEC Web of Conferences* (Vol. 134, Issues 18th International Scientific Conference on LOGI CL-Ceske Budejovice. DOI: 10.1051/matecconf/201713400018

Hawkins, M. A. (2017). Brand network communities: Leveraging brand relationships within the supply-chain. *Journal of Brand Management, 24*(6), 516–521. DOI: 10.1057/s41262-017-0041-9

Huang, L. (2022). Research and Application of Business Law Information Management System Based on Big Data. *Journal of Sensors, 2022*, 1–12. Advance online publication. DOI: 10.1155/2022/5885451

Huang, Z. (2022). Integrated Management System of Instrument and Equipment in University Financial Media Laboratory Based on Hybrid Cloud Architecture. In S. Liu & X. Ma (Eds.), *ADVANCED HYBRID INFORMATION PROCESSING, PT I* (Vol. 416, Issues 5th EAI International Conference on Advanced Hybrid Information Processing (ADHIP), pp. 587–600). DOI: 10.1007/978-3-030-94551-0_46

Hussain, M., Ahmad, S. Z., & Visvizi, A. (2022). Government regulation and organizational effectiveness in the health-care supply chain. *TRANSFORMING GOVERNMENT- PEOPLE PROCESS AND POLICY, 16*(4), 649–662. DOI: 10.1108/TG-06-2022-0090

Iskanderov, Y., & Pautov, M. (2019). Security of Information Processes in Supply Chains. In A. Abraham, S. Kovalev, V. Tarassov, V. Snasel, & A. Sukhanov (Eds.), *PROCEEDINGS OF THE THIRD INTERNATIONAL SCIENTIFIC CONFERENCE INTELLIGENT INFORMATION TECHNOLOGIES FOR INDUSTRY (IITI'18), VOL 2* (Vol. 875, Issues 3rd International Scientific Conference on Intelligent Information Technologies for Industry (IITI) CL-Sochi, pp. 13–22). DOI: 10.1007/978-3-030-01821-4_2

Kokodey, T. A., Lomachenko, T. I., Maidanevych, Y. P., Nekhaychuk, D. V., & Romanova, Y. A. (2020). Effect of world economy globalization and supply chain upon socio-economic processes at the national level. *International Journal of Supply Chain Management, 9*(2).

Korecki, Z., & Adamkova, B. (2018). Implement policies and processes to increase the level of security of the multi-tier logistics chain. *NTAD 2018 - 13th International Scientific Conference - New Trends in Aviation Development, Proceedings*. DOI: 10.1109/NTAD.2018.8551684

Li, X., Aouad, G., Li, Q., & Fu, C. (2008). An nD Modeling Enabled Collaborative Construction Supply Chain Information System. In Q. Zhou & J. Luo (Eds.), *2008 INTERNATIONAL SYMPOSIUM ON INTELLIGENT INFORMATION TECHNOLOGY APPLICATION, VOL III, PROCEEDINGS* (Issues 2nd International Symposium on Intelligent Information Technology Application CL-Shanghai, pp. 171-+). DOI: 10.1109/IITA.2008.551

Li, X., Wang, L., & Fang, L. (2022). Optimal Design of an Information Management System for Government: A Bridge between Government and Citizens. *Mathematical Problems in Engineering*, *2022*, 1–10. Advance online publication. DOI: 10.1155/2022/3127858

Lin, J., & Ghodrati, B. (2012). Information sharing in a spares demand system. In *2012 IEEE International Technology Management Conference, ITMC 2012* (Issue IEEE International Technology Management Conference (ITMC) CL-Dallas, TX PU-IEEE PI-NEW YORK PA-345 E 47TH ST, NEW YORK, NY 10017 USA, pp. 36–44). DOI: 10.1109/ITMC.2012.6306382

Mirarchi, C., Pavan, A., de Marco, F., Wang, X., & Song, Y. (2018). Supporting facility management processes through end-users' Integration and coordinated BIM-GIS technologies. *ISPRS International Journal of Geo-Information*, *7*(5), 191. Advance online publication. DOI: 10.3390/ijgi7050191

Na, S.-H., & Shon, T.-S. (2022). A Study on the Development of Information Security Management System Using RMF. *Journal of Digital Contents Society*, *23*(5), 977–983. DOI: 10.9728/dcs.2022.23.5.977

Naseer, M., Farooq, M., Younas, W., & Raju, V. (2019). Antecedents of employee retention in the pharmaceutical industry of Pakistan. *Journal of Social Sciences Research*, *5*(3), 656–664. Advance online publication. DOI: 10.32861/jssr.53.655.664

Okada, K., Sugimoto, K., Wada, S., Konishi, S., Manabe, S., Matsumura, Y., & Takeda, T. (2024). Development of the Clinical Specimen Information Management System for Multicenter Clinical Studies. In J. Bichel-Findlay, P. Otero, P. Scott, & E. Huesing (Eds.), *MEDINFO 2023 - THE FUTURE IS ACCESSIBLE* (Vol. 310, Issues 19th World Congress on Medical and Health Informatics (MEDINFO) CL-Sydney, pp. 119–123). DOI: 10.3233/SHTI230939

Olson, D. L. (2018). View of IJPR contributions to knowledge management in supply chains. *International Journal of Production Research*, *56*(1–2), 733–742. DOI: 10.1080/00207543.2017.1398427

Park, K. O., & Koh, C. E. (2015). Effect of change management capability in real-time environment: An information orientation perspective in supply chain management. *Behaviour & Information Technology*, *34*(1), 94–104. DOI: 10.1080/0144929X.2014.945961

Pereira, J., Varajao, J., & Takagi, N. (2022). Evaluation of Information Systems Project Success - Insights from Practitioners. *Information Systems Management*, *39*(2), 138–155. DOI: 10.1080/10580530.2021.1887982

Roy, A., Gupta, A. D., & Deshmukh, S. G. (2012). Information security in supply chains - A process framework. In *IEEE International Conference on Industrial Engineering and Engineering Management* (Issue IEEE International Conference on Industrial Engineering and Engineering Management (IEEM) pp. 1448–1452). DOI: 10.1109/IEEM.2012.6837986

Shah, R., Goldstein, S. M., & Ward, P. T. (2002). Aligning supply chain management characteristics and interorganizational information system types: An exploratory study. *IEEE Transactions on Engineering Management*, *49*(3), 282–292. DOI: 10.1109/TEM.2002.803382

Shi, Y., Ying, J., Shi, D., & Yan, J. (2022). Service-Oriented Modeling for Blockchain-Enabled Supply Chain Quality Information Systems. *Security and Communication Networks*, *2022*, 1–16. Advance online publication. DOI: 10.1155/2022/1987933

Tarigan, Z. J. H., Siagian, H., Bua, R. R., & IOP. (2019). The Impact of Information System Implementation to the Integrated System for Increasing the Supply Chain Performance of Manufacturing Companies. In *2018 5TH INTERNATIONAL CONFERENCE ON ADVANCED MATERIALS, MECHANICS AND STRUCTURAL ENGINEERING (AMMSE)*. DOI: 10.1088/1757-899X/473/1/012050

VanVactor, J. D. (2017). Healthcare logistics in disaster planning and emergency management: A perspective. *Journal of Business Continuity & Emergency Planning*, *10*(2), 157. DOI: 10.69554/PAQN9602 PMID: 28376996

Verwijmeren, P. (1998). *Networked Inventory Management by Distributed Object Technology*.

Wang, L., Wang, Y. C., & Zhang, L. (2009). Study on the design of port logistics information platform. In E. S. Qi, G. Cheng, J. A. Shen, & R. L. Dou (Eds.), *IE and EM 2009 - Proceedings 2009 IEEE 16th International Conference on Industrial Engineering and Engineering Management* (Issue IEEE 16th International Conference on Industrial Engineering and Engineering Management CL-Beijing, pp. 376–379). DOI: 10.1109/ICIEEM.2009.5344567

Wang, Y., & Deng, X. (2015). Empirical Study of Agricultural Supply Chain Information System Integration. In Z. Zhang, Z. M. Shen, J. Zhang, & R. Zhang (Eds.), *Liss 2014* (Issues 4th International Conference on Logistics, Informatics and Service Science (LISS) CL-Beijing Jiaotong Univ, Sch Econ & Management, Beijing, pp. 389–393). DOI: 10.1007/978-3-662-43871-8_57

Wang, Y., Lin, J., Osman, Z., Farooq, M., & Raju, V. (2021). Transformational leadership and employee performance in international commercial banking industry in Malaysia: The role of self-efficacy as a mediator under BRI. *Journal of Chinese Human Resource Management, 12*(2), 25–36. DOI: 10.47297/wspchrmWSP2040-800503.20211202

Wang, Y., Xue, W., & Zhang, A. (2023). Application of Big Data Technology in Enterprise Information Security Management and Risk Assessment. *Journal of Global Information Management, 31*(3), 1–16. Advance online publication. DOI: 10.4018/JGIM.324465

Wenhui, Z., Chunmiao, H., Feng, D., Junqiang, G., & IEEE. (2009). Analysis and Configuration of Enterprise Management Information System Based on the Supply Chain Theory. In Z. W. Ye & P. Ma (Eds.), *2009 INTERNATIONAL CONFERENCE ON E-BUSINESS AND INFORMATION SYSTEM SECURITY, VOLS 1 AND 2* (Issues 1st International Conference on E-Business and Information System Security CL-Wuhan, pp. 866-+).

Xiong, Y., Xie, C., & Wang, A. (2008a). A case study of the construction of the auxiliary material order and warehousing management information system. In *2008 International Conference on Wireless Communications, Networking and Mobile Computing, WiCOM 2008* (Issues 4th International Conference on Wireless Communications, Networking and Mobile Computing CL-Dalian, pp. 12440-+). DOI: 10.1109/WiCom.2008.2898

Xiong, Y., Xie, C., & Wang, A. (2008b). A case study of the construction of the auxiliary material order and warehousing management information system. In *2008 International Conference on Wireless Communications, Networking and Mobile Computing, WiCOM 2008* (Issues 5th International Conference on Service Systems and Service Management CL-Monash Univ, Fac Informat Technol, Melbourne, pp. 493–496). DOI: 10.1109/WiCom.2008.2898

Yang, C., & Sun, Z. (2020). Data Management System based on Blockchain Technology for Agricultural Supply Chain. In G. DiFatta, V. Sheng, A. Cuzzocrea, C. Zaniolo, & X. Wu (Eds.), *IEEE International Conference on Data Mining Workshops, ICDMW* (Vols. 2020-Novem, Issues 20th IEEE International Conference on Data Mining (ICDM) pp. 907–911). DOI: 10.1109/ICDMW51313.2020.00130

Yen, Y. Y., Wen, L. J., Ramasamy, S., & Farooq, M. (2023). Sustainable petrol subsidy program in Malaysia. *Asian Development Policy Review, 12*(1), 1–9. DOI: 10.55493/5008.v12i1.4948

Yinbin, L., & Hongbo, L. (2009). Research on DCOR-based integrated information resource management platform of supply chain system. In Q. H. Zhou (Ed.), *Proceedings - 2009 International Forum on Information Technology and Applications, IFITA 2009* (Vol. 2, Issue International Forum on Information Technology and Applications (IFITA 2009) CL-Chengdu, pp. 513–516). DOI: 10.1109/IFITA.2009.186

Zhang, W., Wang, X., & Cui, Q. (2012). Research of the re-manufacturing model and information system design based on supply chain management. In W. Z. Chen, P. Q. Dai, Y. L. Chen, D. N. Chen, & Z. Y. Jiang (Eds.), *Advanced Materials Research* (Vols. 468–471, Issues 3rd International Conference on Manufacturing Science and Engineering (ICMSE 2012) CL-Xiamen, pp. 3031–3037). DOI: 10.4028/www.scientific.net/AMR.468-471.3031

Zhang, X. (2022). Design and Implementation of Management Information System Based on Network Environment. In D. Zhou & Z. Y. Du (Eds.), *Lecture Notes in Electrical Engineering: Vol. 827 LNEE* (Issue International Conference on Information Technology and Industrial Engineering CL-Wuhan, pp. 1076–1080). DOI: 10.1007/978-981-16-8052-6_147

Zhao, X. X., & Zhu, Y. M. (2011). Supply Chain Quality Information Management Methodology and Application System Research. In X. H. Liu, Z. Jiang, & J. T. Han (Eds.), *Advanced Materials Research* (Vols. 418–420, Issues 2nd International Conference on Advances in Materials and Manufacturing Processes (ICAMMP 2011) CL-Guillin, pp. 1812–1816). DOI: 10.4028/www.scientific.net/AMR.418-420.1812

Zhidong, L. (2023). Construction of management mechanism model of soil and water conservation information system. In *Science of Soil and Water Conservation* (Vol. 21, Issue 5, pp. 106–110).

Zhong, Y., Peng, X., Xiao, X., Zhang, Q., & Cheng, Q. (2010). A preliminary study of JDF-based ERP system in the printing enterprises. In G. Z. Chai, C. D. Lu, & D. H. Wen (Eds.), *Advanced Materials Research* (Vols. 102–104, Issue Global Conference on Digital Design and Manufacturing Technology CL-Hangzhou, pp. 851–855). https://doi.org/DOI: 10.4028/www.scientific.net/AMR.102-104.851

Zoubeidi, M., Kazar, O., Mesbahi, N., & Benharzallah, S. (2014). Toward an architecture for the semantic integration in enterprise resource planning. In *Proceedings - 2014 International Workshop on Advanced Information Systems for Enterprises, IWAISE 2014* (Issues 3rd International Workshop on Advanced Information Systems for Enterprises (IWAISE) CL-Natl Engn Sch Tunis, Tunis, pp. 45–50). DOI: 10.1109/IWAISE.2014.10

Chapter 10
Transformative Impacts of AI in Knowledge Management and Decision Support Systems

ABSTRACT

Knowledge Management and Decision Support Systems (DSS) are fundamental components that work together (Agnoli et al., 2023; Shatat & Shatat, 2023). Harmoniously to improve productivity and strategic decision making. In order to promote an innovative and learning culture inside a business, knowledge management is the methodical gathering, arrangement, and distribution of intellectual assets. It goes beyond just gathering data and focuses on turning data into knowledge that can be put to use (Mattioli et al., 2020). Decision Support Systems also serve as technical enablers, giving decision-makers models and analytical tools to help them navigate the intricacies of the modern corporate environment (Isabella et al., 2023). These systems combine information from several sources to provide a comprehensive picture that enables decision-makers to act quickly and intelligently. Knowledge becomes a strategic asset in a dynamic ecosystem created by the revolutionary synergy of DSS and Knowledge Management (X. Y. Hao & Demir, 2024).

10.1 CHAPTER INTRODUCTION

By virtue of efficient Knowledge Management, institutions develop a storehouse of knowledge and insights that are easily incorporated into Decision Support Systems (Hariyati et al., 2019; Zerfass et al., 2020). When decision-makers use historical knowledge and real-time data to negotiate obstacles and seize opportunities, this

DOI: 10.4018/979-8-3373-0513-4.ch010

synergy promotes agility (Bitonti, 2023). Organizational intelligence is essentially driven by the integration of knowledge management and decision support systems, which is advancing enterprises toward a time when wise judgments are the cornerstone of success.

Figure 1. Mind map of knowledge management and decision support system

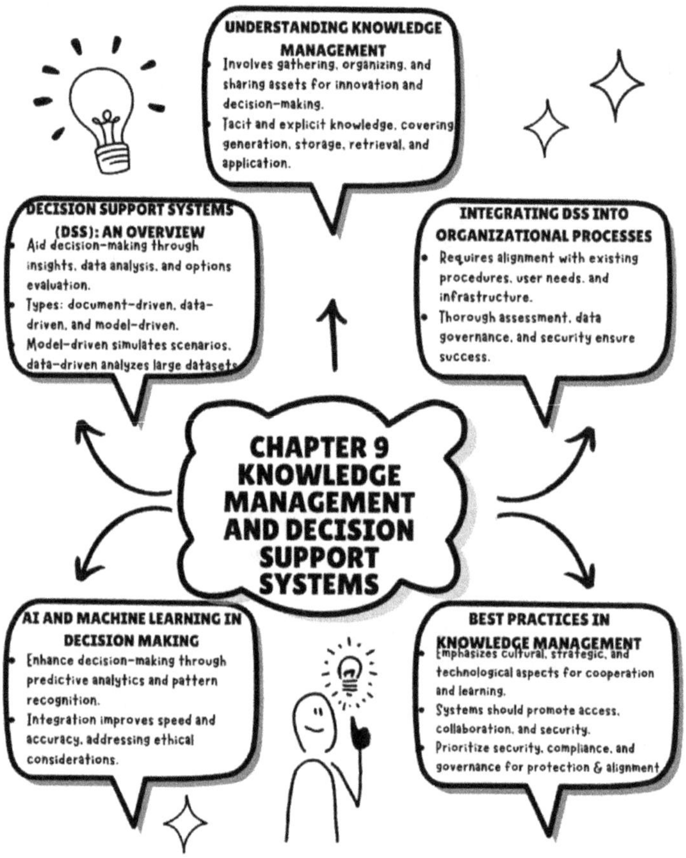

10.2 UNDERSTANDING KNOWLEDGE MANAGEMENT

The methodical and intentional management of knowledge and expertise is known as knowledge management, and its goals are to promote innovation, enhance decision-making, and ease organizational learning. The first step in this process is identifying important knowledge inside an organization(Li et al., 2022; Muir et al.,

2023). This knowledge may be either tacit (derived from personal experiences and insights) or explicit (codified and recorded information). Since tacit information is stored in individuals' thoughts and is not readily transportable, organizations often struggle to record and codify it (Sodhi & Tang, 2021).

The four categories of knowledge generation, storage, retrieval, and application are the components of knowledge management. The process of producing new ideas and insights, often by experimentation and cooperation, is known as knowledge production (Bukhari & Ramzan, 2013; Choudhary et al., 2013; Farid et al., 2013). Retrieval makes ensuring that the information is easily accessible when required, whereas storage involves classifying and structuring knowledge for convenience of access (Arshad et al., 2019; Dr Ramzan, Muhammad; Hussain, Ashfaq; Ahmad, 2019; Ramzan et al., 2019). The last element, application, is using knowledge to resolve issues, guide deliberations, and foster creativity within the company(Dubey et al., 2022).

Knowledge management systems are used by organizations to leverage the combined intellect of their personnel, encourage a culture of ongoing learning, and stimulate innovation(Shafiq & Ramzan, 2015; Shafique et al., 2015; Subhan et al., 2015). These systems often combine organizational procedures that promote cooperation and knowledge sharing with technical resources like databases, intranets, and collaboration platforms. Good knowledge management (KM) enhances decision-making, strengthens problem-solving skills, and boosts daily operations efficiency(Ivanova et al., 2023; Schwering et al., 2022).

Knowledge management deployment is not without difficulties. The corporate culture's aversion to change is one of the main obstacles(Ahmed & Ramzan, 2013; Farid et al., 2013; Malik et al., 2013; Naveed & Ramzan, 2013). Because they fear losing a competitive advantage, are concerned about their job security, or both, employees may be hesitant to share their information. Furthermore, technical obstacles like the absence of user-friendly knowledge management systems may make it more difficult for these projects to be successfully adopted. A comprehensive strategy that takes into account both cultural and technical factors is needed to overcome these obstacles.

10.3 DECISION SUPPORT SYSTEMS (DSS): AN OVERVIEW

A computerized information system called a decision support system helps decision-makers generate insights, analyze data, and weigh different options. DSS are essential for improving the ability of people, communities, and organizations to make decisions because they provide pertinent and timely information in an easy-to-use manner (Chauhan et al., 2023).

DSS's adaptability to a broad range of decision-making situations in many sectors and businesses is one of its core features. These systems may be divided into three categories: document-driven, data-driven, and model-driven DSS. Every category fulfills distinct requirements for decision-making, including financial planning, strategic management, and operational control (Z. Wang et al., 2023).

Model-driven DSS uses analytical tools and mathematical models to simulate situations and forecast results. These models help decision-makers evaluate how different options could affect the company. On the other hand, data-driven DSS makes use of huge datasets to provide trends and insights, helping decision-makers see patterns and make data-driven decisions. The goal of document-driven DSS is to facilitate decision-making processes by organizing, locating, and displaying pertinent documents and data(Gerbeti, 2021).

For DSS to be successful, organizational procedures must be integrated with it. This entails coordinating the system with the objectives, policies, and cultural norms of the company(Marrella & Mecella, 2018; Tian et al., 2023). A deep comprehension of the decision-making requirements, user requirements, and the current information infrastructure is necessary for a successful DSS deployment. Technology and organizational procedures work in concert to guarantee that DSS is woven into the very fabric of an organization's decision-making process (Gerbeti, 2021).

DSS acts as a link between the enormous quantity of data that is accessible and the strategic choices that businesses must make. Because DSS is interactive, decision-makers may experiment with various situations, change parameters, and evaluate possible results. A more dynamic and iterative approach to decision-making is fostered by this involvement. Developments in artificial intelligence (AI) and machine learning (ML) in particular have had a significant impact on the development of DSS. DSS's capabilities have been further improved with the addition of AI and ML, allowing businesses to take advantage of automation, natural language processing, and predictive analytics (Xu et al., 2021).

A paradigm change in decision-making is made possible by AI and machine learning, which enable DSS to forecast future patterns and outcomes in addition to analyzing past data. Decision-makers may get significant insights into prospective possibilities and hazards by using machine learning algorithms, which are capable of identifying patterns and correlations within data. Organizations are able to take advantage of new trends and proactively solve difficulties because to this predictive capabilities.

10.4 INTEGRATING DSS INTO ORGANIZATIONAL PROCESSES

The smooth integration of technologically advanced decision support tools into everyday company activities is a prerequisite for the integration of DSS into organizational processes. With the use of relevant and up-to-date data, decision-makers at all organizational levels from front-line managers to top executives should be able to make well-informed decisions (Peixoto et al., 2016).

A crucial element of DSS integration is its conformity to preexisting organizational frameworks and procedures. This guarantees a seamless shift and staff adoption of these technologies(Ramzan et al., 2013; Zareen et al., 2013).

Developing a thorough organizational requirements assessment, outlining decision-making processes, and pinpointing areas where DSS may have the most impact are all common components of a successful integration. This customized strategy guarantees that the DSS supports the particular needs of the company, promoting a culture of data driven decision-making(Mohamad et al., 2018).

In order to complete the integration process, issues with data security, accessibility, and quality must be resolved. Establishing strong data governance frameworks is essential for organizations to guarantee the precision and dependability of the data included into the DSS. Furthermore, the use of encryption and secure access controls protects private information and gives decision-makers peace of mind about the integrity and confidentiality of the data they use(Sampaio et al., 2022).

The integration of DSS is a continuous process that needs constant review and modification rather than just a one-time application. To maximize the efficacy of DSS, organizations must set up procedures for tracking its performance, getting user input, and making the required modifications. By using an iterative process, the DSS is kept up to date with changing business requirements and technology developments. Effective integration of DSS into corporate operations requires collaboration and communication. Establishing a collaborative culture that encourages workers to share opinions and ideas gained from data provided by the DSS is crucial. To quickly provide pertinent stakeholders with vital decision-support information, efficient routes of communication must be developed.

The incorporation of DSS creates a paradigm change in the dynamics of decision-making by fostering a collaborative atmosphere that fosters a common knowledge of company objectives and makes decision-making more cohesive. In the past, judgments were often decided using intuition and historical evidence. By using machine learning algorithms and predictive analytics, DSS presents a more proactive strategy. This change makes it possible for businesses to see trends, spot opportunities, and take proactive measures to overcome obstacles. As a result, they are better equipped to remain ahead in a business environment that is changing quickly.

10.5 AI AND MACHINE LEARNING IN DECISION MAKING

Fundamentally, artificial intelligence is the creation of machines capable of carrying out operations that would normally call for human intellect(Farooq et al., 2025c). AI systems use sophisticated algorithms to evaluate data and identify trends in order to make more informed and efficient decisions(Farooq et al., 2025a). As a subclass of artificial intelligence, machine learning enables systems to learn from experience and become better over time without explicit programming. It does this by adapting to new data and honing decision-making skills (Hasija & Esper, 2022).

Predictive analytics is a prominent use of AI and ML in decision-making. These technologies may be used by organizations to predict market shifts, detect possible hazards, and project future trends. AI models may identify hidden patterns and correlations in historical data that may be invisible to human observers, giving organizations the ability to remain ahead of the curve and make proactive choices in ever-changing markets(Pasqualino et al., 2021).

Decision support systems (DSS) that use AI and ML improve decision-making processes in terms of speed and accuracy. These technologies have the ability to sort through enormous datasets quickly, giving executives the information they need to make wise decisions. AI's large-scale data processing and analysis capabilities speed up decision-making while lowering the chance of mistake since machine algorithms are unbiased and consistent.

When integrating AI and ML into decision-making processes, ethical issues are vital. As these technologies become more and more integrated into organizational plans, it is critical to address concerns about accountability, transparency, and bias. When it comes to algorithmic decision-making, organizations need to make sure that the prejudices that already exist in society are neither reinforced nor made worse by AI systems.

It is essential for human knowledge and AI-driven insights to work together in harmony. Artificial intelligence (AI) is excellent at processing data and identifying patterns, but human judgment adds ethical concerns, empathy, and contextual knowledge to the decision-making process. Finding the ideal mix between AI-driven data and human intuition is essential for streamlining decision-making procedures.

10.6 BEST PRACTICES IN KNOWLEDGE MANAGEMENT

Organizations looking to capitalize on their intellectual property, encourage innovation, and keep a competitive advantage in the fast-paced corporate world of today need effective knowledge management, or KM(Farooq et al., 2025a, 2025c, 2025b). The best knowledge management techniques emphasize the organizational, strategic, and cultural dimensions of information consumption, using a comprehensive approach that extends beyond technology (Thomas & Paul, 2019).

Developing a culture that promotes cooperation and information sharing is a key component of knowledge management best practices (Farooq, Yuen, et al., 2024; Farooq & Qureshi, 2020; Y. Wang et al., 2021). Employers should provide a climate in which staff members are encouraged to contribute their knowledge, experiences, and thoughts(Farooq et al., 2020; Farooq, Bakhsh, et al., 2023; Farooq & Raju, 2019). Support from the top, acknowledgement of efforts to share knowledge, and the creation of channels for smooth information sharing all contribute to this cultural transformation (Huang et al., 2022).

Systems for managing knowledge are essential for classifying, arranging, and sharing information within an organization(Farooq, Ali, et al., 2019; Farooq, Kalimuthu, et al., 2019; Farooq, Buzdar, et al., 2024). By installing strong knowledge management solutions, staff members may quickly and easily access pertinent information, cutting down on duplication and optimizing processes(Farooq et al., 2022; Farooq, Hafsa Qadir, et al., 2023; Farooq, Rehman, et al., 2019). These systems have to be easy to use, adaptable, and able to include many types of information, such as implicit insights and explicit documentation (Staegemann et al., 2022).

Initiatives for training and ongoing education are essential to effective knowledge management(Farooq, Khalil-Ur-Rehman, et al., 2019). Employers need to fund initiatives that develop workers' abilities, enabling them to stay current on market developments and provide them with the resources necessary to make valuable contributions to the body of knowledge. Initiatives for cross-functional training also promote departmental cooperation and a more comprehensive knowledge of the company(Lee et al., 2005; Stoll, 2010; J. J. Zhang et al., 2009).

Continuous improvement in knowledge management procedures requires the integration of feedback loops. Organizations may find areas for improvement and modify their strategy by regularly assessing their knowledge management procedures, user input, and performance indicators (Lu et al., 2013; Makna & Kirikova, 2011; C. Zhang et al., 2003). The sustainability and efficacy of knowledge management (KM) processes are guaranteed by their adaptability and response to evolving organizational demands (Tootell et al., 2020).

A key component of efficient knowledge management is strategic alignment. Companies should match their KM tactics to the overarching aims and objectives of their businesses. This entails determining which knowledge domains are crucial, ranking them in order of strategic significance, and assigning resources appropriately. An organization's capacity to seize new opportunities and maintain agility and resilience is enhanced by a well-aligned knowledge management strategy. It is impossible to ignore security and privacy issues in the context of knowledge management. It is crucial to protect private data, intellectual property, and sensitive information. Establishing strong security measures, access restrictions, and encryption protocols is critical for organizations to safeguard their knowledge assets from cyber-attacks and illegal access.

10.7 CHAPTER CONCLUSION

Knowledge Management (KM) and Decision Support Systems (DSS) are two intertwined components that play crucial roles in enhancing productivity and facilitating strategic decision-making within organizations. KM involves the systematic gathering, organization, and distribution of intellectual assets to foster innovation, improve decision-making, and cultivate a learning culture. DSS, on the other hand, provide decision-makers with models and analytical tools to navigate the complexities of the modern corporate environment, enabling them to act swiftly and intelligently.

The synergy between KM and DSS creates a dynamic ecosystem where knowledge becomes a strategic asset. Through efficient KM practices, organizations accumulate a repository of knowledge and insights that seamlessly integrate into DSS. This integration empowers decision-makers to leverage historical knowledge and real-time data to navigate challenges and capitalize on opportunities, promoting organizational agility and intelligence.

Understanding KM involves identifying and managing both tacit and explicit knowledge within an organization, encompassing processes such as knowledge generation, storage, retrieval, and application. KM systems leverage organizational procedures and technical resources to encourage collaboration, enhance decision-making, and drive operational efficiency. However, challenges such as organizational culture resistance and technical barriers must be addressed through comprehensive strategies to realize the full potential of KM.

DSS, as computerized information systems, assist decision-makers in generating insights, analyzing data, and evaluating options across various decision-making scenarios. These systems leverage document-driven, data-driven, and model-driven approaches to provide timely and pertinent information, enabling decision-makers to make informed choices. Successful integration of DSS into organizational processes requires alignment with existing frameworks, addressing data security and quality issues, and fostering a collaborative culture that embraces data-driven decision-making.

The advent of AI and machine learning has revolutionized decision-making by enhancing the capabilities of DSS. Predictive analytics, facilitated by AI and ML technologies, enables organizations to anticipate market trends, identify risks, and forecast future outcomes with greater accuracy. While AI-driven insights offer speed and efficiency, ethical considerations regarding accountability, transparency, and bias must be carefully navigated to ensure responsible decision-making.

Best practices in KM emphasize creating a culture of cooperation and information sharing, implementing robust knowledge management systems, investing in employee training and education, and continuously improving processes based on feedback and strategic alignment. Additionally, organizations must prioritize security and privacy to safeguard their knowledge assets from potential threats.

In conclusion, the symbiotic relationship between KM and DSS is essential for fostering innovation, enhancing decision-making, and driving organizational success in today's dynamic business landscape. By harnessing the power of knowledge and technology, organizations can gain a competitive edge and adapt effectively to changing market conditions, paving the way for sustainable growth and resilience.

REFERENCES

Agnoli, L., Urquhart, E., Georgantzis, N., Schaeffer, B., Simmons, R., Hoque, B., Neely, M. B., Neil, C., Oliver, J., & Tyler, A. (2023). Perspectives on user engagement of satellite Earth observation for water quality management. [WE - Social Science Citation Index] [SSCI]. *Technological Forecasting and Social Change, 189*, 122357. Advance online publication. DOI: 10.1016/j.techfore.2023.122357 PMID: 39022384

Ahmed, A., & Ramzan, M. (2013). Effects of job stress on employees job performance a study on banking sector of Pakistan. *IOSR Journal of Business and Management, 11*(6), 61–68. DOI: 10.9790/487X-1166168

Arshad, A., Ramzan, M., Ans, M., & Adeeb, H. (2019). Public perceptions towards media coverage of panama papers in Pakistan. *Media Watch, 10*(1), 165–178. DOI: 10.15655/mw_2019_v10i1_49559

Bitonti, A. (2023). Tools of digital innovation in public affairs management: A practice-oriented analysis. *Journal of Public Affairs*. Advance online publication. DOI: 10.1002/pa.2888

Bukhari, F. Y., & Ramzan, M. (2013). Gender discrimination: A myth or truth women status in Pakistan. *Journal of Business and Management, 8*(2), 88–97.

Chauhan, S., Singh, R., Gehlot, A., Akram, S. V., Twala, B., & Priyadarshi, N. (2023). Digitalization of Supply Chain Management with Industry 4.0 Enabling Technologies: A Sustainable Perspective. [WE - Science Citation Index Expanded] [SCI-EXPANDED]. *Processes (Basel, Switzerland), 11*(1), 96. Advance online publication. DOI: 10.3390/pr11010096

Choudhary, S. A., Ramzan, M., & Riaz, A. (2013). Strategies for career plateau: Empirical investigation of organizations in Pakistan. *Interdisciplinary Journal of Contemporary Research in Business, 4*(9), 712–726.

Dubey, R., Bryde, D. J., Dwivedi, Y. K., Graham, G., & Foropon, C. (2022). Impact of artificial intelligence-driven big data analytics culture on agility and resilience in humanitarian supply chain: A practice-based view. *International Journal of Production Economics, 250*, 108618. Advance online publication. DOI: 10.1016/j.ijpe.2022.108618

Farid, G., Abiodullah, M., & Ramzan, M. (2013). A comparative study of information seeking behaviors of medical faculty working in government and private run medical colleges. *International Journal of Information Management Science, 2*(1), 17–24.

Farooq, M., Ali, W., Younas, W., Khalil-Ur-rehman, F., & Qurashi, Q. A. (2019). the Era of Transformative Marketing: Service Quality of Mobile App Based Taxi Services in Kuala Lumpur. *Proceedings on Engineering Sciences, 1*(2), 49–58. DOI: 10.24874/PES01.02.006

Farooq, M., Bakhsh, A., Hafsa Qadir, B., & Warda, N. (2023). Digital Empowerment: Freedom of Expression Beyond 5G and 6G Networks in Developing Countries. *Pakistan Journal of Social Sciences, 43*(4), 569–584. DOI: 10.5281/zenodo.10448484

Farooq, M., Buzdar, H. Q., Yen, Y. Y., & Bakhsh, A. (2024). Integrating AI in Sustainable Writing: An Empirical Investigation of the Technology Acceptance Model in Asian Social Sciences. *Journal of Logistics. Informatics and Service Science, 11*(3), 324–338. DOI: 10.33168/JLISS.2024.0321

Farooq, M., Cheng, J., Khan, N. U., Saufi, R. A., Kanwal, N., & Bazkiaei, H. A. (2022). Sustainable Waste Management Companies with Innovative Smart Solutions: A Systematic Review and Conceptual Model. *Sustainability (Basel), 14*(20), 13146. Advance online publication. DOI: 10.3390/su142013146

Farooq, M., Hafsa Qadir, B., & Saeed, M. (2023, December). AI-Enhanced Social Sciences: A Systematic Literature Review and Bibliographic Analysis of Web of Science Published Research Papers. *Pakistan Journal of Society* [PJSEL]. *Education and Language, 10*, 1–2.

Farooq, M., Kalimuthu, R., & Reza, M. H. (2019). Measuring and Comparing Brand Equity of Malaysian Banks in the Era of Transformative Marketing. *Global Journal of Emerging Sciences, 1*(June), 96–102.

Farooq, M., Khalil-Ur-Rehman, F., Abdurrahaman, D. T., Younas, W., Sajjad, S., & Zreen, A. (2019). SERVICE QUALITY ANALYSIS OF PRIVATE UNIVERSITIES LIBRARIES IN MALAYSIA IN THE ERA OF TRANSFORMATIVE MARKETING. *International Journal of Qualitative Research, 13*(2), 269–284. DOI: 10.24874/IJQR13.02-02

Farooq, M., & Qureshi, Q. A. (2020). Practical Approach of Environmental Awareness to Broadening Community Participation: A Case Study of Pindad (Persero). *Journal of Management Practices. Humanities and Social Sciences, 4*(1). Advance online publication. DOI: 10.33152/jmphss-4.2.1

Farooq, M., & Raju, V. (2019). Impact of Over-the-Top (OTT) Services on the Telecom Companies in the Era of Transformative Marketing. *Global Journal of Flexible Systems Managment, 20*(2), 177–188. DOI: 10.1007/s40171-019-00209-6

Farooq, M., Ramzan, M., & Yen, Y. Y. (2025a). Artificial Intelligence in Business and Law. In *Transformative Impacts of AI in Management* (pp. 71–94). IGI Global., DOI: 10.4018/979-8-3693-4322-7.ch003

Farooq, M., Ramzan, M., & Yen, Y. Y. (2025b). Exploring the Impact of Artificial Intelligence on Brand Management. In *Transformative Impacts of AI in Management* (pp. 157–188). IGI Global., DOI: 10.4018/979-8-3693-4322-7.ch006

Farooq, M., Ramzan, M., & Yen, Y. Y. (2025c). Exploring the Impact of Ethical Leadership and Employee Engagement on Knowledge Sharing Attitudes in the Asian Digital Economy. In *Transformative Impacts of AI in Management* (pp. 241–264). IGI Global., DOI: 10.4018/979-8-3693-4322-7.ch009

Farooq, M., Rehman, F. K. U., Younas, W., Raju, V., Ahmed, Q. M., & Ali, M. (2019). Investigating Relationship between Net Promoter Score and Company Performance: A Longitudinal Study. *Global Journal of Emerging Sciences*, *1*(1), 1–10. https://www.gjoes.org/wp-content/uploads/2019/04/1-1.pdf

Farooq, M., Saeed, M., Ali, W., & Javid, R. (2020). Online Buying and Customer Satisfaction in the Era of Transformative Marketing. *City University Research Journal*, *10*(2), 274–288.

Farooq, M., Yuen, Y. Y., & Buzdar, H. Q. (2024). Exploring the Research Landscape of Artificial Intelligence Integration with Business Management: A Bibliometric Analysis from 1994-2023. *Journal of Logistics. Informatics and Service Science*, (April). Advance online publication. DOI: 10.33168/JLISS.2024.0410

Gerbeti, A. (2021). Market Mechanisms for Reducing Emissions and the Introduction of a Flexible Consumption Tax. *Global Journal of Flexible Systems Management*. DOI: 10.1007/s40171-021-00283-9

Hao, X. Y., & Demir, E. (2024). Artificial intelligence in supply chain management: Enablers and constraints in pre-development, deployment, and post-development stages. *Production Planning and Control*. Advance online publication. DOI: 10.1080/09537287.2024.2302482

Hariyati, T., Tjahjadi, B., & Soewarno, N. (2019). The mediating effect of intellectual capital, management accounting information systems, internal process performance, and customer performance. [WE - Emerging Sources Citation Index] [ESCI]. *International Journal of Productivity and Performance Management*, *68*(7), 1250–1271. DOI: 10.1108/IJPPM-02-2018-0049

Hasija, A., & Esper, T. L. (2022). In artificial intelligence (AI) we trust: A qualitative investigation of AI technology acceptance. *Journal of Business Logistics*, *43*(3), 388–412. DOI: 10.1111/jbl.12301

Huang, W., Chau, K. Y., Kit, I. Y., Nureen, N., Irfan, M., & Dilanchiev, A. (2022). Relating Sustainable Business Development Practices and Information Management in Promoting Digital Green Innovation: Evidence From China. [WE - Social Science Citation Index] [SSCI]. *Frontiers in Psychology*, *13*, 930138. Advance online publication. DOI: 10.3389/fpsyg.2022.930138 PMID: 35800951

Isabella, G., de Almeida, M. I. S., & Mazzon, J. A. (2023). Editorial: One-way road: the impact of artificial intelligence on the development of knowledge in management. [WE - Emerging Sources Citation Index] [ESCI]. *RAUSP Management Journal*, *58*(3), 249–255. DOI: 10.1108/RAUSP-07-2023-273

Ivanova, S., Kuznetsov, A., Zverev, R., & Rada, A. (2023). Artificial Intelligence Methods for the Construction and Management of Buildings. [WE - Science Citation Index Expanded] [SCI-EXPANDED]. *Sensors (Basel)*, *23*(21), 8740. Advance online publication. DOI: 10.3390/s23218740 PMID: 37960440

Lee, T. S., Lee, D. W., & Kim, J. H. (2005). Introduction of knowledge management system for technical support in construction industries. In Y. Hao, J. Liu, Y. Wang, Y. M. Cheung, H. Yin, L. Jiao, J. Ma, & Y. C. Jiao (Eds.), *COMPUTATIONAL INTELLIGENCE AND SECURITY, PT 2, PROCEEDINGS* (Vol. 3802, Issue International Conference on Computational Intelligence and Security pp. 749–756). DOI: 10.1007/11596981_110

Li, X., Long, Y., Fan, M., & Chen, Y. (2022). Drilling down artificial intelligence in entrepreneurial management: A bibliometric perspective. *Systems Research and Behavioral Science*, *39*(3), 379–396. DOI: 10.1002/sres.2855

Lu, J. W., Chang, N., & Liao, L. (2013). Environmental informatics for solid and hazardous waste management: Advances, challenges, and perspectives. *Critical Reviews in Environmental Science and Technology*, *43*(15), 1557–1656. DOI: 10.1080/10643389.2012.671097

Makna, J., & Kirikova, M. (2011). Patterns-based is change management in smes. In W. W. Song, S. Xu, C. Wan, Y. Zhong, W. Wojtkowski, G. Wojtkowski, & H. Linger (Eds.), *Information Systems Development: Asian Experiences* (Issues 18th International Conference on Information Systems Develolpment (ISD2009) CL-Nanchang, pp. 55–66). DOI: 10.1007/978-1-4419-7355-9_5

Malik, F., Chugtai, S., Iqbal, Z., & Ramzan, M. (2013). Does psychological empowerment bring about employee commitment? Evidence from telecommunication sector of Pakistan. *Journal of Business Studies Quarterly*, *5*(1), 14.

Marrella, A., & Mecella, M. (2018). Cognitive business process management for adaptive cyber-physical processes. In E. Teniente & M. Weidlich (Eds.), *Lecture Notes in Business Information Processing* (Vol. 308, Issue 15th International Conference on Business Process Management (BPM), pp. 429–439). DOI: 10.1007/978-3-319-74030-0_33

Mattioli, J., Perico, P., & Robic, P. O. (2020). Artificial Intelligence based Asset Management. In *SOSE 2020 - IEEE 15th International Conference of System of Systems Engineering, Proceedings* (Issue IEEE 15th International Conference of System of Systems Engineering (SoSE), pp. 151–156). DOI: 10.1109/SoSE50414.2020.9130505

Mohamad, T. N. T., Sampe, J., & Berhanuddin, D. D. (2018). RF and thermal hybrid input for ultra-low power semi-active UHF RFID tags. *Proceedings - 2018 IEEE 14th International Colloquium on Signal Processing and Its Application, CSPA 2018*. DOI: 10.1109/CSPA.2018.8368683

Muir, A. M., Bernhardt, J. R., Boucher, N. W., Cvitanovic, C., Dettmers, J. M., Gaden, M., Hinderer, J. L. M., Locke, B., Robinson, K. F., Siefkes, M. J., Young, N., & Cooke, S. J. (2023). Confronting a post-pandemic new-normal-threats and opportunities to trust-based relationships in natural resource science and management. *Journal of Environmental Management*, *330*, 117140. Advance online publication. DOI: 10.1016/j.jenvman.2022.117140 PMID: 36603252

Naveed, M. Y., & Ramzan, M. (2013). A view about the determinants of change in share prices: A case from Karachi stock exchange (banking sector). *Interdisciplinary Journal of Contemporary Research in Business*, *4*(12), 41–57.

Pasqualino, R., Demartini, M., & Bagheri, F. (2021). Digital Transformation and Sustainable Oriented Innovation: A System Transition Model for Socio-Economic Scenario Analysis. [WE - Science Citation Index Expanded] [SCI-EXPANDED] [WE - Social Science Citation Index] [SSCI]. *Sustainability (Basel)*, *13*(21), 11564. Advance online publication. DOI: 10.3390/su132111564

Peixoto, R., Dias, L., Carvalho, M. S., Pereira, G., & Geraldes, C. A. S. (2016). An automated warehouse design validation using discrete simulation. *IEEE Conference on Intelligent Transportation Systems, Proceedings, ITSC*. DOI: 10.1109/ITSC.2016.7795554

Dr Ramzan, Muhammad; Hussain, Ashfaq; Ahmad, Z. (2019). New Paradigm New Practices and New Professionalism Needed to Meet Modern World Library Challenges. *Library Philosophy and Practice*, 12–19.

Ramzan, M., Arshad, J., Adeeb, H., & Asif, M. (2019). Excessive Use of Instagram causing Anxiety and Depression among Young Adults. *Pakistan Library & Information Science Journal, 50*(3), 45–48. https://search.ebscohost.com/login.aspx?direct=true&db=ofs&AN=138208789&site=ehost-live&scope=site

Ramzan, M., Asif, M., & Mustafa, M. (2013). Impact of trade openness and macroeconomic variables on GDP growth of Pakistan. *A Research Journal of Commerce. Economics and Social Sciences*, *7*(1), 37–47.

Sampaio, R. P., Costa, A. A., & Flores-Colen, I. (2022). A Systematic Review of Artificial Intelligence Applied to Facility Management in the Building Information Modeling Context and Future Research Directions. [WE - Science Citation Index Expanded] [SCI-EXPANDED]. *Buildings (Basel, Switzerland), 12*(11), 1939. Advance online publication. DOI: 10.3390/buildings12111939

Schwering, D. S., Bergmann, L., & Sonntag, W. I. (2022). How to encourage farmers to digitize? A study on user typologies and motivations of farm management information systems. [WE - Science Citation Index Expanded] [SCI-EXPANDED]. *Computers and Electronics in Agriculture, 199*, 107133. Advance online publication. DOI: 10.1016/j.compag.2022.107133

Shafiq, A., & Ramzan, M. (2015). *Determinants of job satisfaction amongst industrial workers.*

Shafique, M. N., Ahmad, H., & Adeel, A. (2015). Growth of Islamic Banking in Pakistan Using Aid Model. *Oman Chapter of Arabian Journal of Business and Management Review*, *5*(4), 40–44. DOI: 10.12816/0019115

Shatat, A. S., & Shatat, A. S. (2023). Artificial Intelligence Competencies in Logistics Management: An Empirical Insight from Bahrain. *Journal of Information and Knowledge Management*. DOI: 10.1142/S0219649223500594

Sodhi, M. M. S., & Tang, C. S. (2021). Supply Chain Management for Extreme Conditions: Research Opportunities. *The Journal of Supply Chain Management*, *57*(1), 7–16. DOI: 10.1111/jscm.12255

Staegemann, D., Feuersenger, H., Volk, M., Liedtke, P., Arndt, H. K., & Turowski, K. (2022). Investigating the Incorporation of Big Data in Management Information Systems. In W. Abramowicz, S. Auer, & M. Strozyna (Eds.), *BUSINESS INFORMATION SYSTEMS WORKSHOPS, BIS 2021* (Vol. 444, Issue 24th International Conference on Business Information Systems (BIS), pp. 109–120). DOI: 10.1007/978-3-031-04216-4_12

Stoll, M. (2010). Integrating information security into quality management systems. In K. Elleithy, T. Sobh, M. Iskander, V. Kapila, M. A. Karim, & A. Mahmood (Eds.), *Technological Developments in Networking, Education and Automation* (Issue International Joint Conferences on Computer, Information, and Systems Sciences, Engineering (CISSE 2009), pp. 455–460). DOI: 10.1007/978-90-481-9151-2_79

Subhan, D. S., Hafeez, D. A., & Waheed, H. (2015). Impact of Energy Consumption on Economic Growth of Pakistan. *International Journal of Mechanical Engineering and Information Technology, 2*(6), 51–60. DOI: 10.18535/ijmeit/v3i9.01

Thomas, A., & Paul, J. (2019). Knowledge transfer and innovation through university-industry partnership: An integrated theoretical view. *Knowledge Management Research and Practice, 17*(4), 436–448. DOI: 10.1080/14778238.2018.1552485

Tian, X., Pavur, R., Han, H., & Zhang, L. (2023). A machine learning-based human resources recruitment system for business process management: Using LSA, BERT and SVM. *Business Process Management Journal, 29*(1), 202–222. DOI: 10.1108/BPMJ-08-2022-0389

Tootell, A., Kyriazis, E., Billsberry, J., Ambrosini, V., Garrett-Jones, S., & Wallace, G. (2020). Knowledge creation in complex inter-organizational arrangements: Understanding the barriers and enablers of university-industry knowledge creation in science-based cooperation. *Journal of Knowledge Management, 25*(4), 743–769. DOI: 10.1108/JKM-06-2020-0461

Wang, Y., Lin, J., Osman, Z., Farooq, M., & Raju, V. (2021). Transformational leadership and employee performance in international commercial banking industry in Malaysia: The role of self-efficacy as a mediator under BRI. *Journal of Chinese Human Resource Management, 12*(2), 25–36. DOI: 10.47297/wspchrmWSP2040-800503.20211202

Wang, Z., Huo, J. Z., & Duan, Y. R. (2023). Manufacturers? strategy for introducing remanufactured products under a government subsidy: Introduce or not? [WE - Emerging Sources Citation Index] [ESCI]. *Journal of Management Science and Engineering, 8*(1), 128–148. DOI: 10.1016/j.jmse.2022.07.006

Xu, Q., Xu, L., Xie, Z. Y., & Jin, M. F. (2021). Does Business Group Matter for the Relationship between Green Innovation and Financial Performance? Evidence from Chinese Listed Companies. [WE - Science Citation Index Expanded] [SCI-EXPANDED] [WE - Social Science Citation Index] [SSCI]. *Sustainability (Basel), 13*(23), 13204. Advance online publication. DOI: 10.3390/su132313204

Zareen, M., Razzaq, K., & Ramzan, M. (2013). Impact of employee retention on performance: The moderating role of employee psychological perception towards retention plan. *Interdisciplinary Journal of Contemporary Research in Business, 4*(10), 822–833.

Zerfass, A., Hagelstein, J., & Tench, R. (2020). Artificial intelligence in communication management: A cross-national study on adoption and knowledge, impact, challenges and risks. *Journal of Communication Management (London), 24*(4), 377–389. DOI: 10.1108/JCOM-10-2019-0137

Zhang, C., Wang, P., Zhao, Y., Lai, Q., & Kong, L. (2003). Network information resources management system based on knowledge mining. *Online Information Review, 27*(2), 129–135. DOI: 10.1108/14684520310471743

Zhang, J. J., Liu, Y., & Song, J. (2009). The scientific research management system of colleges. In C. L. Zhao, Y. W. Wu, J. X. Wang, & Q. T. Liu (Eds.), *2009 2nd International Symposium on Knowledge Acquisition and Modeling, KAM 2009* (Vol. 2, Issues 2nd International Symposium on Knowledge Acquisition and Modeling CL-Wuhan, pp. 289–292). DOI: 10.1109/KAM.2009.298

Chapter 11
Transformative Impacts of AI in Cloud Computing and Information Systems Infrastructure

ABSTRACT

The foundation of contemporary digital landscapes is made up of cloud computing and information systems architecture, which are transforming how companies handle and use data (Farooq, Yuen, et al., 2024; León-Romero et al., 2024). Through cloud computing, which is a paradigm change from conventional on-premise solutions, businesses may access computer resources and services online (Jose et al., 2021). It has a scalable approach that provides affordability and flexibility. Applications, storage, and processing power may all be found in a virtual playground that is the cloud, allowing for easy collaboration and global accessibility (Chenyang et al., 2024; Zhai & Chen, 2024).

11.1 CHAPTER INTRODUCTION

Cloud computing and information systems infrastructure are closely related. Information systems infrastructure includes networks, hardware, software, and data storage components that facilitate the processing and movement of information within an organization. This infrastructure acts as the hub, enabling the smooth integration of different technology components(Chatzimichailidou et al., 2024; Xie et al., 2024). A strong information systems infrastructure is essential for agility and

DOI: 10.4018/979-8-3373-0513-4.ch011

competitiveness as firms depend more and more on digital operations (W. Huang et al., 2022).

The dynamics of data management are redefined by cloud computing and information systems architecture, encouraging creativity and effectiveness(Karim et al., 2024; Okada et al., 2024). Scalable and secure data storage is facilitated by the cloud, and process orchestration is guaranteed by the supporting infrastructure(Cen et al., 2013; Sinclair, 2013; Zhu, 2013). By fostering revolutionary change and advancing organizations toward a future where connection and information flow effortlessly across physical borders, this symbiotic partnership gives them the ability to negotiate the challenges of the digital era (Staegemann et al., 2022).

Figure 1. Cloud computing and information systems infrastructure

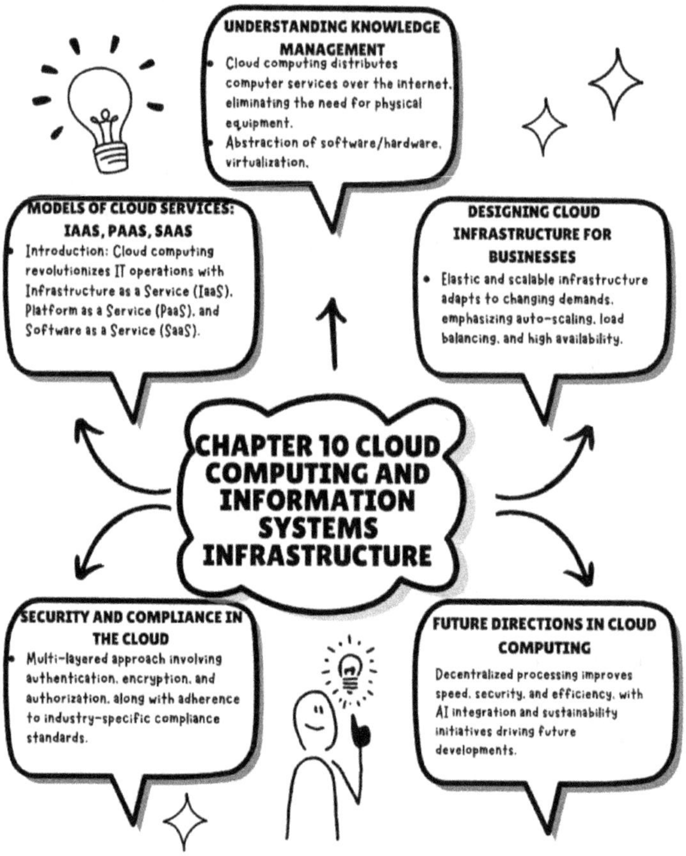

11.2 CLOUD COMPUTING FUNDAMENTALS

A concept known as "cloud computing" makes it possible to distribute computer services via the internet, giving customers access to resources without requiring them to purchase or maintain physical equipment (Solaimani & Swaak, 2023). This fundamental change in computing has become a crucial aspect of the contemporary digital world and has significant consequences for many different businesses (Farooq & Qureshi, 2020; Wang et al., 2021).

The abstraction of software and hardware resources to make them available as online services is the fundamental component of cloud computing(Farooq, Yuen, et al., 2024; Farooq, Ramzan, et al., 2024c). Virtualization technologies, which allow the development of virtual instances of computer resources like servers, storage, and networks, help this abstraction. After then, users may scale their infrastructure up or down in accordance with their unique demands by provisioning and managing these resources on-demand(Farooq, Ramzan, et al., 2024a, 2024g, 2024i). Ease and flexibility are two important features that set cloud computing apart from conventional on-premises systems(Farooq, Ramzan, et al., 2024j). The affordability of cloud computing is one of its main benefits(Farooq, Ramzan, et al., 2024h). Cloud services allow companies to implement a payas-you-go strategy by removing the need for them to purchase and maintain actual gear(Farooq, Ramzan, et al., 2024e, 2024d, 2024f). Users will save a lot of money since they will only pay for the resources they really utilize(Farooq, Ramzan, et al., 2024b, 2024k; Muhammad Farooq, Muhammad Ramzan, 2024). A range of price options and service levels are often provided by cloud providers, enabling businesses to customize their use to match their operating needs and financial constraints (Tootell et al., 2020).

Another important component of cloud computing is scalability(Farooq, Buzdar, et al., 2024; Yen et al., 2023). Businesses are able to quickly scale up or down resources in response to shifting demands and workloads with ease(Farooq et al., 2022a; Farooq, Hafsa Qadir, et al., 2023). In today's dynamic corporate climate, when demand swings and the need for rapid answers to market changes are typical, this adaptability is especially significant(Farooq et al., 2022b; Farooq, Bakhsh, et al., 2023). Cloud computing increases an organization's ability to innovate and compete by enabling quick application deployment and scaling(Farooq et al., 2020).

Collaboration and accessibility are made easier by cloud computing. Users are encouraged to work remotely and collaborate with teams that are geographically separated by the ability to access their data and apps from any location with an internet connection(Buzdar & Farooq, 2020). This accessibility helps to create a more worldwide and integrated company environment in addition to increasing worker productivity(Farooq, Kalimuthu, et al., 2019).

Cloud computing's deployment techniques increase the range of applications for which it may be used(Farooq, 2019; Farooq & Raju, 2019d). Public cloud services provide a common pool of computer resources and are made available to the general public by third-party companies. Contrarily, private clouds provide better security and control as they are exclusive to a single company(Farooq, Ali, et al., 2019; Farooq & Raju, 2019a). Data and apps may be exchanged across public and private clouds thanks to hybrid clouds, which incorporate aspects of both types of clouds (Ghulam et al., 2019; Naseer et al., 2019).

11.3 MODELS OF CLOUD SERVICES: IAAS, PAAS, SAAS

Cloud computing has completely changed how companies run and maintain their IT systems(Farooq, Khalil-Ur-Rehman, et al., 2019). The service models that cloud computing provides—Infrastructure as a Service (IaaS), Platform as a Service (PaaS), and Software as a Service (SaaS)—are among the fundamental components that characterize the technology (Sebrechts et al., 2021).

A basic concept known as Infrastructure as a Service (IaaS) offers virtualized computer resources over the internet. Under this strategy, companies may pay for the virtual computers, storage, and networking components as needed(Farooq & Raju, 2019b).

This gives businesses greater flexibility and scalability by removing the need for them to purchase and maintain physical gear(Farooq & Raju, 2019c). The ability for companies to scale their infrastructure up or down in response to demand is one of the main benefits of Infrastructure as a Service (IaaS)(Farooq, Rehman, et al., 2019). This guarantees that businesses only pay for the resources they use, which is especially advantageous for those with variable workloads. IaaS also makes it possible to deploy apps and services quickly without having to wait for typical hardware procurement delays(Farooq, Muhammad, et al., 2019).

Businesses using IaaS must additionally manage and maintain the middleware, operating systems, and applications that are running on the virtualized infrastructure. Organizations may personalize their environments with this amount of power, but it also means that system management and security are now more of an obligation.

By offering a platform that comprises infrastructure as well as tools and services for developing, deploying, and managing applications, PaaS advances cloud computing. Developers may concentrate on code and creativity instead of worrying about specifics of hardware and operating systems because to this paradigm, which isolates much of the underlying infrastructure(Palomäki et al., 2021; Zhigang, 2021).

PaaS makes development process optimization one of its main advantages. By using pre-built components and services, developers may minimize the time and effort needed to construct and implement applications. Time to market for innovative goods and services is accelerated as a result(Cesaroni & Consoli, 2015a; Li & Yao, 2021). Because PaaS encourages teamwork and creativity among development teams, it is especially beneficial for companies that prioritize application development. Additionally, it makes automated scaling possible, guaranteeing that programs can effectively manage fluctuating workloads(Prabhavathy & Umamaheswari, 2022; Xiao, 2022).

Compared to IaaS, PaaS could provide less customization choices since the underlying infrastructure is abstracted. When using PaaS, organizations need to balance the advantages of quick development against possible limits on customization(Cesaroni & Consoli, 2015b; Wang et al., 2016).

SaaS, or software as a service, offers fully functional and operational software programs via the internet, and it symbolizes the pinnacle of abstraction in cloud computing. This paradigm makes everything available via a web browser, so users don't need to install, maintain, or update software locally(Breeding, 2015; Oduh et al., 2018).

For companies that want to concentrate on their core competencies instead of managing software, SaaS is a gamechanger. Email services, customer relationship management (CRM) software, and teamwork tools are typical SaaS examples(Bican & Brem, 2020).

11.4 DESIGNING CLOUD INFRASTRUCTURE FOR BUSINESSES

Leveraging the advantages of cloud computing for organizations requires careful consideration of the design of an efficient cloud infrastructure. It is possible to achieve optimum performance, scalability, and cost-efficiency with a well-designed cloud architecture. When creating cloud infrastructure for various business requirements, there are a number of important factors to take into mind (Arnone et al., 2016).

The flexibility to scale resources up or down in response to demand is one of the main benefits of cloud computing. It's essential to have an elastic and scalable infrastructure to handle shifting demands. This entails taking into account elements like auto-scaling, load balancing, and the capacity to smoothly add or remove resources as required(Alkhalifah et al., 2022).

Elevated workloads may be accommodated by the infrastructure with scalability and elasticity allowing for automated resource allocation modifications to maintain optimum efficiency and cost-effectiveness(Niros, 2017).

High standards of availability and dependability are necessary for business-critical services and applications. Redundancy and failover techniques should be included into cloud infrastructure architecture to reduce downtime in the case of hardware breakdowns or other problems. This might include load balancing to provide uniform traffic distribution and deploying applications across many availability zones or regions.

Choosing cloud services with built-in redundancy and failover capabilities is a necessary step in planning for high availability. This guarantees that operations will continue even in the event of unplanned interruptions. A significant priority when building cloud infrastructure is security. Companies need to have strong security measures in place to guard against cyberattacks and unwanted access to data, apps, and services. This covers identity and access control, network security, encryption, and routine security audits.

Adherence to industry norms and regulations has similar significance, particularly for enterprises operating in regulated industries like banking, healthcare, and government. To prevent legal and regulatory problems, cloud infrastructure architecture should be in line with applicable compliance standards. Cost Optimization: Although cloud computing's pay-as-you-go approach has cost benefits, it's crucial to minimize cloud costs to avoid unforeseen charges. This entails deciding on the ideal combination of resources, using affordable storage options, and putting effective resource use procedures into place.

Businesses may monitor and manage their expenditure with the use of cloud cost management tools and services, which provide insights into consumption trends and optimization options. Ongoing cost effectiveness may be enhanced by routinely assessing and modifying the cloud infrastructure architecture in response to changing business requirements.

11.5 SECURITY AND COMPLIANCE IN THE CLOUD

Cloud security involves a multifaceted strategy. Strong security procedures are essential to safeguarding the data and infrastructure stored on cloud service providers' (CSPs) platforms. The core elements of cloud security are authorization, authentication, and encryption. Data confidentiality is guaranteed via encryption, even in the event of illegal access(Cloud Security Alliance, 2009). By forcing users to give various forms of identity, multi-factor authentication provides an additional degree of protection (Mallidi et al., 2021). By restricting access to resources, authorization procedures make sure that only those with the proper authority may deal with sensitive information and apps(Habib et al., 2014; Y. Huang et al., 2019).

Organizations themselves need to embrace a shared responsibility paradigm for cloud security in addition to the obligations of CSPs(Aujla et al., 2020; Dora et al., 2022). This entails putting security best practices into effect, including frequent audits, vulnerability analyses, and timely software and system patching. To reduce the possibility of human mistake, companies should also train their staff on security procedures and promote a security-aware culture (Mallidi et al., 2021).

Since organizations must follow industry-specific norms and standards, compliance and security are tightly related in the cloud. Companies have to abide by laws like GDPR, HIPAA, and PCI DSS, depending on the kind of data they manage. In order to provide clients confidence that their services adhere to industry standards, cloud providers often issue compliance certifications for their offerings. Organizations must, however, be aware of their unique compliance needs and make sure the cloud infrastructure they choose complies with them(Mallidi et al., 2021, 2021).

Businesses must carefully consider the geographic placement of their cloud infrastructure to comply with local requirements as data sovereignty and privacy issues gain traction. Certain categories of data must be kept within the boundaries of the nation due to stringent data residency regulations in place in certain nations. A proactive attitude to compliance and a deep comprehension of the legal environment are necessary for navigating these complications.

To keep security and compliance in the cloud, ongoing monitoring and audits are essential. In order to reduce the effect of security events, automated technologies may assist in real-time threat detection and response. Frequent internal and external audits guarantee continued compliance with relevant legislation and provide valuable insights into the efficacy of security procedures(Johnson et al., 2017).

11.6 FUTURE DIRECTIONS IN CLOUD COMPUTING

The emergence of edge computing is one significant development in cloud computing going forward. While cloud services have always been housed in data centers, edge computing moves processing power closer to the customers(Kumar et al., 2022a). Decentralization facilitates quicker data processing and lowers latency, which makes it perfect for applications like Internet of Things (IoT) sensors and autonomous cars that need to respond quickly (Tchuente & El Haddadi, 2023).

Because sensitive data is kept closer to the source, edge computing also improves security and privacy.

Cloud computing services are progressively incorporating machine learning (ML) and artificial intelligence (AI). Specialized AI and ML services are now available from cloud providers, enabling companies to take use of these technologies' potential without requiring a high level of knowledge(Cao et al., 2021; Hallioui et al., 2022). Through this connection, businesses may improve their decision-making processes, get insightful knowledge, and analyze enormous volumes of data (Ji et al., 2020).

Another fundamental change in cloud computing is serverless computing. Developers may concentrate on developing code rather than maintaining the underlying infrastructure when using serverless architectures(Alan, 2023; Ilager et al., 2020). Cloud providers automatically manage resource scaling and provisioning, resulting in more cost-effective and efficient use of processing power. Because serverless computing allocates resources dynamically depending on demand, it is especially advantageous for applications with fluctuating workloads(Alan, 2023; Sun et al., 2020).

In an effort to maximize their cloud initiatives, enterprises are adopting a hybrid and multi-cloud strategy. Hybrid cloud solutions provide scalability and flexibility by combining public and private cloud services with on-premises infrastructure. Utilizing services from many cloud providers helps to improve resilience and prevent vendor lock-in when implementing multi-cloud methods. These strategies let companies take advantage of the advantages offered by various cloud providers and customize their cloud environments to meet certain needs (Siripurapu et al., 2023).

Concerns about security and privacy will always be at the forefront of developments in cloud computing. Cybersecurity threats will evolve, and innovations in encryption methods, zero-trust architectures, and secure access controls will handle them. Cloud providers and enterprises will need to adjust as the regulatory environment changes in order to guarantee continuous compliance and data security(Bourechak et al., 2022; Kumar et al., 2022b).

Cloud computing has a bright future ahead of it when it comes to environmentally friendly and sustainable methods. In an effort to reduce their environmental effect, cloud providers are making more investments in renewable energy sources and using energy-efficient technology(Stoykova & Shakev, 2023; Tchuente & El Haddadi, 2023). Businesses that value sustainability may expect the cloud sector to play a major role in encouraging a more environmentally conscientious computing strategy.

11.7 CHAPTER CONCLUSION

The contemporary digital landscape is fundamentally shaped by the advent of cloud computing and information systems architecture, revolutionizing the way businesses manage and utilize data. Cloud computing, with its paradigm shift from traditional on-premise solutions, offers businesses access to computer resources and services over the internet in a scalable and flexible manner. This virtual playground of applications, storage, and processing power fosters easy collaboration and global accessibility, driving innovation and effectiveness in data management.

Cloud computing, intertwined with information systems infrastructure, redefines the dynamics of data management by providing scalable and secure data storage and ensuring process orchestration through supporting infrastructure. This symbiotic partnership propels organizations towards a future where connectivity and information flow seamlessly across physical borders, equipping them to navigate the challenges of the digital era with agility and efficiency.

Understanding the fundamentals of cloud computing is essential for businesses seeking to leverage its benefits. The abstraction of software and hardware resources, facilitated by virtualization technologies, enables businesses to scale infrastructure up or down based on demand, promoting affordability, flexibility, and ease of use. Cloud computing fosters collaboration, accessibility, and innovation, empowering organizations to deploy applications rapidly and adapt to dynamic market conditions.

REFERENCES

Al Karim, R., Rabiul, M. K., Ahamed, T., Karim, D. N., & Mehzabeen, M. (2024). Integrating Green Entrepreneurial Orientation, Green Information Systems, and Management Support with Green Supply Chain Management to Foster Firms' Environmental Performance. *Sustainability (Basel), 16*(12), 4921. DOI: 10.3390/su16124921

Alan, H. (2023). A Systematic Bibliometric Analysis on the Current Digital Human Resources Management Studies and Directions for Future Research. [WE - Emerging Sources Citation Index] [ESCI]. *Journal of Chinese Human Resource Management, 14*(1), 38–59. DOI: 10.47297/wspchrmWSP2040-800502.20231401

Alkhalifah, A., Alorini, F., & Alturki, R. (2022). Enhancement of E-commerce Service by Designing Last Mile Delivery Platform. [WE - Science Citation Index Expanded] [SCI-EXPANDED]. *Computer Systems Science and Engineering, 42*(1), 49–67. DOI: 10.32604/csse.2022.021326

Arnone, S., Buoni, L., Manieri, A., Mathieu, P.-P., Mazzitelli, G., & Spagnoli, F. (2016). University, Industry and Research Cooperation: the Lazio Pulse Initiative. In L. G. Chova, A. L. Martinez, & I. C. Torres (Eds.), *ICERI2016 Proceedings* (Vol. 1, Issues 9th Annual International Conference of Education, Research and Innovation (iCERi), pp. 3808–3814). DOI: 10.21125/iceri.2016.1902

Aujla, G. S., Barati, M., Rana, O., Dustdar, S., Noor, A., Llanos, J. T., Carr, M., Marikyan, D., Papagiannidis, S., & Ranjan, R. (2020). COM-PACE: Compliance-Aware Cloud Application Engineering Using Blockchain. [WE - Science Citation Index Expanded] [SCI-EXPANDED]. *IEEE Internet Computing, 24*(5), 45–53. DOI: 10.1109/MIC.2020.3014484

Bican, P. M., & Brem, A. (2020). Digital Business Model, Digital Transformation, Digital Entrepreneurship: Is there a sustainable "digital"? *Sustainability (Basel), 12*(13), 5239. Advance online publication. DOI: 10.3390/su12135239

Bourechak, A., Zedadra, O., Kouahla, M. N., Guerrieri, A., & Seridi, H. (2022). At the confluence of Artificial Intelligence and Edge computing in the area of smart applications : Opportunities, Current trends and New perspectives. [WE - Science Citation Index Expanded] [SCI-EXPANDED]. *Sensors (Basel), 23*(3), 1–34. DOI: 10.3390/s23031639 PMID: 36772680

Breeding, M. (2015). INFORME SOBRE SISTEMAS BIBLIOTECARIOS. HACER OPERATIVA LA INNOVACIÓN. In *Library systems report. Operationalizing innovation.* (Vol. 24, Issue 4, pp. 485–496). EPI SCP. http://10.0.12.73/epi.2015.jul.16

Buzdar, A. Q., & Farooq, M. (2020). Memorization of Quran through Mobile Application in the Era of Transformative Marketing. [PJSS]. *Pakistan Journal of Social Sciences*, *40*(2), 689–698.

Cao, K., Hu, S. Y., Shi, Y., Colombo, A., Karnouskos, S., & Li, X. (2021). A Survey on Edge and Edge-Cloud Computing Assisted Cyber-Physical Systems. [WE - Science Citation Index Expanded] [SCI-EXPANDED]. *IEEE Transactions on Industrial Informatics*, *17*(11), 7806–7819. DOI: 10.1109/TII.2021.3073066

Cen, Y., Wang, H., Zhang, Z., & Wang, H. (2013). Design and implementation of cigarette product quality management information system based on ERP and PDM. In Babu, M. S. P., & Wenzheng, L. (Eds.), *Proceedings of the IEEE International Conference on Software Engineering and Service Sciences, ICSESS* (pp. 170–174). DOI: 10.1109/ICSESS.2013.6615281

Cesaroni, F. M., & Consoli, D. (2015a). Are Small Businesses Really Able to Take Advantage of Social Media?: Bournemouth University e-resources. *Electronic Journal of Knowledge Management*, *13*(4).

Cesaroni, F. M., & Consoli, D. (2015b). Are Small Businesses Really Able to Take Advantage of Social Media?: Discovery Service para Universidad Del Pacifico. *Electronic Journal of Knowledge Management*, *13*(4).

Chatzimichailidou, M., Whitcher, T., & Suzic, N. (2024). Complementarity and Compatibility of Systems Integration and Building Information Management. *IEEE Systems Journal*, *18*(2), 1198–1207. DOI: 10.1109/JSYST.2024.3387064

Chenyang, X., Piao, W., Zilun, L., Qing, L., & Yadong, K. (2024). Research on Science and Technology Management Information Security Guarantee System. *Journal of Information Security Research*, *10*(7), 675–681.

Cloud Security Alliance. (2009). Security Guidance for Critical Areas of Focus in Cloud Computing. In *Cloud Security Alliances*. DOI: 10.1016/S1353-4858(99)90042-9

Dora, M., Kumar, A., Mangla, S. K., Pant, A., & Kamal, M. M. (2022). Critical success factors influencing artificial intelligence adoption in food supply chains. *International Journal of Production Research*, *60*(14), 4621–4640. DOI: 10.1080/00207543.2021.1959665

Farooq, M. (2019). Emerging sciences in Social Sciences : An overview, A Research Agenda. *Global Journal of Emerging Sciences*, *1*(October), 183–197.

Farooq, M., Ali, W., Younas, W., Khalil-Ur-rehman, F., & Qurashi, Q. A. (2019). the Era of Transformative Marketing: Service Quality of Mobile App Based Taxi Services in Kuala Lumpur. *Proceedings on Engineering Sciences, 1*(2), 49–58. DOI: 10.24874/PES01.02.006

Farooq, M., Bakhsh, A., Hafsa Qadir, B., & Warda, N. (2023). Digital Empowerment: Freedom of Expression Beyond 5G and 6G Networks in Developing Countries. *Pakistan Journal of Social Sciences, 43*(4), 569–584. DOI: 10.5281/zenodo.10448484

Farooq, M., Buzdar, H. Q., Yen, Y. Y., & Bakhsh, A. (2024). Integrating AI in Sustainable Writing: An Empirical Investigation of the Technology Acceptance Model in Asian Social Sciences. *Journal of Logistics. Informatics and Service Science, 11*(3), 324–338. DOI: 10.33168/JLISS.2024.0321

Farooq, M., Cheng, J., Khan, N. U., Saufi, R. A., Kanwal, N., & Bazkiaei, H. A. (2022a). Sustainable Waste Management Companies with Innovative Smart Solutions: A Systematic Review and Conceptual Model. *Sustainability (Basel), 14*(20), 13146. Advance online publication. DOI: 10.3390/su142013146

Farooq, M., Cheng, J., Khan, N. U., Saufi, R. A., Kanwal, N., & Bazkiaei, H. A. (2022b). Sustainable Waste Management Companies with Innovative Smart Solutions: A Systematic Review and Conceptual Model. *Sustainability (Basel), 14*(20), 13146. DOI: 10.3390/su142013146

Farooq, M., Hafsa Qadir, B., & Saeed, M. (2023, December). AI-Enhanced Social Sciences: A Systematic Literature Review and Bibliographic Analysis of Web of Science Published Research Papers. *Pakistan Journal of Society* [PJSEL]. *Education and Language, 10*, 1–2.

Farooq, M., Kalimuthu, R., & Reza, M. H. (2019). Measuring and Comparing Brand Equity of Malaysian Banks in the Era of Transformative Marketing. *Global Journal of Emerging Sciences, 1*(June), 96–102.

Farooq, M., Khalil-Ur-Rehman, F., Abdurrahaman, D. T., Younas, W., Sajjad, S., & Zreen, A. (2019). SERVICE QUALITY ANALYSIS OF PRIVATE UNIVERSITIES LIBRARIES IN MALAYSIA IN THE ERA OF TRANSFORMATIVE MARKETING. *International Journal of Qualitative Research, 13*(2), 269–284. DOI: 10.24874/IJQR13.02-02

Farooq, M., Muhammad, S., Raju, V., Kalimuthu, K. R., & Qadir, A. (2019). Measuring and Comparing the Desired and Actual Service Quality of Pakistan International Airline. *The Journal of Social Sciences Research, 52*(52), 484–490. DOI: 10.32861/jssr.52.484.490

Farooq, M., & Qureshi, Q. A. (2020). Practical Approach of Environmental Awareness to Broadening Community Participation: A Case Study of Pindad (Persero). *Journal of Management Practices. Humanities and Social Sciences*, *4*(1). Advance online publication. DOI: 10.33152/jmphss-4.2.1

Farooq, M., & Raju, V. (2019a). Impact of Over-the-Top (OTT) Services on the Telecom Companies in the Era of Transformative Marketing. *Global Journal of Flexible Systems Managment*, *20*(2), 177–188. DOI: 10.1007/s40171-019-00209-6

Farooq, M., & Raju, V. (2019b). Want to Stay the Market Leader in the Era of Transformative Marketing? Keep the Customers Satisfied! *Global Journal of Flexible Systems Management*. DOI: 10.1007/s40171-019-00213-w

Farooq, M., & Raju, V. (2019c). Impact of Over-the-Top (OTT) Services on the Telecom Companies in the Era of Transformative Marketing. *Global Journal of Flexible Systems Managment*, *20*(2), 177–188. DOI: 10.1007/s40171-019-00209-6

Farooq, M., & Raju, V. (2019d). Want to Stay the Market Leader in the Era of Transformative Marketing? Keep the Customers Satisfied! *Global Journal of Flexible Systems Managment*, *20*(3), 257–266. DOI: 10.1007/s40171-019-00213-w

Farooq, M., Ramzan, M., & Yen, Y. Y. (2024a). AI in Consumer Behavior Management. In *Transformative Impacts of AI in Management* (pp. 281–294). IGI Global., DOI: 10.4018/979-8-3693-4322-7.ch011

Farooq, M., Ramzan, M., & Yen, Y. Y. (2024b). AI in Customer Service, HR, and Administration. In *Transformative Impacts of AI in Management* (pp. 45–70). IGI Global. DOI: 10.4018/979-8-3693-4322-7.ch002

Farooq, M., Ramzan, M., & Yen, Y. Y. (2024c). AI in Quality Management. In *Transformative Impacts of AI in Management* (pp. 295–312). IGI Global., DOI: 10.4018/979-8-3693-4322-7.ch012

Farooq, M., Ramzan, M., & Yen, Y. Y. (2024d). Artificial Intelligence and Customer Experiences. In *Transformative Impacts of AI in Management* (pp. 95–114). IGI Global., DOI: 10.4018/979-8-3693-4322-7.ch004

Farooq, M., Ramzan, M., & Yen, Y. Y. (2024e). Artificial Intelligence in Administration Sciences. In *Transformative Impacts of AI in Management* (pp. 115–156). IGI Global., DOI: 10.4018/979-8-3693-4322-7.ch005

Farooq, M., Ramzan, M., & Yen, Y. Y. (2024f). Artificial Intelligence in Business and Law. In *Transformative Impacts of AI in Management* (pp. 71–94). IGI Global., DOI: 10.4018/979-8-3693-4322-7.ch003

Farooq, M., Ramzan, M., & Yen, Y. Y. (2024g). Artificial Intelligence in Ethical Business Decision Making. In *Transformative Impacts of AI in Management* (pp. 265–280). IGI Global., DOI: 10.4018/979-8-3693-4322-7.ch010

Farooq, M., Ramzan, M., & Yen, Y. Y. (2024h). Exploring the Impact of Artificial Intelligence on Brand Management. In *Transformative Impacts of AI in Management* (pp. 157–188). IGI Global., DOI: 10.4018/979-8-3693-4322-7.ch006

Farooq, M., Ramzan, M., & Yen, Y. Y. (2024i). Exploring the Impact of Ethical Leadership and Employee Engagement on Knowledge Sharing Attitudes in the Asian Digital Economy. In *Transformative Impacts of AI in Management* (pp. 241–264). IGI Global., DOI: 10.4018/979-8-3693-4322-7.ch009

Farooq, M., Ramzan, M., & Yen, Y. Y. (2024j). Transformative Impact of AI in Education Management. In *Transformative Impacts of AI in Management* (pp. 189–216). IGI Global., DOI: 10.4018/979-8-3693-4322-7.ch007

Farooq, M., Ramzan, M., & Yen, Y. Y. (2024k). *Transformative Impacts of AI in Management*. IGI Global., DOI: 10.4018/979-8-3693-4322-7

Farooq, M., Rehman, F. K. U., Younas, W., Raju, V., Ahmed, Q. M., & Ali, M. (2019). Investigating Relationship between Net Promoter Score and Company Performance: A Longitudinal Study. *Global Journal of Emerging Sciences*, *1*(1), 1–10. https://www.gjoes.org/wp-content/uploads/2019/04/1-1.pdf

Farooq, M., Saeed, M., Ali, W., & Javid, R. (2020). Online Buying and Customer Satisfaction in the Era of Transformative Marketing. *City University Research Journal*, *10*(2), 274–288.

Farooq, M., Yuen, Y. Y., & Buzdar, H. Q. (2024). Exploring the Research Landscape of Artificial Intelligence Integration with Business Management: A Bibliometric Analysis from 1994-2023. *Journal of Logistics. Informatics and Service Science*, (April). Advance online publication. DOI: 10.33168/JLISS.2024.0410

Ghulam, W. A., Ali, W., Ali, S., Khan, M. M., Khan, R. N., & Farooq, M. (2019). Investigating factors influencing brain drain of citizens of Azad Kashmir Pakistan. *Journal of Social Sciences Research*, *5*(3), 782–788. Advance online publication. DOI: 10.32861/jssr.53.782.788

Habib, S. M., Ries, S., Mühlhäuser, M., & Varikkattu, P. (2014). Towards a trust management system for cloud computing marketplaces: Using CAIQ as a trust information source. [WE - Science Citation Index Expanded] [SCI-EXPANDED]. *Security and Communication Networks*, *7*(11), 2185–2200. DOI: 10.1002/sec.748

Hallioui, A., Herrou, B., Santos, R. S., Katina, P. F., & Egbue, O. (2022). Systems-based approach to contemporary business management: An enabler of business sustainability in a context of industry 4.0, circular economy, competitiveness and diverse stakeholders. *Journal of Cleaner Production*, *373*, 133819. Advance online publication. DOI: 10.1016/j.jclepro.2022.133819

Huang, W., Chau, K. Y., Kit, I. Y., Nureen, N., Irfan, M., & Dilanchiev, A. (2022). Relating Sustainable Business Development Practices and Information Management in Promoting Digital Green Innovation: Evidence From China. [WE - Social Science Citation Index] [SSCI]. *Frontiers in Psychology*, *13*, 930138. Advance online publication. DOI: 10.3389/fpsyg.2022.930138 PMID: 35800951

Huang, Y., Debnath, J., Iorga, M., Kumar, A., & Xie, B. (2019). CSAT: A User-interactive Cyber Security Architecture Tool based on NIST-compliance Security Controls for Risk Management. In S. Chakrabarti & H. N. Saha (Eds.), *2019 IEEE 10th Annual Ubiquitous Computing, Electronics and Mobile Communication Conference, UEMCON 2019* pp. 0697–0707). DOI: 10.1109/UEMCON47517.2019.8993090

Ilager, S., Muralidhar, R., Buyya, R., & Soc, I. C. (2020). Artificial Intelligence (AI)-Centric Management of Resources in Modern Distributed Computing Systems. In *2020 IEEE CLOUD SUMMIT* (Issue IEEE Cloud Summit, pp. 1–10). WE - Conference Proceedings Citation Index - Science (CPCI-S)DOI: 10.1109/IEEECloudSummit48914.2020.00007

Ji, H. J., Alfarraj, O., & Tolba, A. (2020). Artificial Intelligence-Empowered Edge of Vehicles: Architecture, Enabling Technologies, and Applications. [WE - Science Citation Index Expanded] [SCI-EXPANDED]. *IEEE Access : Practical Innovations, Open Solutions*, *8*, 61020–61034. DOI: 10.1109/ACCESS.2020.2983609

Johnson, G., Whittington, R., Scholes, K., Angwin, D., & Regner, P. (2017). Exploring Strategy: Text and Cases. In *Pearson Education Limited* (Vol. 159, Issue 3). DOI: 10.1016/S0002-9378(88)80016-4

Jose, B., Ramanan, T. R., & Kumar, S. D. M. (2021). A risk comparison framework for evaluating the impact of telecom cloudification in organizational risk profile. *Telecommunication Systems*, *78*(3), 421–437. Advance online publication. DOI: 10.1007/s11235-021-00827-5

Kumar, D., Singh, R. K., Mishra, R., & Wamba, S. F. (2022a). Applications of the internet of things for optimizing warehousing and logistics operations: A systematic literature review and future research directions. *Computers & Industrial Engineering*, *171*, 108455. Advance online publication. DOI: 10.1016/j.cie.2022.108455

Kumar, D., Singh, R. K., Mishra, R., & Wamba, S. F. (2022b). Applications of the internet of things for optimizing warehousing and logistics operations: A systematic literature review and future research directions. [WE-.]. *Computers & Industrial Engineering, 171*, 171. DOI: 10.1016/j.cie.2022.108455

León-Romero, L. P., Aguilar-Fernández, M., Luque-Sendra, A., Zamora-Polo, F., & Francisco-Márquez, M. (2024). Characterization of the information system integrated to the construction project management systems. *Heliyon, 10*(11), e31886. Advance online publication. DOI: 10.1016/j.heliyon.2024.e31886 PMID: 38841493

Li, J. H., & Yao, M. F. (2021). New Framework of Digital Entrepreneurship Model Based on Artificial Intelligence and Cloud Computing. [WE - Science Citation Index Expanded] [SCI-EXPANDED]. *Mobile Information Systems, 2021*, 1–11. Advance online publication. DOI: 10.1155/2021/3080160

Mallidi, R. K., Sharma, M., & Singh, J. (2021). Legacy Digital Transformation: TCO and ROI Analysis. *INTERNATIONAL JOURNAL OF ELECTRICAL AND COMPUTER ENGINEERING SYSTEMS, 12*(3), 163-170 WE-Emerging Sources Citation Index (ESC. Muhammad Farooq, Muhammad Ramzan, Y. Y. Y. (2024). AI in Management. In *Transformative Impacts of AI in Management* (1st ed., pp. 1–44). IGI Global. DOI: 10.4018/979-8-3693-4322-7.ch001

Naseer, M., Farooq, M., Younas, W., & Raju, V. (2019). Antecedents of employee retention in the pharmaceutical industry of Pakistan. *Journal of Social Sciences Research, 5*(3), 656–664. Advance online publication. DOI: 10.32861/jssr.53.655.664

Niros, M. (2017). *Effective branding strategies using the CET-CC matrix in foreign markets: The Role of Consumer Ethnocentrism and Confidence on Purchase Intention Brand Personality of Telco providers and their effects on Consumer Behaviour View project Consumer Ethnocentrism and Best Branding Practices View project.* https://www.researchgate.net/publication/318110302

Oduh, I. U., Misra, S., Damasevicius, R., & Maskeliunas, R. (2018). Cloud Based Simple Employee Management Information System: A Model for African Small and Medium Enterprises. In A. Rocha & T. Guarda (Eds.), *PROCEEDINGS OF THE INTERNATIONAL CONFERENCE ON INFORMATION TECHNOLOGY & SYSTEMS (ICITS 2018)* (Vol. 721, Issue International Conference on Information Technology and Systems (ICITS), pp. 115–128). DOI: 10.1007/978-3-319-73450-7_12

Okada, K., Sugimoto, K., Wada, S., Konishi, S., Manabe, S., Matsumura, Y., & Takeda, T. (2024). Development of the Clinical Specimen Information Management System for Multicenter Clinical Studies. In J. Bichel-Findlay, P. Otero, P. Scott, & E. Huesing (Eds.), *MEDINFO 2023 - THE FUTURE IS ACCESSIBLE* (Vol. 310, Issues 19th World Congress on Medical and Health Informatics (MEDINFO) CL-Sydney, pp. 119–123). DOI: 10.3233/SHTI230939

Palomäki, J., Laakasuo, M., Castrén, S., Saastamoinen, J., Kainulainen, T., & Suhonen, N. (2021). Online betting intensity is linked with Extraversion and Conscientiousness. *Journal of Personality*, *89*(5), 1081–1094. Advance online publication. DOI: 10.1111/jopy.12637 PMID: 33811638

Prabhavathy, M., & Umamaheswari, S. (2022). Prevention of runtime malware injection attack in cloud using unsupervised learning. *Intelligent Automation & Soft Computing*, *32*(1), 101–114. Advance online publication. DOI: 10.32604/iasc.2022.018257

Sebrechts, M., Borny, S., Wauters, T., Volckaert, B., & De Turck, F. (2021). Service relationship orchestration: Lessons learned from running large scale smart city platforms on kubernetes. *IEEE Access : Practical Innovations, Open Solutions*, *9*, 133387–133401. DOI: 10.1109/ACCESS.2021.3115438

Sinclair, D. R. (2013). Methodologies of anesthesia information management system development. *Journal of Clinical Anesthesia*, *25*(5), 425–427. DOI: 10.1016/j.jclinane.2013.02.009 PMID: 23965189

Siripurapu, S., Darimireddy, N. K., & Chehri, A., B., S., & A.V., P. (. (2023). Technological Advancements and Elucidation Gadgets for Healthcare Applications: An Exhaustive Methodological Review-Part-II (Robotics, Drones, 3D-Printing, Internet of Things, Virtual/Augmented and Mixed Reality). *Electronics (Basel)*, *12*(3), 548. DOI: 10.3390/electronics12030548

Solaimani, S., & Swaak, L. (2023). Critical Success Factors in a multi-stage adoption of Artificial Intelligence: A Necessary Condition Analysis. *Journal of Engineering and Technology Management*, *69*, 101760. Advance online publication. DOI: 10.1016/j.jengtecman.2023.101760

Staegemann, D., Feuersenger, H., Volk, M., Liedtke, P., Arndt, H. K., & Turowski, K. (2022). Investigating the Incorporation of Big Data in Management Information Systems. In W. Abramowicz, S. Auer, & M. Strozyna (Eds.), *BUSINESS INFORMATION SYSTEMS WORKSHOPS, BIS 2021* (Vol. 444, Issue 24th International Conference on Business Information Systems (BIS), pp. 109–120). DOI: 10.1007/978-3-031-04216-4_12

Stoykova, S., & Shakev, N. (2023). Artificial Intelligence for Management Information Systems: Opportunities, Challenges, and Future Directions. [WE - Emerging Sources Citation Index] [ESCI]. *Algorithms, 16*(8), 357. Advance online publication. DOI: 10.3390/a16080357

Sun, L. F., Jiang, X., Ren, H. X., & Guo, Y. (2020). Edge-Cloud Computing and Artificial Intelligence in Internet of Medical Things: Architecture, Technology and Application. [WE - Science Citation Index Expanded] [SCI-EXPANDED]. *IEEE Access : Practical Innovations, Open Solutions, 8*, 101079–101092. DOI: 10.1109/ACCESS.2020.2997831

Tchuente, D., & El Haddadi, A. (2023). One decade of big data for firms' competitiveness: Insights and a conceptual model from bibliometrics. *Journal of Enterprise Information Management, 36*(6), 1421–1453. Advance online publication. DOI: 10.1108/JEIM-03-2022-0074

Tootell, A., Kyriazis, E., Billsberry, J., Ambrosini, V., Garrett-Jones, S., & Wallace, G. (2020). Knowledge creation in complex inter-organizational arrangements: Understanding the barriers and enablers of university-industry knowledge creation in science-based cooperation. *Journal of Knowledge Management, 25*(4), 743–769. DOI: 10.1108/JKM-06-2020-0461

Wang, Y., Hsiao, S.-H., Yang, Z., & Hajli, N. (2016). The impact of sellers' social influence on the co-creation of innovation with customers and brand awareness in online communities. *Industrial Marketing Management, 54*, 56–70. DOI: 10.1016/j.indmarman.2015.12.008

Wang, Y., Lin, J., Osman, Z., Farooq, M., & Raju, V. (2021). Transformational leadership and employee performance in international commercial banking industry in Malaysia: The role of self-efficacy as a mediator under BRI. *Journal of Chinese Human Resource Management, 12*(2), 25–36. DOI: 10.47297/wspchrmWSP2040-800503.20211202

Xiao, X. M. (2022). RETRACTED: Research and Application of Cloud Platform-Oriented Intelligent Information Management System (Retracted Article). [WE - Science Citation Index Expanded] [SCI-EXPANDED]. *Wireless Communications and Mobile Computing, 2022*, 1–8. Advance online publication. DOI: 10.1155/2022/8397780

Xie, J., Jablonski, M., Smith, J., & Navedo, A. (2024). A Graphical Interface to Support Low-Flow Volatile Anesthesia: Implications for Patient Safety, Teaching, and Design of Anesthesia Information Management Systems. *Journal of Medical Systems*, *48*(1), 36. Advance online publication. DOI: 10.1007/s10916-024-02055-1 PMID: 38532235

Yen, Y. Y., Wen, L. J., Ramasamy, S., & Farooq, M. (2023). Sustainable petrol subsidy program in Malaysia. *Asian Development Policy Review*, *12*(1), 1–9. DOI: 10.55493/5008.v12i1.4948

Zhai, Q., & Chen, X. (2024). Design and application of optical communication technology based on machine learning algorithms in physical education teaching information management system. *Optical and Quantum Electronics*, *56*(1), 111. Advance online publication. DOI: 10.1007/s11082-023-05717-5

Zhigang, W. (2021). Research on the Framework of Library Management System Based on Internet of Things. In *Proceedings - 2021 13th International Conference on Measuring Technology and Mechatronics Automation, ICMTMA 2021* (Issues 13th International Conference on Measuring Technology and Mechatronics Automation (ICMTMA) CL-Beihai, pp. 384–388). DOI: 10.1109/ICMTMA52658.2021.00089

Zhu, X. (2013). Web sites information security management based on B/S pattern. In J. Zhang, Z. J. Wang, S. R. Zhu, & X. M. Meng (Eds.), *Applied Mechanics and Materials* (Vols. 263–266, Issue PART 1, pp. 3141–3144). https://doi.org/DOI: 10.4028/www.scientific.net/AMM.263-266.3141

Chapter 12
Transformative Impacts of AI in E-Business and E-Commerce Systems

ABSTRACT

E-business and e-commerce systems have become important elements that are revolutionizing how businesses transact business and engage with their clientele (Gringarten, 2018; S.-C. Huang, 2018; Lepthien et al., 2014). Broader in scope, e-business is the integration of electronic methods into many company operations, including management, cooperation, and communication (R.-T. Huang et al., 2016; Uluta et al., 2018). This all-encompassing strategy breaks down barriers and maximizes the use of available resources while promoting effective workflows (Grewal, 2017; Kumar et al., 2018).

12.1 CHAPTER INTRODUCTION

E-business and e-commerce systems have become important elements that are revolutionizing how businesses transact business and engage with their clientele (Gringarten, 2018; S.-C. Huang, 2018; Lepthien et al., 2014). Broader in scope, e-business is the integration of electronic methods into many company operations, including management, cooperation, and communication (R.-T. Huang et al., 2016; Uluta et al., 2018). This all-encompassing strategy breaks down barriers and maximizes the use of available resources while promoting effective workflows(Grewal, 2017; Kumar et al., 2018).

The online exchange of products and services is the main emphasis of e-commerce systems(Escalas & Bettman, 2005; H. He & Li, 2011). These systems enable transactions over digital platforms, removing geographical limitations, through a smooth

DOI: 10.4018/979-8-3373-0513-4.ch012

integration of business and technology (Arnett et al., 2018; Punj & Hillyer, 2004). Consumers may now easily navigate virtual stores and conduct safe, quick purchases with unmatched convenience(Dreher & Herzfeld, 2005; W. Wang & Seifert, 2018). The incorporation of secure payment gateways guarantees the protection of financial transactions, hence fostering confidence in the digital domain(Bhatti & Qureshi, 2007; Colicev et al., 2018).

Businesses that use e-business and e-commerce systems not only improve operational efficiency but also get priceless insights from data analytics(Alavi, 2012; Zhang et al., 2017). Predictive analysis and real-time monitoring improve decision-making, enabling businesses to quickly respond to market developments. These systems' ability to combine technology innovation with business strategy is driving businesses toward a future where efficiency and connectedness will completely reshape the nature of trade(Christodoulides, 2004; Clermont & Kamsu-Foguem, 2018).

Figure 1. E- business and ecommerce systems

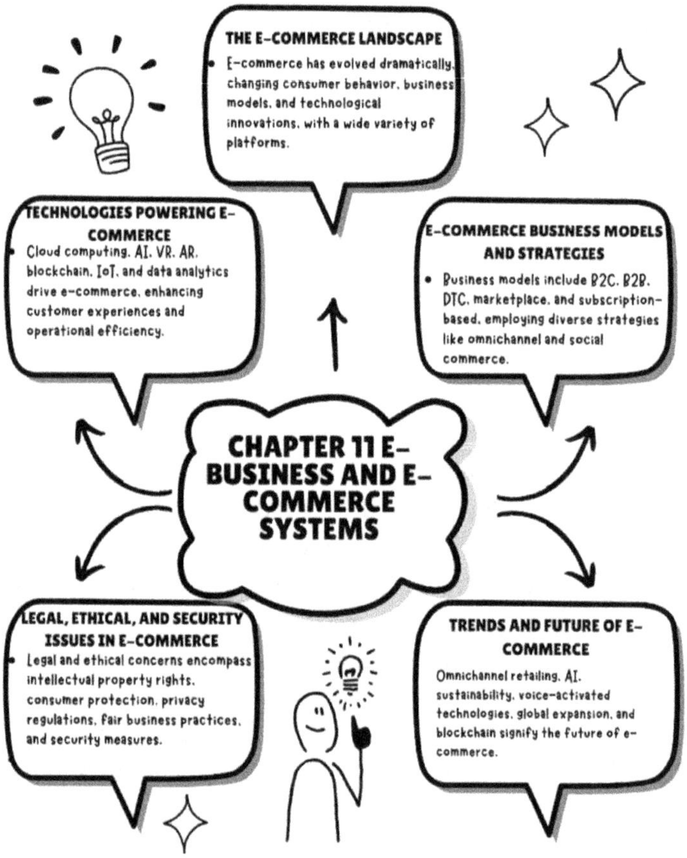

12.2 THE E-COMMERCE LANDSCAPE

Over the last several decades, the e-commerce environment has seen a dramatic transition that has changed how consumers and companies interact(Juana-espinosa & Rakowska, 2018; Shabbir et al., 2023). The purchasing and selling of products and services using the internet is referred to as electronic commerce, or e-commerce(U-mashankar et al., 2017; Žabkar et al., 2010). It has grown to be a crucial component of the world economy, disrupting conventional shopping and creating new channels for companies to connect with customers (Sajid et al., 2022).

The accessibility of e-commerce is one of its main features. Customers may now explore and buy things from the comfort of their homes or while they're on the road thanks to the widespread use of cellphones and the internet(Fock et al., 2013; Gyawali, 2017). Because of its ease, consumers' purchasing habits have changed dramatically, with conventional brick-and-mortar retail declining and internet buying rising(Sfakianaki et al., 2022).

The e-commerce industry is broad, with a wide range of platforms and business models. The digital marketplace supports a wide range of participants, from big international companies to tiny individual vendors(Iftikhar & Khan, 2019; Tuan et al., 2020). Prominent online marketplaces like Amazon, Alibaba, and eBay are well-known brands that link millions of customers and sellers worldwide. Furthermore, companies are using mobile applications and specialized websites to develop their online presence and interact with consumers directly(Gupta et al., 2018; Siti Jahroh, 2019).

Developments in technology have a significant impact on how e-commerce is shaped. Online transactions operate smoothly in part because of the constant development of payment gateways, internet infrastructure, and data security protocols(M. F. Buzdar, Janjua, Khurshid, et al., 2016; W. He et al., 2017). E-commerce has greatly benefited from mobile technology in particular, which allows customers to purchase whenever and wherever they want(M. F. Buzdar, Janjua, & Khurshid, 2016; Jensen & Klastrup, 2008). Technologies like virtual reality (VR) and augmented reality (AR) are also being used into e-commerce to provide customers immersive and engaging purchasing experiences.

The predominance of many business models and tactics characterizes the e-commerce environment. Conventional business-to-consumer (B2C) and consumer-to-consumer (C2C) business models include corporations selling directly to end users or people selling to one another. However, the dynamic character of the e-commerce ecosystem is reflected in the rise of new models like Direct-to-Consumer (DTC) and Subscription-Based. DTC enables businesses to sell directly to customers without the need for middlemen, while subscription-based business models provide goods or services on a regular basis to encourage repeat business(Lim et al., 2011; Seo & Park, 2018).

12.3 TECHNOLOGIES POWERING E-COMMERCE

Cloud computing is a fundamental technology that offers ecommerce platforms with flexible and scalable infrastructure (Farooq et al., 2022b). Large volumes of data may be processed and stored by organizations using cloud-based systems, which guarantees uninterrupted operation even during peak hours (Farooq, Khalil-Ur-Rehman, et al., 2019; Farooq, Hafsa Qadir, et al., 2023). Scalability is essential to managing variations in user traffic and providing a dependable and responsive e-commerce platform(Farooq et al., 2022a; Yen et al., 2023).

In e-commerce, machine learning and artificial intelligence (AI) are essential elements that drive client interaction and customization(Farooq, Kalimuthu, et al., 2019; Farooq, Rehman, et al., 2019). By analyzing past data, preferences, and user behavior, these technologies provide individualized suggestions that increase conversion rates(Farooq, 2019; Farooq, Ali, et al., 2019). AI-powered chatbots improve customer service by answering questions instantly, helping customers through the purchasing process, and enabling a more engaging online experience(Naseer et al., 2019).

With immersive and engaging experiences, virtual reality (VR) and augmented reality (AR) are revolutionizing online shopping for customers(Farooq, Ramzan, et al., 2024i, 2024f). While VR offers virtual stores that let consumers browse things as if they were physically there in a brick-and-mortar store, AR allows shoppers to see products in their real-world surroundings before making a purchase choice(Farooq, Buzdar, et al., 2024; Farooq, Ramzan, et al., 2024j, 2024d).

Blockchain technology is becoming more and more popular in e-commerce because it may improve transaction security and transparency(Farooq, Ramzan, et al., 2024b, 2024a; Muhammad Farooq, Muhammad Ramzan, 2024). Through the use of distributed and decentralized ledgers, blockchain guarantees the security, verifiability, and immutability of every transaction(Farooq, Ramzan, et al., 2024g, 2024k, 2024c). This not only protects financial transactions but also contributes to customer trust-building, fraud reduction, and enhanced ecosystem integrity for e-commerce(Farooq et al., 2020; Farooq, Ramzan, et al., 2024h, 2024e).

A more individualized and effective shopping experience is made possible by the Internet of Things (IoT), which links physical objects and collects data in real time(Farooq, Bakhsh, et al., 2023; Farooq & Raju, 2019d). IoT gadgets, such wearable technology and smart home appliances, make transactions easier and help create a responsive and networked e-commerce environment(A. Q. Buzdar & Farooq, 2020; Ghulam et al., 2019).

Tools for business intelligence and data analytics enable ecommerce companies to extract useful information from enormous databases(Farooq & Raju, 2019a). These insights support better decision-making to increase overall operational efficiency, as well as understanding customer behavior and inventory management optimization.

Technologies like 5G connection, edge computing, and progressive web apps are expected to become more important as the e-commerce scene develops(Farooq, Muhammad, et al., 2019; Farooq & Raju, 2019c). These developments might change how users engage with online platforms by offering quicker and more dependable internet connections, better website performance, and improved user experiences(-Farooq & Raju, 2019b).

12.4 E-COMMERCE BUSINESS MODELS AND STRATEGIES

Business to Consumer (B2C) is a widely used e-commerce business strategy in which companies offer goods or services directly to final customers. Online retail behemoths like Amazon are prime examples of this business model, in which the platform acts as a middleman between vendors and a large customer base. In order to draw in and keep clients, the B2C model places a strong emphasis on delivering a flawless online purchasing experience, prioritizing user-friendly interfaces, and using focused marketing techniques.

Businesses trade with one another when one delivers goods or services, and this is known as the Business to Business (B2B) model. B2B e-commerce platforms emphasize features like order management and interaction with corporate systems, expedite procurement procedures, and provide bulk pricing in order to support effective company operations. The Direct to Consumer (DTC) concept has gained traction, allowing firms to connect directly with consumers by eschewing conventional retail channels. DTC companies often use influencer relationships, content marketing, and social media to increase brand recognition and cultivate a devoted following of consumers.

Marketplace models, such as those seen on Etsy and eBay, unite a number of merchants and customers on one website. These markets offer a wide variety of goods, allowing merchants to reach a wider audience and customers to choose from a larger selection. User experience is the first priority of successful markets, which also employ strong payment and shipping systems and build confidence via reviews and ratings.

Subscription-based business models, which provide customers ongoing access to goods or services in exchange for a monthly payment, are growing in popularity. This business strategy benefits from recurring income streams and client loyalty across a variety of industries, including streaming services and subscription boxes. Companies that use subscription models concentrate on giving special and worthwhile products or services to maintain customers' interest and loyalty.

E-commerce strategies include a range of techniques for consumer interaction, marketing, and operational effectiveness. For example, omnichannel tactics combine online and physical channels to provide a smooth buying experience at several touchpoints. Social commerce makes use of social media sites to find products, read reviews, and make purchases by reaching out to the large user populations of sites like Facebook and Instagram.

Analytics are used by data-driven tactics to better analyze customer behavior, adjust prices, and target marketing campaigns. For example, dynamic pricing modifies prices in response to competition, demand, and other factors in order to maximize revenue and maintain competitiveness. E-commerce companies that are successful make constant adjustments to their models and tactics in order to keep abreast of industry developments, customer preferences, and technology breakthroughs. A customer-centric strategy, flexibility, and innovation are still critical for long-term success in the fast-paced world of e-commerce.

12.5 LEGAL, ETHICAL, AND SECURITY ISSUES IN ECOMMERCE

Legal challenges in the context of e-commerce include a broad spectrum of topics, including intellectual property rights and consumer protection. Privacy rules, like the General Data Protection Regulation (GDPR), require organizations to get informed permission and maintain the protection of personal information (Farooq & Qureshi, 2020). They also demand the appropriate usage of user data. Furthermore, contract law is crucial since it regulates the terms and circumstances of transactions conducted online(Y. Wang et al., 2021). Maintaining adherence to these regulatory standards is crucial for fostering customer confidence and averting legal consequences (Farooq, Yuen, et al., 2024).

In e-commerce, ethical concerns include social responsibility, fair business practices, and transparency(Al-Debei et al., 2008). To build customer trust, online retailers need to be open and honest about their offerings, costs, and guidelines(Masmachuca, 2018; Petruzzellis, 2010). In addition to harming a company's image, unethical actions like misleading marketing techniques or fraudulent advertising may also have legal repercussions(Takeaways et al., 2019; Tsafarakis et al., 2018).

Furthermore, fair labor procedures, employee treatment, and the environmental effects of e-commerce activities are also considered ethical issues. Because online transactions are sensitive, security is still a top priority in the e-commerce industry(Dwivedi et al., 2018; Kouser et al., 2012). Threats to cybersecurity, such as identity theft, financial fraud, and data breaches, put consumers and organizations at serious risk(Farooq, 2019; Jayasuriya & Azam, 2017; Pauwels et al., 2016). To protect consumer data, e-commerce platforms need to invest in strong security measures like multi-factor authentication, secure payment gateways, and encryption technologies(Isa et al., 2016; Johnson, 2017). To maintain a safe online shopping environment and remain ahead of developing cyber risks, regular audits and upgrades are required(Furner et al., 2012).

Because e-commerce is digital, it is vulnerable to intellectual property infringement and counterfeiting. It is possible for dishonest people or organizations to try to steal material, violate trademarks, or offer fake items(Bu et al., 2017; Luan et al., 2019; Mathrani & Ibrahim, 2022). To stop and handle these violations, e-commerce platforms need to have strong security measures in place, such content monitoring systems and intellectual property protection technologies(Farooq et al., 2020; Johnson et al., 2017). Efforts to prevent counterfeiting in the online marketplace may be further strengthened by collaborating with industry associations and law enforcement authorities(Greenberg et al., 2011; Halaweh & Fidler, 2008).

12.6 TRENDS AND FUTURE OF E-COMMERCE

The seamless integration of online and physical channels by firms, known as omnichannel retailing, is rapidly becoming the future of e-commerce(Bommaraju et al., 2019; Isaac et al., 2019). Customers anticipate a consistent online and offline purchasing experience across all platforms, including mobile applications and websites. E-commerce companies will have a competitive advantage in catering to the varied tastes of contemporary consumers if they adopt omnichannel strategies and include features like click-andcollect and augmented reality buying experiences(Delloite, 2019; Finkelstein, 2022).

Artificial intelligence (AI) is revolutionizing the way companies engage with their consumers and is quickly becoming a driving force in e-commerce(Dickson et al., 2017; Farooq & Qureshi, 2020). Chatbots driven by artificial intelligence (AI) give instant support, virtual personal shoppers suggest products that are specific to each customer, and predictive analytics enhance inventory control(Chen et al., 2022; Fesenmaier et al., 2017; Könik et al., 2015). The degree of customization in e-commerce experiences will increase as AI algorithms advance, improving client happiness and loyalty. Consumer tastes are being shaped by environmental awareness, which is driving up demand for environmentally friendly and sustainable goods. Green business strategies, such as using eco-friendly packaging and carbon-neutral shipping, are being adopted by e-commerce companies more and more. Future purchase choices by environmentally concerned customers are likely to be influenced by brands that place a high priority on sustainability in their operations and supply chains.

Voice-activated technologies and smart gadgets are revolutionizing how customers engage with online retailers. With virtual assistants such as Google Assistant and Alexa from Amazon, consumers can make purchases by speaking instructions. Voice commerce, which offers a simple and hands-free buying experience, is anticipated to become more and more popular as these technologies advance(Farooq, Yuen, et al., 2024; León-Romero et al., 2024).

Geographical restrictions no longer apply to e-commerce, which enables companies to access a worldwide customer base (Chenyang et al., 2024; Zhai & Chen, 2024). As customers look for a variety of items from across the globe, cross-border e-commerce is predicted to grow significantly (Chatzimichailidou et al., 2024; Xie et al., 2024). Global marketplace success will go to ecommerce platforms that handle logistical issues, localize experiences, and expedite foreign transactions (Chatzimichailidou et al., 2024; Okada et al., 2024).

Blockchain for Transparency and Trust: Due to its promise to improve transaction transparency and trust, blockchain technology is becoming more and more popular in ecommerce(Farooq, Ramzan, et al., 2024c, 2024a; Karim et al., 2024). A more transparent and safe e-commerce environment is facilitated by blockchain-based supply chain management, decentralized payment systems, and smart contracts. The popularity of this technology is expected to grow as it develops, reducing fraud and enhancing the general dependability of online transactions.

12.7 CHAPTER CONCLUSION

E-business and e-commerce systems have emerged as indispensable elements reshaping the landscape of business transactions and customer engagement. E-business integrates electronic methods into various business operations, breaking down barriers and optimizing resource utilization. On the other hand, e-commerce systems facilitate online exchanges of products and services, transcending geographical limitations and fostering seamless transactions with enhanced convenience and security.

The e-commerce environment has undergone significant transformation, revolutionizing the way consumers and businesses interact. Accessibility remains a hallmark of e-commerce, empowering customers to browse and purchase goods from anywhere at any time, driving the decline of traditional retail and the rise of online shopping. The e-commerce industry encompasses a diverse array of platforms and business models, from global marketplaces to specialized websites, fueled by advancements in technology such as mobile devices, virtual reality, and augmented reality.

Key technologies power the functionalities and experiences of e-commerce platforms. Cloud computing provides scalable infrastructure, while machine learning and artificial intelligence drive personalized interactions and recommendations. Virtual reality and augmented reality offer immersive shopping experiences, while blockchain technology ensures transaction security and transparency. Additionally, the Internet of Things enhances connectivity and data collection, empowering businesses with valuable insights for decision-making.

Various business models and strategies shape the e-commerce landscape, from traditional B2C and B2B models to innovative approaches like Direct-to-Consumer and subscription-based models. These strategies emphasize customer-centricity, operational efficiency, and technological innovation to drive growth and competitiveness in the digital marketplace. Data-driven tactics and omnichannel approaches play pivotal roles in enhancing customer engagement and optimizing business performance.

Legal, ethical, and security considerations are paramount in the realm of e-commerce, encompassing issues such as privacy regulations, fair business practices, and cybersecurity threats. Adherence to legal standards, ethical principles, and robust security measures are imperative for fostering consumer trust and mitigating risks in the digital domain.

Looking ahead, trends in e-commerce point towards the seamless integration of online and physical channels through omnichannel retailing, the increasing role of artificial intelligence in enhancing customer experiences, and the growing demand for environmentally sustainable practices. Voice-activated technologies, global market expansion, and blockchain for transparency and trust are poised to further shape the future of e-commerce, offering new opportunities and challenges for businesses navigating the evolving digital landscape.

In conclusion, e-business and e-commerce systems represent dynamic forces driving innovation, efficiency, and connectivity in the global marketplace. By embracing technological advancements, adopting customer-centric strategies, and upholding ethical and legal standards, businesses can capitalize on the opportunities presented by e-commerce while addressing the evolving needs and expectations of modern consumers.

REFERENCES

Al-Debei, M. M., El-Haddadeh, R., & Avison, D. (2008). Defining the Business Model in the New World of Digital Business. *Proc AMICS 2008,* 2000, 1–11.

Al Karim, R., Rabiul, M. K., Ahamed, T., Karim, D. N., & Mehzabeen, M. (2024). Integrating Green Entrepreneurial Orientation, Green Information Systems, and Management Support with Green Supply Chain Management to Foster Firms' Environmental Performance. *Sustainability (Basel), 16*(12), 4921. DOI: 10.3390/su16124921

Alavi, S. (2012). *Customer Relationship Management and Customer Experience Management Using Business Online Communities.*

Arnett, D. B., Sandvik, I. L., & Sandvik, K. (2018). Two paths to organizational effectiveness – Product advantage and life-cycle flexibility. *Journal of Business Research, 84*(November 2017), 285–292. DOI: 10.1016/j.jbusres.2017.11.010

Bhatti, K. K., & Qureshi, T. M. (2007). International Review of Business Research Papers Impact Of Employee Participation On Job Satisfaction. *Employee Commitment And Employee Productivity., 3*(2), 54–68.

Bommaraju, R., Ahearne, M., Krause, R., & Tirunillai, S. (2019). Does a Customer on the Board of Directors Affect Business-to-Business Firm Performance? *Journal of Marketing, 83*(1), 8–23. DOI: 10.1177/0022242918815894

Bu, L., Durand-Servoingt, B., Kim, A., & Yamakawa, N. (2017). Chinese luxury consumers: The 1 trillion renminbi opportunity. In *McKinsey&Company* (Issue May). http://mckinseychina.com

Buzdar, A. Q., & Farooq, M. (2020). Memorization of Quran through Mobile Application in the Era of Transformative Marketing. [PJSS]. *Pakistan Journal of Social Sciences, 40*(2), 689–698.

Buzdar, M. F., Janjua, S. Y., & Khurshid, M. A. (2016). Customer-based brand equity and firms' performance in the telecom industry. *International Journal of Services and Operations Management, 25*(3), 334. DOI: 10.1504/IJSOM.2016.079516

Buzdar, M. F., Janjua, S. Y. S. Y., Khurshid, M. A. M. A., Farooq, M., Janjua, S. Y. S. Y., & Khurshid, M. A. M. A. (2016). Customer-based brand equity and firms' performance in the telecom industry. *International Journal of Services and Operations Management, 25*(3), 334. DOI: 10.1504/IJSOM.2016.079516

Chatzimichailidou, M., Whitcher, T., & Suzic, N. (2024). Complementarity and Compatibility of Systems Integration and Building Information Management. *IEEE Systems Journal, 18*(2), 1198–1207. DOI: 10.1109/JSYST.2024.3387064

Chen, D. H., Esperanca, J. P., & Wang, S. F. (2022). The Impact of Artificial Intelligence on Firm Performance: An Application of the Resource-Based View to e-Commerce Firms. [WE - Social Science Citation Index] [SSCI]. *Frontiers in Psychology, 13*, 884830. Advance online publication. DOI: 10.3389/fpsyg.2022.884830 PMID: 35465474

Chenyang, X., Piao, W., Zilun, L., Qing, L., & Yadong, K. (2024). Research on Science and Technology Management Information Security Guarantee System. *Journal of Information Security Research, 10*(7), 675–681.

Christodoulides, G. (2004). *E-tail Brand Equity : Scale Development and Validation E-tail Brand Equity : Scale Development and Validation George Christodoulides * Professor Leslie de Chernatony University of Birmingham, UK University of Birmingham, UK University of Nijmegen, The . October 2018.*

Clermont, P., & Kamsu-Foguem, B. (2018). Experience feedback in product lifecycle management. *Computers in Industry, 95*, 1–14. DOI: 10.1016/j.compind.2017.11.002

Colicev, A., Malshe, A., Pauwels, K., & O'Connor, P. (2018). Improving Consumer Mindset Metrics and Shareholder Value Through Social Media: The Different Roles of Owned and Earned Media. *Journal of Marketing, 82*(1), 37–56. DOI: 10.1509/jm.16.0055

Delloite. (2019). Global Powers of Luxury Goods 2019: Bridging the gap between the old and the new. In *Deloitte Touche Tohmatsu Limited.*https://www2.deloitte.com/content/dam/Deloitte/ch/Documents/consumer-business/deloitte-en-cip-global-powers-of-luxury-goods-2019-report.pdf

Dickson, M. T., Ammattikorkeakoulu, M., & Vaatetusalan Koulutusohjelma Opinnäytetyö, V. (2017). *How to Brand and Market a Fashion Label.* https://www.theseus.fi/bitstream/handle/10024/126737/How to Brand and Market a Fashion Label - M. Tereza Dickson.pdf?sequence=1

Dreher, A., & Herzfeld, T. (2005). The Economic Costs of Corruption: A Survey and New Evidence. SSRN *Electronic Journal,July2005.* DOI: 10.2139/ssrn.734184

Dwivedi, A., Nayeem, T., & Murshed, F. (2018). Brand experience and consumers' willingness-to-pay (WTP) a price premium: Mediating role of brand credibility and perceived uniqueness. *Journal of Retailing and Consumer Services, 44*(June), 100–107. DOI: 10.1016/j.jretconser.2018.06.009

Escalas, J. E., & Bettman, J. R. (2005). Consumer Culture Theory (CCT): Twenty Years of Research. *The Journal of Consumer Research, 32*(3), 378–389. DOI: 10.1086/497549

Farooq, M. (2019). Emerging sciences in Social Sciences : An overview, A Research Agenda. *Global Journal of Emerging Sciences, 1*(October), 183–197.

Farooq, M., Ali, W., Younas, W., Khalil-Ur-rehman, F., & Qurashi, Q. A. (2019). the Era of Transformative Marketing: Service Quality of Mobile App Based Taxi Services in Kuala Lumpur. *Proceedings on Engineering Sciences, 1*(2), 49–58. DOI: 10.24874/PES01.02.006

Farooq, M., Bakhsh, A., Hafsa Qadir, B., & Warda, N. (2023). Digital Empowerment: Freedom of Expression Beyond 5G and 6G Networks in Developing Countries. *Pakistan Journal of Social Sciences, 43*(4), 569–584. DOI: 10.5281/zenodo.10448484

Farooq, M., Buzdar, H. Q., Yen, Y. Y., & Bakhsh, A. (2024). Integrating AI in Sustainable Writing: An Empirical Investigation of the Technology Acceptance Model in Asian Social Sciences. *Journal of Logistics. Informatics and Service Science, 11*(3), 324–338. DOI: 10.33168/JLISS.2024.0321

Farooq, M., Cheng, J., Khan, N. U., Saufi, R. A., Kanwal, N., & Bazkiaei, H. A. (2022a). Sustainable Waste Management Companies with Innovative Smart Solutions: A Systematic Review and Conceptual Model. *Sustainability (Basel), 14*(20), 13146. Advance online publication. DOI: 10.3390/su142013146

Farooq, M., Cheng, J., Khan, N. U., Saufi, R. A., Kanwal, N., & Bazkiaei, H. A. (2022b). Sustainable Waste Management Companies with Innovative Smart Solutions: A Systematic Review and Conceptual Model. *Sustainability (Basel), 14*(20), 13146. DOI: 10.3390/su142013146

Farooq, M., Hafsa Qadir, B., & Saeed, M. (2023, December). AI-Enhanced Social Sciences: A Systematic Literature Review and Bibliographic Analysis of Web of Science Published Research Papers. *Pakistan Journal of Society* [PJSEL]. *Education and Language, 10*, 1–2.

Farooq, M., Kalimuthu, R., & Reza, M. H. (2019). Measuring and Comparing Brand Equity of Malaysian Banks in the Era of Transformative Marketing. *Global Journal of Emerging Sciences, 1*(June), 96–102.

Farooq, M., Khalil-Ur-Rehman, F., Abdurrahaman, D. T., Younas, W., Sajjad, S., & Zreen, A. (2019). SERVICE QUALITY ANALYSIS OF PRIVATE UNIVERSITIES LIBRARIES IN MALAYSIA IN THE ERA OF TRANSFORMATIVE MARKETING. *International Journal of Qualitative Research, 13*(2), 269–284. DOI: 10.24874/IJQR13.02-02

Farooq, M., Muhammad, S., Raju, V., Kalimuthu, K. R., & Qadir, A. (2019). Measuring and Comparing the Desired and Actual Service Quality of Pakistan International Airline. *The Journal of Social Sciences Research, 52*(52), 484–490. DOI: 10.32861/jssr.52.484.490

Farooq, M., & Qureshi, Q. A. (2020). Practical Approach of Environmental Awareness to Broadening Community Participation: A Case Study of Pindad (Persero). *Journal of Management Practices. Humanities and Social Sciences, 4*(1). Advance online publication. DOI: 10.33152/jmphss-4.2.1

Farooq, M., & Raju, V. (2019a). Impact of Over-the-Top (OTT) Services on the Telecom Companies in the Era of Transformative Marketing. *Global Journal of Flexible Systems Managment, 20*(2), 177–188. DOI: 10.1007/s40171-019-00209-6

Farooq, M., & Raju, V. (2019b). Want to Stay the Market Leader in the Era of Transformative Marketing? Keep the Customers Satisfied! *Global Journal of Flexible Systems Management*. DOI: 10.1007/s40171-019-00213-w

Farooq, M., & Raju, V. (2019c). Impact of Over-the-Top (OTT) Services on the Telecom Companies in the Era of Transformative Marketing. *Global Journal of Flexible Systems Managment, 20*(2), 177–188. DOI: 10.1007/s40171-019-00209-6

Farooq, M., & Raju, V. (2019d). Want to Stay the Market Leader in the Era of Transformative Marketing? Keep the Customers Satisfied! *Global Journal of Flexible Systems Managment, 20*(3), 257–266. DOI: 10.1007/s40171-019-00213-w

Farooq, M., & Ramzan, M. Y. Y. Y. (2024). AI in Management. In *Transformative Impacts of AI in Management* (1st ed., pp. 1–44). IGI Global. DOI: 10.4018/979-8-3693-4322-7.ch001

Farooq, M., Ramzan, M., & Yen, Y. Y. (2024a). AI in Consumer Behavior Management. In *Transformative Impacts of AI in Management* (pp. 281–294). IGI Global., DOI: 10.4018/979-8-3693-4322-7.ch011

Farooq, M., Ramzan, M., & Yen, Y. Y. (2024b). AI in Customer Service, HR, and Administration. In *Transformative Impacts of AI in Management* (pp. 45–70). IGI Global. DOI: 10.4018/979-8-3693-4322-7.ch002

Farooq, M., Ramzan, M., & Yen, Y. Y. (2024c). AI in Quality Management. In *Transformative Impacts of AI in Management* (pp. 295–312). IGI Global., DOI: 10.4018/979-8-3693-4322-7.ch012

Farooq, M., Ramzan, M., & Yen, Y. Y. (2024d). Artificial Intelligence and Customer Experiences. In *Transformative Impacts of AI in Management* (pp. 95–114). IGI Global., DOI: 10.4018/979-8-3693-4322-7.ch004

Farooq, M., Ramzan, M., & Yen, Y. Y. (2024e). Artificial Intelligence in Administration Sciences. In *Transformative Impacts of AI in Management* (pp. 115–156). IGI Global., DOI: 10.4018/979-8-3693-4322-7.ch005

Farooq, M., Ramzan, M., & Yen, Y. Y. (2024f). Artificial Intelligence in Business and Law. In *Transformative Impacts of AI in Management* (pp. 71–94). IGI Global., DOI: 10.4018/979-8-3693-4322-7.ch003

Farooq, M., Ramzan, M., & Yen, Y. Y. (2024g). Artificial Intelligence in Ethical Business Decision Making. In *Transformative Impacts of AI in Management* (pp. 265–280). IGI Global., DOI: 10.4018/979-8-3693-4322-7.ch010

Farooq, M., Ramzan, M., & Yen, Y. Y. (2024h). Exploring the Impact of Artificial Intelligence on Brand Management. In *Transformative Impacts of AI in Management* (pp. 157–188). IGI Global., DOI: 10.4018/979-8-3693-4322-7.ch006

Farooq, M., Ramzan, M., & Yen, Y. Y. (2024i). Exploring the Impact of Ethical Leadership and Employee Engagement on Knowledge Sharing Attitudes in the Asian Digital Economy. In *Transformative Impacts of AI in Management* (pp. 241–264). IGI Global., DOI: 10.4018/979-8-3693-4322-7.ch009

Farooq, M., Ramzan, M., & Yen, Y. Y. (2024j). Transformative Impact of AI in Education Management. In *Transformative Impacts of AI in Management* (pp. 189–216). IGI Global., DOI: 10.4018/979-8-3693-4322-7.ch007

Farooq, M., Ramzan, M., & Yen, Y. Y. (2024k). *Transformative Impacts of AI in Management*. IGI Global., DOI: 10.4018/979-8-3693-4322-7

Farooq, M., Rehman, F. K. U., Younas, W., Raju, V., Ahmed, Q. M., & Ali, M. (2019). Investigating Relationship between Net Promoter Score and Company Performance: A Longitudinal Study. *Global Journal of Emerging Sciences*, *1*(1), 1–10. https://www.gjoes.org/wp-content/uploads/2019/04/1-1.pdf

Farooq, M., Saeed, M., Ali, W., & Javid, R. (2020). Online Buying and Customer Satisfaction in the Era of Transformative Marketing. *City University Research Journal*, *10*(2), 274–288.

Farooq, M., Yuen, Y. Y., & Buzdar, H. Q. (2024). Exploring the Research Landscape of Artificial Intelligence Integration with Business Management: A Bibliometric Analysis from 1994-2023. *Journal of Logistics. Informatics and Service Science*, (April). Advance online publication. DOI: 10.33168/JLISS.2024.0410

Fesenmaier, D. R., Bharadwaj, N., Stienmetz, J., & Xiang, Z. (2017). MICRO-MARKETING AND BIG DATA ANALYTICS: AN INFORMATION SYSTEM FOR DESTINATION MARKETING MANAGEMENT. In M. Uysal, Z. Schwartz, & E. SirakayaTurk (Eds.), *MANAGEMENT SCIENCE IN HOSPITALITY AND TOURISM: THEORY, PRACTICE, AND APPLICATIONS*.

Finkelstein, S. (2022). *The Role of Marketing in Imagining a Editors :* (Issue June).

Fock, H., Hui, M. K., Au, K., & Bond, M. H. (2013). Moderation Effects of Power Distance on the Relationship Between Types of Empowerment and Employee Satisfaction. *Journal of Cross-Cultural Psychology*, *44*(2), 281–298. DOI: 10.1177/0022022112443415

Furner, C. P., Racherla, P., & Zhu, Z. (2012). Uncertainty, trust and purchase intention based on online product reviews: An introduction to a multinational study. *International Journal of Networking and Virtual Organisations*, *11*(3/4), 260. DOI: 10.1504/IJNVO.2012.048909

Ghulam, W. A., Ali, W., Ali, S., Khan, M. M., Khan, R. N., & Farooq, M. (2019). Investigating factors influencing brain drain of citizens of Azad Kashmir Pakistan. *Journal of Social Sciences Research*, *5*(3), 782–788. Advance online publication. DOI: 10.32861/jssr.53.782.788

Greenberg, R., Wong-On-Wing, B., & Lui, G. (2011). Culture and Consumer Trust in Online Businesses. *Journal of Global Information Management*, *16*(3), 26–44. DOI: 10.4018/jgim.2008070102

Grewal, R. (2017). Journal of Marketing Research: Looking Forward. *JMR, Journal of Marketing Research*, *54*(1), 1–4. DOI: 10.1509/jmr.54.11

Gringarten, H. (2018). Price and Store Image as Mitigating Factors in the Perception and Evaluation of Retailers' Customer-Based Brand Equity. *Journal of Multidisciplinary Research (1947-2900), 10*(1/2), 51–84. http://web.b.ebscohost.com/ehost/pdfviewer/pdfviewer?vid=4&sid=697d26d6-dc2e-4dec-a70b-8dfd81dae130%40sessionmgr104

Gupta, S., Pansari, A., & Kumar, V. (2018). Global Customer Engagement. *Journal of International Marketing*, *26*(1), 4–29. DOI: 10.1509/jim.17.0091

Gyawali, A. (2017). *Impact of Employee Participation on Job Satisfaction, Employee Fairness Perception and Organizational Commitment : A Case of Nepalese Commercial Banks. VIII*(February), 1–13.

Halaweh, M., & Fidler, C. (2008). Security perception in e-commerce: Conflict between customer and organizational perspectives. *2008 International Multiconference on Computer Science and Information Technology, 3*, 443–449. DOI: 10.1109/IMCSIT.2008.4747280

He, H., & Li, Y. (2011). Key service drivers for high-tech service brand equity: The mediating role of overall service quality and perceived value. *Journal of Marketing Management, 27*(1–2), 77–99. DOI: 10.1080/0267257X.2010.495276

He, W., Wang, F.-K., & Akula, V. (2017). Managing extracted knowledge from big social media data for business decision making. *Journal of Knowledge Management, 21*(2), 275–294. DOI: 10.1108/JKM-07-2015-0296

Huang, R.-T., Tang, T.-W., Lee, Y. P., & Yang, F.-Y. (2016). Does proactive personality matter in mobile learning? *Australasian Journal of Educational Technology, 33*(2), 86–96. DOI: 10.14742/ajet.2896

Huang, S.-C. (2018). Social Information Avoidance: When, Why, and How it is Costly in Goal Pursuit. *JMR, Journal of Marketing Research, LV*(June), 382–395. DOI: 10.1509/jmr.16.0268

Iftikhar, M., & Khan, S. (2019). Organizational Empowerment and Turnover intensions:A mediation of Job Satisfaction and Affective Commitment. A Case of Hattar industries, Pakistan. *Journal of Management Info, 6*(2), 1–6. DOI: 10.31580/jmi.v6i2.507

Isa, N. F., Salleh, N. A. M., & Aziz, A. A. (2016). Determinants and Impact of Online Social Interaction on Online Buying Behaviour. *Procedia: Social and Behavioral Sciences, 219*(May), 352–358. DOI: 10.1016/j.sbspro.2016.04.045

Isaac, O., Aldholay, A., Abdullah, Z., & Ramayah, T. (2019). Online learning usage within Yemeni higher education: The role of compatibility and task-technology fit as mediating variables in the IS success model. *Computers & Education, 136*, 113–129. Advance online publication. DOI: 10.1016/j.compedu.2019.02.012

Jayasuriya, N. A., & Azam, S. M. F. (2017). The Impact of Social Media Marketing on Brand Equity: A Study of Fashion-Wear Retail in Sri Lanka. *International Review of Management and Marketing, 7*(5), 178–183. https://econjournals.com/index.php/irmm/article/view/5663

Jensen, M. B., & Klastrup, K. (2008). Towards a B2B customer-based brand equity model. *Journal of Targeting. Measurement & Analysis for Marketing, 16*(2), 122–128. DOI: 10.1057/jt.2008.4

Johnson, G. (2017). *Instructor ' s Manual Exploring Strategy Eleventh edition.*

Johnson, G., Whittington, R., Scholes, K., Angwin, D., & Regner, P. (2017). Exploring Strategy: Text and Cases. In *Pearson Education Limited* (Vol. 159, Issue 3). DOI: 10.1016/S0002-9378(88)80016-4

Juana-espinosa, S. De, & Rakowska, A. (2018). *Public sector motivational practices and their effect on job satisfaction : country differences. 27*(2), 141–154. DOI: 10.1108/EJMBE-02-2018-0027

Könik, T., Mukherjee, R., & Katukuri, J. (2015). Subjective similarity: Personalizing alternative item recommendations. In *WWW 2015 Companion - Proceedings of the 24th International Conference on World Wide Web* (Issue 24th International Conference on World Wide Web (WWW), pp. 1275–1279). DOI: 10.1145/2740908.2741999

Kouser, R., Qureshi, S., & Shahzad, F. (2012). Factors Influencing the Customer ' s Satisfaction and Switching Behavior in Cellular Services of Pakistan. *Interdisciplinary Journal of Research in Business, 2*(1), 15–25.

Kumar, R. S., Dash, S., & Malhotra, N. K. (2018). The impact of marketing activities on service brand equity. *European Journal of Marketing*, EJM-05-2016-0262. DOI: 10.1108/EJM-05-2016-0262

León-Romero, L. P., Aguilar-Fernández, M., Luque-Sendra, A., Zamora-Polo, F., & Francisco-Márquez, M. (2024). Characterization of the information system integrated to the construction project management systems. *Heliyon, 10*(11), e31886. Advance online publication. DOI: 10.1016/j.heliyon.2024.e31886 PMID: 38841493

Lepthien, A., Papies, D., Clement, M., & Melnyk, V. (2014). The ugly side of customer management - Consumer reactions to firm-initiated contract terminations. *International Journal of Research in Marketing*. Advance online publication. DOI: 10.1016/j.ijresmar.2017.02.001

Lim, L., Woodside, A., & College, B. (2011). Literature review and research directions. *The Marketing Review, 11*(3), 205–225. https://doi.org/http://dx.doi.org/10.1362/146934711X589435. DOI: 10.1362/146934711X589435

Luan, L., Kim, A., Zipser, D., Su, M., Lo, A., Chen, C., & Zhang, C. (2019). How young Chinese consumers are reshaping global luxury. In *Mckinsey & Company*. https://www.mckinsey.com/featured-insights/china/how-young-chinese-consumers-are-reshaping-global-luxury

Mas-machuca, M. (2018). BEHAVIORAL PROFILES OF CONSUMERS OF ONLINE TRAVEL AGENCIES. *International Journal for Quality Research 12(3), 12*(3), 703–722.

Mathrani, S., & Ibrahim, S. D. E. (2022). Strategy for Cultural Inclusion in New Product Development Processes: A New Zealand Study. *Journal of Open Innovation, 8*(4), 217. Advance online publication. DOI: 10.3390/joitmc8040217

Naseer, M., Farooq, M., Younas, W., & Raju, V. (2019). Antecedents of employee retention in the pharmaceutical industry of Pakistan. *Journal of Social Sciences Research, 5*(3), 656–664. Advance online publication. DOI: 10.32861/jssr.53.655.664

Okada, K., Sugimoto, K., Wada, S., Konishi, S., Manabe, S., Matsumura, Y., & Takeda, T. (2024). Development of the Clinical Specimen Information Management System for Multicenter Clinical Studies. In J. Bichel-Findlay, P. Otero, P. Scott, & E. Huesing (Eds.), *MEDINFO 2023 - THE FUTURE IS ACCESSIBLE* (Vol. 310, Issues 19th World Congress on Medical and Health Informatics (MEDINFO) CL-Sydney, pp. 119–123). DOI: 10.3233/SHTI230939

Pauwels, K., Aksehirli, Z., & Lackman, A. (2016). Like the ad or the brand? Marketing stimulates different electronic word-of-mouth content to drive online and offline performance. *International Journal of Research in Marketing, 33*(3), 639–655. DOI: 10.1016/j.ijresmar.2016.01.005

Petruzzellis, L. (2010). Mobile phone choice: Technology versus marketing. The brand effect in the Italian market. *European Journal of Marketing, 44*(5), 610–634. DOI: 10.1108/03090561011032298

Punj, G. N., & Hillyer, C. L. (2004). A Cognitive Model of Customer-Based Brand Equity for Frequently Purchased Products: Conceptual Framework and Empirical Results. *Journal of Consumer Psychology (Taylor & Francis Ltd), 14*(1/2), 124–131. http://search.ebscohost.com/login.aspx?direct=true&db=bth&AN=12795612&site=ehost-live

Sajid, S., Rashid, R. M., & Haider, W. (2022). Changing Trends of Consumers' Online Buying Behavior During COVID-19 Pandemic With Moderating Role of Payment Mode and Gender. *Frontiers in Psychology, 13*, 919334. Advance online publication. DOI: 10.3389/fpsyg.2022.919334 PMID: 36033079

Seo, E.-J., & Park, J.-W. (2018). A study on the effects of social media marketing activities on brand equity and customer response in the airline industry. *Journal of Air Transport Management, 66*(September 2017), 36–41. DOI: 10.1016/j.jairtraman.2017.09.014

Sfakianaki, E., Vrechopoulos, A., & Lazaris, C. (2022). Conceptualizing Green Strategies' Effects on Customer Experience in the Context of Omnichannel Retailing. *International Journal on Management of Innovation & Technology*, *19*(5), 2241004. Advance online publication. DOI: 10.1142/S0219877022410048

Shabbir, S. W., Malik, N., Shah, M. A., & Fatima, K. (2023). The Moderating Role Of Perceived Teachers Support In The Impact Of School Environment Quality And Emotional Exhaustion On Fresh Secondary School Students '. *Academic Engagement.*, *7*(6), 58–72.

Siti Jahroh, S. S. C. I. F. (2019). How Important Is Green Marketing Mix For Consumer? Lesson From The Body Shop. *Jurnal Manajemen*, *23*(2), 321. DOI: 10.24912/jm.v23i2.504

Takeaways, K., & Arpizio, C. D. ', Levato, F., Prete, F., Fabbro, E. Del, & De Montgolfier, J. (2019). *Global Luxury Retail in the Digital Era High-end brands adapt their business models for a younger consumer base Chart 1 Sales Growth and Profit Margin by Retail Sector* (Vol. 11). https://www.matchesfashion.com/5carlosplace

Tsafarakis, S., Kokotas, T., & Pantouvakis, A. (2018). A multiple criteria approach for airline passenger satisfaction measurement and service quality improvement. *Journal of Air Transport Management*, *68*, 61–75. DOI: 10.1016/j.jairtraman.2017.09.010

Tuan, L. T., Rowley, C., Khai, D. C., Qian, D., & Masli, E. (2020). *Fostering Well-Being Among Public Employees With Disabilities : The Roles of Disability-Inclusive Human Resource Practices*. Job Resources, and Public Service Motivation., DOI: 10.1177/0734371X19897753

Uluta, M., Erbakan, N., & Fak, U. B. (2018). the Effect of Empowerment on Employees' Job Satisfaction: A Research on Konya Industrial Zone. *MANAS Sosyal Araştırmalar Dergisi*, *7*(1), 589–600.

Umashankar, N., Bhagwat, Y., & Kumar, V. (2017). Do loyal customers really pay more for services? *Journal of the Academy of Marketing Science*, *45*(6), 807–826. DOI: 10.1007/s11747-016-0491-8

Wang, W., & Seifert, R. (2018). BAME Staff and Public Service Motivation : The Mediating Role of Perceived Fairness in English Local Government. *Journal of Business Ethics, 0*(0), 0. DOI: 10.1007/s10551-018-3953-8

Wang, Y., Lin, J., Osman, Z., Farooq, M., & Raju, V. (2021). Transformational leadership and employee performance in international commercial banking industry in Malaysia: The role of self-efficacy as a mediator under BRI. *Journal of Chinese Human Resource Management, 12*(2), 25–36. DOI: 10.47297/wspchrmWSP2040-800503.20211202

Xie, J., Jablonski, M., Smith, J., & Navedo, A. (2024). A Graphical Interface to Support Low-Flow Volatile Anesthesia: Implications for Patient Safety, Teaching, and Design of Anesthesia Information Management Systems. *Journal of Medical Systems, 48*(1), 36. Advance online publication. DOI: 10.1007/s10916-024-02055-1 PMID: 38532235

Yen, Y. Y., Wen, L. J., Ramasamy, S., & Farooq, M. (2023). Sustainable petrol subsidy program in Malaysia. *Asian Development Policy Review, 12*(1), 1–9. DOI: 10.55493/5008.v12i1.4948

Žabkar, V., Brenčič, M. M., & Dmitrović, T. (2010). Modelling perceived quality, visitor satisfaction and behavioural intentions at the destination level. *Tourism Management, 31*(4), 537–546. DOI: 10.1016/j.tourman.2009.06.005

Zhai, Q., & Chen, X. (2024). Design and application of optical communication technology based on machine learning algorithms in physical education teaching information management system. *Optical and Quantum Electronics, 56*(1), 111. Advance online publication. DOI: 10.1007/s11082-023-05717-5

Zhang, X. (Alan), Kumar, V., & Cosguner, K. (2017). Dynamically Managing a Profitable Email Marketing Program. *Journal of Marketing Research, LIV*(December), jmr.16.0210. DOI: 10.1509/jmr.16.0210

Chapter 13
Transformative Impacts of AI in Social Media and Corporate Communication Strategies

ABSTRACT

Social media and business communication strategies have grown to be seen as mutually beneficial. Social media platforms are effective channels that allow companies and their many stakeholders to interact directly (Fangfang et al., 2016; Lu & Koga, 2016; Wencui et al., 2016). Organizations carefully plan their communication strategies in this digital world in order to negotiate the complex web of online connections (Boriev et al., 2016; Chae et al., 2016). Corporate communication strategies on social media have developed into complex narratives that weave responsiveness, authenticity, and openness beyond simple brand promotion (Lin et al., 2016; Tseng et al., 2016). These platforms enable businesses to break through conventional barriers to communication and establish a direct line of contact with their audience. Whether it's engaging images, educational updates, or interactive campaigns, the thoughtful use of content becomes essential in shaping the company's story and image (Cao, 2016; Sokolova & Kratov, 2016).

DOI: 10.4018/979-8-3373-0513-4.ch013

13.1 CHAPTER INTRODUCTION

Social media is a constantly changing environment, therefore navigating it requires flexibility and agility(Lin et al., 2016; Tseng et al., 2016). Businesses use a variety of channels strategically to target different audiences with messages that are consistent with their brand identity.

By this symbiotic relationship, companies actively listen as well as provide information, assessing public opinion and modifying their communication tactics appropriately(Boriev et al., 2016; Chae et al., 2016).

As a crucial part of corporate communication, social media offers a dynamic canvas on which stories may develop, connections can be cultivated, and businesses can sculpt their online identities. In this digital age, the key to an organization's success and continued relevance in the global marketplace is the collaboration of social media and corporate communication strategy(Lu & Koga, 2016; Wencui et al., 2016).

Figure 1. Mind map of social media and corporate communication strategies

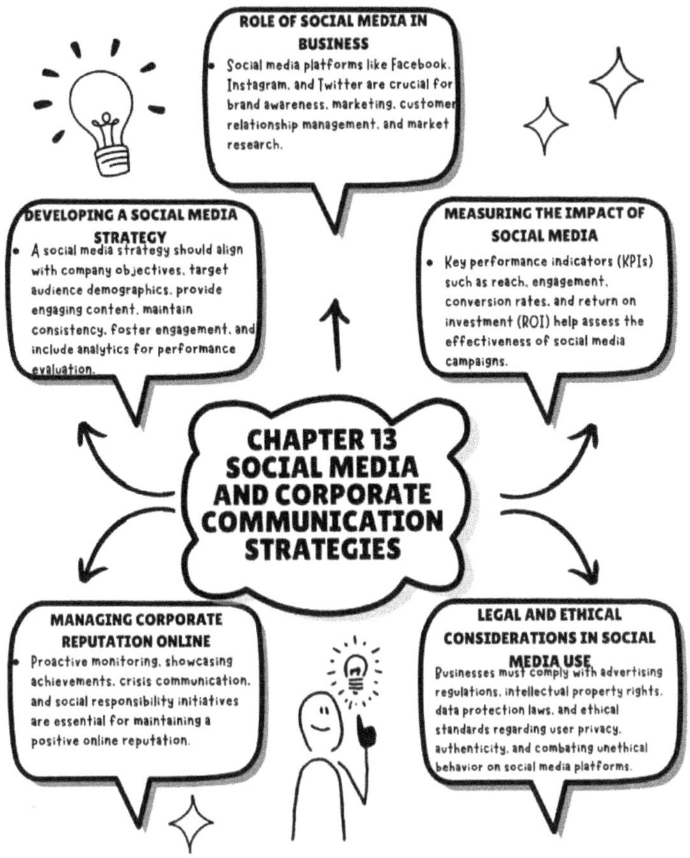

13.2 ROLE OF SOCIAL MEDIA IN BUSINESS

One of the most important parts of social media's function in business is how well it can raise brand awareness. Social media sites such as Facebook, Instagram, Twitter, and LinkedIn provide companies with a wide audience to reach and interact with. Companies may establish a strong online presence and maintain customer awareness by creating and engaging with smart content(Fangfang et al., 2016; Liu & Yang, 2016).

Social media has developed into a vibrant marketplace that allows companies to directly present their goods and services to prospective clients. Product marketing has been transformed by the visual aspect of sites like Instagram and Pinterest, which allow companies to use eye-catching images and videos to draw in customers. In addition to promoting items, this immersive strategy builds a story around the brand and connects emotionally with customers(Lv & Li, 2016; Saleh et al., 2016).

In addition to marketing and increasing brand awareness, social media is essential for customer relationship management. Companies may communicate directly with their clients, answering questions, fixing problems, and getting input(G. Hu, 2016; Yue, 2016). By fostering a feeling of community and trust in real-time, this interaction builds a devoted consumer base. In addition, social media gives users a forum to discuss their experiences, which makes them excellent references that may sway prospective clients(L. Hu, 2016; Shamim et al., 2016).

Social media is useful for trend analysis and market research as well. Businesses may learn about customer preferences and industry trends by keeping an eye on discussions, tracking hashtags, and assessing user activity(Iskra et al., 2016; Park et al., 2016). By using a data-driven strategy, businesses can swiftly adjust to changing market conditions and maintain their competitiveness and customer-focused attitude(Ping et al., 2015).

13.3 DEVELOPING A SOCIAL MEDIA STRATEGY

Understanding the objectives of the company and determining how social media may help achieve them are the fundamentals of creating a social media strategy. Whether lead creation, customer retention, or brand exposure is the main goal, each requires a different strategy(Gisslen & Torne, 2015; Raszka & Jamroz, 2015). A deliberate and significant online presence is guaranteed by a planned alignment of social media operations with corporate objectives(Gisslen & Torne, 2015; Ping et al., 2015; Raszka & Jamroz, 2015).

An additional crucial component of developing a social media strategy is determining the target audience. Businesses can successfully generate content that resonates and interacts with their audience by having a thorough understanding of their demographics, interests, and habits. Different platforms serve different demographics, and selecting the appropriate channels to reach the target audience requires an awareness of this segmentation(Yoon & Jung, 2015; Yuan-jing et al., 2015).

The foundation of every effective social media strategy is content. To draw in viewers and encourage interaction, content creators must provide engaging and relevant material(Iskra et al., 2016; Park et al., 2016). Content, whether it takes the shape of engaging videos, captivating images, or educational blog entries, should always reflect the personality of the brand and provide a consistent message. In order to avoid coming out as too sales-oriented, firms must also create a balance between value-driven material and promotional content(L. Hu, 2016; Shamim et al., 2016; Yue, 2016).

A crucial component of any social media strategy is consistency. Building brand awareness involves establishing a regular posting schedule and maintaining a unified brand identity across all media(Liu & Yang, 2016; Lv & Li, 2016; Saleh et al., 2016). Frequent changes maintain audience interest, and a unified brand image builds credibility and confidence. Additionally, a unified tone and communication style help to build a distinctive and identifiable online presence by contributing to the overarching brand story(Fangfang et al., 2016; Lu & Koga, 2016; Wencui et al., 2016).

In social media, engagement is reciprocal, and companies must take an active role in discussions(Farooq et al., 2025g, 2025i). Fostering a feeling of community requires attending to client inquiries, recognizing feedback, and responding to comments(Farooq et al., 2025j, 2025h, 2025e, 2025d, 2025f). Social media is a tool for connection building as much as for broadcasting, and companies should take advantage of this by interacting with their audience on a proactive basis(Farooq et al., 2025c, 2025a).

A social media plan must include analytics and measurement. Key performance indicators (KPIs) including reach, engagement, and conversion rates may be tracked to get insight into how successful a plan is. By routinely examining these data, companies may improve their strategy, pinpoint winning strategies, and adjust to changing market conditions(Farooq et al., 2024, 2025b).

13.4 MEASURING THE IMPACT OF SOCIAL MEDIA

Establishing quantifiable and precise goals is the first stage in assessing the influence of social media(Farooq et al., 2025k; Muhammad Farooq, Muhammad Ramzan, 2025). Setting clear, reachable goals is crucial, regardless of the objective—for example, raising sales, increasing brand recognition, or increasing website traffic. Metrics like reach, impressions, and engagement provide important information about how successful a social media campaign is(Farooq et al., 2022a, 2022b). Whereas impressions show the total number of times material has been shown, reach shows the number of unique people that have seen content. Clicks, likes, shares, comments, and other forms of engagement show how the audience interacted with the material(Buzdar & Farooq, 2020; Naseer et al., 2019).

By monitoring these KPIs across many platforms, organizations can evaluate the effectiveness of each channel and spend resources efficiently. Social media analytics solutions facilitate data-driven decision-making for organizations by offering comprehensive reports on key performance indicators (KPIs)(Farooq, 2019; Ghulam et al., 2019). Real-time monitoring makes it possible to spot patterns and promptly modify campaigns to increase their effect.

Another crucial component of assessing the influence of social media is conversion monitoring. Through the attribution of certain actions, such completing a form or making a purchase, to social media interactions, companies are able to measure the immediate effect of their efforts(Farooq, Ali, et al., 2019; Farooq & Raju, 2019d). Understanding the customer journey and improving conversion rate methods are made easier with the use of this information(Farooq, Kalimuthu, et al., 2019; Farooq, Rehman, et al., 2019).

Return on Investment (ROI) for social media is a comprehensive statistic used to assess the financial results of social media initiatives(Farooq, Muhammad, et al., 2019; Farooq & Raju, 2019c). It entails weighing the financial return on investment produced by social media marketing initiatives against the associated expenses(-Farooq, Khalil-Ur-Rehman, et al., 2019; Farooq & Raju, 2019b). This covers not only the cost of advertising but also the time and materials needed for community administration and content production(Farooq, Bakhsh, et al., 2023; Farooq, Hafsa Qadir, et al., 2023). A good return on investment (ROI) certifies that the social media approach is successful by showing that the advantages outweigh the disadvantages.

13.5 MANAGING CORPORATE REPUTATION ONLINE

Keeping a company's internet image under check has become crucial for companies. Because of the quick communication and feedback platforms offered by the digital domain, reputation management is a dynamic and difficult undertaking(Farooq et al., 2020; Yen et al., 2023). Monitoring, swaying, and managing an organization's online image are all part of online reputation management, or ORM. Because social media is so important in forming public opinion, companies must actively participate in reputation management initiatives(Farooq & Raju, 2019a).

Proactive monitoring is a crucial component of maintaining a company's internet image. By closely monitoring social media, review sites, and online forums, companies may quickly respond to any unfavorable comments or mentions. Companies may mitigate any reputational harm by exhibiting openness and a commitment to customer satisfaction by swiftly and professionally reacting to complaints.

Creating and selecting content that showcases the company's accomplishments and core beliefs is essential to developing a strong online image (Kim et al., 2021; Mgiba, 2021; Pir & Derinozlu, 2020). Sharing client endorsements, success stories, and behind-the-scenes photos on a regular basis helps to build trust in the business and promote a favorable image(Alagarsamy et al., 2021; Chu et al., 2021; Xie et al., 2020). Social media platforms are useful tools for humanizing the brand and conveying stories, which helps create a compelling and recognizable corporate identity(Enyinda et al., 2021; Nyelele et al., 2023).

Effective communication is essential for managing reputation during times of crisis. Businesses may directly address problems, apologize, and communicate remedial steps using social media (Sulehry & Wallace, 2023). Rebuilding trust requires openness and sincerity, and social media platforms provide a direct line of communication with the public while showcasing responsibility and a dedication to progress(Ghods et al., 2023; Koh et al., 2022; Yan et al., 2021).

Businesses may actively improve their image by actively taking part in social responsibility programs, which goes beyond crisis management. Disseminating information regarding community involvement initiatives, environmental initiatives, and philanthropic donations enhances the company's reputation. Businesses that are socially conscious are valued by customers more and more, and social media gives them a platform to highlight their initiatives.

13.6 LEGAL AND ETHICAL CONSIDERATIONS IN SOCIAL MEDIA USE

Businesses need to be careful to follow the rules regulating their internet activity. This covers advertising guidelines, intellectual property rights, and data protection legislation. Businesses must abide by social media networks' terms of service and community rules in order to avoid legal ramifications(Hosseini et al., 2022; J. H. Zhou & Charoensukmongkol, 2021). There may be penalties, legal repercussions, and reputational harm to the organization for breaking these rules.

When using social media, protecting data and maintaining privacy is essential from an ethical standpoint. User data must be gathered, stored, and used in accordance with industry standards and privacy legislation. Essential components of ethical data management include getting user permission, communicating data practices in a transparent manner, and giving consumers control over their privacy settings. It is morally required for social media communication to be authentic. Companies must to refrain from dishonest strategies like fabricating accounts or using false advertising in an attempt to increase interaction(Atukunda et al., 2023; Fu et al., 2022). Gaining the audience's confidence requires being open and honest about the connections, sponsored posts, and content source. Businesses should also exercise caution when it comes to deception and make sure that the information they post on social media appropriately represents their brand, goods, and principles.

Disinformation, hate speech, and cyberbullying are made more likely by social media. Companies need to speak up against unethical activity on their platforms and have procedures in place to deal with these kinds of problems. This entails carefully monitoring material, encouraging a supportive online community, and responding quickly to any abuse or false information that is found.

13.7 CHAPTER CONCLUSION

In conclusion, the role of social media in business cannot be overstated. Social media platforms such as Facebook, Instagram, Twitter, and LinkedIn offer businesses unparalleled opportunities to raise brand awareness, engage with customers, and drive sales.

One of the most significant aspects of social media's function in business is its ability to enhance brand awareness. Through strategic content creation and engagement, companies can establish a strong online presence and maintain customer awareness.

Moreover, social media has evolved into a vibrant marketplace where companies can directly showcase their products and services to potential customers. Platforms like Instagram and Pinterest, with their visual appeal, allow businesses to leverage eye-catching images and videos to attract and engage customers, thereby transforming product marketing.

Additionally, social media plays a crucial role in customer relationship management, enabling companies to communicate directly with their customers, address concerns, and gather feedback. This interaction fosters a sense of community and trust, leading to a loyal customer base.

Furthermore, social media serves as a valuable tool for trend analysis and market research. By monitoring discussions, tracking hashtags, and analyzing user activity, businesses can gain insights into customer preferences and industry trends, enabling them to adapt and stay competitive.

Developing a social media strategy involves aligning social media activities with business objectives, understanding the target audience, creating engaging content, maintaining consistency, and fostering engagement. Regular monitoring and measurement of key performance indicators are essential for evaluating the effectiveness of the strategy and making necessary adjustments.

Measuring the impact of social media requires setting clear goals, tracking relevant metrics, and analyzing data across multiple platforms. Conversion tracking and return on investment analysis help businesses understand the immediate and long-term effects of their social media efforts. Managing corporate reputation online is crucial in today's digital age. Proactive monitoring, effective communication during crises, and active participation in social responsibility initiatives are essential for maintaining a positive online image.

REFERENCES

Alagarsamy, S., Mehrolia, S., & Singh, B. (2021). Mediating Effect of Brand Relationship Quality on Relational Bonds and Online Grocery Retailer Loyalty. *Journal of Internet Commerce*, *20*(2), 246–272. DOI: 10.1080/15332861.2020.1868213

Atukunda, E. C., Siedner, M. J., Obua, C., Musiimenta, A., Ware, N. C., Mugisha, S., Najjuma, J. N., Mugyenyi, G. R., & Matthews, L. (2023). Evaluating the Feasibility, Acceptability, and Preliminary Efficacy of SupportMoms-Uganda, an mHealth-Based Patient-Centered Social Support Intervention to Improve the Use of Maternity Services Among Pregnant Women in Rural Southwestern Uganda: Randomized. [WE - Emerging Sources Citation Index] [ESCI]. *JMIR Formative Research*, *7*, e36619. Advance online publication. DOI: 10.2196/36619 PMID: 36862461

Boriev, Z., Nyrkov, A., Sokolov, S., & Chernyi, S. (2016). Software and hardware user authentication methods in the information and control systems based on biometrics. In *IOP Conference Series: Materials Science and Engineering* (Vol. 124, Issue 1). DOI: 10.1088/1757-899X/124/1/012006

Buzdar, A. Q., & Farooq, M. (2020). Memorization of Quran through Mobile Application in the Era of Transformative Marketing. [PJSS]. *Pakistan Journal of Social Sciences*, *40*(2), 689–698.

Cao, Y. (2016). Design of College Students' employment management system based on WEB. In J. C. M. Kao & W. P. Sung (Eds.), *MATEC Web of Conferences* (Vol. 63, Issue International Conference on Mechatronic, Manufacturing and Materials Engineering (MMME) CL-Hong Kong. DOI: 10.1051/matecconf/20166305001

Chae, C. J., Choi, K. N., & Choi, K. (2016). Information Interoperability System Using Multi-agent with Security. *Wireless Personal Communications*, *89*(3), 819–832. DOI: 10.1007/s11277-015-3113-8

Chu, M. J., Li, H. Y., Lin, S. N., Cai, X. L., Li, X., Chen, S. H., Zhang, X. K., Man, Q. L., Lee, C. Y., & Chiang, Y. C. (2021). Appropriate Strategies for Reducing the Negative Impact of Online Reports of Suicide and Public Opinion From Social Media in China. [WE - Science Citation Index Expanded] [SCI-EXPANDED] [WE - Social Science Citation Index] [SSCI]. *Frontiers in Public Health*, *9*, 756360. Advance online publication. DOI: 10.3389/fpubh.2021.756360 PMID: 34926380

Enyinda, C. I., Opute, A. P., Fadahunsi, A., & Mbah, C. H. (2021). Marketing-sales-service interface and social media marketing influence on B2B sales process. *Journal of Business and Industrial Marketing*, *36*(6), 990–1009. DOI: 10.1108/JBIM-01-2019-0053

Fangfang, D., Shiwen, W., Peng, C., Lin, M., Lei, Z., & You, S. (2016). Application on "6s" Management Model of Information and Communication safety Management. In F. Zhou & X. Wu (Eds.), *Proceedings of the 2nd International Conference on Electronics, Network and Computer Engineering (ICENCE 2016)* (Vol. 67, Issues 2nd International Conference on Electronics, Network and Computer Engineering (ICENCE) CL-Yinchuan, pp. 506–509).

Farooq, M. (2019). Emerging sciences in Social Sciences : An overview, A Research Agenda. *Global Journal of Emerging Sciences*, *1*(October), 183–197.

Farooq, M., Ali, W., Younas, W., Khalil-Ur-rehman, F., & Qurashi, Q. A. (2019). the Era of Transformative Marketing: Service Quality of Mobile App Based Taxi Services in Kuala Lumpur. *Proceedings on Engineering Sciences*, *1*(2), 49–58. DOI: 10.24874/PES01.02.006

Farooq, M., Bakhsh, A., Hafsa Qadir, B., & Warda, N. (2023). Digital Empowerment: Freedom of Expression Beyond 5G and 6G Networks in Developing Countries. *Pakistan Journal of Social Sciences*, *43*(4), 569–584. DOI: 10.5281/zenodo.10448484

Farooq, M., Buzdar, H. Q., Yen, Y. Y., & Bakhsh, A. (2024). Integrating AI in Sustainable Writing: An Empirical Investigation of the Technology Acceptance Model in Asian Social Sciences. *Journal of Logistics. Informatics and Service Science*, *11*(3), 324–338. DOI: 10.33168/JLISS.2024.0321

Farooq, M., Cheng, J., Khan, N. U., Saufi, R. A., Kanwal, N., & Bazkiaei, H. A. (2022a). Sustainable Waste Management Companies with Innovative Smart Solutions: A Systematic Review and Conceptual Model. *Sustainability (Basel)*, *14*(20), 13146. Advance online publication. DOI: 10.3390/su142013146

Farooq, M., Cheng, J., Khan, N. U., Saufi, R. A., Kanwal, N., & Bazkiaei, H. A. (2022b). Sustainable Waste Management Companies with Innovative Smart Solutions: A Systematic Review and Conceptual Model. *Sustainability (Basel)*, *14*(20), 13146. DOI: 10.3390/su142013146

Farooq, M., Hafsa Qadir, B., & Saeed, M. (2023, December). AI-Enhanced Social Sciences: A Systematic Literature Review and Bibliographic Analysis of Web of Science Published Research Papers. *Pakistan Journal of Society* [PJSEL]. *Education and Language*, *10*, 1–2.

Farooq, M., Kalimuthu, R., & Reza, M. H. (2019). Measuring and Comparing Brand Equity of Malaysian Banks in the Era of Transformative Marketing. *Global Journal of Emerging Sciences*, *1*(June), 96–102.

Farooq, M., Khalil-Ur-Rehman, F., Abdurrahaman, D. T., Younas, W., Sajjad, S., & Zreen, A. (2019). SERVICE QUALITY ANALYSIS OF PRIVATE UNIVERSITIES LIBRARIES IN MALAYSIA IN THE ERA OF TRANSFORMATIVE MARKETING. *International Journal of Qualitative Research, 13*(2), 269–284. DOI: 10.24874/IJQR13.02-02

Farooq, M., Muhammad, S., Raju, V., Kalimuthu, K. R., & Qadir, A. (2019). Measuring and Comparing the Desired and Actual Service Quality of Pakistan International Airline. *The Journal of Social Sciences Research, 52*(52), 484–490. DOI: 10.32861/jssr.52.484.490

Farooq, M., & Raju, V. (2019a). Impact of Over-the-Top (OTT) Services on the Telecom Companies in the Era of Transformative Marketing. *Global Journal of Flexible Systems Managment, 20*(2), 177–188. DOI: 10.1007/s40171-019-00209-6

Farooq, M., & Raju, V. (2019b). Want to Stay the Market Leader in the Era of Transformative Marketing? Keep the Customers Satisfied! *Global Journal of Flexible Systems Management*. DOI: 10.1007/s40171-019-00213-w

Farooq, M., & Raju, V. (2019c). Impact of Over-the-Top (OTT) Services on the Telecom Companies in the Era of Transformative Marketing. *Global Journal of Flexible Systems Managment, 20*(2), 177–188. DOI: 10.1007/s40171-019-00209-6

Farooq, M., & Raju, V. (2019d). Want to Stay the Market Leader in the Era of Transformative Marketing? Keep the Customers Satisfied! *Global Journal of Flexible Systems Managment, 20*(3), 257–266. DOI: 10.1007/s40171-019-00213-w

Farooq, M., & Ramzan, M. Y. Y. Y. (2025). AI in Management. In *Transformative Impacts of AI in Management* (1st ed., pp. 1–44). IGI Global. DOI: 10.4018/979-8-3693-4322-7.ch001

Farooq, M., Ramzan, M., & Yen, Y. Y. (2025a). AI in Consumer Behavior Management. In *Transformative Impacts of AI in Management* (pp. 281–294). IGI Global., DOI: 10.4018/979-8-3693-4322-7.ch011

Farooq, M., Ramzan, M., & Yen, Y. Y. (2025b). AI in Customer Service, HR, and Administration. In *Transformative Impacts of AI in Management* (pp. 45–70). IGI Global. DOI: 10.4018/979-8-3693-4322-7.ch002

Farooq, M., Ramzan, M., & Yen, Y. Y. (2025c). AI in Quality Management. In *Transformative Impacts of AI in Management* (pp. 295–312). IGI Global., DOI: 10.4018/979-8-3693-4322-7.ch012

Farooq, M., Ramzan, M., & Yen, Y. Y. (2025d). Artificial Intelligence and Customer Experiences. In *Transformative Impacts of AI in Management* (pp. 95–114). IGI Global., DOI: 10.4018/979-8-3693-4322-7.ch004

Farooq, M., Ramzan, M., & Yen, Y. Y. (2025e). Artificial Intelligence in Administration Sciences. In *Transformative Impacts of AI in Management* (pp. 115–156). IGI Global., DOI: 10.4018/979-8-3693-4322-7.ch005

Farooq, M., Ramzan, M., & Yen, Y. Y. (2025f). Artificial Intelligence in Business and Law. In *Transformative Impacts of AI in Management* (pp. 71–94). IGI Global., DOI: 10.4018/979-8-3693-4322-7.ch003

Farooq, M., Ramzan, M., & Yen, Y. Y. (2025g). Artificial Intelligence in Ethical Business Decision Making. In *Transformative Impacts of AI in Management* (pp. 265–280). IGI Global., DOI: 10.4018/979-8-3693-4322-7.ch010

Farooq, M., Ramzan, M., & Yen, Y. Y. (2025h). Exploring the Impact of Artificial Intelligence on Brand Management. In *Transformative Impacts of AI in Management* (pp. 157–188). IGI Global., DOI: 10.4018/979-8-3693-4322-7.ch006

Farooq, M., Ramzan, M., & Yen, Y. Y. (2025i). Exploring the Impact of Ethical Leadership and Employee Engagement on Knowledge Sharing Attitudes in the Asian Digital Economy. In *Transformative Impacts of AI in Management* (pp. 241–264). IGI Global., DOI: 10.4018/979-8-3693-4322-7.ch009

Farooq, M., Ramzan, M., & Yen, Y. Y. (2025j). Transformative Impact of AI in Education Management. In *Transformative Impacts of AI in Management* (pp. 189–216). IGI Global., DOI: 10.4018/979-8-3693-4322-7.ch007

Farooq, M., Ramzan, M., & Yen, Y. Y. (2025k). *Transformative Impacts of AI in Management*. IGI Global., DOI: 10.4018/979-8-3693-4322-7

Farooq, M., Rehman, F. K. U., Younas, W., Raju, V., Ahmed, Q. M., & Ali, M. (2019). Investigating Relationship between Net Promoter Score and Company Performance: A Longitudinal Study. *Global Journal of Emerging Sciences, 1*(1), 1–10. https://www.gjoes.org/wp-content/uploads/2019/04/1-1.pdf

Farooq, M., Saeed, M., Ali, W., & Javid, R. (2020). Online Buying and Customer Satisfaction in the Era of Transformative Marketing. *City University Research Journal, 10*(2), 274–288.

Fu, L., Sun, H., & Xu, K. (2022). Whether Social Participation Can Affect the Central Government Public Policy Response to the COVID-19 in China. *Frontiers in Public Health, 10*, 842373. Advance online publication. DOI: 10.3389/fpubh.2022.842373 PMID: 35570925

Ghods, M. J., Moghaddam, L. F., Hosseinabadi-Farahani, M., & Pourebrahimi, M. (2023). The mediation role of self-esteem and hope on the relationship of quality of life and unmet needs of elderly with psychiatric disorders. [WE - Emerging Sources Citation Index] [ESCI]. *Journal of Education and Health Promotion, 12*(1). Advance online publication. DOI: 10.4103/jehp.jehp_163_22 PMID: 37288421

Ghulam, W. A., Ali, W., Ali, S., Khan, M. M., Khan, R. N., & Farooq, M. (2019). Investigating factors influencing brain drain of citizens of Azad Kashmir Pakistan. *Journal of Social Sciences Research, 5*(3), 782–788. Advance online publication. DOI: 10.32861/jssr.53.782.788

Gisslen, L., & Torne, A. (2015). A Semantic Approach to Information Management and Decision Support: An Application to Humanitarian Demining Operations. In J. Brynielsson & M. H. Yap (Eds.), *2015 European Intelligence and Security Informatics Conference (EISIC)* (Issues 2015 European Intelligence and Security Informatics Conference CL-Manchester, pp. 75–82). DOI: 10.1109/EISIC.2015.34

Hosseini, S. A., Moghaddam, A., Damganian, H., & Nikabadi, M. S. (2022). The Effect of Perceived Corporate Social Responsibility and Sustainable Human Resources on Employee Engagement with the Moderating Role of the Employer Brand. *Employee Responsibilities and Rights Journal, 34*(2), 101–121. DOI: 10.1007/s10672-021-09376-0

Hu, G. (2016). Research into College Student Information Management System based on Web. In S. Yingying, C. Guiran, & L. Zhen (Eds.), *Proceedings of the 2016 International Conference on Education, Management, Computer and Society* (Vol. 37, Issue International Conference on Education, Management, Computer and Society (EMCS) CL-Shenyang, pp. 770–773). DOI: 10.2991/emcs-16.2016.188

Hu, L. (2016). Design of dual system teaching management system based on.Net Technology. In J. C. M. Kao & W. P. Sung (Eds.), *2016 INTERNATIONAL CONFERENCE ON MECHATRONICS, MANUFACTURING AND MATERIALS ENGINEERING (MMME 2016)*. DOI: 10.1051/matecconf/20166304004

Iskra, A., Tijan, E., & Aksentijevic, S. (2016). The modem approach to the analysis of logistics information systems. In P. Biljanovic, Z. Butkovic, K. Skala, T. G. Grbac, M. CicinSain, V. Sruk, S. Ribaric, S. Gros, B. Vrdoljak, M. Mauher, E. Tijan, & D. Lukman (Eds.), *2016 39th International Convention on Information and Communication Technology, Electronics and Microelectronics, MIPRO 2016 - Proceedings* (Issues 39th International Convention on Information and Communication Technology, Electronics and Microelectronics (MIPRO) CL-Opatija, pp. 1504–1508). DOI: 10.1109/MIPRO.2016.7522377

Kim, E. H., Yoo, D., & Doh, S. J. (2021). Self-construal on brand fan pages: The mediating effect of para-social interaction and consumer engagement on brand loyalty. *Journal of Brand Management, 28*(3), 254–271. DOI: 10.1057/s41262-020-00211-9

Koh, H. K., Burnasheva, R., & Suh, Y. G. (2022). Perceived ESG (Environmental, Social, Governance) and Consumers' Responses: The Mediating Role of Brand Credibility, Brand Image, and Perceived Quality. [WE - Science Citation Index Expanded] [SCI-EXPANDED] [WE - Social Science Citation Index] [SSCI]. *Sustainability (Basel), 14*(8), 4515. Advance online publication. DOI: 10.3390/su14084515

Lin, C., Li, X., Zheng, M., & Wang, G. (2016). Study on the System and Operation Mechanism of Crisis Information Management in Hazardous Chemicals Accident of Disaster Conditions. In E. Qi (Ed.), *Proceedings of the 6th International Asia Conference on Industrial Engineering and Management Innovation* (Issues 6th International Asia Conference on Industrial Engineering and Management Innovation (IEMI) CL-Tianjin Univ, Tianjin, pp. 463–473). DOI: 10.2991/978-94-6239-148-2_45

Liu, Z., & Yang, Y. (2016). Research on the Construction of Educational Administration Management Information in Colleges and Universities. In S. Yingying, C. Guiran, & L. Zhen (Eds.), *PROCEEDINGS OF THE 2016 INTERNATIONAL CONFERENCE ON EDUCATION, MANAGEMENT, COMPUTER AND SOCIETY* (Vol. 37, Issue International Conference on Education, Management, Computer and Society (EMCS) CL-Shenyang, pp. 652–655). DOI: 10.2991/emcs-16.2016.158

Lu, X., & Koga, T. (2016). Service oriented architecture for global system wide information management. In *2015 IEEE 4th Global Conference on Consumer Electronics, GCCE 2015* (Issue IEEE 4th Global Conference on Consumer Electronics GCCE CL-Osaka, pp. 638–639). DOI: 10.1109/GCCE.2015.7398585

Lv, G., & Li, J. (2016). Design and Implementation of Online Information Management Platform for Athletic Matches. In *Proceedings - 8th International Conference on Intelligent Computation Technology and Automation, ICICTA 2015* (Issues 8th International Conference on Intelligent Computation Technology and Automation (ICICTA) CL-Nanchang, pp. 371–374). DOI: 10.1109/ICICTA.2015.100

Mgiba, F. M. (2021). THE FOURTH INDUSTRIAL REVOLUTION, LOYALTY INTENTIONS AND THE MEDIATING ROLES OF REPUTATION AND PRE-VISIT EXPERIENCES FOR THE VILAKAZI STREET PRECINCT IN SOWETO. [WE - Emerging Sources Citation Index] [ESCI]. *COMMUNITAS, 26*, 124–151. DOI: 10.18820/24150525/Comm.v26.8

Naseer, M., Farooq, M., Younas, W., & Raju, V. (2019). Antecedents of employee retention in the pharmaceutical industry of Pakistan. *Journal of Social Sciences Research, 5*(3), 656–664. Advance online publication. DOI: 10.32861/jssr.53.655.664

Nyelele, C., Keske, C., Chung, M. G., Guo, H., & Egoh, B. N. (2023). Using social media data and machine learning to map recreational ecosystem services. [WE - Science Citation Index Expanded] [SCI-EXPANDED]. *Ecological Indicators, 154*, 110606. Advance online publication. DOI: 10.1016/j.ecolind.2023.110606

Park, J.-K., Cho, S.-Y., & Lee, N. (2016). Information Management System of Solid Waste Landfill based on 3 Dimensional Method. *Jornal of Korea Organic Resource Recycling Association, 24*(4), 39–48. DOI: 10.17137/korrae.2016.24.4.39

Ping, D. R., Sheng, Y. L., & IEEE. (2015). Design and Implementation of Digital Engineering Accounting Management System. In *2015 SEVENTH INTERNATIONAL CONFERENCE ON MEASURING TECHNOLOGY AND MECHATRONICS AUTOMATION (ICMTMA 2015)* pp. 339–342). DOI: 10.1109/ICMTMA.2015.87

Pir, E. O., & Derinozlu, E. (2020). The mediating role of price sensitivity in the effect of trust and loyalty to luxury brands on the brand preference. [WE - Emerging Sources Citation Index] [ESCI]. *UPRAVLENETS-THE MANAGER, 11*(6), 70–84. DOI: 10.29141/2218-5003-2020-11-6-6

Raszka, J., & Jamroz, L. (2015). Reducing human resources in management of information technology (IT) projects. In *Proceedings - 2015 8th International Conference on Human System Interaction, HSI 2015* (Issues 8th International Conference on Human System Interactions (HSI) CL-Warsaw, pp. 115–121). DOI: 10.1109/HSI.2015.7170653

Saleh, M., Misséri, V., & Abel, M. H. (2016). Managing heterogeneous information in a system of information systems. In A. Fred, J. Dietz, D. Aveiro, K. Liu, J. Bernardino, & J. Filipe (Eds.), *IC3K 2016 - Proceedings of the 8th International Joint Conference on Knowledge Discovery, Knowledge Engineering and Knowledge Management,* (pp. 165–172). DOI: 10.5220/0006049101650172

Shamim, S., Cang, S., & Yu, H. (2016). Influencers of information system usage among employees for knowledge creation *A future research agenda.* In S. Cang & Y. Wang (Eds.), *PROCEEDINGS OF 2016 10TH INTERNATIONAL CONFERENCE ON SOFTWARE, KNOWLEDGE, INFORMATION MANAGEMENT & APPLICATIONS (SKIMA),* (pp. 134–141).

Sokolova, O. D., & Kratov, S. V. (2016). Information systems for popularization of scientific and knowledge-based software. In *2016 13th International Scientific-Technical Conference on Actual Problems of Electronic Instrument Engineering, APEIE 2016 - Proceedings* (Vol. 2, Issues 13th International Scientific-Technical Conference on Actual Problems of Electronics Instrument Engineering (APEIE) CL-Novosibirsk, pp. 519–522). DOI: 10.1109/APEIE.2016.7806407

Sulehry, R. S., & Wallace, D. (2023). Identifying the discursive trajectory of social change - a systematic discourse theoretical framework. [WE - Social Science Citation Index] [SSCI] [WE - Arts & Humanities Citation Index] [A&HCI]. *Journal of Language and Politics, 22*(2), 245–267. DOI: 10.1075/jlp.22138.sul

Tseng, K.-H., Chen, K.-H., Chu, C.-L., & IEEE. (2016). Design and Implementation of Flight Information Management System. In *PROCEEDINGS OF THE 2016 IEEE 11TH CONFERENCE ON INDUSTRIAL ELECTRONICS AND APPLICATIONS (ICIEA),* (pp. 61–65).

Wencui, L., & Xinjian, S. LiXiong, Hui, G., Bo, L., Chunying, W., & Ying, Y. (2016). An Information Security Management System Based on “Five-in-one.” In J. Yu & Q. Liu (Eds.), *PROCEEDINGS OF THE 2016 4TH INTERNATIONAL CONFERENCE ON ELECTRICAL & ELECTRONICS ENGINEERING AND COMPUTER SCIENCE (ICEEECS 2016)* (pp. 743–745).

Xie, K. F., Liang, B. B., Dulebenets, M. A., & Mei, Y. L. (2020). The Impact of Risk Perception on Social Distancing during the COVID-19 Pandemic in China. [WE - Science Citation Index Expanded] [SCI-EXPANDED] [WE - Social Science Citation Index] [SSCI]. *International Journal of Environmental Research and Public Health, 17*(17), 6256. Advance online publication. DOI: 10.3390/ijerph17176256 PMID: 32867381

Yan, J. W., You, Y. T., Wang, Y., & Sheng, D. F. (2021). Understanding the Complexity of Business Information Dissemination in Social Media: A Meta-Analysis of Empirical Evidence from China. [WE - Science Citation Index Expanded] [SCI-EXPANDED] [WE - Social Science Citation Index] [SSCI]. *Complexity, 2021*(1), 7647718. Advance online publication. DOI: 10.1155/2021/7647718

Yen, Y. Y., Wen, L. J., Ramasamy, S., & Farooq, M. (2023). Sustainable petrol subsidy program in Malaysia. *Asian Development Policy Review, 12*(1), 1–9. DOI: 10.55493/5008.v12i1.4948

Yoon, I., & Jung, C.-H. (2015). The Effects of Change Management on the Performance introducing Enterprise Resource Planning System: The Moderating Effect of Information System Maturity. *Asia-Pacific Journal of Multimedia Services Convergent with Art, Humanities, and Sociology*, *5*(4), 761–770. DOI: 10.14257/AJMAHS.2015.08.61

Yuan-jing, L., Yu-duo, W., & IEEE. (2015). Design and Development for Information Management System of Property Insurance Faced to Ether-net. In *PROCEEDINGS OF 2015 4TH INTERNATIONAL CONFERENCE ON COMPUTER SCIENCE AND NETWORK TECHNOLOGY (ICCSNT 2015)*, (pp. 436–440).

Yue, F. (2016). A Study of Student Information Management Software. In G. Chen & J. Peng (Eds.), *2016 IEEE INTERNATIONAL CONFERENCE OF ONLINE ANALYSIS AND COMPUTING SCIENCE (ICOACS)* (Issue IEEE International Conference of Online Analysis and Computing Science (ICOACS) CL-Chongqing, pp. 393–396). DOI: 10.1109/ICOACS.2016.7563123

Zhou, J. H., & Charoensukmongkol, P. (2021). The effect of social media use on customer qualification skills and adaptive selling behaviors of export salespeople in China. *Journal of Asia Business Studies*, *15*(2), 278–300. DOI: 10.1108/JABS-12-2019-0377

Chapter 14
Transformative Impacts of AI in Ethics, Privacy, and Regulatory Compliance in MIS

ABSTRACT

A complex interaction between privacy, ethics, and regulatory compliance occurs in the complex field of management information systems (MIS), influencing the field of responsible data management (Hu & Shi, 2021; Koo et al., 2021; Ren et al., 2021; Zhao & Tu, 2021). The moral compass that helps companies navigate the huge sea of information is ethics in MIS (Siyao & Bin, 2021; YOUNG, 2021). This moral need necessitates a dedication to openness, truthfulness, and integrity while managing private information, guaranteeing that choices are based on values that put the well-being of people and society first (Dongfang et al., 2021; Lili et al., 2021).

14.1 CHAPTER INTRODUCTION

As a basic human right, privacy is given top priority in the MIS framework(Liu, 2021; Rusakov V et al., 2021). Safeguarding the security of personal information becomes essential when businesses use data to inform their plans. Implementing strong security measures, cultivating a culture of trust, and giving people control over their personal data are all part of responsible data management(Huang, 2021; Kazemi et al., 2021).

A further level of complexity to MIS is navigating the complicated network of regulatory systems. Following rules and regulations guarantees that businesses stay inside the law, reducing risks and promoting a peaceful coexistence of techno-

DOI: 10.4018/979-8-3373-0513-4.ch014

logical advancements and social mores(Yuan & Yicun, 2021; Zheng et al., 2021). A thoughtful approach to ethics, privacy, and regulatory compliance becomes the cornerstone for sustainable and ethical MIS operations in this constantly changing environment.

Figure 1. Mind map of ethics, privacy and regulator compliances in business

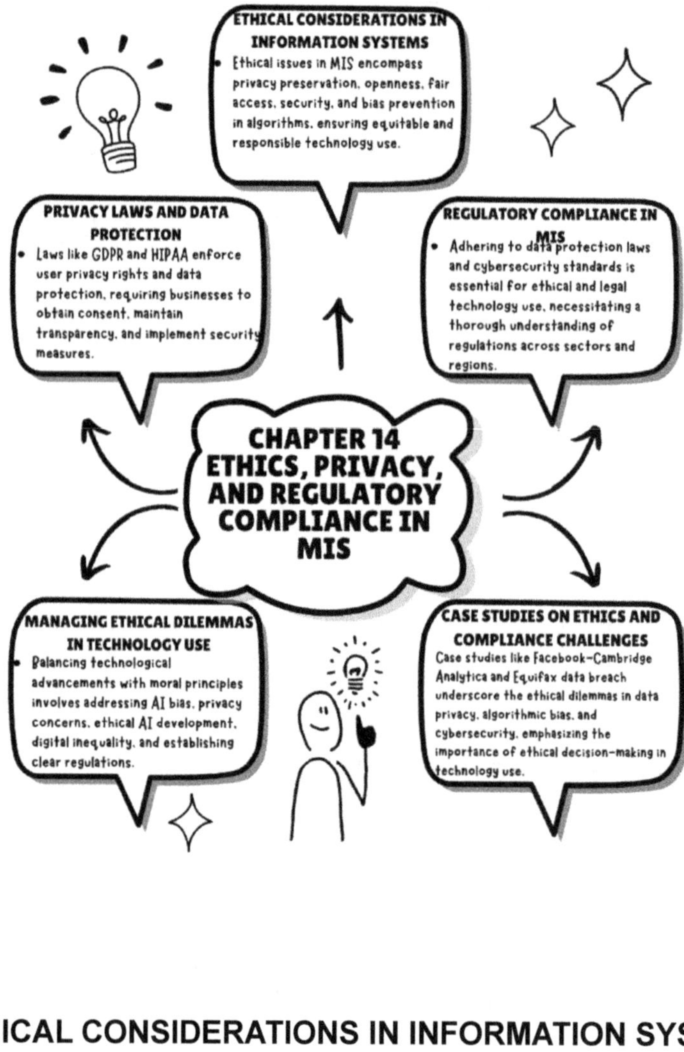

14.2 ETHICAL CONSIDERATIONS IN INFORMATION SYSTEMS

A crucial component of using technology responsibly is taking ethical issues into account when designing information systems. The ethical ramifications of technology's widespread use are becoming more complicated as it continues to progress at an unparalleled rate(Leventhal & Schreyer, 2020; Nedzelskay et al., 2020;

Yousefnezhad et al., 2020). Ethical issues are crucial in guiding the appropriate and equitable use of technology in the field of information systems, which includes data processing, retrieval, and storage (Schiuma et al., 2023).

The preservation of people's privacy is one of the main ethical considerations. Information systems handle enormous volumes of sensitive and personal data, thus it's critical to manage this data responsibly. Establishing strong rules and procedures is essential for organizations to protect people's privacy and make sure that data is gathered, handled, and kept in accordance with moral principles (Grebennik et al., 2021).

An important ethical guideline for information systems is openness. Organizations must be open and honest about their data practices, and users should be informed about how their data is being utilized. Because of its openness, a positive and moral technological environment is promoted by building trust between users and organizations.

Fair access to information systems is a further ethical factor. It is crucial to make sure that everyone has fair and equitable access to information systems as technology becomes more and more integrated into daily life. This entails tackling the problem of the digital divide, putting rules in place to close the gap, and encouraging inclusion while using technology(Genchev, 2020; Sukhorukov et al., 2020). Security is a factor in the proper development and use of technology. Information system security is not just a matter of operation; it is also morally required(Chen, 2020; Zhang, 2020a). Cyberattacks, unauthorized access, and data breaches may all have serious repercussions, including financial loss and privacy compromise. Therefore, as part of their moral obligation to safeguard both its users and the larger digital environment, enterprises must place a high priority on implementing strong cybersecurity safeguards (Talón-Ballestero et al., 2018).

The proper use of machine learning algorithms and artificial intelligence (AI) is included by the ethical issues in information systems. Intentional or inadvertent bias in algorithms may provide biased results(Luo et al., 2020; Matsumoto & Shigeyasu, 2020). Examining algorithms for biases and implementing remedial actions are part of ethical development standards, which guarantee impartiality and fairness in decision-making.

14.3 PRIVACY LAWS AND DATA PROTECTION

The General Data Protection Regulation (GDPR), which was put into effect by the European Union, is one of the fundamental privacy rules. GDPR emphasizes user permission, openness, and the right to be forgotten while establishing stringent rules for the gathering, handling, and archiving of personal data(Changcheng & Chaohu,

2020; Le Queau et al., 2020). In order to guarantee that people have control over their personal information, businesses operating in the EU or managing data connected to the EU are required to adhere to GDPR regulations (Singh & Sethi, 2021).

The Health Insurance Portability and Accountability Act (HIPAA) in the US is primarily concerned with safeguarding the confidentiality and integrity of personal health information. In order to protect sensitive patient data, healthcare organizations are required to abide by HIPAA standards, which place a strong emphasis on data encryption, secure storage, and restricted access (Li et al., 2020).

Other nations have also enacted strong privacy regulations, such as Australia's Privacy Act and Canada's Personal Information Protection and Electronic Documents Act (PIPEDA). Common themes across these rules include the need that businesses get user permission, be open and honest about their data activities, and have security measures in place to keep out unwanted access(Chan et al., 2020; Xie et al., 2020; Zhang, 2020b).

Regarding cross-border data transfers, the Privacy Shield agreement between the European Union and the United States allowed for the easier exchange of personal data while upholding data protection regulations. To retain compliance, companies must, however, keep abreast of modifications to these agreements and modify their procedures as necessary(Long et al., 2020; Yaroslavtsev & Matukhina, 2020). Organizations have an ethical as well as legal duty to comply with privacy regulations. Respecting people's right to privacy increases credibility and trust, which benefits the organization's reputation as a whole. Serious repercussions from non-compliance might include fines, harm to one's image, and erosion of consumer confidence (Chatterjee & N.S, 2022).

14.5 REGULATORY COMPLIANCE IN MIS

Organizations must place a high priority on regulatory compliance in Management Information Systems (MIS) in order to guarantee the ethical and legal use of technology (Farooq et al., 2020; Farooq & Raju, 2019a; Yen et al., 2023). The regulatory framework pertaining to information systems has undergone substantial changes in reaction to the rising dependence on technology and the escalating apprehensions over data security and privacy(Farooq, Khalil-Ur-Rehman, et al., 2019; Farooq, Bakhsh, et al., 2023; Farooq, Hafsa Qadir, et al., 2023). In order to achieve and preserve regulatory compliance in MIS, one must follow a complicated network of regulations and standards that differ across sectors and geographical areas(Farooq & Raju, 2019b, 2019c).

Respecting data protection laws is a crucial component of regulatory compliance in MIS. Strict guidelines for the gathering, handling, and archiving of private and sensitive data are established by laws like the Health Insurance Portability and Accountability Act (HIPAA) in the US and the General Data Protection Regulation (GDPR) in the EU(Farooq, Kalimuthu, et al., 2019; Farooq, Muhammad, et al., 2019; Farooq, Rehman, et al., 2019). In order to maintain compliance, businesses operating in these countries need to have strong data protection measures in place(Farooq, Ali, et al., 2019; Farooq & Raju, 2019d). These measures include encryption, access limits, and frequent audits of data processing procedures(Farooq, 2019; Ghulam et al., 2019).

Cybersecurity is one of the more general topics covered by regulatory compliance. Organizations must keep up with the most recent information security standards and laws due to the constantly changing nature of cyber threats(Buzdar & Farooq, 2020; Naseer et al., 2019). Guidelines for creating, putting into practice, maintaining, and continuously enhancing an information security management system are provided by frameworks such as ISO/IEC 27001(Farooq et al., 2022a, 2022b). Following these guidelines improves an organization's information systems' overall security posture in addition to guaranteeing compliance(Farooq, Ramzan, et al., 2024k; Muhammad Farooq, Muhammad Ramzan, 2024).

Regulatory compliance includes moral issues while using technology(Farooq, Buzdar, et al., 2024; Farooq, Ramzan, et al., 2024b). Businesses have to negotiate a challenging ethical environment while taking into account how their technology affects people individually, in groups, and in society as a whole(Farooq, Ramzan, et al., 2024d, 2024f). This entails tackling problems like algorithmic prejudice, conscientious AI development, and moral use of cutting-edge technology like face recognition(Farooq, Ramzan, et al., 2024h, 2024e).

Respecting moral standards helps one stay out of trouble with the law while also fostering public trust(Farooq, Ramzan, et al., 2024i, 2024j).

14.6 MANAGING ETHICAL DILEMMAS IN TECHNOLOGY USE

Taking care of complicated problems that come up at the nexus of innovation, social effect, and individual rights is part of managing ethical challenges in technology. A bright and inclusive digital future depends on finding a balance between using technology's advantages and respecting moral principles (Anshari et al., 2021).

The proper use of machine learning (ML) and artificial intelligence (AI) technology is one common ethical conundrum. As these technologies advance in sophistication, questions of accountability, justice, and prejudice have grown increasingly pressing. The difficulty of creating AI algorithms that are impartial, transparent, and consistent with moral standards must be faced by organizations. In fields like healthcare, banking, and criminal justice, where the results of biased algorithms may have significant effects on people and communities, ethical issues in AI are relevant. Another major ethical problem when using technology is privacy. Concerns with the right to privacy are raised by organizations' acquisition, retention, and use of personal data. Achieving equilibrium between using data for inventive purposes and upholding the privacy rights of people is a challenging endeavor. Organizations must proactively address these issues in their technological operations, as mandated by regulations like the GDPR and the California Consumer Privacy Act (CCPA), which have been implemented to defend people' privacy (Darnton, 2017).

There are issues with the moral use of cutting-edge technology like biometrics and monitoring instruments. When using such technology, organizations need to take into account the possibility of misuse and violations of civil freedoms. Managing the ethical ramifications of new technologies requires establishing clear regulations, carrying out impact analyses, and maintaining open lines of communication with stakeholders(Rezza, 2016).

Digital inequality is one example of an ethical conundrum, where differences in technology access and proficiency may deepen social divisions. In order to close the digital gap and guarantee that everyone has equal access to the advantages of technology, organizations must use inclusive practices that take into account the wider social effect of their technical breakthroughs.

14.7 CASE STUDIES ON ETHICS AND COMPLIANCE CHALLENGES

A prominent example of a case study that highlights the moral quandaries associated with technology usage is the Facebook-Cambridge Analytica controversy. The political consulting company Cambridge Analytica was found to have collected personal information without permission from millions of Facebook users in

2018. Afterwards, during the 2016 US presidential election, the company utilized this data to produce targeted political ads. Significant ethical questions about user privacy, permission, and the appropriate use of personal data were brought up by this occurrence (Pery et al., 2022).

The Facebook-Cambridge Analytica case highlights the difficulties businesses have in striking a balance between the advantages of data-driven insights and their moral obligation to safeguard user privacy (Farooq, Ramzan, et al., 2024a, 2024g). The ethical ramifications of data collecting and utilization were more widely known as a result of the increasing scrutiny and legislative measures that followed. This case provides a crucial illustration of how businesses must manage the moral dilemmas raised by the use of technology in order to preserve integrity and confidence (Liao et al., 2023).

The ethical issues surrounding machine learning (ML) and artificial intelligence (AI) algorithms are a further relevant example. Organizations in a variety of sectors, such as banking and healthcare, depend on AI and ML technologies to help with decision-making. If these technologies are not properly developed and supervised, they may, however, reinforce prejudice and discrimination(Farooq, Ramzan, et al., 2024c). The ethical issues with technology in human resource management are shown by the example of discriminatory algorithms in recruiting procedures, when prejudices based on gender, ethnicity, or other demographic characteristics are unintentionally ingrained in the algorithms.

Organizations are progressively implementing ethical AI frameworks and rules in order to tackle ethical quandaries. In order to guarantee justice, accountability, and transparency in the use of AI and ML systems, it is imperative to strike a balance between technical breakthroughs and ethical concerns(Gardezi et al., 2023).

As it relates to cybersecurity, ethical issues are equally important. The 2017 Equifax data leak serves as an example of the moral dilemmas businesses have while protecting confidential data. A significant data breach at Equifax, a significant credit reporting agency, resulted in the exposure of 147 million people's financial and personal data. The company's tardiness in patching a known vulnerability in its system was identified as the cause of the incident. The Equifax case serves as a reminder of the moral obligation businesses have to protect the information entrusted to them. Inadequate cybersecurity safeguards undermine confidence in the digital economy while also endangering people's privacy. In order to safeguard its stakeholders, it emphasizes the need of making moral decisions while using technology and calls on businesses to give cybersecurity top priority and swiftly fix any weaknesses.

14.8 CHAPTER CONCLUSION

In conclusion, the chapters on e-business, e-commerce, and mobile technologies underscore the profound impact of digital transformation on modern business operations and consumer behavior. E-business and e-commerce systems have become indispensable components reshaping the business landscape, integrating electronic methods into various operations, and fostering seamless transactions with enhanced convenience and security. The evolution of the e-commerce environment has revolutionized consumer interactions, driving the shift from traditional retail to online platforms and introducing diverse business models fueled by technological advancements.

Key technologies such as cloud computing, machine learning, and blockchain power e-commerce platforms, enabling personalized experiences, ensuring transaction security, and providing valuable insights for decision-making. Various business models emphasize customer-centricity and operational efficiency, while legal, ethical, and security considerations remain paramount in fostering consumer trust and mitigating risks.

Looking ahead, trends in e-commerce point towards omnichannel retailing, artificial intelligence-driven customer experiences, and sustainability practices shaping the future of business transactions. In parallel, mobile technologies have emerged as essential tools transforming business functions and consumer engagement. From the advent of analog mobile phones to the introduction of 5G technology, mobile devices have evolved into multipurpose instruments integral to everyday life.

Mobile application development has become a crucial component of organizational strategy, enabling businesses to optimize workflows, boost efficiency, and establish intimate connections with clients. However, security challenges in mobile applications, such as data leaks and software vulnerabilities, necessitate robust security measures to safeguard sensitive information.

REFERENCES

Anshari, M., Almunawar, M. N., Masri, M., & Hrdy, M. (2021). Financial Technology with AI-Enabled and Ethical Challenges. *Society*, *58*(3), 189–195. DOI: 10.1007/s12115-021-00592-w

Buzdar, A. Q., & Farooq, M. (2020). Memorization of Quran through Mobile Application in the Era of Transformative Marketing. [PJSS]. *Pakistan Journal of Social Sciences*, *40*(2), 689–698.

Chan, Z., Yuxia, X., Chang, L., Guoping, Y., & Zhijun, H. (2020). Design and practice of clinical trial management information system. *Chinese Journal of Clinical Pharmacology and Therapeutics*, *25*(5), 555–558.

Changcheng, X., & Chaohu, H. (2020). Research on university scientific research patent management information system based on BS mode. *Journal of Intelligent & Fuzzy Systems*, *38*(2), 1371–1379. DOI: 10.3233/JIFS-179500

Chatterjee, S., & N.S, S. (. (2022). Artificial intelligence and human rights: A comprehensive study from Indian legal and policy perspective. *International Journal of Law and Management*, *64*(1), 110–134. DOI: 10.1108/IJLMA-02-2021-0049

Chen, Q. (2020). Research on the Implementation Method of Database Security in Management Information System Based on Big Data Analysis. In L. Yang & Z. Xu (Eds.), *2020 INTERNATIONAL CONFERENCE ON ENERGY, ENVIRONMENT AND BIOENGINEERING (ICEEB 2020)*. DOI: 10.1051/e3sconf/202018502033

Darnton, G. (2017). Most approaches to information systems and information systems management are too narrow. In R. P. Dameri & R. Spinelli (Eds.), *Proceedings of the 11th European Conference on Information Systems Management, ECISM 2017* (Issue 11th European Conference on Information Systems Management (ECISM), pp. 85–92).

Dongfang, S., Jiping, C., Yu, Z., Wanqi, Q., & Weiying, L. (2021). Building and application of urban water supply network information management system. *Jishui Paishui*, *47*(1), 96–102.

Farooq, M. (2019). Emerging sciences in Social Sciences : An overview, A Research Agenda. *Global Journal of Emerging Sciences*, *1*(October), 183–197.

Farooq, M., Ali, W., Younas, W., Khalil-Ur-rehman, F., & Qurashi, Q. A. (2019). the Era of Transformative Marketing: Service Quality of Mobile App Based Taxi Services in Kuala Lumpur. *Proceedings on Engineering Sciences*, *1*(2), 49–58. DOI: 10.24874/PES01.02.006

Farooq, M., Bakhsh, A., Hafsa Qadir, B., & Warda, N. (2023). Digital Empowerment: Freedom of Expression Beyond 5G and 6G Networks in Developing Countries. *Pakistan Journal of Social Sciences*, *43*(4), 569–584. DOI: 10.5281/zenodo.10448484

Farooq, M., Buzdar, H. Q., Yen, Y. Y., & Bakhsh, A. (2024). Integrating AI in Sustainable Writing: An Empirical Investigation of the Technology Acceptance Model in Asian Social Sciences. *Journal of Logistics. Informatics and Service Science*, *11*(3), 324–338. DOI: 10.33168/JLISS.2024.0321

Farooq, M., Cheng, J., Khan, N. U., Saufi, R. A., Kanwal, N., & Bazkiaei, H. A. (2022a). Sustainable Waste Management Companies with Innovative Smart Solutions: A Systematic Review and Conceptual Model. *Sustainability (Basel)*, *14*(20), 13146. Advance online publication. DOI: 10.3390/su142013146

Farooq, M., Cheng, J., Khan, N. U., Saufi, R. A., Kanwal, N., & Bazkiaei, H. A. (2022b). Sustainable Waste Management Companies with Innovative Smart Solutions: A Systematic Review and Conceptual Model. *Sustainability (Basel)*, *14*(20), 13146. DOI: 10.3390/su142013146

Farooq, M., Hafsa Qadir, B., & Saeed, M. (2023, December). AI-Enhanced Social Sciences: A Systematic Literature Review and Bibliographic Analysis of Web of Science Published Research Papers. *Pakistan Journal of Society* [PJSEL]. *Education and Language*, *10*, 1–2.

Farooq, M., Kalimuthu, R., & Reza, M. H. (2019). Measuring and Comparing Brand Equity of Malaysian Banks in the Era of Transformative Marketing. *Global Journal of Emerging Sciences*, *1*(June), 96–102.

Farooq, M., Khalil-Ur-Rehman, F., Abdurrahaman, D. T., Younas, W., Sajjad, S., & Zreen, A. (2019). SERVICE QUALITY ANALYSIS OF PRIVATE UNIVERSITIES LIBRARIES IN MALAYSIA IN THE ERA OF TRANSFORMATIVE MARKETING. *International Journal of Qualitative Research*, *13*(2), 269–284. DOI: 10.24874/IJQR13.02-02

Farooq, M., Muhammad, S., Raju, V., Kalimuthu, K. R., & Qadir, A. (2019). Measuring and Comparing the Desired and Actual Service Quality of Pakistan International Airline. *The Journal of Social Sciences Research*, *52*(52), 484–490. DOI: 10.32861/jssr.52.484.490

Farooq, M., & Raju, V. (2019a). Impact of Over-the-Top (OTT) Services on the Telecom Companies in the Era of Transformative Marketing. *Global Journal of Flexible Systems Managment*, *20*(2), 177–188. DOI: 10.1007/s40171-019-00209-6

Farooq, M., & Raju, V. (2019b). Want to Stay the Market Leader in the Era of Transformative Marketing? Keep the Customers Satisfied! *Global Journal of Flexible Systems Management*. DOI: 10.1007/s40171-019-00213-w

Farooq, M., & Raju, V. (2019c). Impact of Over-the-Top (OTT) Services on the Telecom Companies in the Era of Transformative Marketing. *Global Journal of Flexible Systems Managment*, *20*(2), 177–188. DOI: 10.1007/s40171-019-00209-6

Farooq, M., & Raju, V. (2019d). Want to Stay the Market Leader in the Era of Transformative Marketing? Keep the Customers Satisfied! *Global Journal of Flexible Systems Managment*, *20*(3), 257–266. DOI: 10.1007/s40171-019-00213-w

Farooq, M., & Ramzan, M. Y. Y. Y. (2024). AI in Management. In *Transformative Impacts of AI in Management* (1st ed., pp. 1–44). IGI Global. DOI: 10.4018/979-8-3693-4322-7.ch001

Farooq, M., Ramzan, M., & Yen, Y. Y. (2024a). AI in Consumer Behavior Management. In *Transformative Impacts of AI in Management* (pp. 281–294). IGI Global., DOI: 10.4018/979-8-3693-4322-7.ch011

Farooq, M., Ramzan, M., & Yen, Y. Y. (2024b). AI in Customer Service, HR, and Administration. In *Transformative Impacts of AI in Management* (pp. 45–70). IGI Global. DOI: 10.4018/979-8-3693-4322-7.ch002

Farooq, M., Ramzan, M., & Yen, Y. Y. (2024c). AI in Quality Management. In *Transformative Impacts of AI in Management* (pp. 295–312). IGI Global., DOI: 10.4018/979-8-3693-4322-7.ch012

Farooq, M., Ramzan, M., & Yen, Y. Y. (2024d). Artificial Intelligence and Customer Experiences. In *Transformative Impacts of AI in Management* (pp. 95–114). IGI Global., DOI: 10.4018/979-8-3693-4322-7.ch004

Farooq, M., Ramzan, M., & Yen, Y. Y. (2024e). Artificial Intelligence in Administration Sciences. In *Transformative Impacts of AI in Management* (pp. 115–156). IGI Global., DOI: 10.4018/979-8-3693-4322-7.ch005

Farooq, M., Ramzan, M., & Yen, Y. Y. (2024f). Artificial Intelligence in Business and Law. In *Transformative Impacts of AI in Management* (pp. 71–94). IGI Global., DOI: 10.4018/979-8-3693-4322-7.ch003

Farooq, M., Ramzan, M., & Yen, Y. Y. (2024g). Artificial Intelligence in Ethical Business Decision Making. In *Transformative Impacts of AI in Management* (pp. 265–280). IGI Global., DOI: 10.4018/979-8-3693-4322-7.ch010

Farooq, M., Ramzan, M., & Yen, Y. Y. (2024h). Exploring the Impact of Artificial Intelligence on Brand Management. In *Transformative Impacts of AI in Management* (pp. 157–188). IGI Global., DOI: 10.4018/979-8-3693-4322-7.ch006

Farooq, M., Ramzan, M., & Yen, Y. Y. (2024i). Exploring the Impact of Ethical Leadership and Employee Engagement on Knowledge Sharing Attitudes in the Asian Digital Economy. In *Transformative Impacts of AI in Management* (pp. 241–264). IGI Global., DOI: 10.4018/979-8-3693-4322-7.ch009

Farooq, M., Ramzan, M., & Yen, Y. Y. (2024j). Transformative Impact of AI in Education Management. In *Transformative Impacts of AI in Management* (pp. 189–216). IGI Global., DOI: 10.4018/979-8-3693-4322-7.ch007

Farooq, M., Ramzan, M., & Yen, Y. Y. (2024k). *Transformative Impacts of AI in Management*. IGI Global., DOI: 10.4018/979-8-3693-4322-7

Farooq, M., Rehman, F. K. U., Younas, W., Raju, V., Ahmed, Q. M., & Ali, M. (2019). Investigating Relationship between Net Promoter Score and Company Performance: A Longitudinal Study. *Global Journal of Emerging Sciences*, *1*(1), 1–10. https://www.gjoes.org/wp-content/uploads/2019/04/1-1.pdf

Farooq, M., Saeed, M., Ali, W., & Javid, R. (2020). Online Buying and Customer Satisfaction in the Era of Transformative Marketing. *City University Research Journal*, *10*(2), 274–288.

Gardezi, M., Joshi, B., Rizzo, D. M., Ryan, M., Prutzer, E., Brugler, S., & Dadkhah, A. (2023). Artificial intelligence in farming: Challenges and opportunities for building trust. *Agronomy Journal*. Advance online publication. DOI: 10.1002/agj2.21353

Genchev, P. (2020). An approach to support information security risk assessment. In V. Markova & T. Ganchev (Eds.), *PROCEEDINGS OF THE 2020 INTERNATIONAL CONFERENCE ON BIOMEDICAL INNOVATIONS AND APPLICATIONS (BIA 2020)* (Issue International Conference on Biomedical Innovations and Applications (BIA) CL-Varna, pp. 125–128). DOI: 10.1109/BIA50171.2020.9244516

Ghulam, W. A., Ali, W., Ali, S., Khan, M. M., Khan, R. N., & Farooq, M. (2019). Investigating factors influencing brain drain of citizens of Azad Kashmir Pakistan. *Journal of Social Sciences Research*, *5*(3), 782–788. Advance online publication. DOI: 10.32861/jssr.53.782.788

Grebennik, I., Hutsa, O., Petrova, R., Yelchaninov, D., & Morozova, A. (2021). Information Technology Based on Qualitative Methods in Cyber-Physical Systems of Situational Disaster Risk Management. In Y. Murayama, D. Velev, & P. Zlateva (Eds.), *INFORMATION TECHNOLOGY IN DISASTER RISK REDUCTION, ITDRR 2020* (Vol. 622, Issue 5th IFIP WG 5.15 International Conference on Information Technology in Disaster Risk Reduction (ITDRR), pp. 132–143). WE - Conference Proceedings Citation Index - Science (CPCI-S)DOI: 10.1007/978-3-030-81469-4_11

Hu, B., & Shi, W. (2021). Design of a Flexible Exhibition Management Information System for Exhibition Services. *Scientific Programming*, *2021*, 1–10. Advance online publication. DOI: 10.1155/2021/4789408

Huang, L. (2021). Applications of Small and Medium Enterprise Management System Using Edge Algorithm. *Mobile Information Systems*, *2021*, 1–11. Advance online publication. DOI: 10.1155/2021/8730413

Kazemi, P., Lau, F., Matava, C., & Simpao, A. F. (2021). An Environmental Scan of Anesthesia Information Management Systems in the American and Canadian Marketplace. *Journal of Medical Systems*, *45*(12), 101. Advance online publication. DOI: 10.1007/s10916-021-01781-0 PMID: 34661760

Koo, J., Kim, S.-H., & Kim, Y.-S. (2021). Effects of the Government Performance Evaluation System on the Organization Effectiveness of Public Organizations: A Focus on the Interaction Effect of Performance Information. *Socail Science Review*, *52*(1), 33–57. DOI: 10.31502/SSRI.52.1.3

Le Queau, C., Ann Phillips, W., & Srinivasan, A. (2020). Practical use of biobank information management system (BIMS) for clinical-biological annotations in biobanks. *Medecine Sciences*, *36*(3), 285–288. DOI: 10.1051/medsci/2020044 PMID: 32228852

Leventhal, E. L., & Schreyer, K. E. (2020). Information Management in the Emergency Department. *Emergency Medicine Clinics of North America*, *38*(3), 681–691. DOI: 10.1016/j.emc.2020.03.004 PMID: 32616287

Li, Y. Z., Lu, C. J., & Liu, Y. (2020). Medical Insurance Information Systems in China: Mixed Methods Study. [WE - Science Citation Index Expanded] [SCI-EXPANDED]. *JMIR Medical Informatics*, *8*(9), e18780. Advance online publication. DOI: 10.2196/18780 PMID: 32673209

Liao, H. T., Lo, T. M., & Pan, C. L. (2023). Knowledge Mapping Analysis of Intelligent Ports: Research Facing Global Value Chain Challenges. *Systems*, *11*(2), 88. Advance online publication. DOI: 10.3390/systems11020088

Lili, S., Xiaoping, L., Zhen, Y., Yanru, C., & Xianhong, H. (2021). Improvement and effects evaluation of the information system of nursing hierarchy management. *Chinese Journal of Nursing Education, 18*(11), 1018–1022.

Liu, S. (2021). Design and Implementation of High-Skilled Talent Information Management System Based on Multisensor Information Fusion. *Journal of Sensors, 2021*(1), 3812145. Advance online publication. DOI: 10.1155/2021/3812145

Long, F., Chuan, W., Yufen, D., Chuanyong, L., Junjie, Y., & Qiang, L. (2020). Information System of Marine Survey Part 2: The Application Software. In *Hydrographic Surveying and Charting* (Vol. 40, Issue 4, pp. 72–76).

Luo, M., Fan, Z., & Yu, T. (2020). Marine Information Management Service Platform: A GIS Based Study. *Journal of Coastal Research, 557–561*(sp1), 557. Advance online publication. DOI: 10.2112/SI106-126.1

Matsumoto, N., & Shigeyasu, T. (2020). A New Mobile Agent System for Sharing Disaster Information Under Unstable Network Conditions. In L. Barolli, P. Hellinckx, & T. Enokido (Eds.), *Lecture Notes in Networks and Systems* (Vol. 97, Issues 14th IEEE International Conference on Broadband Wireless Computing, Communication and Applications (BWCCA) CL-Univ Antwerp, Antwerp, pp. 222–230). DOI: 10.1007/978-3-030-33506-9_20

Naseer, M., Farooq, M., Younas, W., & Raju, V. (2019). Antecedents of employee retention in the pharmaceutical industry of Pakistan. *Journal of Social Sciences Research, 5*(3), 656–664. Advance online publication. DOI: 10.32861/jssr.53.655.664

Nedzelskay, O. N., Moiseyev, V. V., Bikineeva, A. N., & Bulakina, E. N. (2020). Infrastructure management of software systems of modern "iT" in the automation of production processes. In *IOP Conference Series: Materials Science and Engineering* (Vol. 865, Issue 1). DOI: 10.1088/1757-899X/865/1/012017

Pery, A., Rafiei, M., Simon, M., & van der Aalst, W. M. P. (2022). Trustworthy Artificial Intelligence and Process Mining: Challenges and Opportunities. In J. MunozGama & X. Lu (Eds.), *PROCESS MINING WORKSHOPS, ICPM 2021* (Vol. 433, Issue 3rd International Conference on Process Mining (ICPM), pp. 395–407). DOI: 10.1007/978-3-030-98581-3_29

Ren, P., Nie, M., & Ming, H. (2021). Optimization of Sports Good Recycling Management System Based on Internet of Things. *Wireless Communications and Mobile Computing, 2021*(1), 6415136. Advance online publication. DOI: 10.1155/2021/6415136

Rezza, A. M. (2016). Brand Attitude of Smartphone User: The Role of Brand Knowledge and Self-Congruence. In Abdullah, A. G., Hurriyati, R., Nandiyanto, A. B. D., Adiwibowo, L., Aryanti, T., Adriany, V., & Aripin, A. (Eds.), *PROCEEDINGS OF THE 2016 GLOBAL CONFERENCE ON BUSINESS, MANAGEMENT AND ENTREPRENEURSHIP* (Vol. 15, pp. 381–384). DOI: 10.2991/gcbme-16.2016.68

Rusakov, D. V., & Loseva, D. M. (2021, January). Development of an information system for managing user requests using bitrix. In *2021 IEEE Conference of Russian Young Researchers in Electrical and Electronic Engineering (ElConRus)* (pp. 1055-1058). IEEE.

Schiuma, G., Kumar, S., Sureka, R., & Joshi, R. (2023). Research constituents and authorship patterns in the Knowledge Management Research and Practice: A bibliometric analysis. [WE - Social Science Citation Index] [SSCI]. *Knowledge Management Research and Practice*, *21*(1), 129–145. DOI: 10.1080/14778238.2020.1848365

Singh, V., & Sethi, M. R. (2021). Digital Trade And Artificial Intelligence: Role Of Intellectual Property. *NTUT Journal of Intellectual Property Law and Management*, *10*(1), 45–66.

Siyao, G. U. O., & Bin, X. I. E. (2021, January). An education management assessment model based on information control theory. In 2021 13th International Conference on Measuring Technology and Mechatronics Automation (ICMTMA) (pp. 531-534). IEEE.

Sukhorukov, A., Koryagin, N., Sulyagina, J., Ulitskaya, N., & Eroshkin, S. (2019, May). Digital transformation of airline management as the basis of innovative development. In *International Scientific Siberian Transport Forum* (pp. 845-854). Cham: Springer International Publishing.

Talón-Ballestero, P., González-Serrano, L., Soguero-Ruiz, C., Muñoz-Romero, S., & Rojo-Alvarez, J. L. (2018). Using big data from Customer Relationship Management information systems to determine the client profile in the hotel sector. [WE - Social Science Citation Index] [SSCI]. *Tourism Management*, *68*, 187–197. DOI: 10.1016/j.tourman.2018.03.017

Xie, C., Luo, Y., Yu, X., & IEEE. (2020). Research on the Construction of the Dynamical Mechanism Model for the Military Civilian Integration Sharing of College Educational Resources of Hubei Province. In *2020 16TH INTERNATIONAL WIRELESS COMMUNICATIONS & MOBILE COMPUTING CONFERENCE, IWCMC* pp. 1208–1212). DOI: 10.1109/IWCMC48107.2020.9148562

Yaroslavtsev, A. V., & Matukhina, O. V. (2020). Creating the Web Service of the Laboratory Information and Management System for Analytical Quality Control. In A. V Bogoviz & Y. V Ragulina (Eds.), *Lecture Notes in Networks and Systems* (Vol. 115, Issue Scientific and Practical Forum on Industry, Science, Competences, Integration CL-RUDN Univ, Moscow, pp. 643–649). DOI: 10.1007/978-3-030-40749-0_77

Yen, Y. Y., Wen, L. J., Ramasamy, S., & Farooq, M. (2023). Sustainable petrol subsidy program in Malaysia. *Asian Development Policy Review, 12*(1), 1–9. DOI: 10.55493/5008.v12i1.4948

YOUNG, C. J. (2021). Study on the Health Information Management Practice Program Model for EMR Certification System Education -Focus on Patient Information Management-. *Journal of The Health Care and Life Science, 9*(1), 1–9. DOI: 10.22961/JHCLS.2021.9.1.01

Yousefnezhad, N., Malhi, A., Kinnunen, T., Huotari, M., & Framling, K. (2020). Product Lifecycle Information Management with Digital Twin: A Case Study. In *IEEE International Conference on Industrial Informatics (INDIN)* (Vols. 2020-July, Issues 18th IEEE International Conference on Industrial Informatics (INDIN) pp. 321–326). DOI: 10.1109/INDIN45582.2020.9442208

Yuan, C., & Yicun, H. (2021). Management Information System for Compensation under Multihoming Network Architecture. *Wireless Communications and Mobile Computing, 2021*(1), 6168947. Advance online publication. DOI: 10.1155/2021/6168947

Zhang, X. (2020a). The design and implementation of geologic hazard information management system. *Arabian Journal of Geosciences, 13*(17), 854. Advance online publication. DOI: 10.1007/s12517-020-05874-x

Zhang, X. (2020b). The design and implementation of geologic hazard information management system. *Arabian Journal of Geosciences, 13*(17), 854. Advance online publication. DOI: 10.1007/s12517-020-05874-x

Zhao, B., & Tu, C. (2021). Research and Development of Inventory Management and Human Resource Management in ERP. *Wireless Communications and Mobile Computing, 2021*(1), 3132062. Advance online publication. DOI: 10.1155/2021/3132062

Zheng, H., Zhang, T., Fang, C., Zeng, J., & Yang, X. (2021). Design and implementation of poultry farming information management system based on cloud database. *Animals (Basel), 11*(3), 1–15. DOI: 10.3390/ani11030900 PMID: 33809835

Chapter 15
Transformative Impacts of AI in Applications of MIS to Profit Maximization:
Lessons From the Telecom Industry of Pakistan

ABSTRACT

The telecom industry in Pakistan has undergone significant transformation, transitioning from a monopolistic structure dominated by PTCL to a competitive market driven by liberalization and privatization initiatives (Farooq et al., 2024a, 2024d, 2024b). Today, mobile telephony serves as the industry's backbone, propelled by the proliferation of smartphones and advancements in network technologies like 3G, 4G, and emerging 5G. Key players in the market include Jazz, Telenor Pakistan, Zong, and Ufone, each competing for market share through innovation and aggressive expansion strategies (Farooq et al., 2020; Farooq & Raju, 2019a; Yen et al., 2023).

15.1 CHAPTER INTRODUCTION

MIS plays a critical role in the telecom sector, facilitating operational efficiency, strategic decision-making, and customer relationship management (Chenyang et al., 2024; León-Romero et al., 2024; Zhai & Chen, 2024). By integrating data from various sources, MIS enables real-time monitoring and management of operations, optimization of network performance, and identification of growth opportunities. Additionally, MIS supports strategic decision-making by providing timely insights

DOI: 10.4018/979-8-3373-0513-4.ch015

into market trends, competitive dynamics, and customer preferences, empowering executives to formulate and execute effective strategies (Chatzimichailidou et al., 2024; Xie et al., 2024).

Revenue generation strategies in the telecom sector encompass pricing models and strategies, value-added services, bundling offers, and marketing campaigns(Karim et al., 2024; Okada et al., 2024). Telecom operators utilize subscription-based plans, usage-based pricing, and tiered pricing structures to cater to diverse customer needs while maximizing revenue(Farooq et al., 2024f, 2024e). Value-added services such as mobile banking and entertainment content, bundled with core offerings, enhance customer satisfaction and drive revenue growth(Farooq et al., 2024c, 2024b). Marketing and promotional campaigns raise awareness and stimulate demand, enabling operators to differentiate themselves in the market and attract new customers(Farooq et al., 2024d, 2024a).

Profit maximization techniques in the telecom industry involve cost optimization, revenue optimization through data analytics, and investments in infrastructure and technology. Operators optimize costs through network optimization, resource sharing, and outsourcing, while leveraging data analytics to identify revenue opportunities and prevent revenue leakage(Gupta & Panigrahi, 2023; Y. Wang et al., 2023; Zhidong, 2023). Investments in infrastructure and technology, including 5G deployment and automation solutions, drive operational efficiency and support revenue growth(Dalloul et al., 2023; Godoy et al., 2023).

Successful case studies illustrate the transformative impact of MIS implementation in the Pakistani telecom sector. Examples include improvements in customer satisfaction and retention, operational efficiency, and revenue growth through innovations(Z. Huang, 2022; Na & Shon, 2022). By harnessing the power of data-driven insights and automation, telecom operators have achieved tangible business outcomes, enhancing their competitiveness, and driving sustainable growth in a dynamic market landscape(X. Li et al., 2022; X. Zhang, 2022).

Overall, this chapter focuses the integral role of MIS in revenue generation and profit maximization within the telecom industry of Pakistan, highlighting its importance for driving operational efficiency, strategic decision-making, and innovation in an increasingly competitive and evolving market environment(L. Huang, 2022; Pereira et al., 2022).

Figure 1. Mind map of revenue generation and profit maximization in telecom

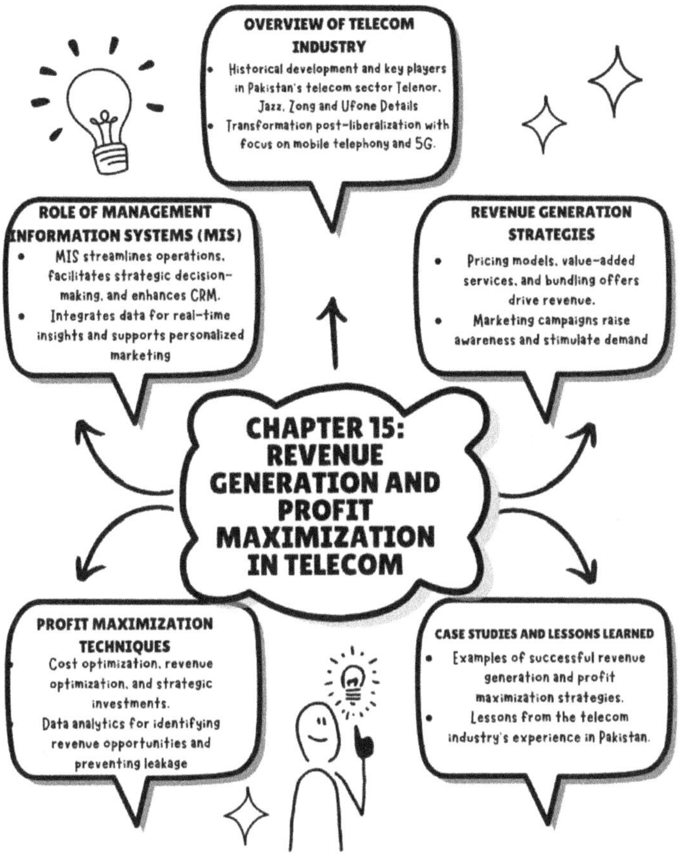

15.2 OVERVIEW OF TELECOM INDUSTRY IN PAKISTAN

The telecom industry in Pakistan has a rich and varied history that has shaped its current landscape. Understanding the historical development, current market landscape, and key players with their market shares provides valuable insights into the dynamics of this vital sector (Butt et al., 2021).

Historically, the telecom industry in Pakistan traces its roots back to the establishment of the Pakistan Telecommunication Company Limited (PTCL) in 1947, which monopolized the sector for several decades (Y. Khan, 2021). During this period, telecom services were limited, expensive, and predominantly landline-based. However, the industry underwent a significant transformation in the early 2000s with the introduction of liberalization and deregulation policies. This led to the privatization of PTCL in 2005, marking a pivotal moment in the industry's history. Subsequently, the government's initiatives attracted foreign investments, fostering competition and innovation in the sector (Ahmad et al., 2020).

Today, the telecom industry in Pakistan boasts a vibrant and dynamic market landscape, characterized by intense competition and rapid technological advancements. Mobile telephony serves as the cornerstone of the industry, with a significant penetration rate and a growing demand for data services. The proliferation of smartphones, coupled with the expansion of 3G, 4G, and now 5G networks, has revolutionized communication and connectivity across the country. Additionally, the emergence of Over-the-Top (OTT) services, such as WhatsApp and Skype, has further diversified the telecom ecosystem, challenging traditional revenue streams (Saman Naz & Moeed Ahmad Sandhu, 2020).

Key players in the Pakistani telecom market include both established incumbents and emerging challengers, each vying for a larger share of the market. Jazz, formerly known as Mobilink, stands as the market leader with a substantial subscriber base and extensive network coverage. Telenor Pakistan, a subsidiary of the Norwegian telecommunications giant, holds a significant market share, leveraging its innovative services and customer-centric approach. Zong, owned by China Mobile, has rapidly expanded its presence in the market, particularly in rural and underserved areas, through aggressive network expansion and competitive pricing strategies. Ufone, a subsidiary of PTCL, remains a prominent player despite facing stiff competition from its rivals (Younas & Kalimuthu, 2021).

Figure 2. Overview of telecom Pakistan (PTA, 2024)

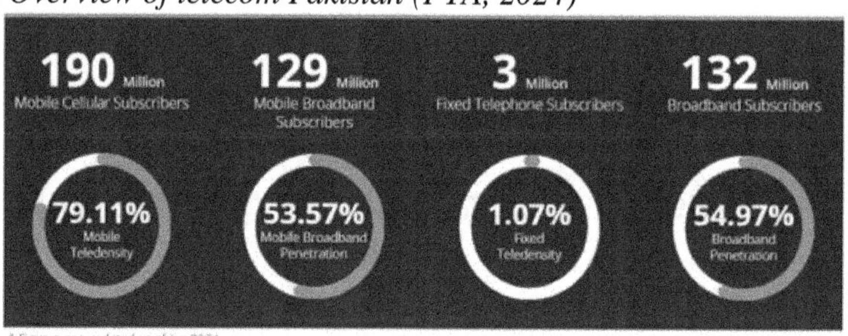

* Figures are updated as of Jan 2024.

Figure 3. Cellular subscribers statistics (PTA, 2024)

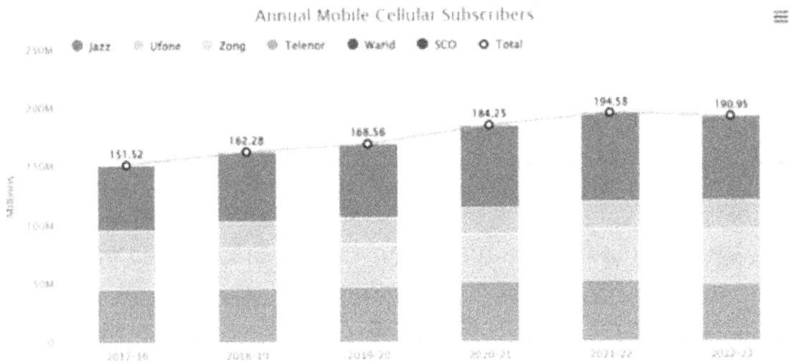

Figure 4. Market share as of Jan 2024 (PTA, 2024)

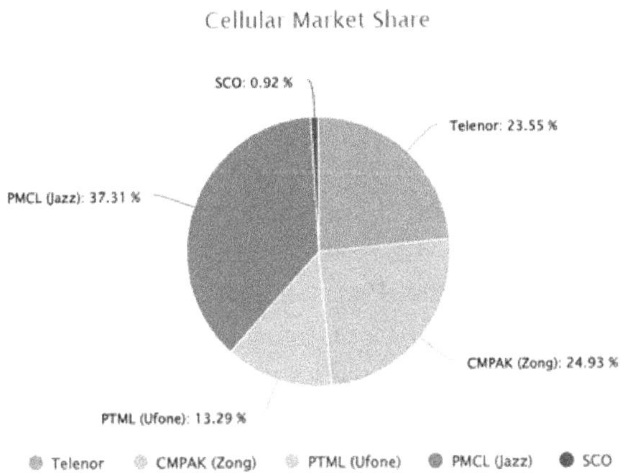

Market share in the telecom industry is a crucial metric for assessing the competitive landscape and the relative strengths of key players. The figure below shows the detailed market situation(Farooq & Raju, 2019b).

In recent years, the telecom industry in Pakistan has witnessed several noteworthy developments and trends that have reshaped its trajectory (A. A. Khan et al., 2016; Ul Haq et al., 2019). The advent of 5G technology promises to revolutionize connectivity, enabling faster data speeds, lower latency, and support for emerging technologies such as Internet of Things (IoT) and Artificial Intelligence (AI). Moreover, the COVID-19 pandemic has underscored the importance of digital connectivity, driving increased demand for broadband services and remote communication solutions (Khuntia et al., 2021).

Looking ahead, the telecom industry in Pakistan is poised for further evolution and growth, fueled by technological innovations, regulatory reforms, and changing consumer behaviors. The rollout of 5G networks, coupled with investments in infrastructure and digital literacy initiatives, is expected to unlock new opportunities for industry players and drive socio-economic development across the country (Oughton et al., 2022). However, challenges such as regulatory uncertainty, infrastructure constraints, and cybersecurity threats remain pertinent and require proactive measures from stakeholders to ensure sustainable growth and inclusive access to telecommunications services (Blouch et al., 2021; Saman Naz & Moeed Ahmad Sandhu, 2020).

15.3 ROLE OF MANAGEMENT INFORMATION SYSTEMS (MIS) IN TELECOM SECTOR

The role of Management Information Systems (MIS) in the telecom sector is paramount, facilitating operational efficiency, strategic decision-making, and effective customer relationship management (CRM) systems. MIS plays a pivotal role in streamlining operational processes and enhancing efficiency across various facets of telecom operations(Imran Hanif & Inayat, 2017; Younas & Kalimuthu, 2021). By integrating data from disparate sources such as network infrastructure, subscriber databases, and financial systems, MIS enables telecom companies to monitor and manage their operations in real-time (Petersen & Daramola, 2020). This includes optimizing network performance, managing inventory, and ensuring timely billing and revenue collection. Through automated workflows and data analytics, MIS empowers telecom operators to identify bottlenecks, allocate resources effectively, and streamline workflows, ultimately improving productivity and reducing operational costs (Mishra et al., 2020).

Moreover, MIS serves as a cornerstone for strategic decision-making within the telecom sector. By providing timely, accurate, and relevant information to key decision-makers, MIS enables telecom executives to formulate and execute strategic initiatives with precision and agility. This includes analyzing market trends, evaluating competitive dynamics, and identifying growth opportunities. Through advanced analytics and predictive modeling, MIS enables telecom companies to forecast demand, assess risks, and develop strategic plans that align with business objectives. Additionally, MIS facilitates scenario planning and what-if analysis, enabling telecom executives to anticipate market shifts and adapt their strategies accordingly (Odusami et al., 2021).

Furthermore, CRM systems powered by MIS play a crucial role in managing customer relationships and driving business growth in the telecom sector. By centralizing customer data and interactions across multiple touchpoints, CRM systems enable telecom operators to gain a comprehensive understanding of their customers' preferences, behaviors, and needs (Kumar et al., 2019; Sharif et al., 2019). This allows telecom companies to personalize marketing campaigns, tailor products and services, and deliver exceptional customer experiences. Moreover, CRM systems enable proactive customer engagement through targeted promotions, loyalty programs, and personalized recommendations, fostering customer retention and loyalty.

Figure 5. Departmental progress reports

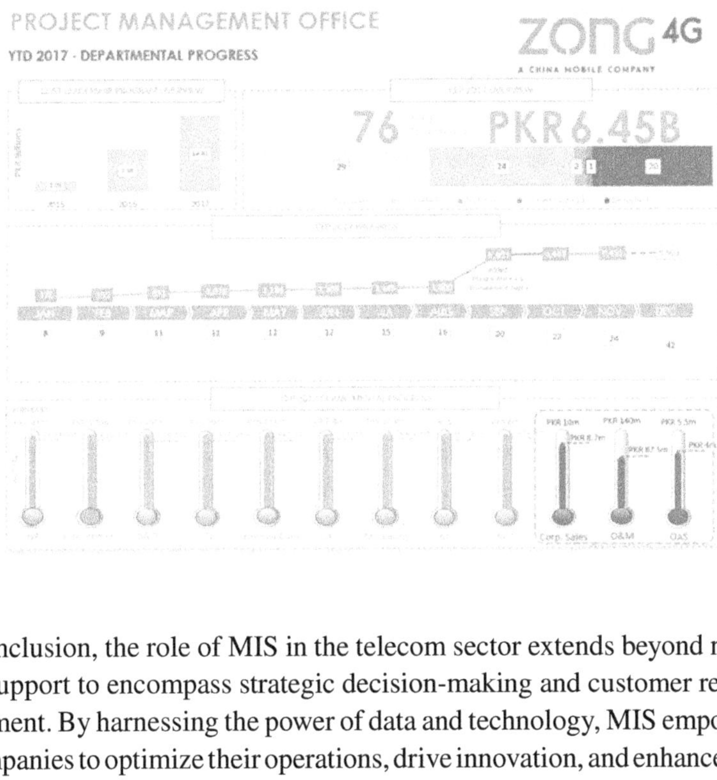

In conclusion, the role of MIS in the telecom sector extends beyond mere operational support to encompass strategic decision-making and customer relationship management. By harnessing the power of data and technology, MIS empowers telecom companies to optimize their operations, drive innovation, and enhance customer satisfaction (Aqeel et al., 2017; Farooq & Raju, 2019c). As the telecom industry continues to evolve in the digital age, the importance of MIS as a strategic enabler will only grow, shaping the future trajectory of the sector and driving sustainable growth and competitiveness.

Figure 6. Annual reporting system

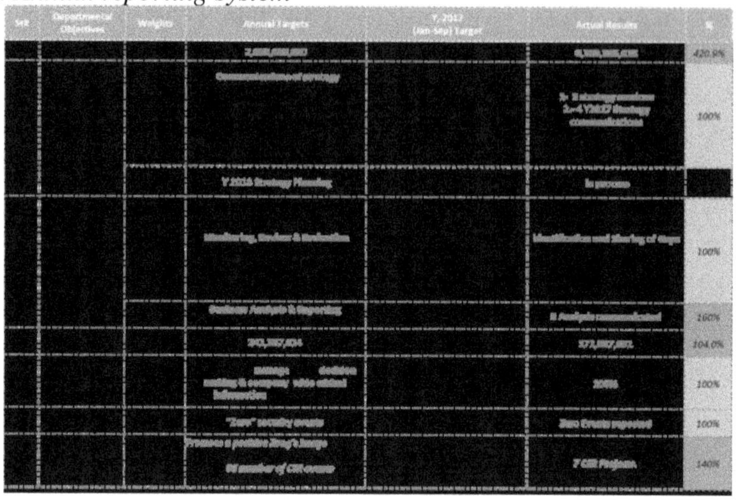

15.4 REVENUE GENERATION STRATEGIES EMPLOYED BY TELECOM COMPANIES

The revenue generation strategies employed by telecom companies are critical components of their business models, as they directly impact profitability, market competitiveness, and customer satisfaction (Idrees et al., 2019; Riaz et al., 2018). This section explores three key strategies commonly utilized by telecom operators to drive revenue: pricing models and strategies, value-added services and bundling offers, and marketing and promotional campaigns (Jamal & Ali, 2017; Majid & Mahmud, 2019).

Pricing models and strategies form the cornerstone of revenue generation for telecom companies, as they determine the cost structure for various services and offerings. Telecom operators employ a variety of pricing models, including subscription-based plans, usage-based pricing, and tiered pricing structures, to cater to the diverse needs and preferences of customers. Subscription-based plans, such as monthly or annual contracts, offer customers a fixed amount of services for a set fee, providing predictability and convenience. Usage-based pricing, on the other hand, charges customers based on their actual usage of services, allowing for greater flexibility and customization. Tiered pricing structures offer different service levels at varying price points, catering to customers with different usage patterns and budget constraints (L. Chen et al., 2021).

Figure 7. Churn prediction mechanism

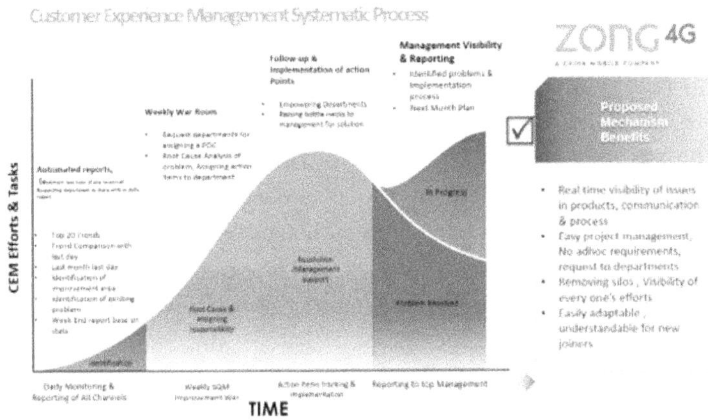

In addition to pricing models, telecom companies employ a range of pricing strategies to maximize revenue and profitability. This includes dynamic pricing, where prices fluctuate based on demand and supply dynamics, allowing operators to capture value during peak periods. Furthermore, telecom operators often bundle services together to create value-added offerings that appeal to customers and drive revenue growth. By bundling services such as voice, data, and messaging, telecom companies can increase average revenue per user (ARPU) while providing customers with greater convenience and value (Keshavarz et al., 2021).

Another key revenue generation strategy employed by telecom companies is the provision of value-added services (VAS) and bundling offers. Value-added services go beyond basic voice and data connectivity to offer customers additional features, functionality, and content. This includes services such as mobile banking, mobile payments, entertainment content, and cloud storage, which enhance the overall customer experience and drive incremental revenue for telecom operators. By bundling these value-added services with core telecom offerings, operators can differentiate themselves in the market, attract new customers, and increase customer loyalty and retention.

Moreover, marketing, and promotional campaigns play a crucial role in driving revenue generation for telecom companies by raising awareness, stimulating demand, and influencing purchasing decisions. Telecom operators invest heavily in marketing initiatives such as advertising, sponsorships, and promotions to create brand awareness and promote their products and services. This includes traditional marketing channels such as television, radio, and print media, as well as digital marketing channels such as social media, search engine optimization (SEO), and email marketing. Furthermore, telecom operators often collaborate with third-party partners, such as handset manufacturers and app developers, to co-promote products and services and leverage their respective customer bases.

In conclusion, revenue generation strategies employed by telecom companies encompass a range of tactics aimed at maximizing revenue, profitability, and customer satisfaction. Pricing models and strategies, value-added services and bundling offers, and marketing and promotional campaigns are key components of these strategies, enabling operators to differentiate themselves in the market, attract new customers, and drive revenue growth. As the telecom industry continues to evolve in the digital age, effective revenue generation strategies will be essential for operators to remain competitive and thrive in an increasingly dynamic and competitive market landscape.

Figure 8. Use of MIS for project management

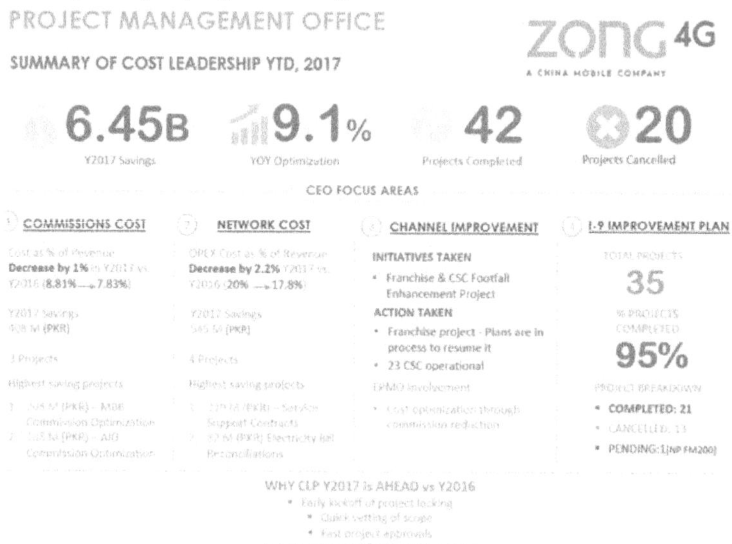

15.5 PROFIT MAXIMIZATION TECHNIQUES IN TELECOM INDUSTRY

Profit maximization is a fundamental goal for telecom companies, and achieving it requires a combination of effective cost optimization, revenue optimization, and strategic investments in infrastructure and technology. This section explores these key techniques employed by telecom operators to maximize profitability in a competitive market landscape (Bensikaddour & Boutte, 2022).

Cost optimization strategies play a crucial role in profit maximization for telecom companies, as reducing operational expenses directly impacts the bottom line. Telecom operators employ various cost optimization techniques, including network optimization, resource sharing, and outsourcing non-core functions(Iqbal & Siddiqui, 2019; Ullah et al., 2019).

Network optimization involves fine-tuning network configurations and traffic management to minimize operating costs while maintaining service quality. Resource sharing initiatives, such as tower sharing and spectrum sharing agreements, allow operators to reduce capital expenditures and operational costs by leveraging shared infrastructure. Additionally, outsourcing non-core functions such as customer service and back-office operations enables telecom companies to focus on their core competencies while reducing overhead costs (Iqbal & Siddiqui, 2019; Ullah et al., 2019).

Revenue optimization through data analytics is another key technique employed by telecom operators to maximize profitability. By leveraging advanced analytics techniques such as predictive modeling and machine learning, telecom companies can gain valuable insights into customer behavior, market trends, and revenue opportunities. This allows operators to optimize pricing strategies, identify upselling and cross-selling opportunities, and personalize marketing campaigns to maximize revenue. Furthermore, data analytics enables telecom operators to detect and prevent revenue leakage through fraud detection and revenue assurance initiatives, ensuring that all revenue streams are fully optimized and protected (Afridi et al., 2018; Tariq & Mat, 2018; Waheed et al., 2019).

Investments in infrastructure and technology are essential for profit maximization in the telecom industry, as they enable operators to expand their service offerings, improve service quality, and enhance operational efficiency. Telecom operators invest heavily in expanding and upgrading their network infrastructure, including deploying new technologies such as 5G and fiber-optic networks. These investments enable operators to offer high-speed broadband services, support emerging technologies such as Internet of Things (IoT), and meet the growing demand for data-intensive applications and services (Ali Shah et al., 2020; Y. Khan et al., 2019; Watto et al., 2020).

Additionally, investments in technology platforms such as billing systems, customer relationship management (CRM) systems, and data analytics tools enable operators to streamline operations, enhance customer experience, and drive revenue growth (Basu et al., 2021).

In conclusion, profit maximization in the telecom industry requires a strategic combination of cost optimization, revenue optimization, and investments in infrastructure and technology. By implementing effective cost optimization strategies, leveraging data analytics to optimize revenue opportunities, and making strategic investments in infrastructure and technology, telecom operators can maximize profitability and sustain long-term growth in a competitive market landscape(Altaf Hussain et al., 2020; Haseeb Riaz et al., 2018; Zakaria & Zakaria, 2008).

As the telecom industry continues to evolve, operators must remain agile and innovative in their approach to profit maximization, adapting to changing market dynamics and emerging technologies to stay ahead of the competition.

15.6 CASE STUDIES: SUCCESSFUL IMPLEMENTATION OF MIS IN TELECOM SECTOR OF PAKISTAN

The successful implementation of Management Information Systems (MIS) has been pivotal in driving transformative changes within the telecom sector of Pakistan(Iliescu, 2022; Lee, 2022; Runge et al., 2022). Through case studies, we delve into distinct instances where MIS has played a crucial role in reshaping operations, enhancing efficiency, and driving revenue growth(Fu & Xu, 2022; B. Guo & Shuai, 2022; G. Wang et al., 2022). The case study section explains the Scenarios how MIS helped telecom companies.

15.6.1 MIS Systems at Ufone -Customer Life Cycle Management

The author had the experience to work as executive churn and loyalty at Ufone in the Customer Life Cycle Management (CLM) from 2011-2013. Telecom in terms of MIS systems is an advanced sector(R. Liu & Wang, 2022; Song, 2022; Tian et al., 2022). As CLM executive authored had the opportunity to interact with operations, customer experience, database, pricing, sales, and information technology teams(Lian, 2022; Liang & Wang, 2022; W. Liu & Wei, 2022). Through using the data base author had the opportunity to lead several campaigns to provide information to more than 12 million customers across pakistan.

Figure 9. Customer journey with Ufone MIS approach

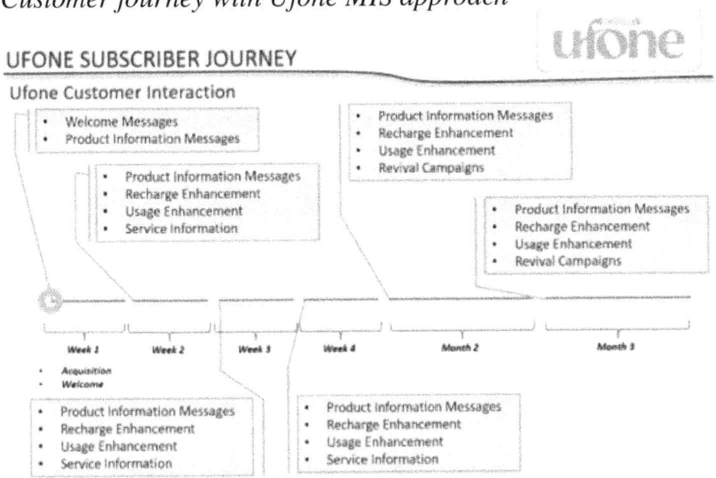

One notable example of MIS implementation in the Pakistani telecom sector is its role in improving customer satisfaction and retention(Y. Liu, 2022; Shi et al., 2022). A leading telecom operator in Pakistan utilized MIS to analyze customer feedback, service usage patterns, and network performance data(Kamenska et al., 2022; Y. Wang, 2022). By integrating data from various touchpoints, including call centers, social media, and network monitoring systems, the operator gained actionable insights into customer preferences and pain points(Xiaobao et al., 2022; Y. Zhang, 2022).

Figure 10. How subscribers usage was tracked!

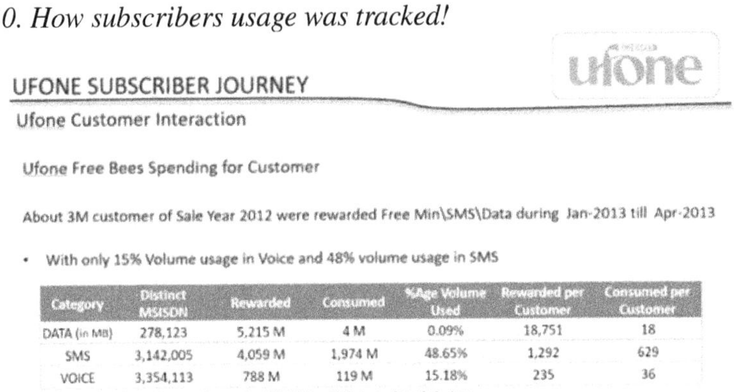
UFONE SUBSCRIBER JOURNEY

Ufone Customer Interaction

Ufone Free Bees Spending for Customer

About 3M customer of Sale Year 2012 were rewarded Free Min\SMS\Data during Jan-2013 till Apr-2013

• With only 15% Volume usage in Voice and 48% volume usage in SMS

Category	Distinct MSISDN	Rewarded	Consumed	%Age Volume Used	Rewarded per Customer	Consumed per Customer
DATA (in MB)	278,123	5,215 M	4 M	0.09%	18,751	18
SMS	3,142,005	4,059 M	1,974 M	48.65%	1,292	629
VOICE	3,354,113	788 M	119 M	15.18%	235	36

Free Resource Calculation was done on Jan-2013 till Apr-2013 due to Data Limitations

Figure 11. Tracking of dormant customers

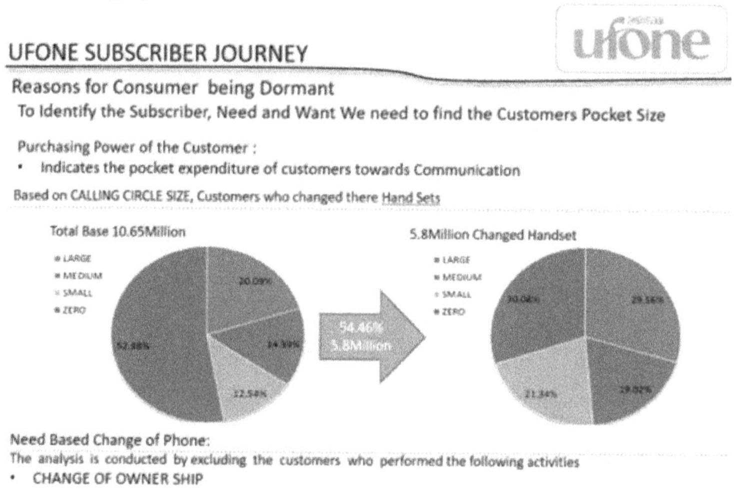

Figure 12. Subscriber interaction with the products

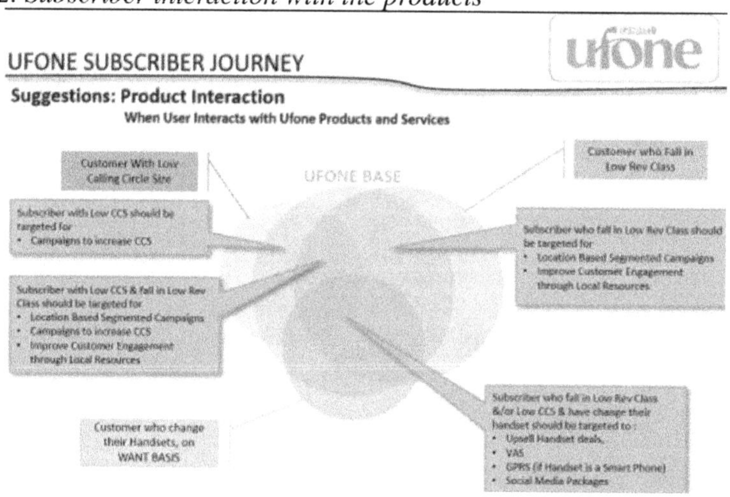

Using this data, the telecom operator implemented targeted initiatives to address common customer grievances and enhance service quality. For instance, they identified areas with network congestion and proactively upgraded infrastructure to improve coverage and reliability. Additionally, the operator launched personalized marketing campaigns and loyalty programs based on customer segmentation analysis, offering tailored promotions and incentives to high-value customers.

Social network analysis is another MIS based interaction tool that telecom companies use. The author had the experience to implement it in Ufone. It helps telecom companies to earn more using the data.

Figure 13. Social network developed by author in Ufone

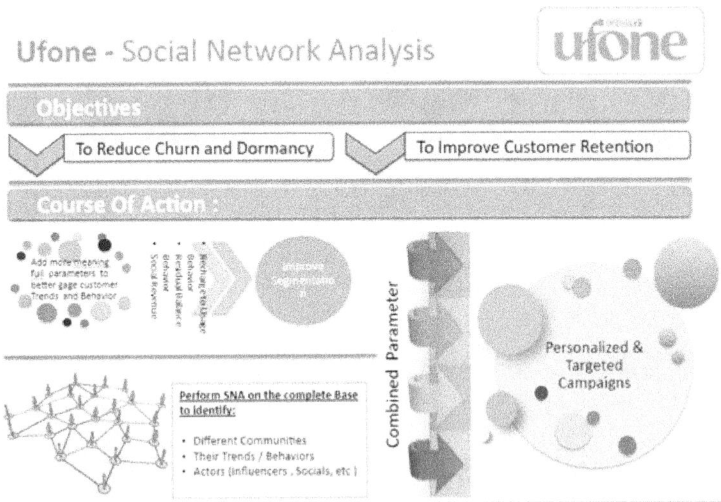

Figure 14. Identification of social communities

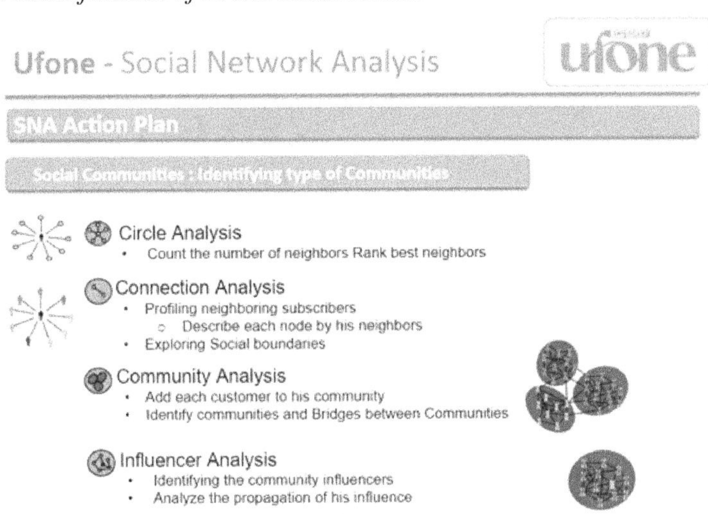

Figure 15. Customer scoring system implemented

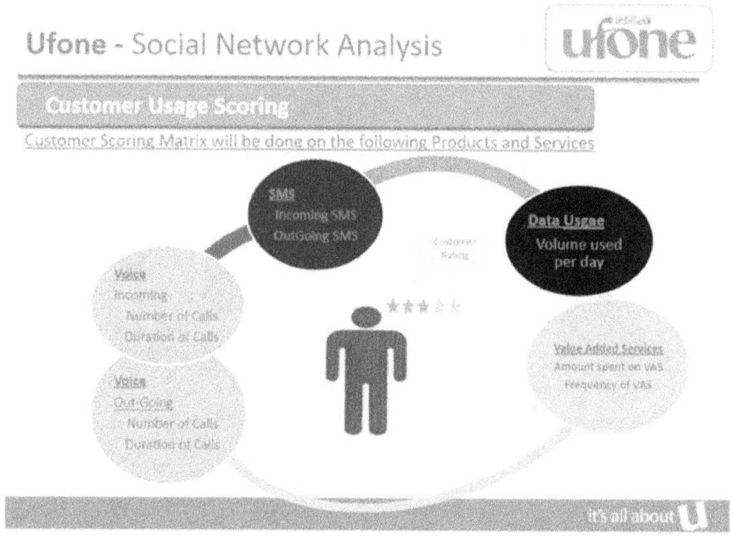

MIS systems also give the ability to companies to see holistic view of their users, their activities and generated revenue.

Figure 16. Churn management nationwide

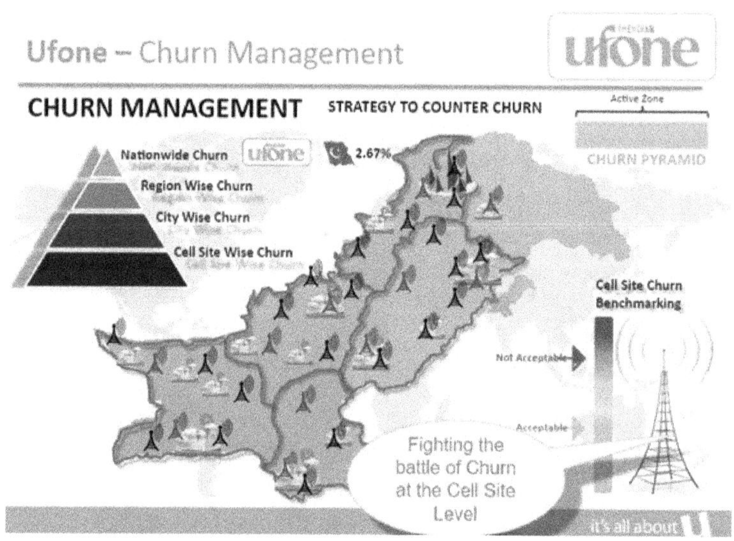

Figure 17. How the MIS system rates each user.

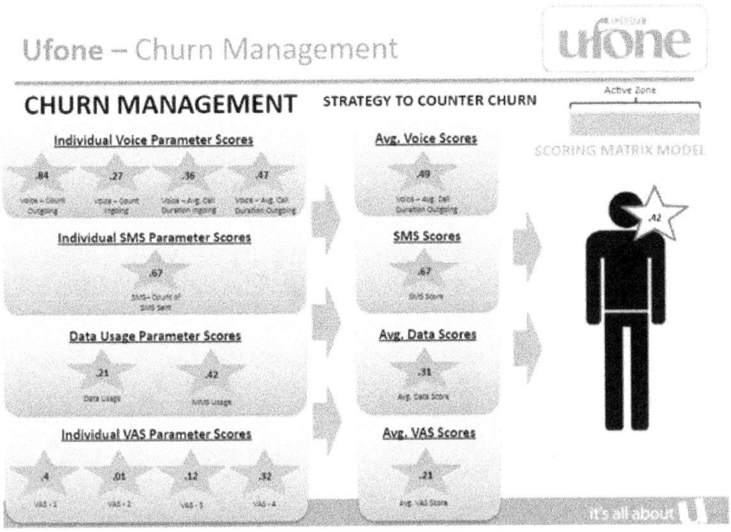

Figure 18. How each user is tracked day wise

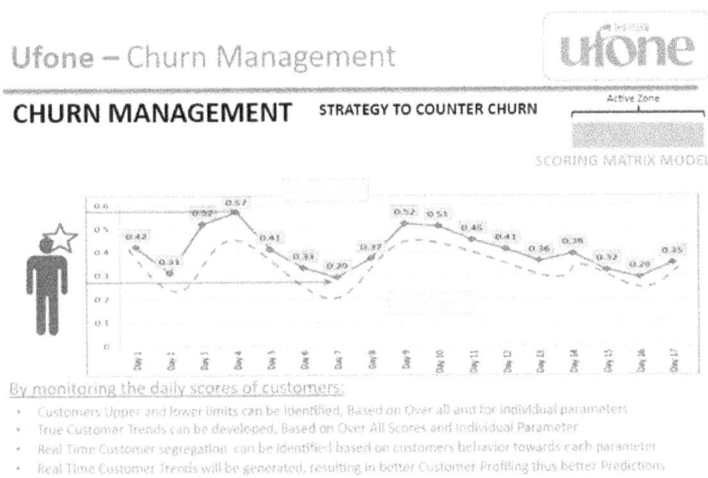

Figure 19. How it works at application level for profit maximization

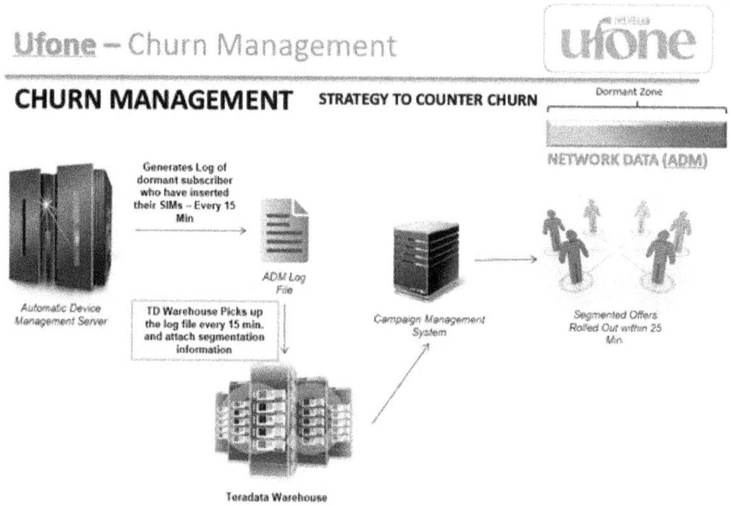

Figure 20. How MIS system works to reward the customers

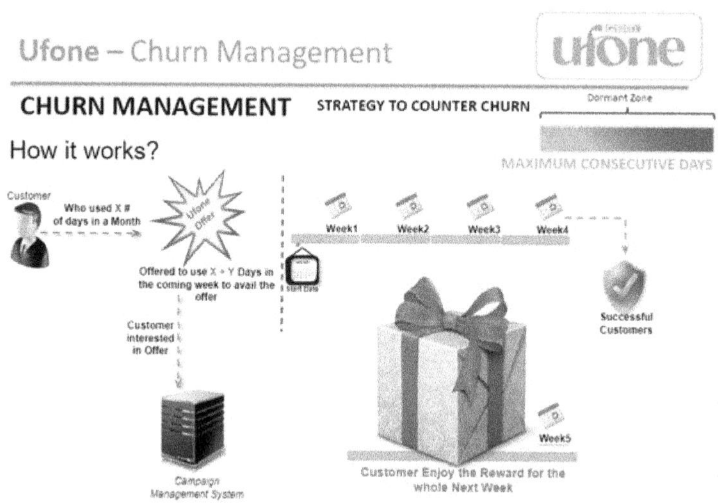

At Ufone to see the respondents response and acceptance level campaigns are designed. MIS helps the professional in this regard to understand each campaign influence.

Figure 21. Ufone earlier days campaigns based on MIS system

The results of these initiatives were remarkable, with the telecom operator experiencing a significant improvement in key customer satisfaction metrics such as Net Promoter Score (NPS) and Customer Satisfaction Index (CSI)(Haiying, 2022; M. S. Khan et al., 2022). Moreover, the implementation of MIS-driven customer retention strategies led to a notable reduction in churn rates, as customers felt valued and appreciated by the operator's proactive approach to addressing their needs.

15.6.2 MIS Systems and ZONG, Telenor- Cost Reduction

Another compelling case study of MIS implementation in the Pakistani telecom sector revolves around enhancing operational efficiency and reducing costs. A major telecom operator leveraged MIS to streamline internal processes, optimize resource allocation, and automate routine tasks across various departments. The author had the opportunity to work with ZONG where ZONG and Telenor has collaborated for network sharing. It was a win-win project for both Telenor and ZONG. Furthermore network sharing is a common practice in the telecom sector between the companies to reduce the cost and maximize the profitability of the company(Jian, 2022; Shin & Choi, 2022).

Infrastructure Level coordination and cooperation required lot of efforts to understand the system and each other's strengths and weaknesses(Zekun et al., 2022; C. Zhang et al., 2022). As network sharing at a certain areas means sharing of the subscribers, revenue share, or possible future growth prospects sharing. In a situation where one network is weak and it shares its network strength with other companies(Y. Chen, 2021; Xie & Luo, 2022). It opens opportunities for weak companies. Thus the MIS system must be strong. A strong customer level and area awareness must be on system provided analytics.

Figure 22. Understanding of competitors for possible collaboration based on MIS analytics

Figure 23. Case study of Telenor's collaboration with ZONG for cost reduction

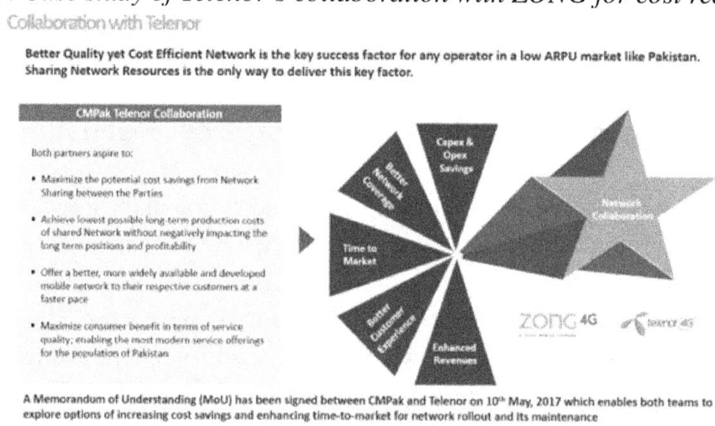

For possible collaboration with another operator companies review lot of possibilities. For instance for telecom companies customers are the main concern(Jin et al., 2021; Xuelei et al., 2021). Network related complaints data can be a key source for collaboration with another operator in an area.

Figure 24. Network related complaints ZONG reports

B.1.b: Network Related Complaints Analysis March and April'17

	Top Areas Identified	Contribution of Critical Areas in Overall Network Related Complaints
Central	Lahore Thokar Niaz Baig, Johar town (Grid C1009)	3.2%
Central	Bhai Peru, Chunian, Raiwand city (Grid C1008)	2.6%
Central	Lahore DHA, Ferozepur road, Gulberg (Grid C1007)	2.8%
Central	Lahore Sabzazar, Chungi Amar Suddu, green town, model town link road (Grid C1005)	2.1%
North	Adiala, Bahria Town, Scheme 3 (Grid N1002)	2.7%
North	F-10 surrounding & I-10 surrounding (Grid N1008)	2.6%
North	Westridge, Saddar, Raja Bazar (Grid N1004)	2.1%
North	Blue Area surrounding & Khanna Pul(Grid N1009)	2.2%
South	Gulshan-e-Iqbal, Gadap, Gulistan-e-Johar, Gulshan-e-Maymar (Grid S1009)	3.6%
South	Lyari, Defence, Clifton, Kemari (Grid S1003)	3.8%
South	North Nazimabad, FB Area(Grid S1010)	4.1%
South	PECHS, Bahadurabad (Grid S1005)	2.2%
These top 12 Areas contribute 33.9% (South 13.9%, Central 10.6% and North 9.5%) to overall network related complaints		

Through the implementation of an integrated MIS platform, the operator gained real-time visibility into key operational metrics such as network performance, workforce productivity, and inventory management. This enabled them to identify inefficiencies and bottlenecks in their operations and implement targeted interventions to address them(Cai et al., 2021; Jiang & Xie, 2021; X. Li, 2021).

For instance, the operator deployed predictive analytics models to forecast network traffic patterns and anticipate capacity requirements, allowing for proactive capacity planning and resource allocation (Thorpe et al., 2021; Zhigang, 2021). Additionally, they automated manual workflows such as billing reconciliation and inventory tracking, reducing the need for manual intervention and minimizing errors.

As a result of these initiatives, the telecom operator achieved significant cost savings and operational efficiencies. By streamlining processes and leveraging data-driven insights, they were able to reduce operational expenses, improve resource utilization, and enhance overall productivity(Z. Guo et al., 2021; Kuzovkova et al., 2021). Moreover, the implementation of MIS-enabled automation solutions resulted in faster response times, reduced cycle times, and improved service delivery, further enhancing customer satisfaction.

Case Study 3: Innovations Driving Revenue Growth

Lastly, MIS implementation has been instrumental in driving revenue growth and fostering innovation within the Pakistani telecom sector. A forward-thinking telecom operator embraced MIS to identify emerging market trends, capitalize on new revenue opportunities, and drive product innovation.

By analyzing market data, consumer behavior, and competitor strategies, the operator identified untapped market segments and unmet customer needs. Leveraging this insight, they launched innovative new products and services tailored to specific market niches, such as value-added content bundles, IoT solutions, and digital payment platforms.

Furthermore, the operator utilized MIS to track the performance of these new offerings, iterate on them based on customer feedback, and optimize pricing and packaging strategies to maximize revenue. Through continuous monitoring and analysis, they were able to identify successful revenue streams and scale them up, while discontinuing underperforming products.

Figure 25. Customer experience initiatives tracking

1- CUSTOMER EXPERIENCE MANAGEMENT

Sr.	ACTION ITEM	CURRENT STATUS	TIMELINE	RESPONSIBLE DEPARTMENT	DESCRIPTION
1	Auto-reimbursement solution for overcharging	In Progress	January 2018	Marketing	[illegible]
2	Reduction in reactivation time on auto suspension	In Progress	February 2018	Marketing/IT	[illegible]
3	Usage notification messages	In Progress	February 2018	Marketing/IT	[illegible]
4	Setting Bundles Usage Priority	In Progress	March 2018	Marketing/IT	[illegible]
5	Mutually exclusive products elimination	In Progress	2nd Quarter 2018	Marketing/IT	[illegible]
6	Promotional SMS governance Model	Not Started	2nd Quarter 2018	Marketing	[illegible]
7	VAS Visibility in ZONG System	Not started	2nd Quarter 2018	Marketing/IT	[illegible]
8	Customer Journey mapping	Not started	3rd Quarter 2018	Marketing/ S&D	[illegible]

The results of these initiatives were striking, with the telecom operator experiencing robust revenue growth and market share expansion. By leveraging MIS to drive innovation and agility, they were able to stay ahead of market trends, meet evolving customer demands, and capture new revenue opportunities in a rapidly changing landscape.

In conclusion, these case studies highlight the transformative impact of MIS implementation in the Pakistani telecom sector, spanning areas such as customer satisfaction and retention, operational efficiency and cost reduction, and revenue growth and innovation. By harnessing the power of data-driven insights and automation, telecom operators in Pakistan have been able to drive tangible business outcomes, differentiate themselves in the market, and stay ahead of the competition in an increasingly dynamic and competitive environment.

15.6.3 MIS Systems Brand Health Tracker as Insights Provider

The author's professional background includes roles at IPSOS and AC Nielsen as Assistant Manager of Customer Experience and Market Research, where they gained valuable experience in analyzing consumer behavior and market trends. This expertise informs their interpretation of the Brand Health Tracker, a comprehensive tool offering insights into the performance of companies within the telecom sector. As the author delves into the Brand Health Tracker report, they draw upon their firsthand experience in market research to provide a nuanced understanding of the data and its implications for the industry(Doutcheva, 2021; Han et al., 2021).

The Brand Health Tracker serves as a vital resource for assessing the competitive landscape of the telecom sector, offering a detailed analysis of various metrics such as switching behavior, brand usage duration, and attitudinal equity. Through their role as Assistant Manager of Customer Experience and Market Research, the author is well-equipped to navigate the complexities of this data and distill key insights that can inform strategic decision-making for companies operating in the sector(Junru et al., 2021; Zeng & Yanchao, 2021).

Within the report, the author highlights significant findings, including the prevalence of non-switchers among telecom customers and the factors driving brand loyalty and churn. They emphasize the importance of understanding customer attitudes and behaviors in shaping marketing strategies and improving brand perception. Leveraging their experience at IPSOS and AC Nielsen, the author provides actionable recommendations for companies to address areas of weakness and capitalize on opportunities for growth.

Overall, the Brand Health Tracker report serves as a valuable tool for stakeholders within the telecom sector, providing a comprehensive overview of market dynamics and consumer sentiment. The author's background in market research enhances their ability to extract meaningful insights from the data, offering valuable perspectives that can inform strategic initiatives and drive business success in a highly competitive industry landscape.

Figure 26. Brand health tracker results

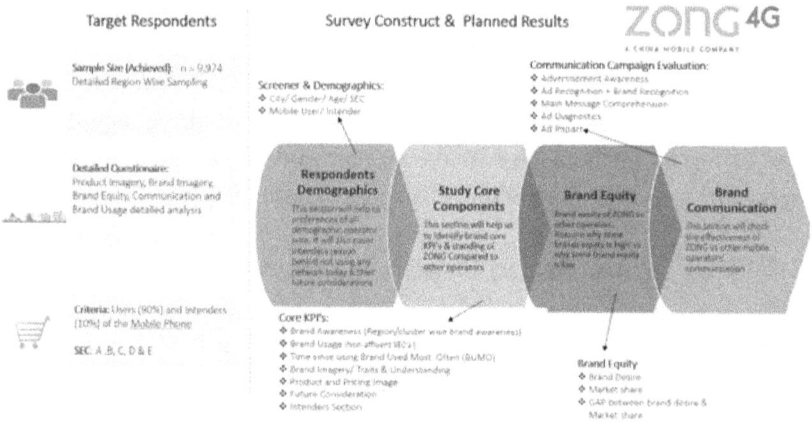

Figure 27. Market effects analysis for brand related decisions in companies

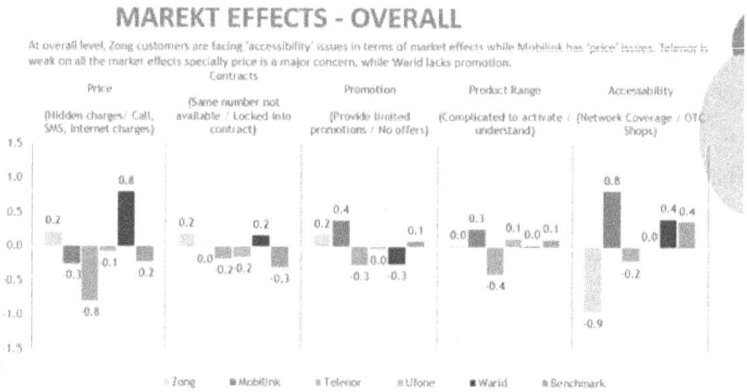

15.7 CHAPTER CONCLUSION

In Pakistan, the telecommunications sector has undergone a major transition, moving away from a monopolistic system controlled by PTCL to a dynamic and competitive market driven by liberalization and privatisation initiatives. Mobile telephony, supported by advancements in network technology such as 3G, 4G, and the forthcoming 5G, has become the essential component of the industry. Prominent rivals such as Jazz, Telenor Pakistan, Zong, and Ufone are vigorously competing to establish market supremacy by employing inventive strategies and expansion techniques.

Management Information Systems (MIS) play a vital role in the telecom business by enhancing operational efficiency, enabling strategic decision-making, and facilitating effective customer relationship management. Management Information Systems (MIS) facilitates the smooth integration of data from several sources, enabling real-time monitoring and management of operations, improving network performance, and identifying possible opportunities for growth. Furthermore, Management Information Systems (MIS) supports strategic decision-making by providing prompt information on market trends, competitive dynamics, and customer preferences.

Revenue-generating strategies in the telecommunications industry encompass pricing models, value-added services, bundled offerings, and marketing initiatives. Telecom operators employ subscription-based plans, usage-based pricing, and tiered pricing systems to cater to the diverse needs of consumers and optimise revenue. Included value-added services enhance client happiness and lead to a rise in revenue. Simultaneously, marketing endeavours enhance consciousness and stimulate demand.

Profit maximisation strategies involve optimizing expenses, maximizing income through data analytics, and investing in infrastructure and technology. Operators employ network optimization, resource consolidation, and outsourcing as cost-saving measures. Additionally, they employ data analytics to identify opportunities for earning revenue and mitigate any potential loss of income. Investments in infrastructure and technology, such as the implementation of 5G and automation solutions, improve operational efficiency and support revenue growth.

Case studies have provided evidence of the substantial benefits of deploying Management Information Systems (MIS) in Pakistan's telecommunications industry. These studies emphasise the improvements in customer happiness, operational efficiency, and revenue growth that have been accomplished using creative methods. Telecommunication operators have achieved tangible business outcomes and enhanced their competitive edge via the utilisation of data-driven analysis and automation. This has resulted in continuous growth in an ever-evolving market landscape.

In summary, the chapter emphasises the vital significance of Management Information Systems (MIS) in generating revenue and optimising profitability in the telecoms industry of Pakistan. Management Information Systems (MIS) are crucial for enhancing operational efficiency, enabling strategic decision-making, and fostering innovation. Consequently, Management Information Systems (MIS) play a crucial role in shaping the future trajectory of the sector and promoting long-term growth and competitiveness.

REFERENCES

Afridi, S. A., Gul, S., Haider, M., & Batool, S. (2018). Mediating effect of customers' trust between the association of corporate social responsibility and customers' loyalty: An empirical investigation from telecom sector. *Pakistan Journal of Commerce and Social Science*, *12*(1).

Ahmad, I., Kim, S. K., Lee, J., & Rho, J. J. (2020). Analytic hierarchy process model for the selection of optimal internet access technologies in rural Pakistan. *International Journal of the Analytic Hierarchy Process*, *12*(2). Advance online publication. DOI: 10.13033/ijahp.v12i2.712

Al Karim, R., Rabiul, M. K., Ahamed, T., Karim, D. N., & Mehzabeen, M. (2024). Integrating Green Entrepreneurial Orientation, Green Information Systems, and Management Support with Green Supply Chain Management to Foster Firms' Environmental Performance. *Sustainability (Basel)*, *16*(12), 4921. DOI: 10.3390/su16124921

Ali Shah, A., Memon, H., Noor, A., Sidra, S., Bhutto, A., & Khan, A. (2020). The Impact of Sponsorship on Brand Equity of Cellular Networks in Hyderabad Pakistan. *Asian Journal of Economics, Business and Accounting*. DOI: 10.9734/ajeba/2019/v13i330171

Aqeel, Z., Hanif, M. I., & Malik, M. S. (2017). Impact of co-branding and brand personality on brand equity: A study of telecom sector in Pakistan. *The Journal of Business and Retail Management Research*, *12*(1). Advance online publication. DOI: 10.24052/JBRMR/V12IS01/IOCABPOBEASOTSIP

Basu, D., Jain, A., Ghosh, U., & Datta, R. (2021). QoS-aware controller and hypervisor placement in vSDN-enabled 5G networks for time-critical applications. In *IEEE INFOCOM 2021 - IEEE Conference on Computer Communications Workshops, INFOCOM WKSHPS 2021* (Issue IEEE Conference on Computer Communications Workshops (IEEE INFOCOM)). DOI: 10.1109/INFOCOMWKSHPS51825.2021.9484544

Bensikaddour, E. H., & Boutte, A. (2022). Proposal of Battery Management Strategy for Small Geostationary Satellite Power System Development. *Revue Roumaine Des Sciences Techniques Serie Electrotechnique et Energetique*, *67*(2), 151–156.

Blouch, R., Bakhsh, K., Shakeel, W., Khan, M. M., & Yasmeen, A. (2021). Linking firms' strategies with firm performance: Mediating role of network value in telecom industry. *International Journal of Productivity and Performance Management*. Advance online publication. DOI: 10.1108/IJPPM-02-2020-0047

Butt, R. S., Wen, X., Hussain, R. Y., & Pervaiz, S. (2021). Motivational Factors of Employees Job Satisfaction and Mediated Model of Happiness at Work: Evidence from the Telecom Sector of Pakistan. *International Journal of Management, Accounting & Economics, 8*(4).

Cai, H., Ouyang, M., Wang, H., & Ma, Z. (2021). Civil Engineering Process File Information Management System. In Z. Li & F. Cen (Eds.), *INTERNATIONAL CONFERENCE ON SMART TRANSPORTATION AND CITY ENGINEERING 2021* (Vol. 12050, Issue International Conference on Smart Transportation and City Engineering CL-Chongqing,. DOI: 10.1117/12.2613749

Chatzimichailidou, M., Whitcher, T., & Suzic, N. (2024). Complementarity and Compatibility of Systems Integration and Building Information Management. *IEEE Systems Journal, 18*(2), 1198–1207. DOI: 10.1109/JSYST.2024.3387064

Chen, L., Po-An Hsieh, J. J., Rai, A., & Xu, S. X. (2021). How does employee infusion use of crm systems drive customer satisfaction? Mechanism differences between face-to-face and virtual channels. *Management Information Systems Quarterly, 45*(2), 719–754. Advance online publication. DOI: 10.25300/MISQ/2021/13265

Chen, Y. (2021). Optimization of Clinical Nursing Management System Based on Data Mining (Retracted Article). *Complexity, 2021*. Advance online publication. DOI: 10.1155/2021/2110154

Chenyang, X., Piao, W., Zilun, L., Qing, L., & Yadong, K. (2024). Research on Science and Technology Management Information Security Guarantee System. *Journal of Information Security Research, 10*(7), 675–681.

Dalloul, M. H. M., binti Ibrahim, Z., & Urus, S. T. (2023). Financial Crises Management in Light of Accounting Information Systems Success: Investigating Direct and Indirect Influences. *Sustainability (Basel), 15*(10), 8131. Advance online publication. DOI: 10.3390/su15108131

Doutcheva, N. Z.-. (2021). *Information Management of Family Caregivers of Children with Medical Complexity.*

Farooq, M., & Raju, V. (2019a). Impact of Over-the-Top (OTT) Services on the Telecom Companies in the Era of Transformative Marketing. *Global Journal of Flexible Systems Managment, 20*(2), 177–188. DOI: 10.1007/s40171-019-00209-6

Farooq, M., & Raju, V. (2019b). Impact of Over-the-Top (OTT) Services on the Telecom Companies in the Era of Transformative Marketing. *Global Journal of Flexible Systems Management*. DOI: 10.1007/s40171-019-00209-6

Farooq, M., & Raju, V. (2019c). Impact of Over-the-Top (OTT) Services on the Telecom Companies in the Era of Transformative Marketing. *Global Journal of Flexible Systems Managment, 20*(2), 177–188. Advance online publication. DOI: 10.1007/s40171-019-00209-6

Farooq, M., Ramzan, M., & Yen, Y. Y. (2024a). AI in Customer Service, HR, and Administration. In *Transformative Impacts of AI in Management* (pp. 45–70). IGI Global. DOI: 10.4018/979-8-3693-4322-7.ch002

Farooq, M., Ramzan, M., & Yen, Y. Y. (2024b). Artificial Intelligence and Customer Experiences. In *Transformative Impacts of AI in Management* (pp. 95–114). IGI Global., DOI: 10.4018/979-8-3693-4322-7.ch004

Farooq, M., Ramzan, M., & Yen, Y. Y. (2024c). Artificial Intelligence in Administration Sciences. In *Transformative Impacts of AI in Management* (pp. 115–156). IGI Global., DOI: 10.4018/979-8-3693-4322-7.ch005

Farooq, M., Ramzan, M., & Yen, Y. Y. (2024d). Artificial Intelligence in Business and Law. In *Transformative Impacts of AI in Management* (pp. 71–94). IGI Global., DOI: 10.4018/979-8-3693-4322-7.ch003

Farooq, M., Ramzan, M., & Yen, Y. Y. (2024e). Exploring the Impact of Artificial Intelligence on Brand Management. In *Transformative Impacts of AI in Management* (pp. 157–188). IGI Global., DOI: 10.4018/979-8-3693-4322-7.ch006

Farooq, M., Ramzan, M., & Yen, Y. Y. (2024f). Transformative Impact of AI in Education Management. In *Transformative Impacts of AI in Management* (pp. 189–216). IGI Global., DOI: 10.4018/979-8-3693-4322-7.ch007

Farooq, M., Saeed, M., Ali, W., & Javid, R. (2020). Online Buying and Customer Satisfaction in the Era of Transformative Marketing. *City University Research Journal, 10*(2), 274–288.

Fu, S., & Xu, B. (2022). Facial Expression Recognition and Beauty Health Management Based on Image Feature Analysis. *Mobile Information Systems, 2022*, 1–11. Advance online publication. DOI: 10.1155/2022/4336840

Godoy, M. P., Rusu, C., Hatibovic, F., Granollers, T., & Ugalde, J. (2023). Addressing Information Consumer Experience through a User-Centered Information Management System in a Chilean University. *Sustainability (Basel), 15*(22), 15998. Advance online publication. DOI: 10.3390/su152215998

Guo, B., & Shuai, L. (2022). Research on Object-oriented Data Model Technology in Tourism Information Management. In S. F. ElZoghdy & M. K. Mohiddin (Eds.), *THIRD INTERNATIONAL CONFERENCE ON ELECTRONICS AND COMMUNICATION; NETWORK AND COMPUTER TECHNOLOGY (ECNCT 2021)*. DOI: 10.1117/12.2629214

Guo, Z., Zhang, X., Gao, Y., Hao, W., Zhang, S., & Du, X. (2021). Design of Information Management System for Large Modular Manned Spacecraft. In *Proceedings of the 16th IEEE Conference on Industrial Electronics and Applications, ICIEA 2021* (Issues 16th IEEE Conference on Industrial Electronics and Applications (ICIEA) CL-Chengdupp. 655–659). DOI: 10.1109/ICIEA51954.2021.9516303

Gupta, B. B., & Panigrahi, P. K. (2023). Analysis of the Role of Global Information Management in Advanced Decision Support Systems (DSS) for Sustainable Development. *Journal of Global Information Management*, *31*(1), 1–13. Advance online publication. DOI: 10.4018/JGIM.320185

Haiying, J. (2022). Conceptual model construction of building information management system based on BIM architecture. *Soft Computing*, *26*(16), 7925–7931. DOI: 10.1007/s00500-022-06851-0

Han, Y., Lei, Y., Bao, Z., & Zhou, Q. (2021). Research and Implementation of Mobile Internet Management Optimization and Intelligent Information System Based on Smart Decision. *Computational Intelligence and Neuroscience*, *2021*(1), 5144568. Advance online publication. DOI: 10.1155/2021/5144568 PMID: 34925490

Huang, L. (2022). Research and Application of Business Law Information Management System Based on Big Data. *Journal of Sensors*, *2022*, 1–12. Advance online publication. DOI: 10.1155/2022/5885451

Huang, Z. (2022). Integrated Management System of Instrument and Equipment in University Financial Media Laboratory Based on Hybrid Cloud Architecture. In S. Liu & X. Ma (Eds.), *ADVANCED HYBRID INFORMATION PROCESSING, PT I* (Vol. 416, Issues 5th EAI International Conference on Advanced Hybrid Information Processing (ADHIP) pp. 587–600). DOI: 10.1007/978-3-030-94551-0_46

Hussain, A., Khan, M. A., Hussain, J., & Khan, M. H. (2020). Nexus of Transformational Leadership and Employees' Job Performance in Telecom Sector Pakistan. *Journal of Business and Social Review in Emerging Economies*, *6*(2), 799–806. Advance online publication. DOI: 10.26710/jbsee.v6i2.1241

Idrees, R. N., Waqas, M., Naqvi, I. H., Imran, A., & Anjum, Z.-U.-Z. (2019). Strategic Human Resource Management Function and HR Staffing: A Case Study of Telecom Sector. *Paradigms: A Research Journal of Commerce, Economics, and Social Sciences, 12*(2).

Iliescu, D. (2022). Some Considerations on Conceptual Modeling for a Laboratory Information Management System. In D. Popescu, L. Barbulescu, E. Popescu, M. Roman, & D. Sendrescu (Eds.), *2022 23RD INTERNATIONAL CARPATHIAN CONTROL CONFERENCE (ICCC)* (Issues 23rd International Carpathian Control Conference (ICCC) CL-Sinaia, pp. 19–24). DOI: 10.1109/ICCC54292.2022.9805898

Imran Hanif, M., & Inayat, A. (2017). Does Compensation Impact on Employee Engagement? Evidence from Telecom Sector of Pakistan. *International Journal of Economics & Management Sciences*, *06*(03). Advance online publication. DOI: 10.4172/2162-6359.1000423

Iqbal, S., & Siddiqui, D. A. (2019). The Impact of Deceptive Advertising on Customer Loyalty: A case of Telecommunication Industry in Karachi, Pakistan. *International Journal of Industrial Marketing*, *4*(1), 39. Advance online publication. DOI: 10.5296/ijim.v4i1.14607

Jamal, A. H., & Ali, H. G. (2017). Mediating role of psychological empowerment between leadership empowerment behavior and job satisfaction : A study of telecom sector of Pakistan. *Journal of Research Society of Pakistan*, *54*(1).

Jian, L. (2022). Design of enterprise human resources decision support system based on data mining. *Soft Computing*, *26*(20), 10571–10580. DOI: 10.1007/s00500-021-06659-4

Jiang, W., & Xie, Z. (2021). The Information Management System of China Forest Products International Trade Based on Internet Platform. In *Proceedings - 2021 6th International Conference on Smart Grid and Electrical Automation, ICSGEA 2021* (Issues 6th International Conference on Smart Grid and Electrical Automation (ICSGEA) CL-Kunming, pp. 343–346). DOI: 10.1109/ICSGEA53208.2021.00084

Jin, Y., Zhao, J., Yu, W., Li, H., Liu, B., Sun, Y., Zheng, Y., He, C., Duan, S., & IOP. (2021). Research on Image Data Management System of Power Transmission Project Based on Geographic Information. In *2020 ASIA CONFERENCE ON GEOLOGICAL RESEARCH AND ENVIRONMENTAL TECHNOLOGY* (Vol. 632, Issue Asia Conference on Geological Research and Environmental Technology (GRET). DOI: 10.1088/1755-1315/632/4/042038

Junru, Z., Bo, Y., Yanfeng, G., Jian, X., & Dingding, L. (2021). Research Status and Prospects of Intelligent Monitoring Technology and Information Management System for Tunnel Engineering. *Chinese Journal of Underground Space and Engineering, 17*(2), 567–579.

Kamenska, L., Moiseenko, V., Shendryk, V., Kamenskyi, S., & Shendryk, S. (2022). Implementation of Distributed Information Systems in Solving Problems of Energy Consumption Monitoring. In I. Karabegovic, A. Kovacevic, & S. Mandzuka (Eds.), *NEW TECHNOLOGIES, DEVELOPMENT AND APPLICATION V* (Vol. 472, Issue International Conference on New Technologies, Development and Application CL-Acad Sci & Arts Bosnia & Herzegovina, Sarajevo, pp. 758–767). DOI: 10.1007/978-3-031-05230-9_90

Keshavarz, H., Mahdzir, A. M., Talebian, H., Jalaliyoon, N., & Ohshima, N. (2021). The value of big data analytics pillars in telecommunication industry. *Sustainability (Basel), 13*(13), 7160. Advance online publication. DOI: 10.3390/su13137160

Khan, A. A., Abbasi, S. O. B. H., Waseem, R. M., Ayaz, M., & Ijaz, M. (2016). *Impact of Training and Development of Employees on Employee Performance through Job Satisfaction: A Study of Telecom Sector of Pakistan*. Business Management and Strategy., DOI: 10.5296/bms.v7i1.9024

Khan, M. S., Khan, M., Bughio, M., Talpur, B. D., Kim, I. S., & Seo, J. (2022). An Integrated HBIM Framework for the Management of Heritage Buildings. *Buildings (Basel, Switzerland), 12*(7), 964. Advance online publication. DOI: 10.3390/buildings12070964

Khan, Y. (2021). COMPARATIVE ANALYSIS OF PREDICTION TECHNIQUES ON THE BASIS OF TELECOM CUSTOMER CHURN. *JOURNAL OF MECHANICS OF CONTINUA AND MATHEMATICAL SCIENCES, 16*(9). Advance online publication. DOI: 10.26782/jmcms.2021.09.00002

Khan, Y., Shafiq, S., Naeem, A., Hussain, S., Ahmed, S., & Safwan, N. (2019). Customers churn prediction using Artificial Neural Networks (ANN) in telecom industry. *International Journal of Advanced Computer Science and Applications, 10*(9). Advance online publication. DOI: 10.14569/IJACSA.2019.0100918

Khuntia, J., Mayya, R., Mithas, S., & Agarwal, R. (2021). Managing Cellphone Services for Customer Satisfaction: Evidence from the Base-of-the-Pyramid Markets. *Production and Operations Management, 30*(2), 438–450. DOI: 10.1111/poms.13276

Kumar, K., Rai, S., & Dugar, A. (2019). Impact of Service Quality on Customer Satisfaction and Loyalty in the Sector of Telecom Service Provider in Delhi-NCR. [IJITEE]. *International Journal of Innovative Technology and Exploring Engineering*, *8*(8).

Kuzovkova, T. A., Saliutina, T. Y., & Sharavova, O. I. (2021). The impact of digital platforms on the business management information system. In *2021 Systems of Signal Synchronization, Generating and Processing in Telecommunications, SYNCHROINFO 2021 - Conference Proceedings*. DOI: 10.1109/SYNCHROINFO51390.2021.9488330

Lee, S. (2022). A Study on the Improvement Model of Administrative Information Dataset Records Management Environment: Focused on the Dataset of Picture Archiving and Communication System. *Journal of Korean Society of Archives and Records Management*, *22*(2), 51–73. DOI: 10.14404/JKSARM.2022.22.2.051

León-Romero, L. P., Aguilar-Fernández, M., Luque-Sendra, A., Zamora-Polo, F., & Francisco-Márquez, M. (2024). Characterization of the information system integrated to the construction project management systems. *Heliyon*, *10*(11), e31886. Advance online publication. DOI: 10.1016/j.heliyon.2024.e31886 PMID: 38841493

Li, X. (2021). Design and Implementation of Project Cost Management Information System Based on Web. In *Proceedings - 2021 6th International Conference on Smart Grid and Electrical Automation, ICSGEA 2021* (Issues 6th International Conference on Smart Grid and Electrical Automation (ICSGEA) CL-Kunming, pp. 288–292). DOI: 10.1109/ICSGEA53208.2021.00070

Li, X., Wang, L., & Fang, L. (2022). Optimal Design of an Information Management System for Government: A Bridge between Government and Citizens. *Mathematical Problems in Engineering*, *2022*, 1–10. Advance online publication. DOI: 10.1155/2022/3127858

Lian, J. (2022). Optimization of Music Teaching Management System for College Students Based on Similarity Distribution Method (Retracted Article). *Mathematical Problems in Engineering*, *2022*, 1–11. Advance online publication. DOI: 10.1155/2022/6444554

Liang, C., & Wang, C. (2022). Coding structure of highway engineering information model. In *Shenzhen Daxue Xuebao (Ligong Ban)/Journal of Shenzhen University Science and Engineering* (Vol. 39, Issue 4, pp. 424–431). DOI: 10.3724/SP.J.1249.2022.04424

Liu, R., & Wang, L. (2022). Information Resource Sharing Based on University Dance Big Data Management and Utilization System Design. *Mathematical Problems in Engineering, 2022*, 1–9. Advance online publication. DOI: 10.1155/2022/4325984

Liu, W., & Wei, S. (2022). Design and Management of Comprehensive Art Student Information Database from the Perspective of Internet plus Education (Retracted Article). *Security and Communication Networks, 2022*, 1–9. Advance online publication. DOI: 10.1155/2022/6494404

Liu, Y. (2022). Design of Financial Information Management System and IoT Application Based on Fuzzy Comprehensive Evaluation (Retracted Article). *Wireless Communications and Mobile Computing, 2022*, 1–11. Advance online publication. DOI: 10.1155/2022/2483306

Majid, M. B., & Mahmud, M. S. Bin. (2019). Knowledge Management and its Impact on Organizational Performance: Evidence from Pakistan. *Annals of Contemporary Developments in Management & HR, 1*(1). DOI: 10.33166/ACDMHR.2019.01.002

Mishra, B., Ghosh, S., & Kanjilal, K. (2020). Evaluation of import substitution strategy in Indian telecom sector: Empirical evidence of non-linear dynamics. *Telecommunications Policy, 44*(7), 101998. Advance online publication. DOI: 10.1016/j.telpol.2020.101998

Na, S.-H., & Shon, T.-S. (2022). A Study on the Development of Information Security Management System Using RMF. *Journal of Digital Contents Society, 23*(5), 977–983. DOI: 10.9728/dcs.2022.23.5.977

Naz, S., & Sandhu, M. A. (2020). Role of Perception of Politics in enhancing Organizational Dissent: Case of Pakistan Telecom Sector. *Journal of Business and Social Review in Emerging Economies, 6*(2), 807–819. Advance online publication. DOI: 10.26710/jbsee.v6i2.1243

Odusami, M., Abayomi-Alli, O., Misra, S., Abayomi-Alli, A., & Sharma, M. M. (2021). A Hybrid Machine Learning Model for Predicting Customer Churn in the Telecommunication Industry. *Advances in Intelligent Systems and Computing, 1372 AISC*. DOI: 10.1007/978-3-030-73603-3_43

Okada, K., Sugimoto, K., Wada, S., Konishi, S., Manabe, S., Matsumura, Y., & Takeda, T. (2024). Development of the Clinical Specimen Information Management System for Multicenter Clinical Studies. In J. Bichel-Findlay, P. Otero, P. Scott, & E. Huesing (Eds.), *MEDINFO 2023 - THE FUTURE IS ACCESSIBLE* (Vol. 310, Issues 19th World Congress on Medical and Health Informatics (MEDINFO) CL-Sydney, pp. 119–123). DOI: 10.3233/SHTI230939

Oughton, E. J., Comini, N., Foster, V., & Hall, J. W. (2022). Policy choices can help keep 4G and 5G universal broadband affordable. *Technological Forecasting and Social Change*, *176*, 121409. Advance online publication. DOI: 10.1016/j.techfore.2021.121409

Pereira, J., Varajao, J., & Takagi, N. (2022). Evaluation of Information Systems Project Success - Insights from Practitioners. *Information Systems Management*, *39*(2), 138–155. DOI: 10.1080/10580530.2021.1887982

Petersen, R., & Daramola, O. (2020). Towards Explainable Direct Marketing in the Telecom Industry Through Hybrid Machine Learning. In O. Gervasi, B. Murgante, S. Misra, C. Garau, I. Blecic, D. Taniar, B. O. Apduhan, A. Rocha, E. Tarantino, C. M. Torre, & Y. Karaca (Eds.), *Lecture Notes in Computer Science (including subseries Lecture Notes in Artificial Intelligence and Lecture Notes in Bioinformatics): Vol. 12254 LNCS* (Issue 20th International Conference on Computational Science and Its Applications (ICCSA), pp. 471–486). DOI: 10.1007/978-3-030-58817-5_35

Haseeb Riaz, Shoaib Akhtar, & Ramsha Aslam. (2018). Total Rewards and Employee Performance : Investigating the Mediating Role of Employee Motivation in Telecom Sector. *Pakistan Administrative Review, 2*(3).

Riaz, H., Akhtar, S., & Aslam, R. (2018). Total Rewards and Employee Performance : Investigating the Mediating Role of Employee Motivation in Telecom Sector. *Pakistan Administrative Review, 2*(3).

Runge, M., Reiche, L. T., Niemann, K. H., & Fay, A. (2022). Universal energy information model for industrial communication. In *IEEE International Conference on Emerging Technologies and Factory Automation, ETFA* (Vols. 2022-Septe, Issue IEEE 27th International Conference on Emerging Technologies and Factory Automation (ETFA) CL-Stuttgart, GERMANY PU-IEEE PI-NEW YORK PA-345 E 47TH ST, NEW YORK, NY 10017 USA). DOI: 10.1109/ETFA52439.2022.9921557

Sharif, M. N., Raza, H., Faizan, M., & Hassan, N. U. (2019). Role of Customer's Orientation and Professional Skill of a Service Provider in the Telecom Sector of Pakistan. *International Journal of Academic Research in Business & Social Sciences*, *9*(10). Advance online publication. DOI: 10.6007/IJARBSS/v9-i10/6815

Shi, Y., Ying, J., Shi, D., & Yan, J. (2022). Service-Oriented Modeling for Blockchain-Enabled Supply Chain Quality Information Systems. *Security and Communication Networks*, *2022*, 1–16. Advance online publication. DOI: 10.1155/2022/1987933

Shin, J., & Choi, B. (2022). Design and Implementation of Quality Information Management System for Modular Construction Factory. *Buildings (Basel, Switzerland)*, *12*(5), 654. Advance online publication. DOI: 10.3390/buildings12050654

Song, Q. (2022). Design and Application of Land Resource Management System Based on Internet of Things. *Wireless Communications and Mobile Computing, 2022*, 1–14. Advance online publication. DOI: 10.1155/2022/2726673

Tariq, B., & Mat, N. K. N. (2018). Understanding the moderating role of government regulations in telecom sector of Pakistan. *Journal of Telecommunication, Electronic and Computer Engineering, 10*, 1–11.

Thorpe, D., Aghili, N., van Neuren, C., & IEEE. (2021). Managing Sustainable Asset Networks using Advanced Information Systems. In *2021 INTERNATIONAL CONFERENCE ON MAINTENANCE AND INTELLIGENT ASSET MANAGEMENT (ICMIAM)* (Issue International Conference on Maintenance and Intelligent Asset Management (ICMIAM) CL-Ballarat. DOI: 10.1109/ICMIAM54662.2021.9715219

Tian, J., Liu, Y., Yang, M., Sun, R., & Zheng, X. (2022). Blockchain Information Sharing Mechanism Based on Embedded System in Project Management System (Retracted Article). *Computational Intelligence and Neuroscience, 2022*, 1–13. Advance online publication. DOI: 10.1155/2022/1835626 PMID: 35965759

Ul Haq, I., Ali, S. M., & Nawaz, M. T. (2019). An Analysis of the Critical Success Factors in ICT Sector of Pakistan. *5th International Conference on Information Management, ICIM 2019*, 45–53. DOI: 10.1109/INFOMAN.2019.8714666

Ullah, I., Mirza, B., Kashif, A. R., & Abbas, F. (2019). Examination of knowledge management and market orientation, innovation and organizational performance: Insights from telecom sector of Pakistan. *Knowledge Management and E-Learning, 11*(4), 522–551. DOI: 10.34105/j.kmel.2019.11.027

Waheed, A., Xiaoming, M., Waheed, S., & Ahmad, N. (2019). The role of social networking sites in effective e-recruitmen; A study of telecom sector in context of Pakistan. *KSII Transactions on Internet and Information Systems, 13*(8), 3842–3861. DOI: 10.3837/tiis.2019.08.002

Wang, G., Li, D., Ge, J., & Wang, T. (2022). Medical informatization of management system for admission office under convolutional neural network. *Expert Systems: International Journal of Knowledge Engineering and Neural Networks, 39*(3), e12780. Advance online publication. DOI: 10.1111/exsy.12780

Wang, Y. (2022). Optimization of the Music Teaching Management System Based on Emotion Recognition. *Computational Intelligence and Neuroscience, 2022*, 1–9. Advance online publication. DOI: 10.1155/2022/4568041 PMID: 35586091

Wang, Y., Xue, W., & Zhang, A. (2023). Application of Big Data Technology in Enterprise Information Security Management and Risk Assessment. *Journal of Global Information Management*, *31*(3), 1–16. Advance online publication. DOI: 10.4018/JGIM.324465

Watto, W. A., Monium, A., Ali, Q., & Ijaz, A. (2020). The Impact Of Ethical Context On Employees In-Role Performance And Citizenship Behavior In Telecom Sector Of Pakistan: The Mediating Role Of Perceived Organizational Support. *International Journal of Environmental, Sustainability, and Social Science*, *1*(1), 25–35. Advance online publication. DOI: 10.38142/ijesss.v1i1.13

Xiaobao, L., Shumin, L., & Kunyan, L. (2022). Establishment and application of hospital clinical trial management information system for improving clinical trial quality. *Chinese Journal of New Drugs and Clinical Remedies*, *41*(3), 146–150.

Xie, J., Jablonski, M., Smith, J., & Navedo, A. (2024). A Graphical Interface to Support Low-Flow Volatile Anesthesia: Implications for Patient Safety, Teaching, and Design of Anesthesia Information Management Systems. *Journal of Medical Systems*, *48*(1), 36. Advance online publication. DOI: 10.1007/s10916-024-02055-1 PMID: 38532235

Xie, J., & Luo, W. (2022). General Surgery Clinical Information Management System Based on Intelligent Data Management (Retracted Article). *Computational Intelligence and Neuroscience*, *2022*, 1–11. Advance online publication. DOI: 10.1155/2022/8601164 PMID: 35958777

Xuelei, L., Enjing, L., Yuetian, L., Kai, H., Yongyi, Z., & Kexin, L. (2021). Research on Function Optimization of University Laboratory Security Access System Information System Based on Environmental Monitoring Laboratory. In *Environmental Monitoring in China* (Vol. 37, Issue 1, pp. 23–28).

Yen, Y. Y., Wen, L. J., Ramasamy, S., & Farooq, M. (2023). Sustainable petrol subsidy program in Malaysia. *Asian Development Policy Review*, *12*(1), 1–9. DOI: 10.55493/5008.v12i1.4948

Younas, W., & Kalimuthu, K. R. (2021). Telecom microfinance banking versus commercial banking: A battle in the financial services sector. *Journal of Financial Services Marketing*, *26*(2), 67–80. DOI: 10.1057/s41264-020-00085-7

Zakaria, M., & Zakaria, M. (2008). Telecom Branding in Pakistan: Network Coverage or Value Added Services. *Academic Journal of Research in Economics and Managment, 11543.*

Zekun, W., Yakun, Z., Xuteng, Z., Wenzhe, T., & Maoshan, Q. (2022). Information management of water conservancy project partnering. *Qinghua Daxue Xuebao. Ziran Kexue Ban, 62*(8), 1351–1356.

Zeng, L., & Yanchao, W. (2021). The internet of things integrated management system of civil engineering laboratory. In Z. Li & F. Cen (Eds.), *INTERNATIONAL CONFERENCE ON SMART TRANSPORTATION AND CITY ENGINEERING 2021* (Vol. 12050, Issue International Conference on Smart Transportation and City Engineering CL-Chongqing, p. 59). DOI: 10.1117/12.2613743

Zhai, Q., & Chen, X. (2024). Design and application of optical communication technology based on machine learning algorithms in physical education teaching information management system. *Optical and Quantum Electronics, 56*(1), 111. Advance online publication. DOI: 10.1007/s11082-023-05717-5

Zhang, C., Xu, X., Duan, L., & Liu, S. (2022). Research on Information Assets Security Management of Electric Power Enterprise Based on Cloud Edge Collaboration Technology. In *2022 4th International Conference on Smart Power and Internet Energy Systems, SPIES 2022* (Issues 4th International Conference on Smart Power and Internet Energy Systems (SPIES) CL-Beijing, pp. 2266–2270). DOI: 10.1109/SPIES55999.2022.10082089

Zhang, X. (2022). Design and Implementation of Management Information System Based on Network Environment. In D. Zhou & Z. Y. Du (Eds.), *Lecture Notes in Electrical Engineering: Vol. 827 LNEE* (Issue International Conference on Information Technology and Industrial Engineering CL-Wuhan, pp. 1076–1080). DOI: 10.1007/978-981-16-8052-6_147

Zhang, Y. (2022). Development Strategy of College Sports Information Management System Using Data Mining in Mobile Internet Environment (Retracted Article). *Journal of Environmental and Public Health, 2022*. Advance online publication. DOI: 10.1155/2022/3895555 PMID: 36159766

Zhidong, L. (2023). Construction of management mechanism model of soil and water conservation information system. In *Science of Soil and Water Conservation* (Vol. 21, Issue 5, pp. 106–110).

Zhigang, W. (2021). Research on the Framework of Library Management System Based on Internet of Things. In *Proceedings - 2021 13th International Conference on Measuring Technology and Mechatronics Automation, ICMTMA 2021* (Issues 13th International Conference on Measuring Technology and Mechatronics Automation (ICMTMA) CL-Beihai, pp. 384–388). DOI: 10.1109/ICMTMA52658.2021.00089

About The Authors

Muhammad Ramzan is a distinguished figure in the realm of academia, holding the prestigious position of Vice Chancellor and serving as a Professor of Management Information Systems at Emerson University in Multan, Pakistan. With a profound educational background, he earned his Ph.D. in the Application of Information Technology from the esteemed Faculty of Computer Science & Information Technology at the University of Malaya, Malaysia, renowned for its QS World Ranking of #65. Dr. Ramzan's expertise extends beyond teaching and research; he actively participates in various administrative roles, exemplifying his commitment to the advancement of higher education. Throughout his illustrious career spanning over three decades, Dr. Ramzan has demonstrated remarkable leadership in both public and private sectors. His portfolio includes significant contributions such as establishing and leading new institutions and departments. Noteworthy appointments include Vice Chancellor at Lahore Leads University, Director General at Punjab Higher Education Commission, and Director/HoD at several reputable institutions including the Information Technology University and Lahore University of Management Sciences. Dr. Ramzan's impact goes beyond administrative roles; he has spearheaded initiatives aimed at enhancing the quality of education and fostering innovation. His accomplishments range from implementing innovative teaching methodologies like the Flipped Classroom Model to establishing vital university structures such as the Office of Research, Innovation, and Commercialization (ORIC). Moreover, he has been instrumental in initiating outcome-based education and introducing contemporary programs like Artificial Intelligence and Cybersecurity. As a consultant to various academic and governmental bodies, Dr. Ramzan's expertise is sought after in areas such as curriculum development, institutional accreditation, and strategic planning. His extensive involvement in committees and task forces reflects his dedication to shaping policies that drive academic excellence. Dr. Ramzan's scholarly contributions are equally impressive, with a prolific publication record comprising 82 research papers in esteemed journals, co-authorship of five books, and numerous conference presentations. His accolades, including prestigious awards such as the Fakhar-e-Pakistan Award for Leadership in Higher Education and the SATKAL Lifetime Achievement Award, underscore his profound impact on the academic landscape. Beyond his professional endeavors, Dr. Ramzan has cultivated international experiences through academic visits and collaborations, enriching his global perspective. With a comprehensive skill set encompassing strategic planning, organizational leadership, and academic governance, Dr. Ramzan continues to shape the future of higher education in Pakistan and beyond.

Muhammad Farooq is a highly accomplished professional, holding a PhD in Management Sciences and serving as a Postdoctoral Fellow with a wealth of experience in both academia and the corporate sector. Currently, he is an Assistant Professor at Emerson University Multan, where he imparts knowledge in various subjects such as Principles of Management, Entrepreneurship, Principles of Marketing, Business Ethics, and Corporate Social Responsibility. His academic journey includes a significant role as an Assistant Professor at TIMES Institute Multan, where he not only taught a diverse range of courses but also supervised PhD and MS research students. The subjects he covered include Research Methodology, Advanced Quantitative Analysis, Strategic Management, Marketing Research, Organizational Behaviour, Marketing Management, Innovation Management, and Entrepreneurship for BBA, MS, and PhD students. In pursuit of cutting-edge research, Dr. Farooq is currently engaged in a postdoctoral project at Multimedia University, Malaysia, focusing on “Business Models Beyond 5G and 6G.” His research output is substantial, with six papers currently in process for Impact Factor Journals and over 15 published in HEC Indexed Journals. His commitment to academic excellence is highlighted by the presentation of two papers at the American Marketing Association and Public Policy Conference 2022. Dr. Farooq's impact extends beyond academia into the corporate landscape. As the Lead Innovation and IT Trainer at Reign Consultancy Malaysia, he played a crucial role in transforming Sudan Telecom's 2G services into a profitable venture in villages. Through Upwork, he provided valuable guidance to startups such as “Smart Ends” in Belgium and facilitated business partnerships for “Stratus Plastics” in Canada. His managerial expertise is evident from roles such as Manager Customer Experience Management at China Mobile (ZONG) and Specialist Customer Lifecycle Management at Telenor. Notable achievements include substantial revenue increases, complaint reduction, and successful project implementations like the Biometric Verification System (BVS). Dr. Farooq is a versatile professional, demonstrating proficiency in teaching, research, and corporate strategy. His dedication to excellence is further illustrated by his extensive list of publications, conference papers, and authored books. As a sought-after expert, he has shared his insights globally, presenting papers in conferences across the USA, Malaysia, Serbia, and Indonesia. In addition to his academic and corporate contributions, Dr. Farooq has authored several books covering topics ranging from business plans to customer experience management. His multifaceted skills encompass teaching, research, revenue generation, project management, and stakeholder management. For those seeking collaboration, consultation, or expertise in the dynamic fields of Management Sciences and Entrepreneurship, Dr. Muhammad Farooq can be contacted at muhammad.farooq@mmu.edu.my or via Whatsapp at +92 3133372345. His rich blend of academic and practical experience makes him a valuable resource for anyone navigating the realms of academia and business.

Hina Adeeb is a communication specialist, researcher and she has 17 years national and International career as radio broadcaster and 10 years in teaching. She started of her teaching career as a Lecturer and currently she is serving as an Assistant Professor in UCP for 7 years. Her primary expertise is "Broadcast Journalism" and her research focuses on "Core Competencies Requisites for Pakistani FM Radio Broadcasters in Digital Era". She earned PhD. in the Radio Broadcasting from the University of Central Punjab, Pakistan. She received a B.S Hons and MPhil. with highest honors and distinction from University of the Punjab, Pakistan. She takes pride to share that she was the pioneer head of UCP Radio & Production house, Patron Performing Arts Society and currently she is the in charge of Pakistan's only Campus Radio FM 92.6 UCP KI DUNYA, that airs its transmission for 24/7& the Patron UCP Dramatics. She has been the member of Academic Council and Member Board of Faculty for Faculty of Media and Communication Studies, UCP. She has published several research articles in HEC Recognized and Impact Factor Journals and also presented papers in various international conferences.

Index

A

D

L

M

T

www.ingramcontent.com/pod-product-compliance
Lightning Source LLC
LaVergne TN
LVHW080607300926
849162LV00005B/1076